The Greek Concept of Justice

The Greek Concept of Justice

From Its Shadow in Homer
to Its
Substance in Plato

Eric A. Havelock

Harvard University Press
Cambridge, Massachusetts, and London, England
1978

Copyright © 1978 by Eric A. Havelock
All rights reserved
Printed in the United States of America
Publication of this book has been aided by a grant from the Loeb Publication
Fund of the Department of the Classics, Harvard University.

Library of Congress Cataloging in Publication Data

Havelock, Eric Alfred.
The Greek concept of justice.

Bibliography: p.
Includes index.
1. Justice. I. Title.
JC75.J8H38   179   78-6064
ISBN 0-674-36220-9

MATRIS

IN PIAM MEMORIAM

Foreword

Scholars of my generation will recognize in my text and notes many evidences of the guidance they have given me, even where the direction of my own journey may seem to have been solitary. It would have been even more so but for the welcome extended to my investigations by Bruno Gentili, a welcome inspired by the force of certain conceptions which have been pursued in parallel to my own. More remotely, but still powerfully, the reader may perceive at work the influences of Bruno Snell and E. R. Dodds. I would also acknowledge the company and criticism that have been afforded me by some scholars of a younger generation who have had the patience in recent years to listen, to comment, and to correct many things that I have said and written and which in their amended form are implicit in this book. To Tom Cole, David Claus, Kevin Robb, Christopher Gill, Michael Gagarin, Jackson Hershbell, Bennett Simon, Joseph Russo, and Alexander Mourelatos I am specially indebted for assistance rendered in this manner, through personal communication and by their published writings. Adam Parry was a companion in much of my endeavor, and my manuscript has lacked the unfailing judgment he would have given it had he lived. A valued association with two other colleagues of Yale University days, Geoffrey Kirk and Hugh Lloyd-Jones, did much by friendly dispute to

vii

sharpen wit and clarify vision. More recently, I have profited from the prompting and sympathetic encouragement of Donald Kagan. To the reader for the Harvard University Press I owe thanks for vigorous criticism of an earlier draft of the book, which produced much improvement in the final version.

Prolonged writing of any kind, creative or scholarly, is a lonely occupation, alleviated in my case by the constant support and informed intelligence of my wife, Christine.

The award of a Senior Fellowship by the National Endowment for the Humanities in 1969–70 afforded me some of the leisure needed to complete this book and is here gratefully acknowledged.

Contents

❦

	Prologue	1
1	From Homer to Plato: The Contours of the Problem	4
2	The Function of Epic in Preliterate Societies	15
3	The Psychology of Rhythmic Memorization	38
4	The Society Reported by Homer	55
5	Some Elements of the Homeric Fantasy	88
6	The Method and Manner of Homeric Storage	106
7	The Justice of the *Iliad*	123
8	The Legalities of the *Odyssey*	139
9	The Moralities of the *Odyssey*	150
10	The Justice of the *Odyssey*	179
11	The Justice of Hesiod: An Essay in Detection	193
12	The Spoken and the Written Word	218
13	The Early History of the Verb "to Be"	233
14	The Justice of Solon	249
15	The Justice of the Pre-Socratics	263
16	The Justice of Aeschylus	272
17	The Justice of Herodotus	296
18	The Justice of Plato	308
19	A Philosophy of the Written Word	324
	Epilogue	335
	Notes	343
	Works Cited	367
	Index	375

Prologue

The present volume resumes that exploration of the growth of the Greek mind which was first undertaken in my *Preface to Plato* (1963). In that work a problem in Platonism—namely, Plato's proposed exclusion of the Greek poets from the curriculum of the Academy—was offered as a point of departure from which to reconsider the cultural role of the Greek poets themselves, in particular Homer and Hesiod. The view presented was that their compositions prior to Plato had constituted an exclusively oral education, in a Greece which had placed minimum reliance upon the written word. It was this oral—that is, poetic—education which Plato proposed to supplant by his own philosophical program. The treatise in which he rejected the poets, namely, the *Republic*, was built round an attempt to conceptualize "justice," usually accepted as the leading Greek "virtue." It is a fair inference that Plato saw the cultivation of justice as lying at the heart of any educational system. This brings up the question: What of justice in the context of an instruction purely oral and poetic? The present work, starting with Homer, addresses itself to this problem directly.

Given this purpose, one is forced to analyze with greater thoroughness the moral function of the poets in archaic Greek culture. But the method proposed does not proceed a priori by looking for moral guidance in their works. Accepting the premise that in general the means of communication tends to condition the content of what is communicated, the investigator finds himself forced to look at things that Homer, Hesiod, or Aeschylus say about justice as in the first instance things said orally and remembered, not written down and read. At this point one touches rather immediately upon questions of cultural history and behavior in a more general and theoretic context. The justice of a Homer or a Hesiod may be considered a purely Greek problem. But once placed in the context of a major transition from the oral to the written word, it becomes a problem in oralism, on the one hand, and in social anthropology, on the other. The oralist school in contemporary America, associated especially with the names of McLuhan and Ong, has drawn a distinction between a linear-literate consciousness and its oral counterpart, on the whole to the disadvantage of the former, and has seen in contemporary culture a revival of oralism, encouraged by many modern technologies of communication. Does the Greek experience have any relevance to such a view? Does it shed any light upon it or support it? As for social (or cultural) anthropology, those familiar with investigations in this field extending over the last century, from Max Mueller and Durkheim through Malinowski to Lévi-Strauss, will realize that I have undertaken to treat the archaic culture of Greece as itself bearing many analogies to societies usually classified as "savage" or "primitive," though the analogy for me lies not in any supposed primitiveness, but in the technology employed for communication. May it be that my account of Homer's function and content (described in *Preface to Plato* as a "tribal encyclopedia") corresponds in important particulars to the function and content of the tribal myth, particularly as interpreted by Malinowski? And if so, what qualifications should be added to distinguish my view of what the Greek "myth" does and how it functions?

In sharp contrast, my story as it moves on out of Homer into Plato, leaving behind a justice orally managed in order to consider a justice formulated in writing, enters a realm usually reserved for philosophers, whether of language, or logic, or ethics. In this latter context, what is likely to be the professional fate of a thesis, here offered, which would regard the achievement of a conceptual syntax, and even of abstract thought, as the fruit of a change of communication, from the ear to the eye, from listening to viewing, from remembering to reading? What is to be made of an argument which seems to be in danger of concluding that ethics was something invented by Plato?

The answers to questions like these might indicate both how far such disciplines are relevant to what I say, and also how far is my distance from them. The answers might, I assume, be controversial. To anticipate what they might be in advance of my text, when it is only in a reading of the text that they are likely to arise, would be premature. The reader who is impatient to know where in the company of anthropologists and philosophers I seem to myself to stand is referred to some tentative comparisons which I have stated in a brief epilogue.

1
From Homer to Plato

❦

The Contours of the Problem

Although we now gain acquaintance with the Homeric poems as they are read between the covers of printed books, there is agreement that they belong to that class of composition commonly described as oral poetry. An examination of their diction, and in particular of verbal formulas out of which the verse is put together, originally suggested this conclusion, which was reinforced by comparison with techniques employed by singers of oral poetry where such can still be found and observed today, particularly in the Balkans.

Homer as Artist

The purpose of epic poetry, ancient or modern, is on the face of it to tell a story, and answers that have been attempted to the Homeric Question have turned very largely on the critic's evaluation of the way the story is told. Such matters as coherence of plot and its relation to incident, consistency or its absence in the delineation of character, and the presence of thematic motifs or imagery where recurrence may be significant have engaged critical attention. The poems are judged in the first instance as works of literary art, successful or not. The focus of interest in them has been aesthetic. As the oral mode of their composition came to be appreciated, this too was evaluated within the same

4

critical context. The formulaic technique was understood as an aid in performing the task of telling the story effectively, mainly (though not exclusively) by assisting fluency either of improvisation or of repetition. Its influence on the poems has been evaluated in terms of style. As for substance, the songs recited by Serbo-Croatian singers, sung or intoned to the accompaniment of a stringed instrument, as Homer's had been, were perceived to celebrate the exploits of heroic figures who for one reason or another had a strong appeal to local audiences. Is not that just what Homer's poems were doing for the ancient Greeks, and were intended to do? Modern analogy in this way reinforced a view of Homer as artist, his art being judged as that of narrative, whether historical or fictive. Like the Yugoslav bard, he was a "singer of tales." Such an approach inevitably leads into the question of authorship, however incongruous such a concept may be in the context of purely oral tradition. The poems represent an accretion of oral materials—on that there is now a consensus. But do they in their present form represent the work of a "monumental composer" (or two such, assigned to the *Iliad* and the *Odyssey*, respectively) who was himself preliterate? Did the resources of oral composition, without benefit of documentation, allow for such length and complexity of construction? Or has the art of writing intervened to make this possible? Such have become matters of scholarly dispute, but they are not of primary concern to the present work.[1]

Homer as Instructor

There is a frame of reference, normally regarded as secondary to the aesthetic, within which it is possible to place the poems, one which was familiar to the ancients. They set less value on Homer as a literary artist after the modern manner than as a didactic author, the teacher of Greece, either by way of accepting this role for him as natural and proper, or by objecting to it because it was performed unacceptably. The earliest Homeric scholar of whom we have record—Theagenes of Rhegium in the latter part of the sixth century B.C.—evaluated the poems as allegorical. The tradition of his critical activity is meager, but his view seems to presuppose that the poet was an author with didactic intentions. This opinion was shared by the philosophers Xenophanes and Heraclitus, the former of whom assumes that "all men have been instructed according to Homer," and links Homer and Hesiod together as teachers of an immoral theology. The latter in separate statements attacks Hesiod as "the instructor of most men" and Homer as unworthy of recitation. Herodotus in a later century, like Xenophanes, links

Homer and Hesiod together, this time as the founding fathers of Greek theology.[2] More remarkable is a statement in one of Aristophanes' plays (*Frogs* 1030–1036):

> Consider from the beginning
> how the master-poets have been the poets of utility:
> Orpheus published our rituals and the prohibition against homicide;
> Musaeus published medical cures and oracles; Hesiod
> works of tillage, seasons of harvest and ploughing; as for divine Homer,
> surely his honor and glory accrued simply from this, that he gave needful instruction
> in matters of battle order, valorous deeds, arms, and men.

Homer and Hesiod are again paired together, but their spheres of instruction are now distinguished, as pertaining to agriculture and warfare, respectively, and are presented in company with religious ritual, oracular wisdom, moral guidance, and medical lore, which are parceled out between two other traditional authorities. The purpose of such poetry is viewed as utilitarian.

The overall debate between Aeschylus and Euripides of which this passage forms a part extends itself to the larger and still more surprising assumption that all poetry is didactic and utilitarian, and that its success as poetry is to be judged by this criterion.[3] Precisely this assumption, some twenty years later, provides the starting point for Plato's proposals to reform the Greek educational system:

> What is to be this education? It is difficult to devise one any better than that which tradition has discovered for us. This of course means "gymnastic" for the body and "music" for the soul. . . . The content of music is discourse . . . factual and fictional . . . you realize of course that initially we start children with tales, mostly fictional, in part factual. . . . Looking at the greater tales, we shall see the models for minor ones. . . . The greater ones are those told by Hesiod and Homer, as well as other poets. They were the composers of fictions related by them to mankind, and which continue to be related.[4]

The fact that the philosopher proceeds to recommend censorship of these two epic composers, far from denying them the role assigned by previous authors, only fastens on them more firmly the category of the didactic, one which Plato makes Homer once more share with Hesiod, in a partnership affirmed even to the extent of using the verb of which they are joint subjects in the dual number. And it is now on the epic tale itself, rather than on incidental material contained in the tale, that the philosopher confers the didactic function.

At a later stage of the same treatise, Plato's position hardens: censorship is no longer enough; the poets must be banned together. He is now legislating not for schoolboys but for philosophers and statesmen. Once more, his hostility to the role of epic in Greek society only serves to make plain what that role in fact was:

> Our next task is a critical examination of tragedy and Homer, the prototype thereof. We are told in certain quarters that these poets understand all techniques and all human affairs pertaining to virtue and vice, not to mention divine matters . . . There are major matters of supreme value on which Homer undertakes to speak, warfare, military leadership, politics and administration, and the education of men . . . If Homer were really competent to educate persons and render them better . . . would he not have acquired a company of disciples and been honored and admired by them . . . Would his contemporaries have been content to let him, and Hesiod too, make their rounds as reciters . . . ?[5]

These notices would seem to indicate that for those who lived within three hundred years or less of the earliest date at which the poems could have been transcribed Homer stood with Hesiod as the original teacher of Greece. The instruction for which he is given credit is not literary or aesthetic, but sociological and utilitarian. It covers technology, including both military skills and (in the case of Hesiod) agricultural techniques, and also civic conduct, morals, and religion.

Is it possible that the ancients were right—that although from the standpoint of a modern critique this view of Homer is indeed secondary and may even seem perverse, it reports a role played by the poems which was in fact the primary one they were called on to play in their own time and circumstance? It is of some interest in this connection to note that Milman Parry himself, always to be remembered as the scholar par excellence of oral style (the French thesis which announced his discovery was subtitled "Essai sur un problème de style Homérique"), was prepared to look beyond style to matters of social substance. In an essay published eight years after the appearance of the thesis and a year after his death,[6] he quotes from Robert Wood (himself quoted in Arnold's essay "On Translating Homer") the story of how, at the end of the Seven Years War, Lord Granville, President of the Council, then mortally ill, would not allow his weakness to afford an excuse to postpone the urgent business of reviewing the terms of the Treaty of Paris, which confirmed the British conquest of North America: "He insisted that I should stay saying it could not prolong his life to neglect his duty." Granville then recited to himself in Greek some lines from the *Iliad* (12.322–328) spoken by Sarpedon to Glaucus:

Dear friend, if indeed we two, this war having evaded,
would evermore be likely ageless and deathless
to exist, neither would I in the front ranks fight
nor would I despatch you into battle that brings glory;
as it is, regardless, dooms of death impend
ten thousand, and no mortal may escape or evade them;
so let us go on; to another shall we his boast extend or he to us.[7]

"He dwelled with particular emphasis on the third line 'Then would I not fight myself in the front rank' which called to his mind the distinguished part he had taken in public affairs."

Parry then goes on to say

> Now I myself, because of the particular training in historical method, read those verses with an understanding which Lord Granville could never have had. I keep in mind, beyond doubt in a way which he never did, certain earlier lines in this same speech of Sarpedon in which that hero states the *moral* grounds which oblige them to high deeds: because their fellow countrymen give them at banquets the best cuts of meat, and keep their cups filled with wine, and have given them broad farm-lands. And then from my understanding of the speech of Sarpedon as a whole, from my knowledge of other early heroic poetries, from the general picture drawn of men of the heroic age by such scholars as Ker and Chadwick, and from what I myself have observed of traditional heroic poetry as it is still sung in the mountains of Hertzegovina, I see that this speech of Sarpedon is really a statement of the *rewards* and the *responsibilities* of prestige in the society of Homer's time—a society in which men were fewer in number, the social group smaller and its members known to one another, the mechanic arts still undeveloped, and warfare of a certain sort the constant condition of life. . . . It was the statement in heroic terms of their own way of life. More than that, it was a *sanction* and an *ideal* for that way of life . . . The hold which Homer had on later centuries, though weaker, was of much the same sort. In one of the dialogues of Plato we find the *Iliad* praised because of the pointers it gives for the chariot racing.

The terms I have italicized call attention to the fact that heroic epic has a moral dimension. The observation is not in itself innovative; the "heroic ideal" has been a commonplace of Homeric criticism. What

8

Parry observes is that the "morality" of a Homeric hero is stated as a set of obligations imposed by a corresponding set of social relations within which his life is lived. These are regulated by general rules of behavior. The ideal (a better term would be ethos) is not conceived a priori as a set of principles to which one aspires, but as a pragmatic response to the general rules which impose "responsibilities" and confer "rewards" for performance. If we are to look in Homer for some prototype of "justice" as originally conceived, it may be here.

The Preliteracy of Early Hellenism

But how could it happen that the epic tale was called upon to perform the didactic functions attributed to it? The outline of an answer begins to emerge if one is prepared to consider that the orality of the poems is not simply a matter of style, chosen by bards who for whatever reason preferred to compose orally, but a reflection of the total orality, that is nonliteracy, of the society in which and for which they were composed. At the time when the thesis of oral composition was proposed, it was generally if unconsciously assumed that this kind of composition had been conducted within a society otherwise literate or partially so, the dates of composition being commonly placed in the centuries between 1000 and 700 B.C., with a preference for the earlier period.[8]

But for Greece, as epigraphical evidence has accumulated, it becomes increasingly difficult to suppose that this is true. No evidence is available for the use of Linear B after the fall of Mycenae, or for the introduction of the Greek alphabet at any date earlier than the last third of the eighth century B.C. A leading authority on Homer and on the poetry of the archaic period has even committed himself to the statement that "the alphabet was not in common use anywhere until the lifetime of Archilochus; and indeed we have no right whatever to believe that the use was common even then."[9] This would seem to imply that a condition of either nonliteracy or semiliteracy—depending upon the scholar's judgment—persisted in Greece to the middle of the seventh century.

If true, this raises a formidable question for the historian. It was precisely in these centuries that Greece invented the first forms of that social organization and artistic achievement which became her glory. Perhaps the start was slow, and from about 1100 to 900 the achievement did not amount to much. Archaeology has made evident the physical ruin of the Mycenaean palace-complexes, and it is usually deduced that with this went also the destruction of those political and social arrangements which had previously rendered commerce, art, and a settled way of life possible. Even this hypothesis of a totally dark age supervening upon the Mycenaean period has lately been questioned. Whatever the truth of it, there is no reason to doubt that, as has recently been emphasized, the centuries after 900 were "dark" only in the sense that so much about them is unknown. If we consider the period from 900 to 650 as a chronological unit, it is obvious that we view in this period, however obscurely, the genesis of that classical culture which becomes evident to documentary inspection only in the sixth and fifth centuries. In what forms had this genesis appeared? The primary one was institutional, embodied in the formation of those corporate identities known as poleis, the Greek city-states. All the essential features of this Greek way of life seem to have been organized and functioning by the tenth century. It has been remarked of the settlements on the Anatolian seaboard which followed the early migrations: "This [some social stability] the Ionian towns with their aristocratic form of government and their federal system had probably achieved to a high degree by the ninth century and to a moderate degree before that."[10] Ionia, it is now agreed, did not become wealthy, in comparison with the mainland, before the middle of the seventh century.[11] A fortiori, the towns of mainland Greece must be deemed already capable by the tenth century of supporting forms of social life which went well beyond the limits of village existence. At the level of technology, these communities were capable of forging iron, and presumably of smelting it, a feat beyond the competence of the Mycenaeans. Their activities in commerce and navigation may not have exceeded Mycenaean standards. Their temple architecture not later than the end of the eighth century can be shown to have anticipated in wood the conceptions and refinements of the archaic age now partially preserved for us in stone. In the realm of the arts, this period saw at its inception the invention and perfection of the geometric style of decoration,[12] followed by the introduction of naturalistic motifs in the so-called orientalizing period, which began, appropriately enough, about the time that the Phoenician letters were put to Greek use. The same period fostered the verbal art of Homer.

The Concept of Cultural Storage

How was it possible for this kind of society to come into existence and subsist over a lengthy period without benefit of documentation? It can be replied that, so far as the architecture and arts of the period are concerned, draftsmen can use geometry without having to read, and that high levels of skill and taste, in materials and design, can be orally transmitted between master and apprentice, father and son. But the question is peculiarly pertinent to the problem of Greek political organization and the social and moral consciousness that goes with it. Hellenism, a culture which came into existence in this period, can be regarded as a rebirth of the Mycenaean or as marking a fresh start, depending on the varying emphasis placed on what seems new and what seems traditional. The truth no doubt lies somewhere between these alternatives. But historians seem agreed that the city-state, considered as an institution peculiar to the Greeks, was, we may say, incubated in this period, as also was the Greek tongue in that classic form which was to enjoy such an extended life in later centuries. Both these phenomena seem to rest upon and also express a sense of Hellenic identity, despite the division of the language into dialects and the endemic tendency of the city-states to fight each other. This sense expresses itself in the recognition of common gods, the observance of common rituals and customs, the acceptance of a common mythology, and, something of equal significance, an assumption of social order and regulated usage shared by all who called themselves Hellenes. It was a culture, in fact, which the barbarian neighbors of this people became aware of and showed some signs of wishing to share. It was what Parry called "the way of life," perhaps best summed up in the two Greek words *nomos* and *ethos* in their earlier usage.[13]

Social anthropology has called attention to the unique ability possessed by our species to take charge of our own development. Upon the genetic inheritance determined by previous natural selection we superimpose a process of cultural evolution under our own management, which becomes especially conspicuous as human society becomes urbanized. To explain how this works, there has been introduced the concept, borrowed from genetics, of cultural information placed in storage for reuse. As the biological information is encoded in the living cell, so cultural information is encoded in language. Human culture is not inherited but learned, and through language transmitted from generation to generation.[14]

A theory applicable to *Homo sapiens* in general may have relevance to the phenomenon of a Greek "culture"[15] occurring in a particular historical situation. But there remains an obstacle. The metaphor of storage implies the existence of a material object that can be so treated. The term "information," though not necessarily referable to a documentary source, tends to carry this coloration. Encoding, another metaphor commonly employed by biologists and anthropologists, is explicitly referable to a written medium, a slip of paper, a punched card. Terms like program, system, and structure, applied to beliefs or institutions or customs characteristic of a given society, evoke the presence of objects which can be seen and touched. If these metaphors have become easy to accept, it is surely because the information upon which modern societies depend has become materialized. It exists as it is documented. The document, whether in circulation or on a shelf, whether book, pamphlet, report, card or code, rule or regulation, law or literature, philosophy or religion, is essentially information placed in storage and resused, corrected, enlarged, redrawn, read, and reread. Ever since the Greeks, the frame of reference and court of appeal, the source of knowledge, the basis of faith and the guide to action, have reposed in documents, whether textbooks or treatises, bibles, poetry or prose, works of fact or fiction—artifacts to be handled, read, taught and indoctrinated, digested, consulted, quoted, and sometimes memorized. It would appear that, as a result, our terminology for dealing with anything expressed in language reflects that condition under which language becomes an artifact, that is, becomes inscribed.[16] Even such a fundamental word as "literature" describes language as it is portrayed in letters, just as "grammar" implies a rationale applied to signs and symbols graphically present on a surface.[17]

The Problem of Preliterate Storage

How can such storage be managed in a culture which is nonliterate, one in which language has not become a visible artifact? To observe the metaphors commonly employed is not just a philological exercise; it exposes the existence of a historical and technological problem which the metaphors have tended to protect from scrutiny. The conditions under which language exists and functions in preliteracy are strictly acoustic: it is the ear, not the eye, which universally confers acquaintance with linguistic information of any kind; it is the ear which is required to assist in storing it. If early Hellenism was preliterate, it must have employed methods of storage which met these conditions. How was it done? Spoken language does not fossilize; the evidential resources characteristic of the literate period which succeeded Homer are not available. The question can be met only by first attempting a theoretic answer, in part logical, in part psychological, with some assistance from the observed behavior of preliterate societies where these have survived for inspection.[18] Such is the task assigned to Chapters 2 and 3, as a preparation for considering the possibilities open to the Greeks, given a similar preliterate condition.

Justice in Preliterate Language

Within the context of such possibilities, as the argument is pursued, the didactic functions ascribed to Homer become explicable: "he" (meaning two major epics bearing his name) constitutes the early Hellenic answer to the problem of oral storage: first, it is the society of early maritime Hellenism, not an antique Mycenaean model, which he reports (Chapters 4 and 5); second, the stories in the poems are told in such a way as to include a mass of directive information covering the nomos and ethos, the life-style and its proprieties, appropriate to the society to which the poems are addressed and which was guided by them. The way in which this "information" is included and so placed in oral storage conforms to the rules as these were theoretically outlined. Seen in this light, the poems constitute two major reports upon propriety both social and personal, practiced as a conservative ethic and implemented in a thousand specific proprieties (Chapter 6). They employ one regulative symbol which was to acquire special significance after Homer, and predictably so because of the way Homer used it. This was expressed in the Greek word *dikē* and its derivatives, a word not easy to render in strictly conceptual terms, but furnishing a prototype of what we might designate as Homeric "justice." The plot of each epic can be seen as indirectly didactic, insofar as it proceeds in a way which has the effect of illustrating and implementing *dikē* as a regulative principle legally in the *Iliad* and morally in the *Odyssey* (Chapters 7-10), though such a distinction should not be pressed too formally.

Justice in Its Literate Formulation

To stop there would be to lay a foundation without indicating the superstructure which it was destined to support. The symbol *dikē*, as incorporated into its derivative form *dikaiosunē*, came to embody a concept central to Greek moral and political philosophy, transmitted by the Greeks to their heirs in the European tradition. In this conceptual sense, justice does not find a place in the Homeric text. Even to speak of it as a regulative *principle* is misleading. Intruding as it does only incidentally in epic narrative, it is first seized upon by Hesiod, who isolates it and converts it into a formal topic of discourse (Chapter 11). This was a pioneering achievement, which I shall suggest he was able to carry out because though still an oral composer, he was able to read a Homeric text which had been alphabetized. Even so, he was able to describe only what justice does or how it behaves, not what it *is* (Chapter 12). The conditions of narrative syntax required for memorization still prevailed, particularly as they limited the usage of the verb "to be," and so made definition impossible (Chapter 13). This did not prevent authors intervening between Hesiod and Plato from exploiting "justice" symbolically, though still not conceptually. Their mentions of it were incidental to other purposes, and their discourse remained poetic, so that the syntax of oral composition continued to prevail in their works. Some advance toward a syntax of definition is perceptible, but it is never quite reached (Chapters 14-16). Plato on the available evidence would appear to have been the first after Hesiod to confront the problem of justice as a topic, converting it into a conceptual entity and making it a normative principle. By the time he wrote, the term *dikaiosunē* had already come into usage as a replacement for *dikē*, indicating that an important extension of the meaning of "justice" was already in the making (Chapter 17). Hesiod had been a proto-literate composer who not only heard Homer but read him. He initiated a didactic mode of discourse which was to lead to philosophy, but the process was completed only when discourse fully "literalized" itself in the systematic writings of Plato (Chapter 18). Given the conditions of Plato's achievement, rejection of previous poetry as a suitable vehicle for the definition and description of justice becomes explicable (Chapter 19).

Justice now exists as a concept; it has passed from shadow to substance with linguistic success, which allows my argument to terminate without treating Aristotle's doctrines on the same subject; unless perhaps to suggest in this place that his "distributive justice" essentially represents a rationalization of Homeric *dikē*. Conceptual methods established by Plato have been extended backward to cover procedures and attitudes rooted in the Greek tradition.

2

The Function of Epic
in Preliterate Societies

❦

The civilizations of Egypt and Mesopotamia, with their apparatus of law, government, and religion, made use of writing as early as the third millennium before Christ, a fact which may tempt us to conclude that an ability to maintain and transmit a cultural identity should be correlated with the existence of some literacy, however limited.[1] But when we consider the time scale within which the social evolution of our species has occurred, it becomes evident that oral cultures have had in the remoter past a more protracted existence than literate ones; and, moreover, to judge from the evidence of artifacts, they appear to have continued to subsist successfully in some parts of the world—South America, for example—in later periods when writing was elsewhere in common use. The Greek cultural experience as late as the period between 1100 and 700 B.C. was nonliterate and was not in this respect unique. Granted that the ability to place cultural information in linguistic storage is crucial to the existence of a culture, it would appear that the means available for this purpose in preliterate societies must differ sharply from those used in literate ones.

The Fixity of Preserved Statement

Yet a first step toward discerning the genius of oral preservation is taken when we examine the genius of the document: why is it "informative" in a sense in which language as it is spoken in the vernacular is not? Why does it furnish a court of appeal and a source of reference? Surely because the statements contained therein, being, as it were, frozen in script, are stabilized and are, as we say, "reliable"; they cannot be changed without changing or replacing the document, and this in effect means that a document preserves information because it preserves the words of the information. It is forbidden to alter the words, and it is also forbidden to alter the order in which the words are placed, their syntax, in short; for the stability of the statement relies upon preserving this order, and upon this stability in turn depends the viability of the document as a court of appeal.

These necessities manifest themselves most conspicuously in the case of verbal formulas governing technical procedures; the order of symbols in an algebraic equation is only an extreme example of the same rule. All syntactical statements which purport to state a formula, a principle, or a truth, or extended statements which compose a plot, a thesis, a theory, or a set of "meanings" which are to achieve the status of permanent or preserved language, are submitted to the control of a written version which *qua* version remains invariable, not subject to the whim of arbitrary manipulation or faulty recollection. The "original," as we say, is always there.

In the Second World War the development of modern explosives and the means to deliver them made possible a massive destruction of the material apparatus of culture. A program of what was called strategic bombing applied to the German and Japanese economies was able to reduce a large proportion of the artifacts to rubble. Buildings, factories, and equipment vanished in fire and dust, particularly in the capital cities. Proportionate destruction of this kind visited on an antique culture, for example, the one in Crete centered on Knossos, would normally finish the culture. But the material basis of German culture could be repaired or moved around during the war: the program of strategic bombing proved a failure, militarily speaking. And after the war, the entire structure in West Germany was remodeled and rebuilt with considerable rapidity. What had not escaped destruction was the documented basis for the culture: the blueprints and their texts inside Germany and, still more, the corresponding documentation available elsewhere in Europe or the United States. Information, accurate and specific, was available in fixed statements both linguistic and mathematical. If this entire hoard of information had been destroyed, then indeed a cultural regression would have occurred. But this destruction would have had to be worldwide, for modern Western culture rests upon a foundation of documented storage which is now international.

An example on the constructive side, involving not the reconstruction of a literate culture but its transfer, is furnished by the settlement of New England. Both law and religion, furnishing the nexus of New England behavior patterns, traveled across the Atlantic not only as incorporated in the personal habits of the settlers but in the books and documents that they brought with them or else imported after arrival. It was not for nothing that Harvard College acquired institutional form out of a parcel of books donated for this purpose and that one of the early tasks set before some of the settlers was to compose technical handbooks for navigation, architecture, and the like, modeled upon the stored information already available in England. In short, the settlers were readers, who not only listened to the weekly sermon but read earnestly in the texts made available.

The Code[2] of Linguistic Propriety

In the behavior of language without benefit of documentation, where is the principle of fixed order first perceptible? Surely in the grammar of the language itself. This, in the case of English, requires such conventions as are indicated in the distinctions between the various parts of speech and their functions: a subject normally precedes a predicate and requires it, and must share with it an agreement as to number and so forth. But this kind of order is only formal and analytic. It deals solely with the abstract properties of words. There is a second level of grammar, which we might call the grammar of linguistic propriety, or "anthropological grammar."[3] This requires that combinations of words make sense, as we say, in agreement with the common experience of the group using the language. So the linguistic convention excludes from the normative such statements as "man bites dog" or that grapes are gathered from thorns or figs from thistles. It disallows the injunction that we should "love enemies." Such statements, if they are made, reflect deliberate paradox: they violate comon sense, as we say; they imagine the culture which happens to use this language as being stood on its head.

Such proprieties in the arrangements of words extend to the language with which members of the linguistic group describe their interrelations, their behavior toward each other. The linguistic sounds "friend" and "enemy" are habitually paired with other sounds respectively appropriate to each, such as "love" versus "hate" or "dear" versus "dangerous." Aside from this kind of pairing, words of a given language when pronounced may automatically identify not only various persons as types, but also the relationships in which they are normatively involved. The way the family is arranged, so that family behavior is regulated from generation to generation, is laid out in words which when severally pronounced identify the relationships between the members, and tend to memorialize and conserve the usages which the relationships require. At the simplest level words like *father, mother, son, daughter, grandfather, grandmother,* as they come up when pronounced in actual and not theoretic speech, are accompanied by certain automatic reflexes on the part of the father speaking to or of his son, or on the part of the son speaking to or of his father, and so on. The linguistic sound "father" describes a person who is always older than the person denoted by the sound "son," and at first also stronger. However, he is going to die, perhaps soon, in the normal course of events, while the son is likely to be still alive. The father will be responsible for the son up to a given age and, depending upon the culture pattern, may in old age expect reciprocal support from the son. These expectations will be reflected in the syntax in which the words are regularly employed, and such expectations constitute a body of information continually available for reuse by succeeding generations.

An example of the way this works, in a culture in which the family structure was far more elaborate than ours, can be supplied from the text of Homer. It is found in that moving lament for Hector which on the lips of Helen brings the *Iliad* toward its close. The modern translator[4] renders the relevant terms that she uses as follows:

Hector, of all my lord's brothers dearest by far . . .
I have never heard a harsh saying from you, nor an insult.
No, but when another, one of my lord's brothers or sisters, a fair-robed
wife of some brother, would say a harsh word to me in the palace,
Or my lord's mother—but his father was gentle always, a father
indeed—then you would speak and put them off and restrain them
by your own gentleness of heart and your gentle words.

The five English expressions "my lord's brothers," "lord's sisters," "wife of some brother," "my lord's mother," and "his father" are renderings of five separate Greek words, each distinct from its fellows, each denoting a separate type of person within the family complex. They therefore imply a set of five different relationships in which these people stood to Helen, and she to them. In the English version they have all been translated into appendages of her husband. The Greek vocabulary denotes that Helen, by marrying Paris, became a member of a complex family group system with which she would normally enjoy complex relations and from which she could normally expect support, for they all have specific roles to play vis-à-vis her, and the roles are indicated by the words. The pathos of her isolation is that she has been rendered a woman without this kind of family. The marriage therefore has not worked, but its failure is not one we would understand in modern terms. It does not concern herself and Paris alone. This kind of vocabulary implies a set of proprieties; as it implies them, it also recommends. The words, becoming part of the custom of the language, embody the assumption that the relationships thus denoted will continue to be so, and therefore that behavior appropriate to the relationships will also continue to be so. In this way the language itself carries the tradition of the culture.[5]

A nonliterate culture can in this way maintain a basic identity for itself simply by maintaining the stability of its vocabulary and syntax. The vernacular can do this. Using such a vocabulary, one retains after acquisition the information whom to marry and whom not, whom to consort with and whom not, whom to love, whom to hate, what to eat, what to wear; one learns automatic responses to given situations; cultural expectations are supplied.

Being so supplied, they confer on the user a "command" over his tongue: he continually prescribes as he speaks for others or for himself. "As soon as we look at actual speech communities we see that variation in speech is first universal, second highly patterned, and third closely correlated to cultural and subcultural situations. That is to say, people not only know their own language, they know how to use it. People talk the way they do not solely because they possess an abstract systematic knowledge of their knowledge. They also have a command of the knowledge, and by now research in the ethnography of speaking—the scientific description of the use and understanding of language in a culture—has clearly established that command is as patterned as knowledge."[6]

Individuation and Disorder

This kind of stored information works automatically; its directive power over behavior is exercised below the level of conscious thought. Yet its location resides in the individual brains of members of the group. Can these individuals be relied on to respond automatically and always to the common signals of the language, to obey them with consistency? Will the signals be implemented by responses which are automatic reflexes? Will a man and a woman always mate according to the rules, whatever they are, of mating? Will they automatically treat their children according to prescribed modes of nurture and protection? Will they remain content with property duly inherited? Will they always perform the tasks allotted to them by group modes of division of labor? Or will they intermittently wish to behave eccentrically, in terms of the common code? Will they wish to trespass, secretly to steal or openly to rob by violence? Will they use hostility toward friends rather than their proper enemies? Will they simply withdraw into idleness and sloth?

These are random examples of the phenomenon of human individuation,[7] perceptible in the behavior of the human brain and extending to differentiation in the shapes of human bodies. Although it is true that animals exhibit some individuation within a given species, its degree is limited; the social behavior of an animal group in terms of mating habits, food gathering, rearing of offspring, and the like proceeds according to programs which seem self-fulfilling. In human society the component members can behave on the one hand as though they were members of a herd and on the other as though they were living outside the herd. Man's behavior in culture reflects the tension between these opposed tendencies, and the tension is reflected in the way language is used. For its role is paradoxical: on the one hand, the accepted mores, a stability of expected relationships, are woven into its syntax; on the other, it can be spoken in ways to justify the repudiation of what is expected; it can be spoken, as it were, defiantly as well as conventionally; it can be used to express the arrogance of the individual over against the claims of the common consensus. Human societies, unlike animal ones, contain inherently the seeds of their own instability. The individuation which renders this possible is itself a function of language.

When Captain Cook anchored for the first time in Matavai Bay in Tahiti in April of 1769, he encountered a culture of perhaps fifty thousand persons which was preliterate. The society was a structured one,

> not settled in villages but scattered visibly in single huts in small groups all round the verge of flatland, less visibly throughout the valleys and over the uplands. The high valleys also gave refuge to the fugitive and to the oppressed; for there was a class structure and varying degrees of prosperity, there could be oppression; and though desperate warfare was rare it was not unknown, briefly . . . The remains

of Tahitian building are not those of forts but of marae—the coral stone structures of courtyard and "altar," small or large, that almost innumerably dotted the land, the centers of religious ceremonial for families or communities or craft-groups; highly important when they belonged to chiefly families, the importance of whose members themselves might be measured by their seats on the marae, immensely tapu or sacred, surrounded with sacred trees, ministered to by a priesthood, the very language of whose invocations was an esoteric thing; less important as social rank declined, yet, whether the center of human sacrifice or of a more ordinary ritual, the abode of awe and the visiting-place of gods. Tahitian society, that is—as was to become apparent to the European mind only gradually—Polynesian society in general, was in its own terms a profoundly religious society.

The responsibility for the oral maintenance of this structure seems to have rested upon a given class of specialists, the *arioi*: "They were a trained and graded society, celebrating in dance the seasonal festivals and those that marked the great events of communal life—like the birth, marriage or inauguration of *ari'i*—and providing a great part of the mime, drama and wrestling that were favorite diversions. They toured the island group in fleets of consecrated canoes, were met with gifts and with joy; their god was the god of peace and fertility. It is probable that Cook was entertained by *arioi* more often than he knew."

And yet, however stable the social proprieties which regulated individual behavior in this oral society, the governmental structure was unstable, a fact which baffled Cook continually. With whom was he to deal? On the one hand, "chiefs, the *ari'i*, were sacred in their degrees; most sacred of all were the *ari'i rahi*, particularly the three great heads of clans who might in some sort present to men from a different world the quality of 'kings.' The *ari'i* commanded and was obeyed . . . An *ari'i* firstborn was regarded with particular veneration, all the more if male: he was recognized immediately as the head of the family and his father, or his mother, took on the role of regent."

And yet, on the other hand, the arrangements for transferring power from one generation to the next seem to have been unstable:

> But the power of the *ari'i rahi* or his regent was not equal to his privilege, his social consequence; he could not command the obedience of other chiefs, even in his own district; there was great scope for personality. Hence Wallis' acceptance of Oborea, or Purea, as a queen, the magic of her name in England; hence Cook's bafflement, sometimes, as his experience continued, over who might be the really great man with whom he should deal. . . . These chiefly families were not

merely related [which explains Purea's seeming primacy in Wallis' eyes], but at times bitterly divided; and it was the result of bitter family dissension and war, caused by Purea's overweening ambitions for her young son, that as a defeated person she now took a subordinate role to that of Tuteha, the organizer of victory. Cook learnt a little of this and was to learn a little more on the tour of the island which he made with Banks in the last days of June.[8]

These descriptions, quoted from Captain Cook's modern biographer, J. C. Beaglehole, expose a paradox within a naive or primitive society—primitive, that is, from the standpoint of the literate mind—a paradox with which all societies of *Homo sapiens* have to contend: a formal stability enforced by tradition and predictable in its operation is continually disturbed by the assertive intervention of personal behavior which is unpredictable.

The syntax of the vernacular of itself does not provide adequate means for controlling or correcting the effects of such individuation.[9] It is, to be sure, normative, but the conventions which are implicit in it are already being violated or threatened with violation. What is needed is language applied to the purpose of warning against this possibility and suggesting means of correction when it occurs. Society will need some form of managed language beyond the vernacular. The linguistic signals governing behavior will have to be made more explicit.

The Oral Directive

It will be thought that these conclusions coincide with the emergence of a body of law, oral or written, promulgated by chiefs, judges, courts, kings, oligarchs, to which obedience is required from members of the group and enforced by penalty. But this way of looking at it oversimplifies the historical process by accelerating it. Literacy has made modern societies familiar with the notion of laws in the plural existing as a corpus of institutions, procedures, and penalties for violation. These, however, are only the end product of a need experienced in developing societies to formulate special statements of many kinds which are framed to guide, control, and correct. Let us call these directives, varying in influence and importance, but framed as explicit statements of what ought to be done. Essentially, they express social information to be applied and reused; its relative importance for the community, historically speaking, will vary according to the varying spans of time during which the directives are expected to be effective.

They can therefore be meaningfully classified in ascending order of duration.

There is the ukase, to use a conveniently archaic term, issued by a governmental authority, essentially a "proclamation"—a term etymologically faithful to the orality of the original procedure—assembling a levy for war, announcing a treaty of peace, imposing a tax, and the like. The intended effects are temporary, lasting a matter of days, weeks, or a few months. Their memory can consequently afford to be correspondingly short-lived. But in an oral society it must remain memory. Next, there are the judgments rendered by that social mechanism, whatever it may be, which governs contractual relations, marriage, divorce, inheritance, crimes of theft, murder, and the like. These depend for their effectiveness upon the conservation of precise wording, however simple; in an oral society such conservation is guaranteed against the vagaries of personal willfulness or bad memory only by the presence of listeners, that is, witnesses who witness the oaths and hear promises given and received. Again, the effect required will last only as long as the situation lasts which called them forth. Oaths exchanged to settle a marriage contract are not likely to serve as a court of appeal, that is, to be remembered, after the marriage is dissolved or ended by death. The same is true of a treaty governing relations between groups which are altered or severed by war. Family genealogies, another form of explicit statement affirming family claims to status or privilege, while they constitute directives for reuse by successive generations, are not likely to survive the lapse of four or five of these without alteration. Familial connections and continuities are always fluid; in preliterate society oral genealogies are discarded and new ones furbished. The elaborate genealogical codes of the Old Testament are indeed codes, the fruit of craft-literate composition, not of living oral memory.

Ephemeral as these may be, they rest upon or are framed in general agreement with a second set of directives which have a longer life and a wider validity. These may be said to support and guarantee the foundations of social behavior. One group can be viewed as technological in the sense that they describe special procedures to be followed with some precision: they will describe the divinities to be worshiped by the group and their attributes and in particular the cult performances required for this worship, which conserve what a literate observer would call the "beliefs" of the group. The same applies to certain skills: the calendar governing agriculture, if agriculture is practiced, and the star map governing navigation if such is practiced, furnish examples.

A contrived language, moreover, requires a skill of its own, and the society is likely to entrust to specialists the linguistic task of framing its vocabulary and idioms. If these are taught to the group as a whole, it then becomes a partner in the act of preservation; if hoarded in secrecy, then group behavior takes the form of obedience to directives issued on authority.

Nomos and Ethos

There remains one body of cultural knowledge which, whatever the form of government, must in an oral society become communal. This can be described as a general awareness of custom-law, apprehended not in the shape of specific edicts but as a body of maxims or sayings which describe the proprieties of behavior both personal and social. These proprieties constitute the mores of the society, to use a Latin term; in the Greek, they are conveniently identified in the words *nomos* and *ethos* in the singular, or *nomoi* and *ethe* in the plural: the custom-laws, the folkways, the habits of a people. It is of interest to note that by etymology both these terms, which when literalized can be rendered as "law" and "ethics," signify in their original usage not principles or beliefs but localized human activities, that of distributing or managing land in the case of nomos, and that of living in a place or a haunt in the case of ethos. Their inspiration is behavioristic, not philosophic, legal, or moralist.[10]

This body of maxims (as they become when incorporated in contrived statements) represents the common consciousness of the group, its sense of what is fitting, decorous, and seemly. It corresponds somewhat to the literate notion of equity, whether legal or moral. It reflects the more permanent proprieties of the society, over against which the particular decisions of a governing body have to be framed. Both represent forms of knowledge placed in storage, but of varying lengths of validity. In Scotland, where the forms of oral communication lingered longer than elsewhere in Europe, the two can be seen as late as the early seventeenth century still operating side by side:

> Obedience to tradition was supplemented as a means of achieving cooperation by the institution of the Baron Court. This had two functions. On the one hand, it served as a place where the tenants of a laird's estate, often comprising many farmtouns, could come together and interpret custom. On the other, it acted as the laird's private court of jurisdiction through which he could exert his control over society, compel payment of rents and services due to himself and punish crimes

committed by the peasant against himself or against the community. Some of the little courthouses have still survived, like the one at Ceres in Fife with its motto carved over the door: "God Bless the Just."[11]

Finally, any society will wish to preserve some sort of history of itself. This is obviously true of literate societies, especially as they take the form of nation-states with ambitions which require patriotic sentiment and expression and which have to be validated by a presumed historical past. But the desire seems to attach itself to preliterate communities as well. Its psychological basis may be simply the need to assert and preserve the identity of the culture group by relating the group to the environment in which it lives. For the cosmic scene seems to wear the appearance of permanence; it does not die as men do; it is always around. And since men do not wish to die—for whatever mysterious evolutionary reason—they seek permanence by claiming group connection with what is permanent. So the oral history, besides reporting group achievement in the form of victories over other groups, feats of prowess or daring and the like, will connect the group, first with its ancestors, and then with the gods who produced these ancestors. For the gods have their generations, representing the cosmos from the beginning. They have generated the group and they preside over its achievements. In literate terms, we are inclined to call such preserved statements national epics. But their function and provenance are more general than this description would suggest.

Overall, the knowledge that has been stored in the form of wisdom or of history in this manner will wear the appearance to literate eyes of being "religious." The whole secular body of knowledge and skills has to be preserved in linguistic formulas which are ritualistically memorized and in reenactments which are ritualistically performed. The gods, standing at the apex of group history, preside over the whole body of knowledge. They authenticate it. They represent not so much an article of faith as a means of identity.

Rhythmic Memorization

The total of special statements required by an oral culture can be regarded as representing an act of storage at a second level superimposed upon the primary level of storage in the linguistic syntax, or "anthropological grammar." Surely, then, at this secondary level, the rules for preservation, which alone will make storage effective as a control over behavior, will continue to require stability in the statements made, so that they survive without being subjected to arbitrary alteration or faulty memorization. But now, this rule has to go beyond what is found in the general proprieties of word connection; it must in the case of explicit statements require that the words composing them and their syntactical relations both remain unchanged. Specific statements are now required which per se can survive without modification.

We are asking of an oral culture this question: Do you have any device, the equivalent of documentation in a literate culture, which is available to guarantee that a series of words shall be preserved in the oral memory in an order of relationship which does not change as this series is transmitted from mouth to mouth and memory to memory? One which preserves a unique syntax between uniquely chosen words and not just a general syntax of the language? Yes, comes the answer, there is one way to do this: the words have to be arranged in a rhythmic sequence which is independent of the words themselves considered as words but to which they have to respond acoustically. The mouth, which has learned to arrange speech sounds to conform to the grammar of the linguistic code, must now learn the further trick of so selecting these sounds that they not only "make sense" but set up a kind of music in the ear both for speaker and listener which is governed by rhythmic periods which repeat themselves. The recall of this kind of "music," to be sure, itself makes some demand on the memory, but the act of recall is relatively easy because rhythms are repetitive; that is their essence; they can provide a spell, a standardized incantation to which the words of a required statement can be fitted so that as pronounced they reproduce the rhythm. Once so placed, they remain relatively immune to arbitrary change or imperfect recollection, for their order cannot be shifted.

Preservation after this rhythmic fashion will involve a new order of memorization,[12] lying outside the ability to learn a language code. Whether this secondary ability is genetically encoded as language is, or whether it is only a learned ability, part of the open program which man devises for himself, is an unsolved question. The fact that our literate habits of reading appear to discourage habits of oral memorization and recitation might seem to support the second alternative: what man learns for himself he can also unlearn and discard.

The inability of the vernacular to carry out this required duty can be tested by resorting to that simple device whereby a message concocted by A for transmission to D is first written down and the written version laid aside. It is then recited privately to B, who recites it privately to C, who recites it privately to D, who then writes down what he thinks he has been told. For example, the original might run: "If you want to get to the manor house, go as far as the elm tree on the far side and turn left toward the setting sun 'till you see the roof of the barn." The two written versions when compared will never agree and will sometimes diverge widely, usually through substituting one related object for another, simplifying the syntax, or complicating it. Thus: "To get to the farm, go beyond the oak on the edge of the field and turn to your west and you will come to the barn." Sometimes a livelier imagination on the part of recipients will embroider the statements with fresh information, such as "crossing the ditch beside the field" or "catching sight of the top of the barn roof."

But in rhythmic language the problem of preservation is solved, as can be seen at its simplest level in the nursery rhyme. Take as an example "Sing a song of sixpence, a pocket full of rye." The verses of this familiar ditty illustrate both the primary and secondary levels of storage language, that of linguistic propriety and also that of rhythmic determination. Linguistic propriety forbids that the queen rather than the maid should be the person hanging out the clothes, though the rhythm would permit this. It forbids that the blackbirds be baked in a sty rather than in a pie or in any receptacle not designed for cooking. It requires that a dish set before a king be dainty or accompanied by an adjective of equivalent approval. But rhythm, together with rhyme, alliteration, and assonance, themselves all varieties of rhythm, alone guarantees that the song be of "sixpence" rather than "tenpence"; that "rye" be present to rhyme with the "pie," that the "baked" objects are "blackbirds," that the sequence in the narrative descends from king to queen to maid, that the queen eats "honey" rather than caviar, and so forth.

The Saying

Rhythm is the genus of which meter is only a species. It is a principle of composition more extensive than meter. At the acoustic level it can be set up by assonance, alliteration, and the like;[13] and at the level of meaning it can be generated by parallelism, antithesis, and the simpler figures of speech, like chiasmus. Many of these terms, to be sure, describe language or words only as they have been framed under literate conditions, that is, as they are written. But when we speak of a "saying," we select a term which, like the "winged word" of Homer, rather aptly describes the primary form of preserved oral speech, for the "saying" implies the use of some words specially chosen to express an item of wisdom which is repeatable. An appropriate illustration can be cited from the "saying" which happens to head the collection known as the Book of Proverbs in the Old Testament:

My son, hear the instruction of thy father
and forsake not the law of thy mother,
for they shall be a chaplet of grace unto thy head
and chains about thy neck.

The rythmic devices which at the acoustic level contribute to the memorization of this statement, and hence to its survival value, can be properly observed only in the original. But even the English translation brings out the system of balances, parallelisms, and contrasts which at the thematic level contribute to the total rhythm of the saying. The sentiments are arranged in pairs: the first couplet lists two directives referring to two parallel figures, father and mother, while at the same time exploiting the antithesis between father and son and the correspondence between instruction and law. The second couplet lists two parallel statements which are linked to the two preceding directives as a commentary upon them and are put together with the aid of similar parallelism and antithesis.

Though it is unlikely that extensive collections of sayings like the Book of Proverbs would come into existence without the aid of inscription, the component parts are framed according to oral rules. It is essential to the rhythm set up in a saying that it is complete in itself and does not allow of extension. It does have relatives in the oral repertoire, so to speak, which are longer, like the parable, the fable, and the ritual incantation. Very often, as in the case particularly of the fable, the versions now in circulation in literate cultures are themselves the product of literate paraphrases in which some of the original rhythmic elements have been suppressed. This was possibly true, for instance, of the fables of Aesop as they were available for literate Greece, though if their models were Egyptian, these would have been inscribed at a time when Greece was still nonliterate, and so would have attained the form of prose paraphrase at an early date. But even in prose versions, the thematic rhythm of parable and fable persists, reminding us of their genesis and function in an oral culture. Nor must we forget the humble nursery rhyme, which can sustain a single memorized narrative statement, but within its own unique metric. The readiness of children to memorize this form of speech suggests that it may have served from time immemorial as a training in the handling of rhythm. The child thus becomes accustomed to managing the acoustic aids to memorization. They are the oral equivalent of instruction in reading. Hence the proclivity observable in children for indulging in nonsense-language chosen for its sound values as a mnemonic. The nursery rhyme has proved ephemeral so far as the cultural record is concerned, though indications of its wide use can be found in some corners of surviving Greek literature. Considered in terms of its length and self-containment, it resembles an extended saying. It can be regarded as a preparation for more meaningful and lengthy efforts of memorization which are to come later as the capacity of the brain is more effectively mobilized.

The fact that the rhythms of all these forms of preservable speech, whether acoustic or thematic, are self-contained places narrow limits on what they can say. The parable or fable or nursery rhyme comes to a stop. If it did not, its unique rhythm would be destroyed. None of them admits of extended statement; none of them is open-ended.

The Epic

Yet a culture which had reached the stage of seeking to incorporate its traditions in memorizable speech would surely wish them to take the form of an extended statement, a connected report, which would command attention and provide a verbal nexus round which the consciousness of the culture could rally. The saying or the parable can furnish clues to the consciousness of a people, but not the key to that consciousness. To achieve extension of statement required the invention of an extendible rhythm, achievable by simplifying and formalizing it, converting it into a repetitive meter, which produces what may be described as a series of sayings of roughly equal acoustic length, following one another as a series of waves in extended duration. The oral memory by this method is led on to recall the sequences, and so master a whole program of instruction. Such, it is suggested, is the genesis of the epic as it has subsisted in all oral cultures.[14] It arises in response not to artistic impulse but to functional need. It constitutes a massive attempt at oral storage of cultural information for reuse.

Verbal rhythm, therefore, can be structured in varying modes and at varying levels of regularity and complexity. In its most regular form, we view it as poetry, an art form which manipulates the prose of the vernacular to its own special purposes. So far as we tend to regard this purpose as exotic or esoteric, we do violence to its fundamental nature. It is not to be denied that it is an art, provided this term is understood in the Greek sense as an act of contrivance, a technology of spoken language. But the poetic management of speech is prompted in the first instance not by exotic inspiration or by individual genius but by the functional need of human beings to cope with the stable preservation of a social organism.[15] Poetry viewed in the overall context of the history of human culture is a mechanism for oral storage. Under literate conditions, where documentation has applied the resources of literate technology for preserving important statements, the original function is lost. Stripped of its service to society, poetry is freed to explore and express the esoteric, the untypical, and the individual. For many centuries this was only partially true; the great literate epics of Europe, of which the *Divine Comedy* and *Paradise Lost* are exemplars, were still composed with oral ends in mind. They represent a halfway house between orality and the documented literacy of a culture fully prosaic.

The Enclave of Contrived Speech

Within a strictly nonliterate culture, storage will range in coverage from the closed saying through the ritual hymn to the longer myth and the extended epic. Obviously, the extension of length would make increasing demands upon brain energy, a problem to be examined in the next chapter. But we can generalize and say that an oral culture will found itself on a compendious body of stored information, directive or descriptive, which is expressed in rhythmic language apart from the vernacular and which can be thought of as an enclave of contrived speech existing within the vernacular. Its vocabulary is likely to be specialized to some extent when compared with vernacular converse, but such specialization, whether a result of archaic survival or invented contrivance, will be such as to increase the rhythmic capacity of the statements. To this enclave the oral society will entrust the overt expression of its nomos and ethos, its mores, its "values," to use a literate and rather misleading term. While the syntax of the vernacular tongue will betray the proprieties of behavior practiced by the group, the enclave will memorialize their importance; it will describe what happens when they are contravened; it will admonish and alert; above all, it will energize in language the sense of identity of the group.

I have noted that to contrive a special language would call for a degree of skill requiring the services of specialists. Given the diversities of human talent, such skill is likely to become a specialized province. More accurately, the specialists supply the models and modes of a living art which the popular ear can memorize and also imitate in varying degree. In modern parlance, priest, bard, prophet, and sage define separate types of specialist. They can be thought of as representing originally divergent aspects of a common craft, the exercise of which gave such specialists their power in oral society. It is to be noted that with the onset of craft literacy the rituals of cult became incorporated in documented formulas, that is, in liturgies, incantations, and the like, which are likely to be hoarded in varying degrees of sanctity, which means secrecy. Hence the power of the priest in craft-literate societies, as for instance in Jewish society after the reign of Solomon, tends to increase at the expense of the minstrel and the prophet. The priest has acquired the functions of a scribe. Whether it is realistic to imagine that in purely oral societies the sacred office and the secular, of priest and of bard, respectively, were formally divided from each other is very doubtful.

The Management of the Enclave

The common office and honor of such specialists in the community rested upon their control of the information contained in their poetry, information which their art rendered transmissible between the generations. They were the "authorities," but equally, the acceptance of this authority in the absence of documentation rested upon the degree to which their songs, hymns, incantations, epics, and dances were communicated to the populace at large and held in the memories of the individuals thereof. This would require the constant participation of their audiences to guarantee the safe transmission of the whole verbal enclave of contrived speech. The situation altered when a craft-literate monopoly over documentation allowed its practitioners to control an interpretation of sacred writings not otherwise available. In the linguistic sense, all oral societies had to be functionally "democratic," if that much misused term is allowable.

If it is a mistake to seek to separate the bard from the priest and prophet in oral society, it is equally mistaken to view him as a mere entertainer. Entertainment was, to be sure, one of the objectives of performance, a matter to be taken up in the next chapter, but this was subordinate to the performer's functional role as the reciter of preserved statements. A festival of recitation, of song and epic accompanied by dancing, was no more or less sacred, and so protected, than a ritual sung before a shrine, nor was it any more or less entertaining. The notion of poetry as the expression of purely aesthetic values in the modern literate sense must be given up as we approach the poetry of preliteracy. Cook's impressions of the Tahitian specialists who managed the songs, recitations, dances, and rituals of the contrived word have been already cited. Although ignorant of the language, Cook was able to become aware of the existence of a speech specially contrived. The *marae,* those family structures of coral stone containing courtyard and altar surrounded by sacred trees, were "ministered to by a priesthood the very language of whose invocations was an esoteric thing." But was it? Were its rhythmic structure and functional purpose any different in essence from the performances in mime, dance, recitation, and song which were managed by the *arioi* who celebrated "the seasonal festivals and those that marked the great events of communal life?"[16] Cook, equipped with the presuppositions of a literacy in which such performances had become only entertainment, could view the *arioi* only as "strolling players." Their true social function eluded him.[17]

Scottish society in the prefeudal period, although organized on very different lines and in a very different historical context, already neighbor to the literacy of Europe, could still utilize for purposes of legal and social observation the resources of an enclave language:

> We know little about the organization of the native peoples anywhere in Scotland before David's reign, but Celtic society was clearly tribal, based on a real or fancied kinship between every freeman and the head of his tribe. The tribes apparently occupied fairly distinct areas of the country, had reached the stage of individual ownership of land among the tribesmen, were organized in social strata (the law of the Britons and Scots mentioned earls, thanes, freemen, and carls) and possessed differing tribal laws that were memorized by hereditary wise men who handed them down unaltered to their sons. It would be wrong to imagine either simplicity or uniformity in such arrangements—a primitive society is usually a complex one, and social muddle may have formed one reason why the Norman kings wished to introduce the strict and tidy forms of feudalism.[18]

The observation that such formulary speech was transmitted from father to son raises the larger question: Did oral society make any provision for teaching any part of the code as contained in rhythmic speech to children and adolescents? We should distinguish here between specialized information transmissible within families of specialists and that which could be viewed as constituting a program of general education for the society as a whole. The practices observed in Tahiti seem to reveal a degree of partnership between the populace and the specialists who performed and recited constantly before audiences who listened and may have participated. The effect of constant performance would be to diffuse a memory of the contrived language among the populace as a whole; the oral wisdom thus became transmissible between the generations simply by its reiterated recital.

There is a Homeric passage which may reflect a more structured method of guaranteeing the continuity of the tradition. Andromache, lamenting the fate of her son after his father, Hector, has fallen in battle, commemorates the lot of the male orphan in the following words (*Il.* 22.490–499):

The loss of a father isolates a child from other children;
he hangs his head, his cheeks streaked with tears.
In his destitution the child resorts to his father's associates,
tugging one by his cloak and another by his tunic.
They may take compassion on him and one will hold out a cup to him for just a sip;
the taste will touch his lips but will not touch his palate.
But another boy with living parents will beat the boy out of the banquet,
hammering him with fists and harrying him with insults.
"Beat it! Your father is not a member of our banquet. You have not got a father."
And in tears the child resorts to his widowed mother.

In a later age when the institution described had fallen into disuse, the passage was felt to be an inappropriate digression and was obelized.[19] It can be suggested, however, that it lifts for a brief moment the veil which normally shrouds those proceedings which were adopted in an oral society for educating children. The male child attended the common mess table of his elders (the Greek word rendered "associates" also means "messmates"), the one to which his father was assigned; his father's presence guaranteed his own right to attend. Why was attendance important to him? The passage celebrates only the consumption of food and drink, but he could get these from his mother. Such symposia, however, were also the occasion for musical performances accompanying the recital of encomia, songs, and epic narratives.[20] The practice continued throughout Greek history, though in later and literate conditions its character changed; musical recital from memory was replaced by bookish quotation, as in *The Professors at Dinner,* a work by an author of the late second century after Christ which purports to describe the learned conversation at one of these occasions. Literacy had banished any need for the presence of the younger generation, who now learned to read in schools. But in an oral culture, the boys, listening to their parents celebrate, themselves mastered to some degree the skills of contrived speech. In such a social context, assisted by private tuition, a hero like Achilles would himself learn the art of singing the deeds of heroes. Learning these, he would learn also to be "a speaker of words" as well as a "doer of deeds." In the last third of the fifth century B.C. Aristophanes produced a comedy called *The Banqueters* which featured fathers and sons at mess tables. The institution was still in being at that time or it could not have been exploited by the dramatist for comic purposes. The "father-and-son" banquets included in the program of male friendly societies in American small towns may reflect, however remotely, the same felt need for this type of association.

Social Propriety versus Personal Morality

To this account of what I have styled the enclave of contrived speech supporting an oral culture, two footnotes can be added. What precisely is the content of the ethos and the nomos? Such codes of behavior, in order to survive, must be expressible in survivable language, and such language relies on memorization. But the limits of the living memory for this purpose are finite, even if more extensive than is true of literate memories. The enclave of rhythmic speech is therefore circumscribed both as to the quantity and the variety of statements made, when compared with the illimitable resources of documentation. The habit patterns to be memorialized will be correspondingly economical, implemented by an energy which is limited in application so that possible responses to situations, as these are signaled in the language, are less diverse, eccentric, individualistic than would be possible in a culture of literate and reflective storage.

They therefore carry the strong stamp of tradition, unfriendly to innovation, hostile to reformist improvement or speculative interrogation. What, then, is the primary ethical quality of such behavior? It resides if anywhere in the terms which identify propriety, seemliness, and appropriateness. Good conduct is that which is appropriate in the circumstances and it will be so signalized, for this label simply indexes adherence to a norm implicitly accepted by the whole group and incapable of reflective change.

A modern illustration can relevantly be cited from the example of an American statesman who through the circumstances of his upbringing was kept in unusually close touch with the oral genius of his language and culture. Certain speeches of Abraham Lincoln have always been accepted as particularly adapted for memorization and recital on formal occasions. This is because their verbal rhythms, employing echoed repetition, parallelism, assonance, and balanced contrast, respond to the rules of acoustic harmony of the English tongue, and because their content usually reflects the basic values of American society of the time. This ethos and nomos was largely, though not exclusively, biblical; it was often a matter of oral comprehension.

Thus it is relevant to note that his Gettysburg Address, a conspicuous example of these arts, included propriety as the normative term to describe the occasion on which the speech was delivered: "We have come to dedicate a portion of that field as a final resting place for those who here gave their lives that this nation might live. It is altogether fitting and proper that we should do this."

Again, in his Second Inaugural, the same accent recurs:

> Fellow countrymen: At this second appearance to take the oath of the presidential office, there is less occasion for an extended address than there was at the first. Then a statement, somewhat in detail, of a course to be pursued, seemed fitting and proper. Now, at the expiration of four years, during which public declarations have been constantly called for from every point and phase of the great contest which still absorbs the energies and engrosses the attention of the nation, little that is new could be presented. . . . It may seem strange that any men should dare to ask a just god's assistance in wringing their bread from the sweat of other men's faces; . . . woe unto the world because of offenses, for it must needs be that offenses come, but woe to that man by whom the offense cometh [a biblical quotation] . . . shall we discern therein any departure from those divine attributes which the believers in a living god always ascribe to him?

The doctrinal context of this speech is Judeo-Christian, and in that sense literate, but the profound feeling that violation has been imposed upon a normative order and that this is unseemly and unfitting and untraditional, and that the cure lies in a return to propriety, responds to the deepest instinct of preliterate man.

If such be the overriding rule which determines moral behavior in the oral community, it follows that an oral community is incapable of conceiving of a personal morality apart from the communal, or indeed of understanding the concept of formal morality at all except in the sense of preserving a given set of behavior patterns in stable harmony with a given culture. This is as much as the oral memories employed in the culture can manage; they will expel the eccentric act and the imaginative question. I. A. Richards narrates an incident which occurred in Peking during his oral presentation of the climactic scene in Hardy's novel *Tess of the D'Urbervilles.* "As the students listened to the description of the raising of the black flag, signifying that Tess had been hanged, they burst into spontaneous applause, the only applause to occur in the course. When asked to explain the reasons behind this surprising reaction, their protocols revealed this answer: Tess had been an unfilial daughter and had failed to pay her father proper respect. The Chinese wanted her punished and at last, that great writer, Thomas Hardy, saw that she got what she deserved: death by hanging."[21] It would seem that in this instance Richards, despite the fact that his class consisted of "forty highly motivated and intelligent Chinese students," was really confronting the reactions of a culture orally conditioned to accept the proprieties enforced by any existing legal system.

The Pragmatism of Oral Ethic

Nevertheless, this truth about oral "morality" contains a paradox which can puzzle us. Though the patterns of behavior are closely knit, the maxims, the sentiments, not to mention the myths and the stories which make up the corpus of the embodied wisdom, will not hesitate to celebrate in their formulas and their plots the most diverse types of behavior. Conciliation and aggression, contentment and greed, courage and caution, advance and retreat, responsible action and selfish withdrawal, pride or humility, defiance or submission, are all likely to find their advocates in the maxims, proverbs, and exemplars of such a tradition with a bewildering lack of moral uniformity, quite unlike the more uniform pieties of the biblical Book of Proverbs. The fact seems to be that without benefit of a documented speech which will arrange the terms of conduct according to fixed principles, oral wisdom is more free to express pragmatic attitudes which vary according to the necessities of various situations as they arise: it can index the contradictions of daily living. In human societies instability continually competes against stability, the relations of human beings admit of flux, they require constant ad hoc adjustment, a process carried on continually within the pattern of overall adherence to group identity and stability. The oral ethic recognizes this: within the overall realm of propriety as it is conserved, there is recognized to exist not a single rule of conduct but many rules reflected in preserved statements which are pragmatic, empirical, and can appear contradictory. When an anthropologist stumbles upon a pocket of pure preliteracy—and the importance of such encounters cannot be overestimated—literate inspection is likely to find things that seem, from its own moral standpoint, to be puzzling, bizarre, or even illegal. It is precisely these irregularities that are likely to contain significant clues to the character of the culture that is encountered.

Does all this mean that oral cultures are innocent of ethics, unguided and unguarded by morality or moral law? On any objective judgment their behavior social and personal so far as it has been observable has been neither more nor less kindly or cruel, cooperative or divisive, than that of modern societies of the present century. What may be said is that oral societies are innocent of principles systematically stated by which the inconsistencies common to ordinary life can be judged.[22] If we are willing to identify the moving principle of modern morality by the term "justice," conceptually defined and consistently applied, we must allow that societies relying exclusively on oral storage for their existence could get on very well without it. But might they still be aware of a justice of a different and prior order, identifiable as a rule of propriety embedded in action, recognizable not as principle but as procedure, working with varying effects to maintain an overall stability?

3

The Psychology of
Rhythmic Memorization

Oral doctrine can persist as such only when framed in statements which are immune to change, a condition achievable by placing the diction within rhythmic patterns which require the words to maintain their given order. So far so good. But how persuade the memory to conserve this rhythmic order? One may reply that the arrangement of words in the meters of poetry assists verbal memorization; there is no doubt of that. But verbal memorization remains a difficult thing. In speech we still prefer to pour out the vernacular in immediate response to temporary situations. This lively converse is the easiest to indulge in; it takes least mental effort and presumably always has. How persuade the brain to substitute for this vernacular practice the memorization of an enclave of contrived speech?

Rhythmic Hypnosis

Rhythmic pronunciation of words in a given order is not in itself enough. There are other resources to draw on which lie at the root of the whole notion of rhythm. In its primary manifestation as employed in culture, rhythm arises in physical motions of parts of the human body. The column of air compressed within the human throat can be constricted or released to assist articulated speech. But its energy need not

38

be devoted to this purpose. It can be controlled by the rhythmic movements of the vocal organs to produce sheer melody, a rhythmic acoustic operation. In parallel with these motions, the arms and legs can be mobilized to produce rhythmic movements which harmonize with the vocalic sounds, whether the result is identified as gesture or as dance.[1] Such motions are then supplemented by material instruments from which a fresh set of sounds can be manufactured in rhythmic order by the application of hand or mouth: by percussion applied to a surface, as in the drum, cymbal, or castanet; by plucking or striking upon stretched cords, as in the lyre, the harp, and the lute; and by compressed air applied by mouth or bellows to a hollow reed or pipe. Of all the tools invented by our species, these were not the least important.[2]

There are grounds for thinking that these types of rhythm are more memorizable by untutored brains than patterns of words taken by themselves. When performed, therefore, in consonance with uttered speech, rhythm to rhythm, they have the effect of assisting memorization of the words and reinforcing the act of their recall. It would appear that all preliterate cultures employ these resources for assisting the act of storage of necessary information.[3]

Why are such rhythms more easily memorizable? The common-sense reply would be that we have keen enjoyment in making them; there is a human relish in regularized rhythm that seems to reflect some degree of programing in our genes. Why would the pressures of natural selection have pointed in this direction, if it is true that they do? What superior survival value for our species does rhythmic performance possess? It seems difficult to supply any answer other than the assistance given by body rhythms to increase the memorization of language, language being the source of the hoard of information which alone guarantees that type of superior survival achieved by man. Whatever the truth of this speculation, it is beyond dispute that the biological functions necessary to life have their encoded pleasures to guarantee their ready performance; we eat, sleep, excrete, and propagate ourselves by the guidance of appetite. Should we not also have to admit that the readiness of our response to physical rhythm betrays similar seeds of encoded pleasure? A drum and fife band passing down the street, the great operatic aria for which the audience has been waiting, the exaltation produced by a massed choir, the summons of the jazz band which draws us to the dancing floor, the compulsive spell of a rock and roll concert—all these invite a response on the part of the listener which he may find irresistible: it is noteworthy that in normally literate societies it is in particular the young and the semiliterate whose responses to these performances can become instinctive. What is perhaps peculiar to the pleasures of rhythm as distinct from those of the biological functions is that they are pleasures intensified by participation in group activity. Hence their ability to set in motion the mechanisms of mass suggestion, which can in extreme cases lead to hysteria. This fact again suggests that this particular type of encoded pleasure has been evolved to serve the needs of human communication.

Dance, song, and instrumental playing therefore command an immediacy of response which language alone cannot, even when rhythmically arranged. To place cultural information in the memory, a difficult task, preliterate societies indulged in a marriage between the rhythms of song, dance, and instrument on the one hand and the rhythms of contrived statement on the other. So the act of memorization, which alone can support the tradition and make it effective, is converted into submission to a spell,[4] which by the employment of effects almost hypnotic can engrave upon the memory the required body of doctrinal information.

The poets of the neoclassic revival, nurtured on a heritage written and preserved in printed books, were not in a psychological position to appreciate this fact. The verse of Dryden and Pope is a highly literate phenomenon, and it is understandable that Wordsworth, reacting against it, should commit himself to a preference that poetry return to the simplicities of the vernacular. In this commitment he turned his back on the traditional sources of poetic statement, and it is fortunate that he did not consistently practice what he preached. The ability to evoke with some correctness the original powers and functions possessed by preserved speech was appropriately reserved for that most romantic of the romantics:

Drive my dead thoughts over the universe
Like withered leaves to quicken a new birth!
And, by the incantation of this verse,
Scatter, as from an unextinguished hearth
Ashes and sparks, my words among mankind!
Be through my lips to unawakened earth
The trumpet of a prophecy! O, wind,
If winter comes, can spring be far behind?

In Tahiti, as previously recounted, Captain Cook encountered a professional group, a highly organized enclave of singers, dancers, actors, and musicians revered by the society that they served. To him they seemed to be nothing but "strolling players"; for their own people they were the guardians of wisdom, historical, theological, legal. It was a classic confrontation between representatives of the two cultures, the preliterate and the literate. How would the latter understand that the former relied on the use of rhythm in all its forms to guarantee the continuity of the tradition, of the social mores, of cultural identity? Most of Polynesia, after two centuries of contact with literate cultures, is now losing or has already lost acquaintance with these clues to its own oral past; for the need has vanished. The modern explorer, until very recently at least, could, however, encounter the same phenomena in some African cultures. In Gambia, for instance, "the oral historian, integral to tribal life in much of Africa, has the duties of keeping the chronology of his tribe and region, and in many cases . . . is also called upon as an entertainer, propagandist and envoy." He would recite "while two assistants provided soft music on their korahs, 21-string African lutes that are played with both thumbs . . . At other times he would accompany himself on the balafong, a xylophone with bars made of hard wood . . . Now and then he would emphasize the narrative with a pointed finger, a lifted eyebrow or a big smile . . . A crowd of men and young children . . . listened with closed eyes and whose heads moved to the sound of the korah music."[5]

Narrative Syntax

In preliterate societies, a tradition sufficient to sustain cultural identity can transmit itself successfully between the generations only when musical rhythm and the spoken word enjoy an intimate connection, a partnership which is organic. What is likely to be the effect of such a partnership upon the quality and content of the statements that are made? Using the model of modern opera, one would easily conclude that words uttered under such conditions would be more lyrical, dramatic, emotive, or passionate than is normally the case in common speech. But this falls short of comprehending the latent or controlling principle which informs the syntax of preserved speech in an oral culture. Modern opera is a phenomenon of literate societies and relies on a connection between music and words which is too superficial to supply the explanation. Given preliterate conditions, it is possible to discover a simple law at work. Rhythm in all its forms, vocal, instrumental, choreographic, involves physical motion regularized in recurrent patterns, and this motion is of organs of the human body. As performed in union with words uttered, the rhythms are likely to tempt the brain to choose for utterance words which themselves describe action and movement. The verbs used in such statements will be such as will signalize action in the form of doings or happenings, of actions or events. The subjects of such verbs will therefore have to be agents or represented as agents, actors in the framing of a perpetual drama of representation. In the drama of the preserved word, the acts of the agent will themselves tend to be described as though they were performed in rhythmic patterns rather than according to the untidy and undiagramed activities of current living. The content of the preserved statement, just as its form is made by creating an enclave within the vernacular, will itself tend to represent an enclave of activity of a special kind within what might be called the vernacular activity.

In short, in a nonliterate culture in which cultural information has to be memorized, the words of the information are likely to show a strong preference for a syntax of narrative rather than a syntax of analysis. The subject of the informative statement is likely to be a person, and the items of his performance are likely to fall into rhythmic patterns of their own which echo at some distance the actual rhythms of the musical performance. This system is born of mnemonic necessity, for words thus woven into a system to suit the rhythm of the performance are easier to recall along with the performance itself.

In terms of the possible logic of human discourse, an important result follows: oral storage is unfriendly to what we might call an "is" statement; that is, it is unfriendly to the use of the verb "to be," or its equivalent in whatever tongue is in question, used simply as the verb "to be," meaning either essence or being, either what is logically true or metaphysically existent.[6] Oral information is likely to be unfriendly to such a statement as "The angles of a triangle are equal to two right angles." If, however, you said, "The triangle stood firm in battle, astride and poised on its equal legs, fighting resolutely to protect its two right angles against the attack of the enemy," you would be casting Euclid backward into Homeric dress, you would be giving him his preliterate form. However, triangles are not personal agents and Homer was not very interested in them.

Oral storage is therefore hostile to the expression of principle or program as such, aside from describing actions or events which are programed. We can say if we like that oral man does not think like that: it is better, however, to restrict our argument to determining what is likely to be said, in preference to what may be thought, and the main point to make is that the syntax of what is said is likely to be governed by the syntax of what can be rhythmically memorized. Oral storage is hostile to the expression of laws and rules which are stated as such in terms which are connected by the timeless present. It is unfriendly to statements which place cause and effect in analytic relationship. It is often said that primitive speech is hostile to what we call abstractions or concepts. This way of putting the matter focuses upon the supposed properties of individual words, and it is not very satisfactory. The oral song and the oral history can evoke what we would call abstractions and make statements about them. The issue turns not on the individual word, but on how it is made to behave in oral speech. It will tend to turn itself into an agent, doing something or having something done to it.

Once it is perceived that active narrativization of some kind is a rule which has to be applied to statements preservable in the oral memory, it becomes possible to understand the extensive role played by myth and epic in the storage mechanism of nonliterate societies. But evidence for the operation of the same rule is available in other areas of discourse—areas that also serve the storage needs of oral societies. Legal regulations, for example, when framed for the use of either oral or craft-literate societies, are turned into case law or participial law: "If a man commits a certain act he shall do or suffer accordingly"; "If his ox shall gore another man he shall pay so and so"; or else, "The man doing a given act shall be declared without the law"; and so forth. In a theistic context, the law is addressed to the hearer as a personal command of the god: "Thou shalt not do so and so." The kind of legal statement that is avoided is the one that would say, "Murder is definable as a crime punishable by death"; "Ownership of property implies responsibility for its maintenance"; "Personal liability proportionate to the investment made"; and so forth. In short, in order to frame a legal directive, a situation is conceived and stated, cast in the form of an event or an action by a given agent, not in the form of a general principle within which a given case might fall. The law code of Hammurabi and the various Hebraic law codes incorporated in the Pentateuch all exhibit this kind of syntax.[7] The formulas themselves are sometimes poetic, but they need not be so; but whether poetic or not, they reflect the oral necessity to frame a memorizable rule as an action performed.[8]

All types of information stored in the oral repertoire are thus likely to be cast in narrative form, to be represented as doings. To describe the geography of an island, you do not state its position relative to coordinates; you say, "If you sail two days toward the setting sun, you will come to a cliff facing you on which there stands a temple." If you report a catalogue of items, they will be described as acts committed in succession: "Ten ships came from Athens and they were led by X and Pylos sent twenty ships and so-and-so commanded them." If you report a genealogy, it will not be a table of affinities but "A loved B and lay with her and begot C," and so forth.

The Russian psychologist A. R. Luria has put on record the mentality of a human subject he encountered who possessed a phenomenal memory. The mentality was explored and tested in a psychological laboratory. The subject, who happened to be a journalist, had a freakish capacity to memorize and recall extensive lists of objects and items or just words which had been presented to him without previous preparation or warning. Recall would take place "fifteen or sixteen years after the session in which he had originally recalled the words. Yet invariably [these sessions] were successful. During these test sessions S would sit with his eyes closed, pause, then comment 'Yes, yes . . . this was a series you gave me once when we were in your apartment . . . you were sitting at the table and I in the rocking chair . . . you were wearing a gray suit and you looked at me like this . . . now then I can see you saying . . .' And with that he would reel off the series precisely as I had given it to him at the earlier session."[9]

This report makes clear that the mnemonic trigger for repeating the list had to be a narrative situation, a little story within which the list is embedded. But the list itself is also retained in narrative form: "When S memorized a list of nouns he needed a few seconds pause after each item. This gave S time to get a visual image of the object and set it at a particular point in an imagined background, commonly at intervals along a familiar street. Once that was done he could just walk along the street from either end or starting at any point enroute and report the things he had placed there."

As a secondary effect of this need to convert items of information into a series of active situations, S continually allowed the items themselves to turn themselves into agents, or in the words of the report: "Words for him were indissolubly bound up with visual and other images." It is probable that the mnemonic secret of such images lay in the fact that they moved; they were active.

This particular subject obviously had a brain of a peculiar order, a genetic "sport." In fact, he found many conceptual operations difficult, and after trying several jobs he ended up as a professional mnemonist, a showman performing before audiences who provided lists of articles and materials of all kinds which he could memorize after one hearing.

The available report on him fails to note any symptoms of rhythm in his verbal recall, and it may be he had none, but it is recorded of him that a sympathetic understanding of poetry eluded him because "such vividly concrete images arose to every detail of a poem, sometimes with idiosyncratic associations, that he could completely lose the sense." One wonders if this does not report the way in which a literate mind may fail to comprehend a nonliterate mentality. Is not the evocation of such images the primary business of oral poetry rather than a statement which "makes sense," ethical or philosophical?

Such a subject, to be sure, required to exercise his mnemonic ability upon lists prescribed for him by literates, is exercising himself upon the storage of documented knowledge. He is unlikely to be able to represent in any complete fashion the habits of recall which are normative in a totally oral culture. But his reliance on the syntax described accords with one of the linguistic requirements on which oral memory has relied for uncounted millennia before the age of literacy.[10]

Performative Statement

Aside from information of this order, preserved by an oral society for purposes which are obviously utilitarian, there is that body of oral law, which might be styled ethical or moral, designed to express, and therewith to recommend, the proprieties of behavior and attitude which are followed by members of the society in their relations with each other. Here, too, the activist syntax has to prevail as long as the form of the directive remains truly oral. This is obvious in the case of parable and fable, which place their moral in the context of a little narration. It is equally true of the maxim and proverb as long as they remain in the truly oral form of the saying without benefit of literate compilation and summarization. The saying, I have said, is the primary unit of oral storage; it is therefore rhythmic. But it is also activist, so to speak. Such short directives, constantly on the lips of the members of an oral culture and continually transmitted to the memories of their children, are either phrased in an imperative enjoining a given action or are framed as short, pregnant situations which describe something that has happened and will happen again, or they employ brief dialogue, an exchange of speech between two agents. To be sure, the oral maxim can use a shorthand which approximates to what I have called an "is" statement. The tendency is evident in that collection of sayings attributed to the seven wise men of Greece, though this collection is an amalgam of oral echoes combined with literate paraphrasing. Such axioms, however, never go so far as to adopt the syntax of the "copybook maxim"—a phraseology which itself betrays the fact that oral, narrativized diction can be taken over by literacy and adapted to the syntax of documented speech. One must guard against the deception of literate reflexion. For example, "Honesty is the best policy" is not a true oral saying.

Mythos and Epic

The role of activist syntax already visible in the framing of the short directives now becomes more evident in the extended statement. The overall total of cultural guidance, the general education of the group, is entrusted to a tribal narrative. It is this which constitutes the enclave of contrived speech par excellence, a record of agents performing acts which syntactically constitute events in time, a series of grand happenings, perhaps recited as epic, perhaps mimed as drama, holding within its ample grasp a large body of useful information and ethical teaching made available as the narrative gives opportunity.

The terminology for what I have described as the oral enclave of contrived speech is inevitably borrowed from the Greek experience. The term "epic" is in fact late and sophisticated, reflecting postliterate categories. The Greek who lived before the age of achieved literacy would have spoken simply of mythos, which basically means just an oral utterance, as, for example, a command or a precept, or even a conversation, although the word from the beginning was also extended in its application to describe an uttered story, a tale or a narrative. This is to say, a sense of the seminal narrative quality inherent in all types of preserved speech as previously described seems to have been caught up in the earliest usages of a word which we now transliterate as "myth." There was no original Greek basis for drawing those distinctions between saga, epic, myth, and folk tale which have become part of the apparatus of modern literate criticism. For that matter, under literate conditions we commonly draw a distinction between a story and a statement. We have difficulty conceptualizing forms of speech which are both story and statement. Mythos is the original oral term for both. Any preserved speech, that is to say, any storage, any history, any directive preserved in an oral culture, has to be cast in the form of a mythos. This is the fundamental explanation of what is called myth in early cultures, and also illustrates how, given our literate split between the tale and the statement, the story and the fact, we are led astray by the modern conception of myth and try to find its explanation in nontechnological factors, in terms of some esoteric experience presumed to be available to precivilized peoples.[11]

The element basic to all such types of language is the activist syntax required to assimilate descriptions of deeds performed by agents or of events which happen to agents. Though the word *mythos* is Greek and therefore reflects the Greek cultural experience at its oral stage, there seems no inherent reason why it should not be properly used to identify those similar kinds of linguistic enclaves as they exist and are recited in other oral societies.

Thus, to resort to African experience once more, the Myth of the Bagre, lately transliterated and translated by the efforts of scholarship, and therefore now existing for literates in a printed text,[12] represents "a great myth used in annual ceremonies to transmit to successive generations of the Lo Dagaa people an image of their society and the mysterious powers who guide it." As in the case of the Tahitians encountered by Cook two centuries ago, its perpetuation appears to depend upon a special group of professionals, and yet "a majority of the Lo Dagaa . . . will be initiated into it at some stage in their lives." The material recited

> is divided into two great cycles both recounted over a number of weeks . . . the white Bagre into which neophytes are first initiated tells how the various staple crops of the area were first discovered and what natural events should control the sequence of their harvesting. The successive stages of this myth are recounted to the neophytes by their guides at the appropriate season for the harvesting and preparation of each crop so that they are actually enacting the ritual which is being described to them exactly as it was enacted by the first men on the earth . . . the black Bagre tells with great simplicity and power about the first successful coupling of the primal pair taught to the woman by the boa constrictor, the first murder, the first hunting expedition, the first smelting of iron, and many other cardinal events in the evolution of human society . . . so the initiate finally emerges with an extraordinarily rich and complex though not comprehensive picture of his society, its origins, its rituals, and its ways of life.[13]

It can be allowed that even this myth is not a pure example of preliterate composition. But whether or not it has been contaminated by craft-literate procedures transmitting Muslim versions of Old Testament doctrine, and even after we allow for its inevitable manipulation as it is transferred by literates into transliteration and then translation,[14] it survives as a valuable contemporary example of the way in which the recited enclave does become an enclave, nourished within the vernacular by professional expertise yet communicable to the populace at large. It entertains, but its entertainment is incidental to its functional purpose as a vehicle of oral storage of cultural information and cultural directives.

One might think that the contrivers of the enclave had to do no more than take over the habits of the vernacular story teller. This character surely has always exhibited his talents by the fireside or at the well or in the marketplace in oral societies without apparent benefit of professional expertise. This is not quite true, at least not in oral societies, where the telling of a tale has its own repertoire of motifs and language. The character of the enclave, however, is determined by mnemonic necessities which lie beyond the range of common usage. The vernacular tale is in essence an ephemeral phenomenon. It cannot constitute a fixed statement, nor will it hold fixed statements within it. Even if we admit that oral themes may persist in story telling, still the tale of them as it is told is too fluid, too subject to the personal whim of the narrator, too obedient to the temporary interests of a given moment or audience, too casual in composition. Even as it repeats itself in colloquial narration, it undergoes alteration from version to version.

Fixed rhythm alone will guarantee that kind of preservation which will approximate to documentary fidelity as known in a literate society, and this is likely to encourage if not require some specialization of idiom and vocabulary which is placed at some distance from the vernacular. The memorization of an extended enclave, a master statement, a comprehensive cultural mythos, requires an open-ended rhythm; and this means a regular and recurrent one, repeating itself with minor variations line after line, a rhythm, in fact, which we may be tempted to call an epic meter. Dramatic reenactment, however, and therefore the drama itself, cannot be excluded as a possible parallel mode of preservation in oral cultures, and this format would presumably entail the use of more than one meter, and of nonepic meters. However, it is probable that the epic tale, rather than the dramatic reenactment, is the prototype of all lengthy statements preserved in an oral culture. What is the advantage which epic meter gains over those unique rhythms that accompany short statements? The answer is very obvious: a regular meter repeating itself in periods which are roughly identical opens up the possibility of an extended sequence of statements which can be linked together in memorization. The memory will be beguiled into anticipating the next statement and the next in the course of its obedient response to the regular repetition of the measure, whether that measure be quantitative or accentual.[15]

Gods and Heroes as Agents

The word spoken is itself a form of action and it is to be expected that the agents, that is, the characters, human or divine, whose performance dominates the orally preserved word will exercise their effects by rhetoric as well as by specific acts. The narrative situation constructs itself in such a way as to provide them with audiences who invite exhortation, admonition, advice, reproof, hostility, or friendship, or with whom such colloquy is interchanged. Rhetorical dialogue is a central element in all oral epic. In effect, as agent speaks to agent in the course of a developing piece of action, the speech spoken operates also outside the frame of the story, addressing itself to the listener or to the reciter, who then as he repeats it addresses, as it were, himself. The task of the enclave is, after all, to reiterate in memorizable form the social directives of the society concerned. Such coded information so often takes the form of "we must do so and so" or "let us do so and so" or "this is the thing that must be done." What is more natural than that the necessary narrative frame should take frequent opportunity to make occasion for exhortation, reproof, admonition, encouragement, condemnation, challenge, and the like in the course of which the assorted maxims, the proverbs, the moral law of the community will find a natural place in the mouths of the speakers.

Thus in the West African Bagre myth, two characters, an older and a younger brother, and two others, an old man and an old woman,[16] take leading roles in a converse which indirectly becomes a vehicle for unfolding the traditional wisdom. Such dialogue in oral epic may come close to drama and to dramatic reenactment, as is evident from many scenes preserved in the Book of Genesis in which the teaching of fundamental truths is communicated indirectly in this way.

The agents who serve as what we call characters in epic stories must therefore in some sense be supermen, and may be superwomen if the society concerned is not exclusively patriarchal. Their acts and sayings are framed and preserved in the enclave as the containers of the tribal wisdom, a fact which can enforce the conclusion that it is not just epic poetry *qua* poetry that comes into being to serve the functional needs of cultural continuity. The same is true of that typical epic character that we style the hero. Only kings, queens, princes, military commanders, landowners, men of special power or prowess are suitable vehicles for the didactic purposes required of the narrative. Better still, let it be a god who performs the necessary acts and makes the necessary speeches. This should warn us against too literate an approach to the preliterate style. In literate terms, a hero becomes a study in a special kind of psychology, and the god becomes an embodiment of religious belief or the focus of religious practice. The oral enclave of preserved speech, however, utilizes heroes and gods as part of the apparatus of memorization. The essence of their presence is that what they do or say is more likely to be remembered than if they were ordinary mortals.

The god, however, has a special role in the apparatus. His actions and decisions are used as a symbolic equivalent for natural phenomena which need to be translated into acts by agents in order to be accommodated in the memory. It is often said that the presence of deities in the mythology of so-called primitive peoples is caused by failure of comprehension; they are used to supply a causation for mysterious natural forces not otherwise understood. But the miraculous character of the acts they may perform is not the real clue to their function. They serve as a kind of shorthand, supplying a narrative framework in which flood and fire, earthquake, storm, shipwreck, the sacking of cities, the failure of crops, epidemics, and the like can be described as the acts of agents without impairing the essential quality of the phenomenon. A kind of mythic understanding, valid for its purposes, takes the place of that chain of cause and effect in which literate speech would seek to arrange the same phenomena.

In a well-known story of Joseph Conrad's, a member of the crew is stoking the boiler of a river steamer as it slowly makes its way up the endless green vistas of the Niger. He knows he has to keep stoking, for the god inside the boiler needs warmth. He also knows he has to watch the water gauge, for the god is always thirsty; and if the supply runs short, the god will in his rage burst out of the boiler and overwhelm him. This is a rather simple paradigm of the way in which the god apparatus functions in orally memorized discourse. The action of heat on water to produce a resultant steam pressure and the action of heat on hot air to produce a resultant explosion are chains of cause and effect which describe what happens in terms of law and which utilize a language which classifies the facts under forms of matter and energy in order to do this. The preliterate version of the same connected events short-circuits the explanation and makes it into a much simpler and more effortless picture of an agent with given powers and passions. The angry god bottled up in the boiler is something that the stoker can both remember and express in his own vocabulary. But the concreteness of his vision does not prevent him from being an effective servitor of the god: that is, an efficient boiler tender. As he stokes up the god to keep him comfortably warm, he also interrupts this process to pour water into him to keep him comfortably wet. This is the way the god likes it, and being continually placated by the proper ceremonies, he produces the results which his servant seeks. The boat's paddlewheel revolves; the journey proceeds. A narrativized comprehension has been carried far enough not only to live with the phenomenon but within limits to use it. What, of course, the African cannot do without a literate training is to make an engine. This kind of language can express his acceptance of the engine and describe the proper way to live with it. It cannot help him to invent the machine in the first instance because he cannot rearrange his experience in terms of cause and effect.[17]

It is also observed by literate minds that the acts and decisions of such gods are not ethical or moral in our sense. The one essential characteristic of a god is not his superior morality but his superior durability and the same may apply to demigods and even in limited cases to heroes. Immortality in the agent accords with what is felt to be the necessary permanence, the survival of the stored information of which he is the instrument. All oral epic tries to deal with death. Is it possible to surmise that man's puzzling awareness of his own mortality and his resistance to it may arise from his self-identification with that knowledge preserved in the oral enclave, a knowledge whose immortality seems a necessary condition of the survival of the society? Was it reserved for Plato to rationalize this possibility in his *Phaedo,* making the immortality of the soul a function of the immortality of the Forms?

Teaching by Indirection

The oral tradition, though so profoundly interwoven with the life of its society, so intimately in control of its activities, its sense of identity, its patterns of behavior, carries out all its instruction by indirection. The living memory does not easily hold doctrines unredeemed by entertainment; the pill has to be sweetened.

We can see this most evidently in the way in which information in our sense, for example, historical or geographical, is actually incorporated. The listener is not given a list to memorize. This is provided incidentally in a narrative which he will want to sing and recite, in a condition of exaltation perhaps, and so incidentally recall the information included. A striking instance of this didacticism by indirection is furnished by the so-called Song of Deborah preserved in the Book of Judges in the Old Testament. A true survivor of preliterate Hebrew, unique of its kind, it contains a register of the Hebrew tribes and their geographical locations, furnishing the earliest extant linguistic identity for what was to become the nation of Israel.[18] But this information is not given directly as such; the song, a little epic in its own right, now much corrupted in our present text, which may well be only a truncated version of the original, celebrates a memorable victory of the Hebrew invaders over the resident Canaanites. The battle as it was conducted in a storm, the rout, the death of the Canaanite commander, all hold the listener in rapt attention. However, while some of the tribes rallied to provide the victory, others preferred to stay aloof. The song therefore indulges in encomia of the ones who provided the muscle, while addressing savage reproaches to others for their neutrality. As it does so, the names, the characters, and the locations are recapitulated, and while the audience to whom the song was recited "at the watering places" would relish the story, they also would memorize the composition of their nation and so realize the identity of themselves as a people. Admittedly, this reverses the values by which a modern literate critic would judge the composition, but those values reflect the categories of a different culture.

Successful composition therefore consists not in invention of a plot, as it would in a literate context, but in the contrivance of relevance between a plot and its didactic content. The story must proceed in such a way as naturally to lead into situations which illustrate what proper behavior is, positively or negatively, and provide occasion also for continual inclusion of that vast store of maxims which encapsulate the culture. To the extent that the story teller gets carried away by his story and is tempted to invent novelties, he will be a less successful poet in the terms required by the oral condition.

The situations described in the story are therefore typical rather than unique, as also are the characters, for all the vitality with which they act and speak. But typical need not mean ideal. This is an interpretation which must be guarded against. Viewing the enclave of contrived speech performing its function in society, we may be tempted to describe its content as providing models, patterns, or paradigms of character and action suitable for imitation. Aside from the suggestion implicit in these words that the tradition is somehow documented when of course it is not, they might also induce us to believe something else, namely, that it offers ideal characters performing actions which follow the proprieties proper to the society which uses the tradition. To be sure, propriety and seemliness provide the best operative definition of oral mores—not so much a definition as a validation; the "done thing," to use a schoolboy phrase, is the "right thing." But it would be an error to draw the conclusion that what the agents actually do in the required narrative is itself governed by propriety. Memorized narrative likes to follow rhythms not only metrical but thematic, and this kind of rhythm encourages patterns of polarization between agents and between episodes. Warfare as a subject of epic has mnemonic advantages, as does any hazardous enterprise. It follows that plots of memorized speech will offer heroes and sometimes gods who, so far from providing copybook models of approved action, will illustrate the proprieties by defying them. They will do this successfully for a time; the logic of the function of storage will, however, require that penalty be paid in the end, or redress achieved or balance restored. In short, the teaching of the tradition tends to be carried out negatively rather than positively, or at least it tends to formulate situations which are ethically negative before correcting them. There are unlikely to be agents of total villainy; they may show hostility to man or society perhaps, but as we say, they have redeeming features; whether tyrants or tricksters, they are not wholly rejected from the tradition. Their presence in African mythology and traces thereof in Hebrew myth indicate a desire to sum up the entire gamut of experience, good and bad, as known to the society. It is this total bundle that constitutes the cultural information hoarded for reuse.

A qualification must be added. Some records of oral traditions now available, the Old Testament being the leading example, show evident signs of having been reworked within a more literate framework, and in the interests of a more literate view of the human condition. Good and bad, righteous and wicked, have been sorted out from each other, with the effect that the agents whose performance is described in the stories become paradigmatic figures of virtue and vice.

Justice as Propriety

I suggested at the end of the previous chapter that if justice be identified as the central principle of modern morality, conceptually defined, oral societies could get on very well without it. What they did rely on for cohesion—as does any society—was a set of proprieties, of general rules of behavior which in sum total constitute "what is right." We may now be forced to admit that these "rules" are not abstracted from what is done—that is, they occur incidentally—and that they need not add up to a system which can be consistently formulated. All societies, it may be acknowledged, recognize right from wrong in particular cases. The "way of life" (in Parry's phrase) settles what the distinction is. The business of epic storage is to conserve this life-style and ensure that it is transmitted. It therefore transmits running instructions concerning "the right of it" in given cases. But the symbol or symbols of right which are employed in the story need not be expected to behave as principles. Rather they will be likely to appear as indexes to a process or procedure, indicating specifics, not generalities. They have to observe the narrative rule: being reported only as they occur incidentally in active situations, the subjects of assertion or appeal. Nor is it to be expected that such symbols would behave with that consistency which a philosopher would demand.

4
The Society Reported by Homer

❦

In Plato's words, "It is now time to consider tragedy and its master, Homer," a promise which in his *Republic* he proceeds to fulfill by considering Homer almost exclusively. If it is theoretically correct to identify any culture complex as a system which subsists and flourishes by placing information in storage for reuse; if a preliterate culture can do this only by the use of memory; if memory requires rhythm; if at an advanced level mnemonic needs are met by the construction of an enclave of contrived rhythmic speech, shaped to conform to the rules by which such information is memorized; if, finally, the Hellenic culture was one which arose under preliterate conditions: How then did such a culture subsist and flourish? Where was its enclave? If we assign Homer to the required role, does this not explain that view of him as a didactic poet which prevailed in the three hundred years after his inscription? Clues to the answer can be sought only in his text, assuming that that text preserves in a unique fashion the accent, the idiom, the vocabulary of a wholly preliterate composition. Does it exhibit the functions and conform to the rules of oral storage? Is it didactic by indirection? Is mythos used as the matrix of nomos and ethos? More particularly, do the poems report and recommend an oral morality innocent of conceptual content, pragmatic, procedural, and flexible? What are the discernible lineaments, if any, of a Homeric "justice"?

But an initial obstacle stands in the way of responding to such a question, and it will have to be removed in order to make room for an answer. There is a commonly held view that "Homer," though now admitted to have "lived" in the period of early Hellenism (I use his name as a convenient shorthand), was a poet of the Mycenaean age, meaning that it is the culture and life-style of Mycenae that is described by and large in his poems. "The Greece Homer describes is a network of well organised kingdoms capable of joint military action; its kings live in luxurious stone-built palaces adorned with gold, ivory and other precious metals . . . The scenes attributed to the shield made for Achilles by the god Hephaestus argue a high degree of artistic competence . . . In order to find a plausible setting for the Greece Homer describes, we need to go back to the Mycenaean age, to the twelfth or more likely the thirteenth century at latest." This is the published opinion of one authority and it is very recent (1976). Another has stated (1956) that "neither poem has any trace of a *polis* in its classical political sense. *Polis* in Homer means nothing more than a fortified site or town." In these two judgments,[1] both the material and the political conditions described in the poems are assigned to a society which had ceased to exist perhaps four hundred years before the date of final composition. Several of the chapters of *A Companion to Homer* (1962), a standard work, express the same point of view, at least so far as the material conditions are concerned.[2]

Homeric Fantasy

If a contrary judgment can be rendered, this must mean that Homer's text is ambivalent. The Mycenaean hypothesis is not formed in a vacuum: there are elements in the text that can be viewed as supporting it.[3] Yet it will be my contention that the poems essentially report a society which both in its material and its political aspects is contemporary with their final date of composition. To indicate if possible that this is so, and to disentangle those elements which have the effect of disguising that it is so, is a necessary task before the content and the style of Homer can be examined, and the hypothesis tested that he does in fact constitute a cultural encyclopedia.

Essentially, the Mycenaean disguise is a form of fantasy. But since even the suggestion of fantasy may disturb some who wish Homer to be valued at his true worth, I may call attention to an advantage which its presence would confer on him, both as poet and as the teacher of Greece. If his Greek is artificial and archaic, it is also international (in the pan-Hellenic sense), a lingua franca in which the mythos could be sung in city-states of competing dialects and ambitions. If the actors on his stage are portrayed as Mycenaeans, they could function as ancestors and prototypes of all Greeks living everywhere, while at the same time behaving in contemporary fashion; distance from the present furnishes universality for the context in which the conditions of the present are stated or suggested. They have been put into the costumes of a legendary past, which is, however, supposed to be relived in the present.[4]

This kind of advantage is illustratable from English experience during the sixteenth and the seventeenth centuries. The historical plays of the period, in particular those of Shakespeare, mirror the life-style and the moral concerns of Elizabethan and Jacobean men and women, commoners or gentlemen. But the action is made distant from the present by being played out in the historical past by figures who in some ways were not in the least like Elizabethan and Jacobean gentlemen. Compared with gentlemen of the present, they were larger than life, heroic after their kind, because remote and ancestral and royal. And yet the audience hearing them speak at the same time recognized their membership in the contemporary scene.

In a different genre, the ladies and gentlemen of Tennyson's Camelot were put there to express and justify Victorian manners and values. Their effectiveness at the time in doing this for the epoch in which they were created was reinforced by their apparent membership in a chivalric and idealized society of the past. Both these comparisons have their limits as illustrations of Homeric poetry. They involve works of written literature contrived and conceived by individuals at a given moment in time, not compendia shaped by time and tradition over centuries of oral art. But they do illustrate the advantage that is gained when contemporary experience is reported in such a way as to place a historical distance between the report and the audience for which it is intended.

Homeric Reality: The City

What then is Homer's contemporary scene? Each epic supplies a possible answer, by including an episode which has the effect of presenting precisely a "scene" inserted into the story. In the *Iliad*, Patroclus has fallen, and his borrowed armor has passed to the enemy. Achilles' need for fresh equipment is met by Hephaestus. The listener is transported from the battlefield to the workshop, to watch the manufacture and decoration of a chef d'oeuvre, the great shield.

On it he made two cities of mortal men
which were beautiful . . .

The ordered scenes that follow are a report of civic life: a marriage procession, the women standing at the street doors to watch; an agora held to arbitrate the blood price for a man slain; a state of war, a city besieged, a proposal to negotiate, a decision to resist; a raid on cattle in the hinterland; then, the peaceful pursuits of agriculture, plowing, reaping, the midday meal in the shade, the vintage, the merrymaking, the cattle in the farmyard, the predators on the range, the sheepfolds, the holiday, and the dancing. Only the *basileus* who owns the farm, a privileged domain (*temenos*), recalls the antique, but what is he? He is there in the field with his staff, beside the three sheaf binders and the children who are helping, while he watches the reapers. This is no Mycenaean king but a country squire among his hired hands.

In the *Odyssey,* the shipwrecked hero manages to swim ashore, naked and exhausted. But the hazards of his voyaging are over. He finds himself welcomed by a highly civilized community, which clothes, feeds, entertains, and honors him before dispatching him homeward. Though presided over by a "king" and "queen" living in a palace, this community has the physical contours of a city-state adjacent to the sea and committed to maritime skills and commerce, which the description takes pains to emphasize. It has a city wall, streets, agora, temples, and public buildings, and also harbor, dockyards, and fleet, laid out according to plan. Here, it has been suggested, is an idealized version of a Greek maritime colony, the royal court supplying a touch of Mycenaean fantasy.[5]

In the first of these civic portraits the accent is on land, on agriculture, and land warfare; in the second, on ships and seamanship and commerce by sea. They complement each other, being obverse and reverse of that Hellenism and Hellenic consciousness which are reported in the poems. They will appear conjointly in the *Works and Days* of Hesiod. If most critics have allowed neither passage due weight as an indicator of a social context for both poems, this is because of their inclination to treat them precisely as inserts, in which the narrative temporarily lapses from its task of reporting Mycenaean tradition. The same kind of treatment has been accorded Homeric descriptions of

Troy, in which such items as the temples of Apollo and Athena and the monumental statue of the goddess are viewed as "anachronisms."[6] A demonstration that the reverse is the truth, that it is the Mycenaean memories which are the anachronisms, retained in stories otherwise firmly founded in the life-style of the Greece of historical times, must depend upon an examination of the warp and woof of Homer's text. An example, a running sequence of nearly four hundred lines, can be furnished which at first sight will seem unpromising.

The Catalogue of the Ships

Nowhere has the argument for prehistoric control over content been more effective than in the case of the catalogue of Greek forces included in the latter half of the second book of the *Iliad*. Here surely is a document with prehistoric credentials guaranteed by the long list of place names attached to sites forgotten or deserted in classical times. If, however, even this list in the text now transmitted is demonstrably relevant to contemporary Hellenism, we can anticipate a fortiori that a similar effect may be demonstrable in the bulk of both epics. There is a narrative excuse for inserting it, as there has to be: the Greeks in an excess of war-weariness, after nine years of trying to take Troy, have broken ranks in a mad rush to their ships. They are rallied and in assembly renew their resolve to continue hostilities after being reminded of the augury of victory given to them nine years ago. The war takes on a fresh start at this point, and in preparation for it the Greek ranks are mustered in a review which is complemented by a similar review of Trojan forces, as though two massed armies were drawn up against each other on the plain (*Il.* 2.484–877).

Since the mythos of a war against Troy requires that the Achaean army arrive by ship, the respective numbers of the Achaean contingents are reported in terms of numbers of ships. The Trojan side, being represented as defending a city, is in contrast represented as wholly land-based, though in the case of the more distant allies of the Trojans this would not seem to be very realistic. The Achaean catalogue is much the longer, 266 lines (494–759), as against 62 lines for the Trojan side (816–877). It is a review of forces now present on Trojan soil supposedly led by Agamemnon and preparing for battle. Given this intention, one is entitled to ask the question, simply and perhaps naively, "Why, after all, a catalogue of ships rather than of men?" In fact, the listing is both of men and of ships; the manner of their combination bears some inspection.

The poet invokes the direct aid of the Muses, who are invited not to prompt his own memory but to speak in their own voices. He makes it quite clear that their task is to enumerate the Greek heroes by name—"who were the leaders and lords of the Achaeans"—and to deliver a record of "all who came up before Troy" (492), a total number for which the poet's own voice and resources are quite inadequate (488–490). To this appeal he then appends one more line, as follows: "Moreover I will declare the ships' commanders and the total of the ships." The line reads as an afterthought, as though the ships were a supplementary item which required to be added. Moreover, the "author" of the line uses the first person, substituting himself in place of the Muses. Is he a "second author," revising the composition of a "first," his task being to convert a list of land-based forces into a maritime list? Confirmation of this inference depends upon an analysis of the way in which the catalogue itself is put together.

It opens with fifteen lines (494–508) devoted to an enumeration of the names of the Boeotian chieftains and towns, all framed in a narrative syntax which describes how they variously "commanded" and "dwelt in" or "held" or "inhabited." Two more lines are then appended as follows: "Of these, fifty ships went, and in each young men of the Boeotians 120 did go." Is it perhaps a little odd that the ships not only appear as an appendix to the heroic catalogue but emerge in the guise of troops on the move (the verb is used otherwise only of persons), as though the poet's mind's eye remained focused on his land forces? The next list is shorter; using the same narrative syntax, it covers the inhabitants of the district of Orchomenos and their rulers accompanying them, and then adds the single line: "For them thirty ships marched in file." Why use such a curious verb, again appropriate to a military rather than a naval contingent? It is elsewhere applied to persons or animals in motion and could scarcely describe ships beached in rows at Troy, particularly since the catalogue occasionally inserts the notice of crews "embarking." To be sure, it might conceivably describe ships disposed in line of battle, but is this likely? The next seven lines list in similar syntax the Phocaean commanders and those who inhabited the various towns of the district, to which the poet then appends the following: "Along with them forty ships followed" (524). Why, it may be asked, should the ships be following the men? The verb regularly describes the "company" that constitutes the following of a chieftain; these ships, then, are presented as an entourage. The same list then reverts to the chieftains as subject and to a purely military terminology:

They organized the ranks of the Phocaeans and disposed them
as they donned their harness to the left of the Boeotians

Are we to infer that the line about the ships is an intrusion into a
description otherwise focused upon the land-based military formation?

In a majority of the succeeding lists which make up the total
Achaean catalogue, the ships are added to each list in similar fashion as
a kind of appendix to a military formation and are presented as either
"followers" or as troops "marching in file." The first formula is the
commoner, used in the case of Ajax and the Locrians (534), the
Euboeans (545), Athens and Menestheus (556), Argos and Tiryns
(568), Elis (618b–619), the Western Isles (630), Odysseus and Ithaca
(637), the Aetolians and their leader (644), the Cretans and their
leaders (645), the kingdom of Protesilaus and Podarkes (709), the
district of Ormenius and its leader (737), the district of Argissa and its
leaders (747), the Magnesians and their leader (759).

The second formula is used at the end of the Pylian list (602), the
Aegean Islands list (680), and the Ithome list (733). It seems designed
to supply a stylistic variation, to relieve monotony.

But besides adding or inserting individual lines like footnotes, the
poet occasionally achieves the same objective by means of a syntactical
trick, applied in the first instance to the Lacedaemonian list (581–590).
A series of generic relative clauses—"they who," etc.—itemizes the inhabitants of Lacedaemonian towns. This is topped off by the apodosis:

Over them [genitive] ruled Menelaus.

But the next line adds, also in the genitive:

even over sixty ships.

This insertion alters the object of the verb but is made possible by the
ambiguity of the Greek genitive plural. That it is an insertion, and
arbitrary at that, is revealed as the line completes itself:

They donned their harness apart

Here translators can be seduced into rendering the harness as though it
referred to naval equipment (so, for example, Lattimore: "Ships mar-
shalled apart"), but it does not. The device which allows ships to be
aligned in apposition with troops so that the troops are virtually converted into ships is used four more times, being applied to the Arcadian

list (610), the Phthia-Achilles list (685), the Pherae-Admetus list (713b), and the Methone-Philoctetes list (719).

These peculiarities become explicable on one hypothesis: an original catalogue of the components of an army viewed as organized for operations by land has been converted into an expedition by sea. The conversion has been carried out summarily and mechanically. As further evidence of this, one notes that in the case of the land-locked Arcadians the poet has realized the absurdity of including them as navigators since they were "innocent of navigational skill" (614), and has felt obliged to supply as an explanation the donation to them of no less than sixty ships from Agamemnon (612–613)!

Concluding his catalogue, the poet repeats the definition of its content first supplied when he invoked the Muses (487):

These were the leaders and lords of the Danaans.

No more talk of ships. Then the Muse is invited to tell the poet which was the best warrior and which the best team of horses, and the answer is supplied at some length (763–779). At 780 the whole army is discovered proceeding on the march to battle (its feet firmly planted on the ground).

The possible origins and original components of the muster of land forces has properly been the subject of lively speculation. Was it an original Mycenaean muster list?[7] Does it combine two different catalogues, one geographic, a gazeteer of prehistoric Greece, the other biographic, a list of the names of legendary heroes with genealogical and anecdotal notes? Whatever may be the proper answer to such questions, one basic fact seems to emerge, which, given our traditional way of looking at the *Iliad,* is a little disconcerting. An original catalogue of a land expedition has been manipulated into the shape of a naval expedition which formed no part of the original catalogue. Its artificiality is confirmed by the round numbers of ships, extravagant if not absurd, which are attributed to a good many of the contingents.[8]

At what period and in what interest would such a manipulation have been attempted? On behalf of a Mycenaean context, it can be argued that ships are appropriate if this Achaean force is to be an expedition which has to reach Troy before laying siege to the city. The Mycenaeans were seafarers, even though representation of ships in art becomes common only in the Hellenic period. On the other hand, the narrative context of the catalogue calls for a muster of two confronting armies on a plain, for which ships as such are an irrelevance. More important, if the catalogue had been composed as an original record of a legendary naval muster at Aulis, preparatory to the expedition (an event recalled in the preceding context), then it would not have had to be edited.

A reasonable solution would be that an original version was based on a concept of the Greek hero as a warrior fighting on land. The desire to modify this ideal so that it could take naval form, the hero assuming the guise of the seaman, would be likely to arise in the eighth and seventh centuries at the earliest, the period of Greek colonization, when Greek naval activity expanded aggressively, when enormous demands were made on navigational skills, and when the Greek temperament responded in a fashion historically unique in terms of the sheer concentration of activity, the amount of risk taken, the degree of bold and imaginative exploration pursued under hazardous conditions—unique, that is, by the standards of previous empires of the Near East and uniquely concentrated in a span of two hundred and fifty years culminating in the organization of the Athenian overseas empire. What a literate critic would style as editing is in fact an oral manipulation, and aside from its congruence with the known facts of Greek naval activity in the late geometric and orientalizing period, is it not reasonable also to place this manipulation in that period of bardic activity which saw the perfection of the Homeric language as an enclave of contrived speech deeply colored by contemporary Ionian experience?

It was suggested sixty years ago that whatever is genuinely prehistoric in the catalogue has been amalgamated through the processes of continual oral reformulation with a kind of navigator's guide to the Aegean orally composed and sung and dating from the Ionian period.[9] The conversion of the heroology into a ship's catalogue coincides with such a conclusion, though it does not confirm it. In support, it has been pointed out that many groups of inhabitants in the Trojan list are located by their relationship to rivers or river mouths, in some cases with epithets indicating water quality (825, 839, 845, 849–850, 854, 869, 877). The location of supplies of fresh water was of first importance to navigators in antiquity no less than it was later to Captain Cook. The initial composition of songs recording this information is plausible in the period which immediately preceded successful colonization of the Black Sea in the seventh century. There are also some indications in the

Achaean portion that point to hinterlands (*ēpeiroi*), estuaries, and fore-shores as of interest to the catalogue. A terminus ante quem of 650 B.C. or even later for its consolidation, and then its inscription, in present form, would be reasonable.

One arguable objection to such a dating lies in the omission from the Greek list of Samos and also of Chios, the reputed home of the Homeridae, and also in the failure of Homer anywhere to mention Phocaea and, for that matter, Smyrna. The sailors of Samos and Phocaea, according to Herodotus, had pioneered in long-distance naviga-tion in the archaic period, and Samian archaeology reveals the earliest known Greek temple on a grand scale. It has, however, been pointed out that the geographic nexus of the existing catalogue, taking the two lists together, is Rhodes.[10] Is the catalogue in its final form a Rhodian product? We remember the possibility that the alphabet was born in Rhodes. Was it perchance applied to the transcription of an original Achaean prehistoric listing which had uniquely survived in Linear B when nothing else did, Linear B being a medium whose usefulness was restricted to such purposes? If this is true (and it is only guesswork), such a list was then edited by a bard or bards of the late eighth or seventh century in the interests of a mythos which had to be shaped to reflect the conditions of a maritime epoch. Nevertheless, the control of the antique ancestral memory over those who made the maritime adaptation remained firm. Forgotten cities and dynasties and grandeurs still had their rolling rhythms and their ring of pride for those who listened and could repeat them. The Achaean catalogue remains a com-ponent of that historical fantasy to the celebration of which both Homeric poems address themselves.

The Trojan Catalogue

Troy's troops, by contrast, are land-based, not an expeditionary force despatched overseas. The occasion for their muster is furnished when Iris descends with a message from Zeus. At the moment of her arrival (2.788–789):

They were uttering addresses-in-agora at the doors of Priam,
all of them assembled-in-agora, both the young and the elders.

She then admonishes Priam (796–797):

Ever are utterances [*mythoi*] without number dear to you,
as once in time of peace. But war without stint has arisen

Troy is conducting public business under peaceful conditions in an agora, translatable as a town meeting, whether or not a given place for such meeting is implied. It is held in front of the doors of the royal palace, a setting that maintains the blend of the contemporary and the antique. The proceedings are about to be interrupted by an armed attack from outside, a situation which has its analogue in the *Odyssey*, where the first speaker in an agora hastily convoked inquires anxiously: "Are we threatened?" The divine messenger—she is really only a scout who has been posted as a lookout (792–793)—warns that a large expedition is advancing over the plain to attack the town (801). Turning to Hector, she urges him to take charge (803–806):

Many are the "accessory peoples" [*epikouroi*] through the great town of Priam;
various are the tongues of the varied, even of many-sown mankind;
for them should each man give signal, even to those whom he commands,
and of them should he be leader, having set in order the citizens [*poliētai*]

These directives are most reasonably referable to the military dispositions of a city-state of early Hellenism, not on the mainland, but in Anatolia, where the inhabitants might include allies, ethnic minorities here treated as citizens, who live in the city but follow the leadership exercised by their own local authorities. The rule of these authorities is expressed by the regular Greek verb *archein*, not the archaic *anassein*. To meet a military threat, the citizen body is mustered in separate companies officered by their local leadership. Iris inserts an aphorism in her advice suggesting that language communication may be a problem. It is interesting that Leaf's commentary admonishes the reader at this point to ignore lines 803–804; any critic committed to the proposition that the prehistory of Homer is to be taken seriously would have to do this.

Where would one find a Greek city inhabited and governed on these lines if not at Miletus or Smyrna or Phocaea, to take obvious examples of Hellenic settlements with mixed populations constantly threatened from the landward side by the non-Hellenic natives of the area? To be sure, the mythos of the *Iliad* requires Troy to be situated at a distance from the coast, but so were the Ionian settlements.

Hector's response to the scout's alert is automatic (808–810):

He at once dissolved the agora; they all made for their arms;
the gates were all opened and the people streamed out,
both foot and horse, and a great shouting arose

65

But in order to fight effectively, this citizen body has to be mobilized. This occurs on the slope of an eminence facing the city (815):

There were the Trojans then marshaled by groups and the accessory-peoples

The ensuing list of Trojan contingents, though less than a quarter in length, follows the same formula as the Greek list, with the omission of the ships: given peoples, sometimes named and sometimes not, are identified as inhabitants of named cities or regions, and paired in each case with names of one or more commanders. Troy leads off, then the cities of the Troad and the Hellespont, then the Thracians from east to west, then back to Anatolia to cover the Paphlagonians, Alizonians (whoever they may be), Mysians, Phrygians, Maeonians, Carians, and Lycians. The effect produced is to represent the opponents of the Achaeans as constituting a kind of "empire" (though Priam is not mentioned). The composition is heterogeneous and some of the personal names bear the mark of sheer invention. Even if the lines referring to Greek Black Sea settlements (853–855) are excised, the Sestos and Abydos which are listed as on the Hellespont are not likely to be intended as references to prehistoric sites. The ethnography and geography in general reflect the Anatolia known or guessed at by the Ionians. The Phrygians and Maeonians (that is, Lydians) and the Lycians "beyond Xanthus" do not belong in the heroic age, nor probably the silver mines of inner Anatolia, nor perhaps even the Thracians. Miletus may or may not owe its inclusion to its Mycenaean origins, but the mixed blood of its inhabitants due to intermarriage with the Carians is a fact attested for the seventh century, as in the instance of Thales the philosopher. Its people, according to the catalogue, "speak bad Greek," and the heights adjacent to the city are called "Lice Mountain," which sounds like a nickname. Nastes, one of the two Milesian commanders (the other bears an invented name), "joined the war like a girl clad in gold, poor fool," and was killed by Achilles. The hint of malice in these notices is more likely to reflect an attitude on the part of Ionian neighbors of Miletus, especially from the islands, in the historic period, than any tradition descending from the heroic age, and in a list otherwise barren of topographical detail there are a few touches added to the descriptions of the Lydian and Milesian territories which would be available to a bard familiar with the coastline and immediate hinterland in the same period. To be sure, the Ionian cities (with the one exception) are omitted, as also elsewhere in Homer. But the omission is needed to protect the fantasy, with which the audiences were invited to identify as being supposed descendants of heroic progeny.[11]

Books have been written about Homer which would allow the reader to suppose that Troy scarcely existed except as the necessary objective of the Achaean heroes. In fact, it is a metropolis. Its city walls and gates, its streets, houses, and temples are described in Books 3, 6, 22, and 24. Its "people" are a *"laos"* or a *"demos."* Its Athene temple, housing a monumental statue of the goddess, is visited by the Trojan women in procession to supplicate the statue. The incongruity between this kind of city and the meager dimensions of the fort that has actually been uncovered by archaeologists has long been acknowledged. Troy in Homer has Greek language, Greek gods, Greek manners, and a Greek life-style. It endures the perils common to Greek city-states. It could be Miletus or Ephesus, Sybaris, Syracuse, Athens, or Corinth, a composite picture. The fantasy takes over when Priam's household is described: the fantastic numbers of his progeny, the dimensions of his palace, the autocracy and the empire with which he is implicitly invested. But it is fantasy.

Life-Style in Ithaca

The plot of the *Odyssey* revolves around the return of a missing husband and father, whose property in his absence has been occupied by interlopers. The adventures by land and sea which accompany his attempts to return home, though probably more familiar to the common reader, are only a subplot inserted into the main theme, which is domestic. Matters are set in motion when Athene, patroness and protector of the absent hero, descends from Olympus in disguise to pay a visit to the household in Ithaca at present deprived of its master. The mise-en-scène as it unfolds may furnish a second example of the realities with which Homer's text is dealing (1.103–104, 106–112):

and she stood in the township of Ithaca before Odysseus' front door at the
threshold of the yard . . .
There she found the suitors, those men of might. They at this time
were enjoying themselves in front of the doors with (a game of) draughts,
sitting on ox hides of animals that they had personally killed.
Orderlies and servants were busy about them,
some mixing wine and water in bowls,
others using porous sponges to wash down the tables
before setting them out, and others again were putting around plenty of
meat.

There are those who would insist that this scene, if not actually Mycenaean, at least reconstructs a reminiscence which is prehistoric and therefore heroic in the accepted prehistoric sense. They are assisted in this view by the fact that many words used to describe physical objects and human actions operate at two alternative levels of reference. They can be translated to refer to the world of historic Greece; they can also be rendered in a way that will either neutralize this reference or convert it into a grandiloquent equivalent which confers on them a prehistoric, not to say heroic, flavor. Thus the "township" can be generalized to mean simply the "land" of Ithaca; Odysseus' "front door" becomes "the entry of the gate of Odysseus," and the "yard threshold" becomes "the threshold of the courtyard." The "busy servants" become "ready squires." These examples are taken from Butcher and Lang's archaizing transla-tion. While a small part of Homer's vocabulary has connotations which are exclusively prehistoric, the bulk of it has experienced semantic changes which respond to the altered economic and social conditions of the Hellenic period. The Greek word *aulē*, for example, could be taken to indicate the courtyard of a Mycenaean palace complex com-plete with vestibule, porticoes, and entrances. It could also indicate the yard in front of a large farmhouse. Which is it in this case? Can this really be a Mycenaean forecourt when in a later context its vestibule is alluded to as a place where farm animals can be tethered (20.189). In the present instance the unwanted guests of the house are outside in the yard playing a game and sprawled on the rough hides of the animals they have eaten, presumably to protect themselves from the dirt. The scene continues (114, 115–120):

Telemachus was sitting despondent among them . . .
Would his father ever come back and scatter the suitors to the winds
and resume his proper estate and control of his property?
He had noticed the stranger before they did
and went straight out to the front door, for he did not want
to leave such a visitor standing at the door

So he welcomed hm, offering him refreshment preliminary to learning what he has to say (126–130, 132–134):

They went inside the lofty house.
Taking the stranger's spear, he propped it against a long pillar
inside the spearholder [a kind of umbrella stand], in which as well
Odysseus' spears were standing many of them,
and conducted him to a chair . . .

and set a stool for himself beside it out of earshot
of the suitors to avoid upsetting the guest with the shouting
and putting him off his food.

Such a precaution presupposes architectural arrangements of the simplest sort. The setting is unpretentious; the manner is formal yet homely. Telemachus' problem is practical: how are the rights over his father's property to be preserved in his absence?

The guest's hands are then washed and he is fed; the suitors enter the hall, sit down on benches and chairs, and eat and drink, and are then entertained by song. The style in which these operations are described is ceremonious and flavored with the antique. But there is nothing exculsively antique, let alone heroic, about what is happening.

Voyaging, Fighting, and Farming

Telemachus, speaking close to the stranger's ear to avoid being overheard, explains that the owner of the house is away, perhaps drowned at sea, perhaps killed ashore, no one knows. There is no thought of any written communication that might arrive to break the silence. But he would like to know to whom he is speaking (170–172, 175–177).

Who are you? Where have you come from? Where is your city and your parents?
What sort of ship have you arrived in? How did the sailors
bring you to Ithaca? And who did they claim to be? . . .
Are you a newcomer? Or are you indeed a traveler with previous guest privileges in our house?
Many are the men that have come to it from time to time,
for the man I speak of liked to move around in the world.

It is no hero of Troy that Telemachus is thinking of. His father is an Ionian merchant mariner, a roving spirit, a lavish entertainer, now long absent on a voyage and given up for lost. And the stranger is another such, expected to identify himself by name, by city, by patronymic, in accordance with a formula which is still quoted by Xenophanes in the closing years of the Archaic Age.[12] Telemachus does not view his visitor as a chieftain accompanied by retainers but as a merchant who has embarked on a ship somewhere, managed by a crew who are strangers to him—that is, they are for hire or are in business of their own.

The visitor in reply gives his name, patronymic, and geographic base (181–188).

I rule over the Taphians, those ready oarsmen,
and have just landed here with ship and company
in the course of a voyage to men of alien speech
to Temese to fetch bronze. I am carrying iron.
My ship is here lying off out in the country away from the city
in Reithron harbor beneath wooded Neeion.
Your house and mine share guest privileges, so I asseverate;
to confirm, you can go and ask Laertes, that aged sire

These few words are enough to outline a state of affairs which pertains to the conditions of maritime commerce and overseas colonization. To expose this with full clarity, it is not enough simply to note that a cargo of iron is an anachronism in a description of what is supposed to be a Bronze Age culture. We are not in the Bronze Age at all. The location of the scene is that pertaining to any Greek maritime town of the early Hellenic period, whether in Ionia, the islands, the mainland, or in the west. Very few such towns survive for archaeological inspection in the condition of that time. Emporio, on the southern tip of Chios, would fit quite well.[13] For that matter, so might Ithaca, in which for mythic purposes the tale is located, whether or not Reithron and Neeion are really Ithacan names. The Greek township of this period is what it still remained in the fifth and fourth centuries, a complex consisting of a town site, unfortified, but surrounded by a wall, a protected beach, separate but nearby, and an agricultural hinterland. All such were ports of call for the island-hopping navigators of the period as they transacted their business across the eastern Mediterranean. They were all seafarers, ready oarsmen, as well as farmers and traders.

Their expanding commerce was bringing them into contact with non-Greek peoples of Anatolia, Africa, Sicily, and Italy, "men of alien speech." Metallurgy has become an important item in this commerce. Politically, the townships or city-states are all autonomous. Their narrower interests can involve them in military confrontations. Yet economically, this Hellenic culture can become viable and remain so only if communications and trade are kept open.[14] This depends upon a system of safe conduct for all voyagers who put in at the ports of fellow Hellenes, as they have to, as well as on the right to break a journey or voyage. The problem is handled by maintaining "correspondents" in all the cities, just as overland travel and commerce was handled in Europe before the nineteenth century. Only in an oral age, these cannot be literally "correspondents." They are posting hosts and guests of each other with an obligation of mutual entertainment and protection, provided when bona fides and proof of identity can be furnished. Later, the system is going to expand to a point of producing whole communities of resident aliens who are citizens of one town but are doing business in another.

The mention of Telemachus' grandfather, Laertes, provides occasion for a description of his situation (189–193):

. . . Laertes, that aged sire. They say he has stopped coming to the city
and instead keeps away in the country. He has his troubles,
with an old woman to help him who prepares food and drink for him;
what time his limbs are wearied
as he toils up the terrace of his vineyard plot

Here is the agricultural hinterland contiguous to the city. The visitor has traversed it on his way from the roadstead, thus gaining the opportunity to learn about Laertes. It is inhabited by farmers of the township who come into town to do business, visit relatives and the like, but it is a long walk, too far for an old man who just manages to keep up his terraced vineyard with the help of an aged female housekeeper. He labors as Hesiod's farmer labors, and as hard as he does, and for both of them the living that is attained is not far above the subsistence level, but it can be improved by trade and travel, a line of business which the son has taken advantage of. The son, more prosperous, has a country mansion on the outskirts of the town. By Aristophanes' day the Attic standard of living had improved, but a dozen of his plays will attest a similar relationship between town and country.

The poet's song must not neglect his duty to his audience. He must invest his contemporary report with the aura of romanticism. So his Ionian trader becomes a "lord over the Taphians," that mysterious name (does it mask a reference to Samos or Phocaea?), just as though he were a Mycenaean autocrat, and to get the copper he wants he has to go as far as "Temese," another legendary name, apparently invented. The aged grandfather is dignified as a "hero,"[15] not, however, meaning a warrior in the accepted modern sense of "heroic," for he certainly is not that, but in the antique Homeric sense that he is a stout man, an epithet acceptable for minstrels, heralds, doctors, princes, and just plain citizens. The visitor continues (194–199):

So here I am. The fact is they told me he was in town—
I mean your father. But now it seems the gods stop him from his road.
But Odysseus cannot have died.
He must have been detained somewhere in the wide seas
on some island sea-beset. Violent people have got hold of him—
savages, I expect—who keep him in forcible detention.

I am no prophet, he continues, but (203–205)

I wager he won't be away long from his own country,
not though his bonds be iron.
He is an ingenious man, he will think of a way to get back.

Such observations as these treat Odysseus not as a warrior who has been absent for nearly twenty legendary years besieging Troy, but a traveler like the speaker, trading by sea with dangerous customers on some distant shore who have temporarily detained him. The visitor then takes a closer look at Telemachus and exclaims (207):

Aren't you Odysseus' son grown up?

He notes the resemblance, adding that (209–212)

Odysseus and I had been together in the old days quite a bit
before he embarked for Troy, which was also
the destination of so many other Argive chieftains . . .
I have not seen him since . . .

In this way the poet hastily restores to Odysseus his role as a hero in a myth of long ago. But he does not stay there, for Telemachus promptly replies (214–220):

Guest-friend, to tell you the truth,
if I am his, that is what my mother says, but I myself
don't know; a man's own descent is not a thing one knows oneself.
I wish I had had the fortune to be the son of the kind of man
who when old age overtook him remained in possession of his property.
As it is, of all men he is most out of luck.
However, in responding to your question, they say I am his son.

To which the traveler offers courteous consolation by way of a compliment to Telemachus' mother (222–223):

Well, the gods have not left you lineage without a name,
considering you are what you are, and Penelope is your mother.

The boy cannot remember his father. The wanderer has been away long enough to make it possible for Telemachus to be illegitimate. And now, growing up fatherless, he can neither inherit the property waiting for him when his father dies nor take control of it himself, for he lacks the credentials. How often must precisely such situations have risen under the conditions of maritime voyaging which prevailed in the geometric and archaic periods of Greek enterprise?

Domestic Proprieties

The visitor, however, while conversing with his host, cannot help noticing what seems to be an unusual situation in this house. Can't you explain to me, he continues (225–229):

What's going on here—the eating, drinking, and the crowds? Why need you do this?
Is it a celebration or a wedding? Certainly not a love-feast.
They look to me as though they were deliberately insulting you
while eating and drinking in your own house. It's a disgraceful spectacle
for anyone to encounter; any man of sense would take grave offense at it.

Domestic celebrations and entertainments are a common feature of this culture, always accompanied by food. Weddings, reunions, complimentary dinners, and the more intimate occasions when friends club together to bring their own contribution—any of these a visitor might have expected to find had he chanced on the occasion. But the present company astonishes him by their incivility to their presumed host. They don't fit any proper occasion. They are violating one of the basic norms of the society to which he is accustomed. The question gives Telemachus his opportunity to explain more clearly the facts underlying his despondency (232–243):

This house was once wealthy and very respectable
when the man of whom we speak was in town . . .
. . . but now he is a man utterly unknown.
I would not feel so badly
if he and his company had been overcome in the Trojans' township
or he had died in the arms of his friends, his warfare spun through to the end.
The Panachaeans would have made him his monument for that
and his son thereafter would have gained name and fame.
But as it is, the hurricane has blown him away from name and fame.
He is gone unknown, unnoticed, and the tears and grieving
he has left to me.

73

The visitor's notions of where Odysseus may be, and why, must be set straight. To make the story—the fantasy—work, Telemachus briefly restores him to his heroic context in the Trojan legend, and then promptly removes him from it again. The roles of son and father, and the son's motives in what he says, belong to the contemporary Ionian scene. While it is true of all societies that material security and social status are usually connected, in this society the one is a function of the other. A man's name is his identity, and the greater the name and fame, the Greek *kleos,* the greater his social role and the more effective the rights he can exercise, and upon these rights the security of his property depends. Its retention to life's end depends upon a career not only successful but known and accepted by the community, by one's friends and connections, who are the only witnesses there are to affirm these rights. The affirmation depends upon oral report, by word of mouth, for written documents are not available. With equal force, reliance on such social awareness—one's *kleos*—is transferable from father to son so that the son can come into his inheritance; but only provided, first, that the father's life story is known and his deeds proclaimed; second, that the life is capped by ceremonial burial, also in the presence of witnesses who can state it; and third, that the son's paternity is acknowledged by the same witnesses so that he can come into his father's place. In the present instance, none of these things has happened: an anonymous father lost to record and knowledge cannot confirm his son's position in the community and his indisputable right to the property.

Such reflections as these of Telemachus mirror a society in which not only communication but all record is wholly oral, dependent upon speech and statement pronounced, repeated, and remembered. No Linear B is operating here to supply a legal framework which is visually operative. Some accumulation of wealth is possible, but its inheritance is always at the hazard of foreign travel and foreign wars, which in this case are imagined to be taking place in "the Trojan township," that is, against another Greek city-state. Yet the citizens of that same state are all Greeks, "Pan-Achaeans," sharing a common culture, a common trading economy, members of cities which are continually fighting each other. This is no confederacy ruled over by Mycenaean bureaucrats. It is the world in which Archilochus lived, of soldier-adventurers, "Pan-hellenes" off to Thasos for pillaging maybe, or to seize homesteads, maybe fallen in the fighting, maybe drowning on the way there or on the way back, all hope and ambition frustrated.

However [Telemachus continues], I have other troubles:
all the powerful top men [*aristoi*] in the islands . . .
all who lord it in craggy Ithaca—
all these are suitors for my mother's hand and devour our house.
She can neither say no nor say yes.
So they go on eating and consuming our house.
It won't be long before they finish me off too.

(244–245, 247–251)

No need to say more. Here is a prosperous estate, one among dozens in the area, well worth acquiring through marriage to the putative widow, well worth dividing up among the rivals for her hand, if it comes to that. It is not a prize that the lowly can afford to compete for. Heads of houses all over the area, including adjacent islands, are in the market. The exaggeration of numbers of eligibles stretches plausibility, but is once more appropriate to the context of heroic fantasy, for in the end Odysseus will have to take them all on, and win. The procedure they have adopted is to camp upon the widow's doorstep and wait for her choice to be announced. Her husband has disappeared, so why shouldn't they do this? But they have gone too far. They have taken over the manor, give orders to the servants, eat on the premises, a violation of the unwritten law. You have a right to bring some pressure on a woman in this circumstance, but not that kind of pressure. The exercise of *hubris* has become their hallmark: it has been so stigmatized by the visitor. It will become the moral issue upon which the dénouement of the plot will turn when it begins to appear that the husband after all is not dead. But how are they to know it, how is anyone to know it? No reader of such contexts could mistake Odysseus for a Mycenaean king, paymaster of an armed retinue and lord over a subservient peasantry. The visitor, at last in possession of the full facts, grasps the obvious conclusion (253–254):

I see! You do indeed need Odysseus—and he is gone.
He would be the man to lay hands on these unconscionable suitors . . .

and he recalls the Odysseus that he knew (257): what a fighter (256), what a guest, what a drinker (258), what a voyager, what a friend (259–264)! It is an opportunity to recall the heroic dimensions of the chief character, a man who would soon finish off the suitors (265–266). But realism returns:

However, that is on the knees of the gods.
Will he return to wreak vengeance in his own home, or will he not?

We still do not know.

Political Realities

But heroic reminiscence now gives way to realism as the visitor next addresses himself to the present situation: what Telemachus has to do is to plan a method of getting rid of the suitors (270), so he must pay close attention to the following advice (272–280):

Tomorrow call to assembly the Achaean sires
and make a statement to them all and the gods must give testimony for it.
Enjoin upon the suitors that they disperse to their own places;
as for your mother, if her inclination is to marry
she must go back to her father's hall; he is a powerful man.
They will make ready a wedding and arrange to furnish all the bride gifts
that should accompany a cherished daughter.
What you have to do
is to take the best ship you can with a crew of twenty . . .

Telemachus in fact must make up his mind to leave home temporarily, risky as that may be. He must sail away in search of news of his father, positive or negative. In either case the tidings he may acquire, if properly confirmed (282–286), will clarify his own position (287–296). Such a risky step must be protected by preliminaries. He must call a town meeting (agora); the story comes to grips with current political realities.

The procedures will be oral, and are to be addressed to the necessity of placing on the public record a situation which requires a solution and stating what that solution ought to be. The statement to be made will be validated before witnesses, in the first instance the members of the meeting, in the second instance the gods, a necessary presence to support promises, oaths, or threats which the speaker lacks power to implement directly.

The agora is duly summoned, and its proceedings are reported in the second book with continuing realism. A committee of elders is in charge, before whom Telemachus appears as a plaintiff or litigant. But the mythos prepares for his entrance by resorting briefly to fantasy, in order to present him as a heroic protagonist (2.2–5):

He rose from his bed, even the dear son of Odysseus;
he donned his clothing and hung his sharp sword upon his shoulder,
and beneath his nimble feet bound fair sandals,
and went forth from his chamber in likeness to a god in presence.

Descriptions of the absent father had qualified the realism of his contemporary situation as a missing voyager with some touches of the antique. It was a mythic necessity. Here the same thing is done for the son. About to face the ordeal of confronting the agora, he is temporarily converted from a frustrated, cynical, and helpless human being into a youthful Mycenaean demigod. Formulas appropriate to this purpose are employed: the sword, the sandals, the divine appearance. So he makes his entrance, still at the heroic level (10–14):

He progressed into the agora and held in hand a bronze spear,
not alone, for at his side followed two swift-footed hounds.
Wondrous the grace that Athene shed upon him;
and him all the people beheld marveling as he came in;
and he sat down in his father's seat.

Divine agency is employed to assist the conversion. This is indeed a Mycenaean prince seated in the throne room, before whom stand obedient courtiers. The incongruity is evident given the actual setting of the action. Where has this seat been for the last twenty years?

A Civic Society

The society with which Telemachus has to deal and of which he is a member is the "polis according to Homer."[16] When his father at a later stage of the story has returned, but in a disguise, with the intention of regaining control of his property by stratagem, he is brought into contact with the same kind of community. Connection with his own people begins in the country cottage of his swineherd, which serves as his first temporary home, from which he will enter his own house unrecognized. Eumaeus' services will be used to aid this purpose. Such is the arrangement required by the plot. But his original proposal to Eumaeus is not couched in these terms. He says (15.307–310):

I have a mind to depart for the town [*astu*]
to beg, in order to avoid being a burden on you
. . . through the city [*ptolis*]; I will by myself in my necessity
go to and fro waiting for people to extend a cup or a morsel to me.

This takes for granted the existence of an urban center with streets where he can beg as a matter of course, a method of self-support acceptable for the destitute (cf. also 18.1–2), rather than sponging perpetually on Eumaeus. He then adds, or rather the poet does for him (313–314):

Perhaps I will go to Odysseus' house
and give a message to Penelope . . .

Thereafter, as persons in the cottage prepare to leave, the formula employed describes them as going "to the city," never to the megaron, the
house of Odysseus. Thus when Eumaeus on the orders of Telemachus
leaves to tell his mother that her son is now safe: "he put on his sandals
and went cityward" (16.155). As he returns, Telemachus asks him,
"What are they saying in town?" (16.461), and then "intending to go to
town himself" (17.5) he tells his pig man (17.6, 9–11):

Look here, dad, I am going into the city to visit with my mother. . . .
Do you take this hapless stranger into the city
to beg his dinner from any who choose to give him
morsel or cup?

Upon this Odysseus comments: "Better for a beggar to beg through the
city than through the countryside" (18). But he would wait until the
day warms up, for as they have been saying, "It is some way to town"
(25). Telemachus in fact "reaches the house well built" (28), which
seems to imply it is on one of the streets, and after speaking with his
mother, apparently leaves the house to encounter his spearman, Piraeus,
who "was bringing a stranger to the agora through the city" (72).
Odysseus and the pig man have stayed behind in the cottage. But the
moment comes when "they bestirred themselves to go cityward" (183),
and the man addresses the master: "Since your desire is to go cityward
this day . . ." (185). The story continues: "So he brought the lord into
the city . . ." (201).

As they got near town they came to a spring
built up and fair-flowing whence the citizens [*politai*] drew water.

(205–206)

When they arrive at the house Antinous, the leading suitor, angrily
asks Eumaeus, "Why did you bring this person cityward?" (375). This
kind of urban phraseology is employed casually and unconsciously. The
urban center thus envisaged is regularly equipped with an agora and a
set of seats for the council (15.468; 16.361; 17.72); the ship of Telemachus is berthed in the city's harbor (16.327 ff.).

The climactic episode is confined within the walls of the house.
The great hall provides an operatic stage set for the grand battle which
extinguishes the enemy. Yet the banquet in the house which immedi-

ately precedes it is in fact timed to coincide with a civic festival in the town (20.155–157):

Dinner will be served early;
the suitors will not be away from the hall long
but will return early; it is a feast day for all.

One hundred and twenty lines later the poet inserts into his narrative his own statement as an aside (275–277):

Heralds through town a holy hecatomb of the gods
were conducting; and the long-haired Achaeans were gathering
in the shade of a grove of far-shooting Apollo.

This deity, it turns out, is selected for his symbolic association with the archery which Odysseus will soon practice with such deadly effect.

We need not, therefore, be surprised if the suitors, beleaguered and desperate within the house, look for a way to get outside to reveal their plight to the people and get help from them (22.132). They cannot manage it, though they assume the popular response would be swift if they could. Only after their death does the news of the massacre penetrate to the town, leading to an aftermath which is described at the conclusion of the epic.

A Maritime Complex

The portrait of the Homeric polis that emerges from references like these is the more convincing for being incidental, furnishing a background for action which is taken for granted. One episode in the epic provides occasion for explicit statement. Odysseus, recalling the encounter with the Cyclops, describes these creatures as follows (9.106–108, 112–115, 125–130):

To the land of the Cyclops overweening and traditionless
we came; who trusting in the immortals
neither plant any growing thing with their hands nor plow . . .
They have no agoras-of-counsel nor traditions
but dwell in the heights of lofty mountains
in hollow caves, and each sets his rules
over children and wives, nor do they reck anything of each other . . .
The Cyclops lack the presence of ships vermilion-cheeked
nor among them are valiant craftsmen of ships who could labor-to-build
ships well-benched that might perform their several (things)
proceeding to the cities of mankind—the many (things)
such as men to each other in ships convey—
men who might have labored to build the island well-settled.

These lines, by describing what the Cyclops do not have, provide a negative definition of what Odysseus does have. He is a citizen of a city-state equipped with architectural features "well-built" and familiar from the historical period, founded on the joint practices of agriculture and maritime commerce, containing a population in which craftsmen enjoy prestige, and which is always prepared to colonize unoccupied territory —typically, in this case, an island. Appropriately enough, the definition is uttered before an audience who are members of a similar type of community. Over and above the physical details, the statement reveals a condition of cultural consciousness. The confrontation has pitted a Greek who is aware he enjoys the advantages of civil society against a barbarian who does not.

Civic Behavior of the Greek Army

The *Odyssey,* it might be argued, being later in composition than the *Iliad,* may more closely reflect the Hellenic condition of the eighth or even the seventh centuries. But as we have seen, this type of evidence bearing on what may have been the contemporary realities of Homer's world is not confined to the *Odyssey*. The existence of the city-state in its Hellenic form and its situation as a member of a maritime complex have colored the narrative of the *Iliad*. It can even be perceived to intrude where we would least expect it, in the conduct of the Greek army. Ostensibly, this is an expedition camped on foreign soil, divorced from any civic base. Yet, aside from the frequent assemblies held by the army which take on the appearance of town meetings (to be reviewed in a later chapter), the same army shows a recurrent tendency to behave like a city.

For example, in city-state warfare, it was standard practice to inter-rupt the rhythm of conflict to allow both sides to recover the dead under truce for burial. Homer interrupts the momentum of his own plot in order to introduce a copy of this practice. Is this a concession to what a contemporary audience would expect to be included in a complete picture of warfare? Or again, on the face of things, the Greeks represent an expedition dispatched overseas to raid foreign territory, determined to sack a city to which they lay siege in order to acquire booty. But when they suffer a serious reverse at the hands of the local forces, instead of fighting a rearguard action preparatory to reembarkation, they with all deliberation set about constructing a protective wall with gates, which they then proceed to defend while their fleet remains beached or anchored on an adjacent roadstead. To destroy this fleet by fire becomes the objective of the opponents. The result for the course of the narrative is the introduction of an epic of siege warfare lasting a considerable space. The Greeks have become a Greek maritime settlement, its navy in harbor, its population protected by fortifications on the landward side against assault from the natives in the hinterland. To force open the (city) gates becomes the objective of the attackers; to retain their naval resource becomes a basic objective of the defenders. Is this a prehistoric memory, or instead an evocation of a peril which continually confronted the Greek colonies? The poet himself seems aware that the whole episode tends to undermine the mythic fantasy, which requires that prehistoric heroes capture Troy. He tells us in his own person that the subsequent ravages of nature have removed all trace of these elaborate works from the plain. The explanation wears the air of an apology.[17]

The heroic ethos of the story is nowhere more evident than in the description of battle, where we would expect it. Conflict is personalized as warrior challenges warrior, pursues or flees, is wounded or killed. The proper names and lineages by which the actors in these scenes are identified seem to have the authentic prehistoric ring. The mythos simplifies the normal confusion of combat, as it has to, by personalizing it.

Yet there is more than one trace of the disciplined military organization characteristic of interstate warfare in historic times. References to hoplite tactics have been detected by scholars in Books 12, 13, and 16,[18] but the effect is more pervasive than that. Actual fighting breaks out in Book 4. The order is given for a general advance (4.427–432):

Rank upon rank, the lines of the Danaans began to move
steadily battleward; to his own men orders were given by each
of the captains; the men marched in silence; you would hardly believe
such a mass of people were keeping pace, holding their voice in their breasts
in silence, wary of their commanders' signals; all over them
glittered the panoply they wore as they marched in file.

This would just as well describe a civic army under company commanders advancing against an opposing force as it would a hypothetical Mycenaean army. It explains why it came so natural to Tyrtaeus, the poet of hoplite warfare, to frame his patriotic exhortations in Homeric terms and why Aristophanes and Plato, citizens of the polis of the fifth and fourth centuries, could without question still designate Homer as the accepted source for military education. As for the armor and weapons and military paraphernalia of the story, the details are Hellenic, or at least no more prehistoric than they are Hellenic. The short and the long spears, thrown or thrust, the helmet, of bronze or leather, the cuirass, greaves, the sword, the bow and arrow, the horses, and even the chariots, are the common property of soldiers at all stages of Hellenic history. The point has been made that, if the warriors ride to battle and then dismount from their chariots, this procedure represents an imperfect memory of Mycenaean practice. It might just as well reflect the fact that in Hellenism the chariot was an item of display and of sport which was required to have its place in the epic, as it does conspicuously in the chariot race of Book 23, but not as a serious military weapon. The equipment of the Homeric warrior is not easily distinguishable from that employed by the armed citizen of a city-state, and attempts to prove otherwise have yielded meager results.[19]

Domestic Architecture

Priam in the *Iliad*, Nestor, Menelaus, and Alcinous in the *Odyssey* are kings who live in palaces; three of them have queens for consorts. The life-style on the whole is regal (with exceptions), as is the architecture, so far as it is indicated. These buildings, the seats of a centralized authority, are reminiscences of Mycenae, part of the Homeric fantasy. But they intrude into a physical setting which as it emerges in incidental references is otherwise essentially urban, and we might say decentralized. The city of the Homeric poems is built on a street plan, and the streets are broad—a regular epithet. Paris and Hector occupy private horses in Troy, and the women of the city pass in popular procession through the streets to the temple. The house of Odysseus is a manor on the outskirts of the town but within hailing distance of neighbors. Its architecture has a part to play in the plot, which requires a degree of realism in description. When the house is first seen by its owner after twenty years absence, its appearance is appropriately magnified; he is after all a beggar, brought up against the building which symbolizes his real status (17.260–268):

Approaching now were Odysseus and the divine swineherd;
they came and stopped and about them rose the great cry
of the polished lyre; (the bard) was beginning a song for them,
even Phemius. Odysseus seized the swineherd's hand and spoke:
"Eumaeus, so these (are) the fair halls of Odysseus I see;
they are easily recognizable, a sight to see among many;
this (part) to that is (connected), its courtyard has been well fashioned
with wall and coping stones, the doors are fitted nicely,
double-folding. No man could outdo this!"

This is a gentleman's house, not a palace. It bears comparison with other buildings of less expensive construction; due notice is taken of the masonry and the fine carpentry employed on the doors. Further details, as they are furnished, are homely. In order to reach the main door, one crosses through the dung of mules and cattle lying in heaps (17.296); the courtyard is a farmyard where the pigs are turned out of their sties to root for food (20.164); and the colonnades are pens or stalls where goats and cattle are tethered (20.176, 189). (Even at Sparta the horses were tethered in Menelaus' yard and the chariot stood up against the gateway, 4.40.) Because Odysseus' house has an upper story and a staircase, attempts have been made to relate the architecture to that of the palace of Nestor. But did the wooden houses of the city-state even in the early period never have second stories? The main hall contains armor and weapons hanging on the wall, long disused and dirtied by smoke from the fire (16.284–290). The suitors must be denied the use of this equipment, so Odysseus instruct his son to "lift and deposit them in a corner of a *thalamos*[20] up above" (16.285), to "deposit them inside" (19.4–9). Telemachus then has the women segregated in their quarters, so that he can "deposit them in a *thalamos*" (19.17–19). Is this an "armory" or a more humble repository? It is upstairs, we infer, where the women might observe what was going on unless confined behind doors. The nurse tells Telemachus that he will need a servant to carry a light behind him. The route to this *thalamos* therefore is pitch dark. In fact, Athene holds the light for both of them, and Telemachus observes the illumination cast on the roof beams and the tops of the pillars (33,38).

When later the situation of the suitors becomes critical, the goatherd, traitor to Odysseus, guesses where the arms have been hidden —"inside and nowhere else"—so he "ascends" to the *thalamos* "along the 'breaks' (*rhoges*) of the hall." This word is unique, and no one has been able to determine what it means. Some translators, under the spell of the fantasy, interpret it to refer to a "clerestory," as though the operation was being conducted in a small cathedral.[21] On a second visit to this room the goatherd is caught and "strung up to the roof beams." Where have these arms been put? Most plausibly, in a loft or garret above the second story under the roof beams. You need a light to get there, which would reflect against the roof of the hall if the door to the loft were left open, and, in fact, Telemachus later remembers ruefully that he had forgotten to shut it. Such architecture implies the ridge-roof, probably thatched, typical of the early temples and houses of the Hellenic period, in contrast to the flat roof of prehistoric palaces. The *Iliad* likewise is familiar with this type of roof (23.712). Any house of size would have such a lumber room, a place of storage for unwanted objects; it is as true of modern houses as of Hellenic ones. Do the "breaks of the hall" refer to the gaps between the ceiling joists, which would have to be traversed carefully by anyone using the loft?

Just before the traitorous goatherd makes his move to get the armor, an alternative means of rescue for the wooers is proposed, namely, that they get outside the hall to alert the neighbors to their predicament and ask for help. The front door is commanded by Odysseus; there is no exit from the rear. But there is one alternative exit; it is a doorway which Homer calls an *orsothura* "in the wall at the outermost of the threshold." It leads to something called a *laure* and is closed by folding doors. Odysseus stations the swineherd there to prevent access to it. Why, asks one of the suitors, can't someone ascend the *orsothura* and tell the people? The traitor says no: the doorway is near the courtyard and the mouth of the *laure* is difficult; a single man could hold many at bay (22.126–138). What is the architectural arrangement envisaged? Does an elevated "postern" lead to an elevated gallery "above the topmost level of the threshold" or to a "clerestory," or else a corridor which runs all round the house? Such suggestions are in keeping with the fantasy concept, but the elaborate additions to the architecture which they require are implausible. Etymology and popular usage alike suggest a humbler meaning for *orsothura* and for *laure*. The *orsothura* can be literally translated as an "arse-door," a "rears," near the main exit to the hall and leading to a "privy" (*laure*) which is also accessible from the outside, so that one could get out of the hall by going through it. The floor of this convenience is elevated for hygienic reasons and is reached by steps from inside the hall; the hall entrance to it is carefully closed by double doors to keep out the smell. The whole arrangement serves the needs, first, of diners inside the house and then of those outside, who can use it without going into the house. Homeric descriptions may sometimes gain clarity in the light of the early architectural arrangements of New England.[22]

Some Homeric Occupations

In the *Iliad* a certain Polydamas, who on the Trojan side plays the role of prudent counselor giving advice which is neglected only at peril, reproaches Hector in a crisis for assuming that because he is a warrior he is also a superior tactician and backs up his advice with the following (*Il.* 13.730–733):

To one God gives works of war,
to another the dance, to a third the lyre and song,
to another in his breast Zeus places good sense,
whereof many of mankind reap benefit.

This formulaic definition of types of achievement no doubt reflects a bias on the part of the bardic profession—a bias discernible elsewhere in both poems. The passage classifies society in terms of the roles played (*erga,* functions); the role of the warrior is only one among many. This is not the language of a warrior-oriented society. In parallel can be set a passage from the *Odyssey.* After Eumaeus has brought his master, disguised as a beggar, into the house, a suitor objects that they have beggars enough crowding round the dinner table waiting to be fed. Why add one more? Eumaeus, disavowing responsibility, uses the following formula to explain (17.382–387):

Does anyone ever invite a stranger, going to fetch him from elsewhere,
except he be a member of those who are craftsmen [*demiourgoi*],
a prophet, a healer, a carpenter,
or a bard inspired whose singing gives pleasure;
these indeed are the invited ones all over the boundless earth,
but a beggar would not be invited to consume one's own substance.

"Public worker" is a literal rendering of the term usually translated as "craftsman." The itinerant bard was regarded as a man of skill like the carpenter; both belonged to a class of skilled practitioners who were available on call and whose services were prized, payment often being made in kind, such as board and room. If they are strangers (*xenoi*), they are not citizens of the city where their services are available. These services are pan-Hellenic, indicating a considerable mobility of labor. Heroic fantasy is not friendly to the presence of craftsmen whose activities by definition were the reverse of military. But this does not prevent Odysseus from playing the role of a skilled carpenter who constructs his own bedroom and boat, operations described with technical detail (*Od.* 23.188–204; 5.243–262; Calypso provided sailcloth). Even Lycaon, one of Priam's sons, makes chariot rails out of the wood of a fig tree. He has gone into the orchard to cut it, and that is where he was when Achilles seized him (*Il.* 21.35). The women in both epics are skilled spinners and weavers and regularly represented as such regardless of social status, whether they are playing the role of housewife (Andromache and Penelope) or of a housewife costumed as a queen or princess (Helen and Arete). To be sure, in their character of warriors the male personalities of the epics carry the right kind of equipment. But very often they are betrayed in the performance of common tasks undertaken by ordinary people. Priam, lord of a farflung empire, preparing the arrangements for ransoming Hector's body, himself goes and lifts the lid of the chest where his best clothes and blankets are stored and brings them out (*Il.* 24.228). He takes a stick and chases the inquisitive neighbors out of the house (247). His surviving sons are peremptorily told to get a wagon ready and load in it all the things he is carrying (262). They hastily and rather nervously attend to this matter in the manner of grooms or teamsters doing a job (266–277). Priam then steps into his own chariot and drives it, preceded by the wagon (322–324). As the narrative of his embassy to Achilles gathers momentum, he becomes just an old man, like any other in similar circumstances, but also a surviving father easily scared but with enough courage for his task. This is no Mycenaean or Cretan potentate. Alcinous, for all the dignity which surrounds him in his court, personally goes through the ship provided for his guest and stows away the gifts under the thwarts so that they will not get in the way of the rowers (*Od.* 13.20). Hot baths must be ready for Hector and Odysseus. To be sure, they do not have to get the baths themselves; Andromache and Penelope have servants. But the attention given to details of this sort is suggestive. Lurking below the heroic level in both poems there is detectable a layer of feeling, a focus of attention, which is almost bourgeois in quality. The "warriors" of the *Odyssey* whose joint effort vanquishes the "enemy," that is, the suitors, consist of two authentic heroes in the fantasy sense, namely, the father and son, and two farm laborers, treated not only as friends but as comrades in arms.[23] In the background there is the essential support of two women. Penelope and the nurse. Their most dangerous opponent turns out to be another farmhand turned traitor.

Finally, there are the similes, forming a constant feature of both epics and reporting what is done in farm and field and household, the productive skills, the behavior of animals and weather, including the all-pervasive sea. These are not prehistoric memories; this has long been acknowledged.[24] But are they merely late intrusions into a composition which is otherwise prehistoric in inspiration and content? Surely not. If a poet seeks constantly to illuminate whatever he is narrating by using

comparisons, and using them habitually, the thing compared and the
comparison must have some congruence, some connection recognized as
intimate.

In sum, the stories and episodes of both epics are fashioned in such
a way as to take for granted a polity and life-style which are contemporary, meaning that they reflect Greek life as it was lived in the period
when the poems assumed their final compositional form. The characters
live and behave as people in that society would live and behave even
though they often wear the fancy dress of Mycenaean legend. The institutions, the domestic proprieties, the military and maritime dispositions,
the agriculture, the commerce, the architecture and art, and we may add
the recreations, are those of the early maritime complex of Hellenic city-
states, originating perhaps in the tenth century, but attaining their full
development in the eighth and seventh centuries. The local geography,
the agriculture, the commerce, the seafaring, the endemic warfare, the
legalities of family and property, the citizen's identity, the oral procedures for decision making, all seem to be versions in embryo of the
essential elements out of which the societies of Solon and Pericles
evolved—adapting, enlarging, codifying, complicating, but never depart-
ing from them. Both the *Iliad* and the *Odyssey* reveal a veiled portrait of
Greece in the historical period. That is why a citizen of Periclean
Athens could still feel himself to be a "Homeric man."

If the period thus reported in both epics was also nonliterate, we
can reasonably expect, on the analogy of practices in other oral societies,
that the epics will not confine themselves to story telling. They are
likely to use the mythos as a vehicle of storage, a repository of the
pragmatic values of their audience. The epics may constitute that enclave of contrived speech constructed according to the rules of oral
memorization which oral societies find necessary for this purpose. For
the performance of such a function, the Mycenaean fantasy could
provide an essential support, giving to the cultural index a distance and
a solemnity which the living memory would welcome. The mores of the
present are transposed into the past; historical Hellenism becomes a
prehistoric tradition. It is this hypothesis which now remains to be
tested.

5

Some Elements of the
Homeric Fantasy

❦

The spell of the antique is strong in both epics, pervasively so in the associations surrounding proper names and epithets carried by some of the principal actors. Though the situations related in the stories belong to early Hellenism, the Hellenes are always archaized as Achaeans, Argives, or Danaans, a nomenclature not applicable (in this reference) in the historical period. Achilles, Ajax, Idomeneus, Hector (as well as some less conspicuous examples) have been doubtfully identified in the Linear B tablets, and the personality of Agamemnon still more doubtfully in the Hittite records.[1] Odysseus, by contrast, may be a name without a pedigree.[2] Mycenae "rich in gold" was in historical times a village, and Troy an uninhabited site.

Adversary Relationships

Format no less than nomenclature shows the effect of traditional influence insofar as the ways in which the plots of both epics are constructed reflect the rules required for ease of memorization, rather than those required by a desire to record facts of contemporary history.

When Odysseus landed on his native soil to explore the reception he might meet with, he had already been accepted by the Phaeacians on their island utopia. If realism prevails in the harsh conditions on Ithaca, it is romanticism which had colored his reception in Phaeacia. Arriving at the palace of the king, the suppliant is graciously raised from the hearth, promised a convoy on the morrow which will take him home, and is presented by his host to an assembly, his guise transfigured by Athene's miraculous power. The order is given to equip a ship for him. He is then conducted in the company of the leading men of the city to a formal banquet for which the king has been careful to provide appropriate entertainment. The bard Demodocus receives a ceremonial summons to attend the banquet and recites a lay (8.73–78, 81–82):

The muse aroused the singer to sing the fames of men—
a song whose fame then reached to wide heaven—
the strife [*neikos*] of Odysseus and Achilles—
how on a time they contended [*dērisanto*] in luxuriant banquet of the gods
with terrifying utterances. The king of men, Agamemnon,
rejoiced in his heart when the best of the Achaeans were in contention
[*dērioonto*] . . .
. . . It was then that the beginning of woe toppled over
for Trojans and Danaans because of the counsels of Zeus.

This saga, otherwise unrecorded except by commentators on the passage, sounds like an alternative version of the *Iliad*. Its theme is an angry confrontation between two powerful men in the Greek army the result of which brings an avalanche of trouble upon both Trojans and Achaeans, this being in accordance with some decisions made by Zeus himself. These terms are identical with those set forth in the preface to the *Iliad*, with the difference that Odysseus is substituted for Agamemnon as the opponent of Achilles.

Both versions illustrate what seems to be one of the laws controlling the composition of mythos for oral commemoration. The action has to take the form of confrontation between two or more parties. It is stories of confrontation and struggle which are most seductive to the memory and which give most pleasure in recall. War is a subject preferred to peace. This meets one of the theoretic requirements of memorized speech, which likes to follow not only metrical but thematic rhythms, taking their most obvious form in a pairing arrangement between two contending parties. Agents who have to dominate the action are placed in adversary relationships. The Greek terms are *neikos* and *eris*. The tale best remembered is the tale of a duel. The characters become wrestlers, battlers, fighters—*agonistae* (this term, however, is post-Homeric). The competitive element in Greek culture has recently attracted scholarly attention; I suggest here that in an orally managed culture the verbal record of what is going on is likely in any case to be created around competitive antagonisms between the personalities who are required as actors. The character of the record is governed in this respect by mnemonic considerations.

This principle of composition is characteristic of all epic as a genre. Its traces recur. The most natural way to incorporate confrontation at the center of narrative is to arrange the story within the context of the waging of war. A great war partly recollected and partly invented in oral epic becomes the necessary vehicle to serve as a repository for the storage of cultural information of the people whose exploits are sung in this way. This is not to say that such oral storage does not respond to certain realities in human history. Most language groups that have won for themselves cultural identities have done so in part by fighting their neighbors. But the point to bear in mind is that the compulsion to sing what is memorizable inevitably tends to compose history as though it consisted almost exclusively of military history. Such epics build themselves in response to the need to store and repeat and remember information. But that information covering the ethos and the nomos of ordinary daily life remains buried in the military context, so that the historical consciousness of the language group concerned becomes somewhat distorted. It is probably true that war as a way of life after the fashion of the *Iliad* has been a concept in part foisted upon Western culture by the mnemonic requirements of oral epic.[3]

What is here being proposed is a functional, technical explanation of that poetry which we style "heroic." Its existence is usually explained in terms of the human consciousness, the supposed ideals of the people for whom such poetry was sung, and the same explanation is responsible for our imagining a society of warrior-aristocrats for whom such poetry was composed, whether in Greece or elsewhere. This is close to romantic nonsense. No society at any stage of the development of human civilization could ever have lived continuously as the Homeric so-called heroes are represented as living in the *Iliad*. In fact, as we have seen, below the level of the military narrative the outline of a perfectly normative society, political and familial, becomes evident. The Trojan War itself is a narrative fantasy designed to evoke sympathetic response from a culture which was all too familiar with wars but never on such a total scale or with such concentration.

Action arranged as confrontation serving as a principle of composition can take a second form, that of the dangerous journey in which an individual or family are pitted against both natural and human enemies through which they thread their way toward a satisfactory terminus which is supposed to be a return home.[4] It is relevant to observe that the original Hebrew epics which lie behind the biblical narrative of events up to the beginning of David's reign combine these two principles of composition: first, the journeys of the patriarchs in search of homes new and old; then the journey of the Israelites to seek a new home; then the "Wars of Jehovah," still traceable in the books of Joshua and Judges, supposedly waged with the aim of occupying Canaan, but represented as a final homecoming to a land long promised—in short, a Hebrew *Odyssey,* or several *Odysseys,* followed by a Hebrew *Iliad.*[5] Hazardous journeys conceived on a grand scale are, like wars, part of the story teller's stock in trade, and for the same reason. They are memorizable. Both types provide an overall context, a kind of portmanteau of memory, within which cultural data can be contained and recollected as the remembered rhythm travels the same road over again.

The Trojan War and the *nostos* of Odysseus, respectively, are therefore fantasies which serve as excuse for the presence of nonfantastic elements. They carry the hallmarks of fantasy, one of which is exaggeration of dimension. The war is a ten-year war, the journey home is a ten-year journey. The war pits a host of warriors assembled from the entire Achaean world against a city which we are encouraged to imagine is not just any city but an imperial capital wealthy and populous. The fighting is carefully structured in a series of duels and confrontations capped by an inspired and miraculous onslaught on the part of a single man who is supposed to take on the forces of Nature herself as his antagonists. The war even invades heaven, dividing the deities into warring camps.

The equally fantastic journey is so designed that in the course of confronting alien hazards, hostile men and creatures, storm, hunger, and shipwreck, the protagonist alone surives through a combination of superhuman skill, prudence, and daring. His total isolation is then pitted against a group of enemies numbering over a hundred. He reveals himself to them with some advantage of surprise, and the fantastic encounter has the improbable result that he kills them all together. The mythos has to make some concession to the probabilities by supplying him with one divine and three human assistants of inferior age and rank.

Kings and Queens

If the remembered mythos requires to be cast in the form of a narrative of acts by living agents, and if the cultural function of such narrative is enhanced by historical fantasy, the agents concerned must inevitably show some tendency to enjoy an enlarged status and inflated importance. In the context of military confrontation they become generals, commanders of great masses of men; in their civil aspect they become kings and queens and princes and princesses, grandiose versions of members of that public for whose benefit the oral epic is being composed. It is in any case very difficult to describe the confusions of actual conflict coherently except in terms of the leadership, as readers of *War and Peace* are well aware.

Agamemnon in his civil aspect becomes a monarch "who holds power over all Argives and the Achaeans obey him" (*Il.* 1.78–79). This is fantasy. The extent of his actual authority and status, as revealed in the course of the story, is a very different affair. His opposite number in civil life is Priam with his consort Hecuba, an absolute monarch of an empire vaguely defined and never operative in the actual plot. There is less fantasy in the portrait of Odysseus in the *Odyssey*, mainly because the plot requires his humble disguise, but he is not infrequently identified as the monarch ruling over Ithaca in its entirety, a status directly at variance with the existence of all the magnates who want to marry his putative widow. More obviously, the polity of the Phaeacians, though exhibiting a life-style which is obviously a utopian version of that current in the Hellenic maritime polis, is represented as enjoying the rule of a beneficent monarchy exercised by an idealized king and queen.

The commingling of romanticism and realism can be appreciated by analyzing the way in which this king summons an agora at the beginning of the eighth book of the *Odyssey* to deal with the problem of the mysterious visitor in their midst. The poet makes clear that it is indeed an agora (8.5 and 12), but because of the monarchical setting the council of elders is summoned by the king first. They are in effect represented as his courtiers and accordingly take their seats (4–6). Only then is the herald dispatched to perform his function of going through the city to summon the meeting. He addresses "each man," but the object of his address is then described as "leaders and counsellors of the Phaeacians" (11). The agora fills up, and then the stone seats are again occupied, this time in the proper order (16), implying the presence of two different bodies, one consisting of the standing citizens, the other the seated council. But no deliberation follows. The king stands up, harangues and gives orders, and leads his princes in a kind of ceremonial exit to escort the stranger to the palace for a banquet. There is no mention of the termination of the agora; its existence has been forgotten.

Exaggeration of Dimension

The inflation of rank and station required by fantasy finds its counterpart in the exaggeration, already noted, of numbers and quantities, a persistent trait observable in all oral epic. Priam is equipped with fifty married sons who require fifty bedrooms plus apparently twelve daughters and sons-in-law with twelve bedrooms (*Il.* 24.41–50). Apparently, by the time Priam confronts Achilles they have all been wiped out (24.494), though earlier in the narrative the poet seems to allow for survivors (260). The household of Odysseus requires the services of fifty maid servants (*Od.* 22:421; so also Alcinous 7.603); the competitors for Penelope's hand number 108 plus eight servitors, one herald, and one bard (16.247–251). How, we may ask, could the estate of Odysseus, even imagining him to be monarch of all Ithaca, accommodate these numbers not for a single year but for a ten-year orgy? No wonder that the dimensions of his megaron have to be extended to accommodate such a horde. In fact, they are presented as a muster of leading men drawn from Ithaca and the adjacent islands and mainland. The poet supplies a catalogue of their kingdoms. All this is complete fantasy.

Equal exaggeration is extended to the material resources employed by this society. The meals eaten in the *Iliad* and the *Odyssey* are gargantuan. The gifts proffered by Agamemnon to Achilles as part of the reconciliation are perhaps conceivable as worthy of an oriental monarchy, but they would bankrupt any Greek state. Apparently, a large part of them is supposed to be in storage on Trojan soil during the campaign, loot accumulated and guarded during nine years of fighting (*Il.* 9.122–148, with 149–156, a supplementary list of towns; at 19.238 a retinue is needed to produce them). The gifts heaped upon Odysseus by the Phaeacians are less imperial (no women are included) but equally extravagant (*Od.* 8.392–394, 403–405, 424–428, 438–442; 13.10–19, 13–19 [an additional levy], 363–370). These lists in the *Iliad* and the *Odyssey* are repetitive and obsessive; the narratives make a point of stressing that the objects are to be counted (*Il.* 9.121) and placed on display (*Od.* 8.424; *Il.* 19.172, 189), to be looked at as at a modern wedding ceremony. The magic vessel which transports Odysseus to his home transports also his hoard, which on arrival has to be carefully stowed away in hiding by Athene's instructions (*Od.* 13.363–371). The epics glory in conspicuous consumption. Such descriptions reinforce the spell over the memory of the listeners. A culture in reality based on meager economic resources and a simple life-style will respond to their fascination with a kind of vicarious greed. Readers of the Count of Monte Cristo will recognize a modern Odysseus, not merely by his early persecution, his adventures, and his disguise, but by that rich and mysterious hoard of treasure which his adventures gained for him.

These examples of romantic dimension are not very subtle; they could be multiplied with ease.[6] Fantasy, however, can also intrude at a level which could be described as purely verbal and which may elude notice because its effects are unconscious. Inherently, it is achieved by the fact that so much of Homer's vocabulary operates at two levels, in the sense that given words can describe relationships or acts which are either Mycenaean in the fantasy sense or Hellenic in the contemporary and realistic sense. Four such can serve as typical examples of this verbal behavior: the Greek words *basileus, heros, skeptron,* and *megaron.*

The Title *Basileus*

The reader of Homer does not need to be reminded how frequently the poet employs the word *basileus,* which is commonly translated to mean a "king." This coloration derives from its association as a title with three men: Agamemnon and Priam in the *Iliad* and Alcinous in the *Odyssey.* Its appearance in the contexts controlled by these personalities is rather infrequent. But all three of them in the epic mythoi are represented as enjoying a status which is unique and royal, equivalent to our monarch or sole ruler, occupying palaces, and ruling over empires, in the case of Agamemnon and Priam, or over a city and people, in the case of Alcinous. In these contexts, it is implied that their rule is autocratic.

Basileus is employed to identify Agamemnon in the opening lines of the *Iliad:* a plague had descended on the army because "Apollo was angry with the king." More explicitly, after Achilles has quarreled with Agamemnon, Nestor admonishes him in the following terms (1.277–281):

Do not contend or strive in confrontation with a king,
seeing that never is the portion of honor like to that of other men

which is assigned to a scepter-holding king to whom Zeus has given glory;
you may be the stronger because of your divine birth,
but he is the superior for he rules as lord over more people.

The position of Agamemnon is unique precisely because of the extent of his authority. He is a monarch, Achilles is not. The word which describes his exercise of power is *anassein;* the correlative noun is *anax,* which recurs in the formula "Agamemnon, lord-king of men." *Basileus,* therefore, in this context is treated as the equivalent of *anax.*

The poet takes occasion to underline the same status of Agamemnon as he describes the military review which occupies Book 2 (100–101, 107–109):

Lord-king Agamemnon stood up,
holding the scepter that Hephaestos had wrought . . .
. . . Thyestes left it to Agamemnon to wield
to rule as lord-king over many islands and Argos.
He leaned on it and addressed the Argives.

Though the title *basileus* is not used, this is fortuitous. The verb once more in *anassein,* to exercise the power of an *anax,* a monarch.

Again in Book 9, as Nestor tactfully opens up the subject of a possible conciliatory move on Agamemnon's part toward Achilles, he ceremoniously addresses him (9.96–99):

Son of Atreus renowned, lord-king [*anax*] of men Agamemnon,
in you I shall cease, with you I begin, for that over many
peoples you are lord-king [*anax*] and Zeus has put into your hands
scepter and formularies that you may administer counsel to them.

Once more the particular title *basileus* does not occur, but we infer from correlation between this and other passages that in the case of Agamemnon *basileus* is equivalent to *anax,* itself a Mycenaean title.[7]

The same rule seems to be followed for Priam, who carries the title *anax.*[8] It is only in the conclusion of the epic that Achilles takes occasion to note the extent of Priam's empire (24.543 ff.), whereupon the poet calls him *"basileus"* (24.680) and finally "god-nurtured *basileus"* in the last line but one of the poem.[9] Throughout the *Iliad* his name recurs formulaically in the role of paterfamilias;[10] at the realistic level of the concluding episodes he becomes simply an aged man, with corresponding titles.[11]

In the seventh book of the *Odyssey* Alcinous likewise occupies a large and luxurious palace and apparently rules authoritatively over his people. The title *basileus* is attached to him with some regularity (7.46, 55, 141, etc.).

The same title in the same monarchical sense is occasionally linked associatively with Odysseus. Mentor, reproaching the agora of Ithaca for their indifference to the memory of Odysseus, exclaims (2.230–233):

No need for any man to be of ready kindness and gentle,
even a scepter-bearing *basileus* . . .
. . . since no man now remembers Odysseus
or the people whom he ruled as lord-king [*anassein*] and as a father was gentle to them.

The complaint is repeated in the same terms by Athene on Olympus (5.8–12), and when Odysseus disguised first greets Penelope, he compares her ceremoniously to

. . . a blameless *basileus* who god-fearing
among many men and mighty ruling-as-lord [*anassōn*]
sustains justices-that-are-good . . .[12]

(19.109–111)

It is proper to isolate these examples of a term otherwise used with a different coloration, for the contexts recall the conditions of monarchy as it was exercised among the Mycenaeans. The coloration is prehistoric and constitutes a forceful element in the fantasy, suggesting that the leading personalities of the poems were themselves prehistoric and therefore that the society described is also prehistoric and monarchical.

The fantasy was continued in the plots of Athenian drama produced during the fifth century. These for the most part mirror the preoccupations of contemporary society, which, however, are transferred into the lives of kings and queens, reigning prehistorically for the most part in such centers as Thebes, Athens, Argos, and Sparta. Such monarchies at the time when the plays were offered for performance were antiquarian curiosities. But the dramatic action acquired obvious advantages when it focused on the lives of a few powerful people, men and women. It became at once intensified and simplified. The *basileis* and *anaktes,* the kings and lords who thus reappear in the post-Homeric era, induce the modern reader of Homer to accept with some readiness the proposition that Homer's world was likewise a monarchical world. So indeed it was felt to be by its audiences insofar as they submitted readily enough to the required fantasy. But equally they were aware of a second level at which the society of Homer operated within contemporary concerns, the level of the city-state.

This can be appreciated by noticing the second level at which the term *basileus* is used, one which would correspond to its original meaning in the prehistoric period,[13] if the decipherment of Linear B tablets is to be trusted. It has been discovered in them and has been translated as "feudal lord" or as "mayor," being taken to identify local officials of towns subordinate to Knossos and Pylos, and under the authority of the kings who lived there. In Homer it is more often pluralized than used in the singular of a monarch. All the leading characters of the *Iliad* can be styled *basileus,* and from time to time they constitute a committee of *basileis* which functions as a kind of council of war.[14] The city-state ruled by Alcinous in the *Odyssey,* it turns out, contains twelve *basileis* besides Alcinous himself. Antinous, leading spirit among the suitors of Penelope, is styled *basileus* (24.179). The question arises: Can these really be "kings"? Does the translation not convey a misleading suggestion? Should they even be equated with "princes"?[15] Princes after all are members of royal courts. Is not the whole concept of royalty inapplicable to societies in which these pluralized *basileis* lived? By following the logic of its pluralization, *basileus* can be used as an adjective—a *basileus*-man—and even more surprisingly, the adjective can be compared in degree: a man can be "more of a *basileus*" than another. The inference is that *basileus* at this level of meaning indicates any person of importance, and importance can be a matter of degree. The term, in short, should be equated with many others in Homer which equally indicate people we would call "magnates," "leading men," and the like: "O leaders and magistrates" was a favorite form of address—*hēgētores* and *medontes.* At other times we hear of the *stratēgos* and the *kosmētōr,* the "army leader" and the "organizer"; of the *archos,* or "ship's captain"; the *dunamenos,* or "man of power"; the *aristos,* "the top man" applied to the suitor who will win Penelope, 16.76); the *koiranos,* the "authority." All these terms can be pluralized. The suitors of Penelope are described in the following terms:

All who have power over the islands being top men [*aristoi*]
and all who have authority [*koiraneousi*] through craggy Ithaca

The formula is repeated by Eumaeus and by Penelope (16.122; 19.130).

I noted above the extraordinary number of these suitors. These are not royal personages or monarchs; they are gentlemen, country squires, local potentates in their communities. The verbs which express their exercise of power are really applicable to the exercise of what we would call "influence." But it is equally true that the same words at the level of fantasy can recall the autocracies of Mycenae. The problematic status of Telemachus, an issue central to the developing story, is debated early in the epic (*Od.* 1.383–404), in terms which illustrate the fluid confusion of archaic and contemporary within the same vocabulary: (1) Ithaca is ruled by a hereditary monarchy (386–387); (2) the monarchy is not hereditary (400–401); (3) there is no monarchy, but a large number of local authorities (393–394): (4) winning such authority is prized for the prestige and money it brings (391–393; cf. below, Chapter 6: "The Sentiments of Sarpedon"); (5) "lord-king" (*anax*) is the title of a man of property (397–398).

At the realistic level the "aristocracies," so called, of Homer are small-town elites, not formally defined by birth or inheritance, though inheritance can become an issue, as in the *Odyssey*. Status depends on money and wealth more than on military effectiveness. But because of the double reference, on the one hand to prehistoric kingdoms half-remembered, on the other to contemporary city-state conditions in which the leading men run things as leading men always do, the citizens who listened to these sagas could feel a confused identification of themselves as the demos and *laos* who lived in the city-state, or as members of a real class of influential families whose decisions could guide the city provided they were approved in the agora, or finally as kings and princes living in Mycenaean palaces with hordes of mythical retainers.

In this guise they thought themselves to be the heirs of Homer living the life of true Greeks on the heroic scale insofar as an aspiration to emulate past ways was instilled by a recital of the epics. This is the secret of those "ideals" which historians have ascribed to the Greeks without knowing quite where they came from, or indeed what they were. The fantasy was essential for this purpose. It supplied not merely cultural identification for the Hellenes of the historic era but an intensified consciousness, so that they were capable of living in two worlds at once.

A fantasy which was functional for the Hellenes has become an intellectual trap for moderns, creating the presumption that Homeric society was one of "tribal kingship," supposedly intermediate between Mycenae and the city-state of historical times.[16] There is no hard evidence that such a polity in such a period ever existed. The portrait of

Alcinous and his court and his master-mariners in the seventh book of the *Odyssey* has been superimposed upon a life-style which, as previously indicated, is that of a Greek maritime colony. To be sure, his court has many parallels with the so-called courts established by those individuals who from time to time exercised authority in the Greek city-states in the early Hellenic period, and who are styled "tyrants," which is a transliteration but also in effect a mistranslation of the Greek *tyrannos.* The tyrants were popular leaders, usually acclaimed by the agoras of their respective cities, vested with powers which, though short-lived, were to prove beneficial to the demos, and generous in their patronage of poets and musicians. Their era would coincide with the last period of oral composition, when the epics were achieving their final form, and it cannot be excluded that behind the portrait of Alcinous there is concealed the gratitude of a bard to his patron.

The "Scepter"

The *basileus* in his monarchical aspect carries a *skēptron*, but not the scepter of medieval and Renaissance usage when the availability of a literate bureaucracy had rendered the scepter ceremonial. In Homer it is a club or staff held in the hands as a symbol of oral authority—the right to speak[17]—as opposed to the duty to listen. This symbol of a common object is also used ambivalently. It refers to a procedure carried out in two different modes. In a passage of the second book of the *Iliad* already noted Agamemnon's monarchical authority is given a legitimacy conveyed by the fact that his scepter had descended to him ultimately from the gods. Similarly, Nestor's tactful admonition to Agamemnon in Book 9 recalls the fact that "scepter and formularies are placed by Zeus in your hands." In this sense the scepter is behaving prehistorically. We might say that its possession is a monopoly of the Mycenaean throne. But at the beginning of the *Iliad,* as the quarrel opens between Achilles and Agamemnon, Achilles is holding a scepter which he dashes on the ground, exclaiming

Now indeed do the sons of the Achaeans
wield it in their hands, even the managers-of-rights, who the formularies
do conserve under Zeus

This would seem to describe the scepter as representing an authority vested not in any monarch but in a body of magistrates, specialists who had the duty to preserve the "dooms" which in Book 9 are supposed to be solely in the hands of the monarch. It is tempting to infer that in Book 9 Nestor is commemorating the prehistoric practice which allowed the king to hold in his hand the tablets of the law inscribed in Linear B, whereas Achilles in Book 1 commemorates the guarding of the law in historical times through oral memorization entrusted to officials especially trained for this task. This is consistent with the import of a scene described as embossed upon Achilles' shield which describes a litigation between two parties in purely oral terms.[18] Such would be the necessary practice in the city-state of early Hellenism; and the combination of two such different memories in a single epic, though inconsistent in themselves, would accord with the mingling of fantasy and reality necessary to the epic's function as a cultural encyclopedia.

The Megaron

One of the commonest nouns in the diction of Homer and of Greek tragedy is *megaron,* a hall, or the plural *megara,* halls. The "megaron type" has become a technical term in architectural history inspired by the palace plans uncovered at Mycenae and Pylos from which the Greek temple plan is viewed as derivative. Accordingly, elaborate attempts have been made to identify Homer's description of a megaron, particularly the megaron of Odysseus, with the prehistoric model.[19] Such labor is misapplied. In its Mycenaean aspect the megaron is supposed to be fronted by an *aulē,* a court, with colonnades (*aithousai*) and perhaps a forecourt, porticoes and gateways. However, we have already viewed the suitors for Penelope's hand sitting in front of Odysseus' house on hides spread over the dung-laden farmyard. In more grandiose settings Zeus in the *Iliad* not infrequently assembles his family council in a complex which is recognizably Mycenaean. If prehistoric memories play much part in the politics of the *Iliad,* the place to look for them is in the councils held on Olympus. Zeus for the most part is a true monarch, a Mycenaean autocrat, though there is a powerful consort by his side, and both of them sit on thrones. His court is strictly limited in numbers, a *boule* without an agora; it consists of blood relatives, including females, who are equal in rank to the males. Meetings are held in Zeus's house (20.10, 15.85) in a kind of throne room, with perhaps an anteroom and a forecourt with a colonnade and seats (20.11). It is this architectural complex which resembles what archaeologists describe as the "megaron of the classic Mycenaean type," though the descriptions are not wholly consistent. When the members of the court meet and are seated, there is a "session" (8.439), but a session is equally an occasion for drinking

(20.101, 15.86 ff.) and for eating (15.95), so that the throne room is in effect also a dining room, where if Zeus is absent Themis becomes the presiding deity (15.95), perhaps because Hera has arrived late (15.84), though it is significant that Themis, goddess of law, is elsewhere at the realistic level (*Od.* 2.69) assigned the symbolic role of "seating and dismissing the agora," where law was administered. At the opening of Book 20 the narrative describes Zeus in the role of a summoner of an agora, uniquely so. The mass audience is provided by the rivers, nymphs, and springs (20.7 ff.). Nevertheless, they are somehow accommodated in the forecourt, a fact which allows Zeus to address them. There may be a blend here of fantasy and reality: the fantasy being the Mycenaean palace, the reality a civic agora surrounded by colonnades with a council house at one end. The fact is that the megaron continued to symbolize any dwelling of superior status, from a palace to a farmhouse. It remains a poetic word, a fantasy word. The personage who in Balfe's opera sings "I dreamt that I dwelt in marble halls" is certainly no character out of Homer, but the fantasy in which the building exists is Homeric all the same. The proportions of Odysseus' megaron would be required to accommodate over a hundred guests plus fifty maids plus more servitors unspecified; its dimensions for poetic purposes have to be heroic, but only for poetic purposes.[20]

The "Hero"

The illusion of a supposed "tribal kingship" is only part of a larger misconception about the society reported in Homer's poems, one that is summed up when we speak of the age of Homer as a "heroic age" and of his epics as "heroic poetry." No conception is more firmly rooted in the modern mind. Yet its existence is one more tribute to the power of Homer's fantasy to control our reading of his surviving text. The term "hero" in the sense in which we use it, the romanticized sense, is only rarely reflected in Homeric usage. Before Odysseus completes his account to Alcinous of his visit to Hades, his narrative pauses, and this allows the king to ask him (11.371–372):

Did you see any of your godlike comrades who with you
followed to Ilium together and there met their fate?

Odysseus responds by adding a supplement, in which he recounts how he conversed with Agamemnon and Achilles, sought to converse with Ajax, viewed as in a spectacle Minos, Orion, Tityos, Tantalus, Sisyphus, and listened to converse from Heracles. The narrative device has the effect of placing this list of names in a special classification, in which three of the great dead of the Trojan War are included with mythical figures who may be regarded as pre-Trojan. The inference is encouraged that certain leading characters of the *Iliad* have been consigned by tradition to a category of supermen and were so accepted by the audience at epic recital. But they are such because, being dead and gone, they belong to a remote past. When Odysseus is about to leave Hades, he waits a moment (11.628–629):

. . . if perchance one might still come
of the hero men who perished aforetime

When in the last book of the epic the ghosts of the slain suitors encounter company in Hades, they discover Achilles commiserating with Agamemnon (24.24–25):

Son of Atreus, we used to say that to Zeus the thunderer
you above all hero men were dear for all your days

The formulaic expression "hero men" in both these instances is applied to "ghosts," and the same is true of one usage of "hero" in the opening lines of the *Iliad,* an unlucky place for it to occur, so far as Homeric interpretation is concerned, for it can mislead the reader into supposing that "hero" is a title routinely conferred upon all Greeks who fought at Troy. The wrath of Achilles, we are told, was the agent which (1.3–4)

did hurl to Hades many stalwart ghosts
of heroes, but made of the men [*autous*] takings for dogs
and all birds

To speak of a "stalwart ghost" is for Homer a contradiction in terms, and when the same formula is reused in the eleventh book (l. 55), the poet prefers more logically to speak of "stalwart heads." The intention of his introduction is to place the label "hero" summarily upon those stalwarts who fought at Troy, but being now dead they have to become, rather awkwardly, "stalwart ghosts." It is almost as though the notion of "heroes" as a class, described in the *Iliad* as falling at Troy, and now constituting a vanished generation, is taking shape in the poet's mind, and this is borne out by another passage (*Il.* 12.23) where it is recalled how by Simois and Scamender "fell the race [*genos*] of godlike men."

For the poet himself, the characters of his *Iliad* are by now becoming legendary.

But otherwise, as applied to the living, the reference of hero is commonplace: particularly in the formula of address used, for example, by Agamemnon in the episode in Book 2 already noted where he has mustered the army:

O Danaans, my dear heroes, servants of Ares

This is simply a general's address to his army as "fellow soldiers." The so-called heroes consist of all ranks, as is clear from another formula which speaks of Athene's spear in the following terms (*Od* 1.100–101):

wherewith she subdues the ranks of hero men,
even those with whom the daughter of the mighty sire is angered.

It appears to describe under the guise of divine action what happens when troops break ranks in panic. Again, when Achilles summons an agora to witness his reconciliation, the general audience which is expected to attend (and which includes civilians) is twice described by the formula "hero-Achaeans."[21]

Nor, as we might be tempted to think, does *hērōs* necessarily mean a fighting man. It can stand as an epithet of the bard, the herald, the craftsman, not to mention the Phaeacians, that peaceful society of master mariners. The two companions of Achilles who in the last scene with Priam have taken Patroclus' place and wait on Achilles (*therapontes*) and take orders from him along with the servants (24.590, 643) are called "heroes" (474, 573), but Achilles is not. In short, the hero was any stout fellow, whatever his status and function, as indicated by the pertinent entry in the earlier editions of Liddell and Scott's *Greek Lexicon*: "applied to any free man of the ante-Hellenic age," an observation regrettably omitted from the latest edition. It should be added that the epithet is frequently attached to the aged, somewhat like our "sire."

Since whole books have been and will continue to be written on such things as heroic poetry, Homer and heroism, Homer and the heroic tradition, and the like, it may be pertinent to add a footnote on the probable origins of the concept of the heroic as applied to a type of society and a genre of poetry. In post-Homeric Greek, a *hērōs* is someone dead, but bearing the reputation of important achievement in life, often in the role of supposed ancestor, such as the founder of a city, the "eponymous" of a tribe. Such "heroes" were frequently the object of local cults. This usage seems to have only tenuous connection with a presumed "heroic age" of Trojan warriors, the seeds of which appear to have been sown when Hesiod inserted in the myth of the Four Ages of Man a fifth, which he put in fourth place, consisting of those who fought at Troy, by which he means the characters in the Homeric poems.[22] The intimacy of Hesiod's relationship to these poems will be explored in a later chapter. Hesiod himself was canonized by the Greeks of the fifth and later centuries, and his "heroic age" was accepted by Aristotle as a formal historical category: "The leaders of the ancients alone were heroes: the people were just human beings." This view allows the philosopher to use the phrase "in the heroic times" as a chronological definition. From the Hellenistic age the concept passed to Rome, was accepted by Cicero and the Augustan poets, canonized by Horace, enshrined in Virgil's *Aeneid,* and passed in its Latinized version first to the Normans and then to the Renaissance. Milton is perfectly familiar with it:

> Th' Heroic Race
> That fought at Theb's and Ilium.

Applying the term deliberately to Samson, who

> heroicly hath finished
> A life heroic,

he enlarges it out of its Greek context and converts it into a general historical type. During the eighteenth and nineteenth centuries this late classical conception of the heroic was applied to early European societies and their sagas, so far as known. The tendency of Germans to romanticize their Teutonic and Nordic origins had a considerable effect upon German scholarship, nor should the widespread influence of Wagnerian opera be forgotten. English publicists like Carlyle could commit themselves to a whole view of human history summed up in such a title as *Heroes and Hero Worship.* Finally, the concept has been extended in the twentieth century to cover the surviving oral poetry of the Balkans and to the characters commemorated therein.

If the characters of the *Iliad* and *Odyssey* are "heroes" in any meaningful sense, it is only because they gave to the early Hellenes a sense of identity and of history rather larger than life size. But they could not have done this if they had been restricted to representing purely hypothetical personages living a life-style distinct from that of the Greek city-state.

The noun *kouros* (*kourētēs*),[23] a "youth," "young man," "fellow," or "wight," has a coverage of meaning similar to that of *hērōs*, coextensive with the population portrayed. The warriors of the *Iliad* are *kouroi*, and so are those who wait on them (*Il.* 19.248); so are the suitors in the *Odyssey* (17.174), and also those who wait on them (*Od.* 1.148); so are the peaceful seafarers who inhabit Alcinous' kingdom, so are the statues holding lamps which illuminate his banquet hall (8.35, 40, 48; 7.100), and so also the male inhabitants of Athens (*Il.* 2.551). The term is worth mentioning, as an appendix to *hērōs*, if only because its usage in Homer faithfully corresponds to the wide dispersion of *kouroi* (not to mention *korai*) as funerary statues in the orientalizing and archaic periods of the Greek city-state. Homeric epic and Hellenic art alike report a concept of manhood (and womanhood) which, as noted in the previous chapter, is coextensive with the citizenry of the Greek polis.

6
The Method and Manner of Homeric Storage

The historical-social context in which the poems are placed is that of early Hellenism. We return to the next question: Are they just stories, or are they also storage mechanisms, supplying to a nonliterate society its cultural identity, preserving and recommending its mores, as these are memorized in the course of recital, for stable transmission between the generations? Is this done not only rhythmically but by indirection, in obedience to mnemonic laws which require a narrative framework for useful knowledge which is to be made transmissible under such conditions? The presence of fantasy in the poems supplies an initial clue to the answer. If epic performing its cultural function is to become an enclave of contrived speech existing within the vernacular, some artificiality of composition and content becomes necessary. Both language and setting become slightly exotic. This exoticism, by placing a distance between auditor and material, invests the material with an authority which attains sway over his imagination.

The complete case for Homer's oral didacticism must rest on an examination of what his preserved text actually says and how he says it. Does it conceal a kind of encyclopedia of Greek manners and mores, values and proprieties?[1] I defended this view fifteen years ago, in an examination of the first book of the *Iliad*, where the typicality of the

sample was taken for granted. An exhaustive survey of the text undertaken on these lines would require several volumes of commentary, in
lieu of which I offer two further samplings here.[2]

The Sentiments of Sarpedon

The values of Homeric man are commonly characterized by the
term "heroic," and seldom more so than in the case of a well-known
episode on the battlefield of the *Iliad*.

At the opening of the twelfth book the Trojans are discovered
assaulting the wall and fosse which protect the Greek encampment. At
its conclusion they have broken through. But, says the poet, they would
not have succeeded if Sarpedon, son of Zeus, had not been aroused by
Zeus to lead the Lycian allies of the Trojans in a frontal assault. The
venture will cost him his life. Preparing for it, he makes an address to
Glaucus, his companion-in-arms and second-in-command. The passage
(12.310–328) has long commended itself to scholar and common reader
alike for the nobility of its sentiments. It reads like a serene statement of
values at once aristocratic and morally elevated, characteristic, so it is
supposed, of all that was best in the Homeric code. The spoken words
do indeed convey by indirection a fragment of the social code of Homer's
society. But its precise character, as Milman Parry perceived, is both
more specific and more pragmatic than the modern reader may at first
imagine. It can be effectively elucidated if it is designated as Passage A
and divided into two parts, the terms of which are to be compared with
those of four other contexts in the epic, designated as B, C, D, and E.

A
Part One

Glaucus, why have we two been honored most
with seating and meats and cups filled full
in Lycia, and all look at [us] as on gods,
and we have and hold a section by the banks of Xanthus
fair with vineyard and plowland for growing grain.
Therefore, now it is necessary, in the front ranks of Lycians being set,
to stand ground and in burning battle to engage,
so that a man may speak this word, even one of the Lycians well armed:
"Indeed, not unrenowned through Lycia do they rule lordly
even the "kings" [*basileis*] we have, and they eat fat sheep
and selected honeyed wine; yes, the force (of them)
how goodly it is; indeed, among the front ranks of the Lycians they fight."

Part Two

Dear friend, if indeed we two, this war having evaded,
would evermore be likely ageless and deathless
to exist, neither would I in the front ranks fight
nor would I despatch you into battle that brings glory;
as it is, regardless, dooms of death impend
ten thousand, and no mortal may escape or evade them;
so let us go on; to another shall we his boast extend or he to us.

(12.310–328)

This translation reflects the formulaic character of the expressions used, so far as this is possible in English, even at the price of some awkwardness of expression. To modern ears the speech carries a chivalric ring of noblesse oblige. It is commended for its "high temper" and for the sentiments that "great honors must be deserved," that "courage thrives on danger and the hero does not care if this means his own death."[3] Before going overboard in such appreciation, it is salutary to examine what precisely Sarpedon is made to say, lest our own literary and literate consciousness betray us into placing upon the passage moralistic values which are not there. Each part gives a reason for entering a battle, which in the present case is particularly hazardous. The two reasons are quite different: The first points out in realistic terms that such military responsibility is what kings are paid for, to put it crudely. The second in more general terms argues that since no man lives forever and we all want to triumph, it is worth accepting the fifty-fifty chance of winning rather than losing. The conjunction between the two parts is responsible for a general impression that the sentiments expressed are elevated.

Sarpedon belongs to the class of *aristoi,* the leaders of the community, the magnates, the *basileis,* who in return for performing military service for the society are rewarded, first, with public respect, second, with food and drink furnished free, and third, with property. They have the return obligation to give military leadership, presumably in the protection and service of the society. These privileges are conferred: they are neither appropriated by conquest nor gained by birth and inheritance. The system that is here reported is an early form of that institution which became accepted and formalized in the sixth- and fifth-century city-states, namely, the public support of benefactors of the state, which in Athens was provided in the form of maintenance in the Prytaneum. Xenophanes in his own day protested the practice of honoring athletes in this particular way. It may be surmised that special grants of land to favored persons bred a system subject to abuse and that it was discontinued, as might be indicated by some of the reforms of Solon in Athens. Here, regardless of the fact that they are located in Lycia, in embryo are institutions of the city-state both described and prescribed— it is implied that there is a reciprocity of performance between the population and their leaders in this matter and that this reciprocity constitutes an item of the nomos of the society.

Content aside, what is the form in which this fragment of nomos-ethos is cast? The report is stated by indirection: it is woven into the narrative context of a recited poem in which specific agents engage in action or speech addressed to specific occasions of time and place which the listener is invited to remember and which he is likely to remember. These specifics can be stripped away from the passage, leaving a residue which describes habitual relationships or patterns of action and management in which reside the values of the culture in which the actors are imagined as performing. The verbal elements thus removable become the following:

310 Glaucus, why have we two . . .
312 in Lycia
313 by the banks of Xanthus
315 now . . . of Lycians
317 the Lycians
318 through Lycia
321 of the Lycians

This leaves as the general statement of nomos-ethos the following:

310   *basileis* [subject supplied from 319] are honored most
311   with perquisites of food [that is, payment in kind]
312   and universal regard
313   their property is a section of land
314   suitably fertile
315–316 "kings" are expected to take front rank positions in battle
317   when they do, the troops, observing the fact,
318   voice pride in the reputation of their "kings," approving their powerful status
319–320 and their enjoyment of perquisites, noting their especial prowess in exposing themselves in front-rank positions

While in appearance Sarpedon's statement is spontaneous and personal, a reaction to a unique situation in the narrative and therefore itself unique, it is in fact a generic statement, a compendium of common-places reporting and also recommending certain institutions and atti-tudes which are normative for the audience to which the poem is addressed.

The Moral Formula

If the contents of the statements made are as typical as this analy-sis suggests, if they memorialize social relationships which are accepted as habitual, we would expect that their verbal expression would be equally formulaic, reflecting the necessarily formulaic character of any information of this sort which is preserved rhythmically in the oral memory; that is, we would expect them to recur elsewhere in the epic if prompted by an appropriate context. The expectation is confirmed if we turn to an episode in Book 4 (251 ff.).

There, Agamemnon, rallying his army, addresses in turn the mem-bers of the Greek leadership, directing them to show initiative. To Idomeneus he says:

B

Idomeneus, I honor you exceedingly beyond the Danaans fast mounted,
whether in war, or for works of other sort,
or in banquet when the sparkling wine of the elders
the top men [*aristoi*] of the Argives in the crater do mix.
To be sure, other Achaeans long haired
may drink their portion, yet your cup ever more full
stands there, as also in my case, to drink from as the spirit commands:
so bestir yourself for war like the man you boast to be

(4.257–264)

Approaching the contingents of Menestheus and Odysseus, Aga-memnon reproaches them for holding back:

C

You two, it is expected, in the front ranks being set,
will stand ground and in burning battle engage;
for you two are first to hear the call of the feast I hold,
what time a feast for the elders we Achaeans get ready;
then it is the cooked meats you want to eat and the goblets
to drink of honeyed wine as much as you two please,
but now you would like to look on . . .

(4.341–347)

Later, in Book 8, the Greek offensive peters out, and the Trojans take over. Diomede's chariot turns tail in the rout. Hector taunts him in the following terms:

D

You, son of Tydeus, they did honor exceedingly, even the Danaans fast mounted,
with seating and meats and cups filled full,
but now they will not honor you; your fashion is a woman's after all.

(8.161–163)

Metrical comparison can establish a variety of rhythmic units within the hexameter structure which are shared between Sarpedon's speech and the three comparable passages. Even the dual number is common to passages A and C. The term "formula" as it is commonly applied stylistically to Homeric composition describes these units. But it is also possible to adopt a different and more extended conception, one of substance, which may be called the "moral formula," constituting an encapsulated statement of a fragment of nomos-ethos. Does a comparison between these various passages and the Sarpedon speech suggest that we are viewing, or rather hearing, a reiteration of such moral formulas, placed as they are in quite diverse narrative contexts?

Passage A, lines 310–312 and 315–321, celebrates the connection between honor on the one hand, which includes social status plus perquisites, and willingness to take front-rank positions on the other. The connection is necessary (*chrē*, 1.315). The statement has directive force; the case is self-applied to Sarpedon and Glaucus.

Passage B repeats this necessary connection, applying it to the case of Idomeneus.

Passage C repeats it, applying it to Menelaus and Odysseus, and restates the directive force ("it is expected," 1.341).

Passage D repeats it, applying it to the case of Diomede. The addition of this last instance indicates, what is obvious otherwise, that Trojan and Greek sentiments on the subject are identical and reflect identical types of society.

Repetition of content involves much verbal parallelism. Whole lines and half lines are reused. Thus:

A line 311 equals D line 162.
A 315b equals A 321b with variant.
A 315–316 equals C 341–342 with variants.

These lines carry the nub of the oral directive, namely, the notion of honor, which is thematic, and obsessively repeated: A 310, 318, B 257, D 161, 163.

Fragments of variant phraseology echo each other:

A 310 "we have been honored most" is echoed in B 427 "I honor you exceedingly beyond" and in D 161 "they honored you exceedingly."

A 311 "cups filled full" is echoed in B 262 "your cup ever more full."

A 311 and 320 "meats" and "honeyed wine" correspond to C 346–347 "cooked meats" . . . "honeyed wine."

B 260 "the top men in the crater mix" corresponds to C 344 "a feast for the elders we get ready."

B 263 "to drink from as the spirit commands" corresponds to C 346 "to drink as much as you two please."

And as noted, even the dual number of A 310 and 322 recurs in C 341, 343, 346.

Such echoes are commonplaces of oral composition, but the point to be made is that they are here placed at the service of expressing a nomos-ethos statement which is itself also a commonplace.

Social status and choice food and wine were not the only privileges in return for which a *basileus* was expected to give military leadership. He also enjoyed possession of choice landed property:

A

and we have and hold a section by the banks of Xanthus
fair with vineyard and plowland for growing grain

(12.313–314)

Earlier in Homer's narrative, in Book 6, Glaucus had narrated to Diomede the romantic history of his ancestor Bellerophon, how he had been dispatched to the king of Lycia with the intention that he should be executed, but the king, becoming convinced of Bellerophon's divine descent,

E

gave to him half of all his kingly [*basilēidos*] honor,
and for him the Lycians sectioned a section superior to others
fair with vineyard and plowland for growing grain.

(6.193–195)

The reuse of a hexameter describing the property indicates a transaction which itself follows a social formula. The first line reproduces the color of Homeric fantasy: Bellerophon is the recipient of royal favors conferred by a monarch. The second, though applied to the Lycians, describes the actualities practiced in the city-states of early Hellenism: the people made the grant of land to him. This accords with the probability that the perquisites of entertainment are likewise enjoyed at public expense. The text of Sarpedon's speech at lines 310 and 311 seems to support this inference. In the *Odyssey* we hear of the entertainment enjoyed by the *dikaspolos,* presumably in recognition of his services as judge and arbiter of disputes. The same form of compensation—namely, "gifts"—given to *basileis* is vigorously criticized by Hesiod.

Sarpedon's words also record the specific way in which status is experienced: "and all look at us as on gods" (A line 312). This definition of what makes a person important is characteristically concrete: when you appear in public all heads turn toward you. Orally phrased speech uses a physical act to describe a relationship which a literate mind would express abstractly.

The same formula recurs with enlargement in the *Odyssey.* Arētē, consort of Alcinous in Scheria, was an unusual woman (7.67, 69–74):

Alcinous has honored her as upon earth no other woman is honored . . .
so verily has she been honored and is still honored
on the part of her children dear and Alcinous himself
and the people who, looking at her as on a god,
welcome her with speech when she proceeds uptown,
for woman as she is, she lacks not goodly sense,
and for them for whom she thinks well, even men, she resolves their disputes.

As in the Sarpedon example, the context in which this formula is used calls attention to it as an expression of social status: the "honor" enjoyed by the queen is reiterated four times. Furthermore, this status is accorded by the attitude of the people (*laoi*), among whom she moves with easy familiarity, and there is a hint that she enjoys this respect as an arbitrator of disputes regardless of sex. The whole context exhibits the characteristics of a "moral formula," as can be seen by comparing another description of the effective speaker (8.170–173):

The god puts shape as a crown on his sayings [*epē*] and they at him
gaze in pleasure and he speaks-in-agora securely
with gentle respect and he is preeminent in the agora
and as he goes up town all look at him as on a god.

The exercise of his skill in arbitration is not here mentioned, but a passage in Hesiod's *Theogony* (80–96) combines in a single context formulaic descriptions of the *basileus* and the effective speaker, the popular regard accorded them, the exercise of judgment, the settling of disputes, the assembled agora, the gentle respect, the popular regard (again), and preeminence in the agora.

Do such cross-comparisons justify the inference that when Sarpedon uses the formula "they look at us as on gods," the poet assumes, and his audience will assume, that the social functions of Sarpedon as *basileus* include not only military but judicial duties? This raises an interesting and problematic question: do such routine ethical formulas carry with them a bundle of related associations from one context to another even when these are unstated, so that the formulaic phrases are not merely ornamental but socially functional? If one is able to hear Homer's text as the continuing voice of an oral culture affirming its norms and values, an affirmative answer becomes probable.

The Formula within Narrative

The scattered ethos formulas so far reviewed, placed as they are in diverse narrative contexts, betray linkages which indicate we are hearing a recording of such proprieties. Political, legal, and military leadership is exercised by *basileis,* whose power, privileges, and property nevertheless depend upon popular approval, which is granted on the basis of reciprocal obligation: the popular voice is effective as it is exercised in the agora; command of effective rhetoric is as important for leadership as military prowess. The apparently high-flown character of the sentiments of Sarpedon may be tinged with Homeric fantasy to give the illusion of a heroism of the past. But they are in fact expressed within the limits of contemporary realities.

Our business here, however, is not with the precise character of institutions thus memorialized. What we are to observe now is the verbal mechanism required to make the record memorizable. In effect, the text devotes itself to the pronunciation and reiteration of a set of maxims, of ethos formulas. These, however, can occur only as suggested by relevance to a specific narrative context, so that the syntax of the maxim becomes entangled with the syntax of narrative. The "pure" ethos formula would say, or rather read: "Kings are honored most with seating and meats and cups filled full." The oral instinct is to voice such a sentiment only as part of a story of action in which the personal agent performs the maxim or utters it in relation to what is going on at the moment. Only so does the oral memory, seduced by the tale, accommodate the ethos which it is required to assimilate.

This means that although the concealed maxim could be phrased as a proposition with subject treated generically and predicate in the present-general tense, this theoretic syntax becomes infected by the circumstances of the narrative so that the proposition "kings are especially honored by seating, etc., and possess special divisions of land, etc.," becomes "Glaucus, why are we two honored in Lycia and have and hold property, etc." However, both Sarpedon's speech and the parallel passages B, C, and D hew close to the syntax of generalization because they are all expressed in the present tense: "we are honored . . . I honor you . . . the top men mix the wine . . . your cup is full . . . you two it is expected." When, however, we consider passage E, "gave him half his honor . . . the Lycians sectioned a section," we realize that infection of the syntax of the maxim can go so far as to transfer it into a specific act performed in historic time, replacing the proposition "for a king the people divide a division" with "the Lycians divided a division." It is in this disguised form that the ethos formulas of oral poetry are most consistently expressed and therefore may evade the notice of the literate mind.

The second part of Sarpedon's speech still awaits inspection.

A
Part Two

Dear friend, if indeed we two, this war having evaded,
would evermore be likely ageless and deathless
to exist, neither would I in the front ranks fight
nor would I despatch you into battle that brings glory;
as it is, regardless, dooms of death impend
ten thousand, and no mortal may escape or evade them;
so let us go on; to another shall we his boast extend or he to us.

(12.322–328)

These sentiments, by shifting from the present actualities of Part One to the hypothetical idiom of an unfulfilled condition—"if only"—have the effect of elevating the entire speech to a reflective level. The ability to achieve this by the conjunction of two different sets of formulaic sentiments marks the genius of the composer of this part of the Homeric narrative. However, the gist of what is now being said remains realistic: Sarpedon does not say "if only we could be sure of surviving this war" but "if only we could have got out of fighting it." Such is the form of the verb employed. His observation is rueful rather than heroic. The obligation to fight once hostilities have started has to be accepted; otherwise, no honors, perquisites, and the rest. But equally, fighting involves the hazard of either survival or death, a fifty-fifty proposition as viewed by the dispassionate eye of the Homeric calculator: "triumph will either be ours or our opponent's."

But aside from content, what of the form in which these sentiments are now cast? It emerges that the narrative straitjacket which usually draws the ethos formula into its syntax, so that a proposition (in our terms) is stated as an event, sometimes relaxes its grip. The "if only we two" sentiment is tied to the syntax of the persons performing in the present action, but it is succeeded by the statement "dooms of death impend ten thousand and no mortal may escape or evade them." This is a genuine generalization in the sense that it is not imprisoned in the specific, albeit the syntax remains dynamic. Homer's text contains many such, but they are vastly outnumbered by the types of concealed maxim previously noted.

This unusually reflective character perceptible in Part Two of Sarpedon's statement should not trick us into identifying the quality of the statement with some quality in the mind of either Sarpedon or his poet. Overall, the statement is not personal, as can be seen by reviewing once more its analogues elsewhere in the *Iliad*. We recall the battle in Book 8 which offered occasion for Hector to taunt Diomede, reminding him that his status and perquisites, those of a *basileus*, depended on military prowess. At a later stage in the same battle Hector harangues his own troops as follows:

F

If only I, even I,
were deathless and ageless all my days,
I would be honored as Athene and Apollo are honored
as (surely) as now this day brings evil to the Argives.

(8.538–541)

In a later battle in Book 13 the same threat or boast is placed in his lips in a different version. He is now addressing Ajax:

G

If only I, even I, a child of Zeus the aegis bearer
were all (my) days and Hera did bear me—
I would be honored as Athene and Apollo are honored
as (surely) as this day brings evil to the Argives.

(13.825–828)

The refrain which recurs in these sentiments constitutes one more statement of the vital importance of honor, this time extravagantly expressed: "I would be honored as gods are honored." This is Hector's egotistical aspiration; the personal pronoun is obsessive. It could be achieved for him if his parentage were divine, as it should be (passage G), that is, if he were a god, or alternatively if he did not grow old and die, even as gods do not (passage F). For one passionate moment Hector feels he really is divine and exultantly announces the contrasting mortal doom of his enemies: they will have to die. It is all an illusion, but the two formulas of aspiration poignantly express a contradiction which lay at the heart of the cultural assumptions of the early Hellenes. Their great ones enjoyed divine descent or at least claimed such because they were great. But they were either killed in their prime or grew senescent and died like everyone else. They were denied the immortality of their own putative past.

In Sarpedon's statement a change of syntax translates an arrogant boast into a general reflection. The formula of aspiration to divine descent "if only I were a child of Zeus" is ignored in favor of the kindred formula "if only we were [all] ageless and deathless forever": this is what we would all like to be, regardless of gods. It is an ethos formula reused by the poet of the *Odyssey*: the portals of Alcinous' palace are guarded by dogs (*Od.* 7.91 ff.), cast in silver and gold by Hephaestus, "deathless existing and ageless for all days." They too have divine ancestry, and this time the survival denied to men is given to sculpture. There is some irony, conscious or not, in the formula's application in such a context.

As placed on Sarpedon's lips, the aspiration becomes a reflection upon our common mortality, for the apodosis by which it is concluded replaces the notion of honor by that of survival: "I would not enter the fight . . ."; to which the composer then conjoins the general maxim: "dooms of death await us all and no man may evade them" (though one could evade a war and so win temporary survival). In so doing, he adds that speculative touch which lifts the level of all he has said. Such is the method of combination[4] by which oral genius working with the formulaic material of contrived speech achieves artistic intention.

Nomos and Ethos

This essay in disentanglement has been applied to a few lines selected from a poem of many thousands. The reader familiar with the peculiar style of the Homeric hexameter may, however, begin to realize that the passage in question bears a strong family resemblance to literally hundreds of others that could be quoted. The sublimity of Homer, a quality which has often evoked the admiration of poets, critics, and translators, is usually described in terms of elevated moral sentiments. The impression created of grandiosity and universality may be due less to ethical elevation than to moral realism. The narrative is placed at the service of reporting the way in which the affairs of men were commonly and properly transacted in a culture in which social relations were more direct and personal than has become possible in societies where advanced literate communication and literate relationships tend to prevail.

The lines in question present themselves as, in effect, a piece of social reporting. What is reported can be viewed from one point of view as accepted behavior in a given situation, from another as a definition of given social relationships, and from a third as a definition in embryo of institutions operative and accepted in the society which employs them. These are sophisticated descriptions of what I have described as a fragment of the nomos-ethos of the early city-state. It is difficult to find an alternative to this hyphenated and archaic description simply because the terminologies of modern speech, like code, behavior, relationship, institution, law, and the like, reflect the results that occur when social proprieties become documented, fixed, and visibly apprehended.

The kind of nomos-ethos formula which I have been disentangling is a unit of meaning. Such units will reproduce themselves in the poems; they are not unique statements. Often whole lines incorporating a nomos-ethos statement will recur in diverse contexts, and these typical statements are easily observed. More often they will recur in variant versions or will be made up of parts which can recur in separation from each other. The skill of the composer will be shown by the act of combination. This semantic raw material, as opposed to metrical raw material, provides the whole battery of short nomos-ethos statements which can occur in separation or in suitable combinations, making up more compendious statements. These units of composition are "formulas of meaning" in a larger sense than is applicable to the term "formula" when used by metrical analysts.[5]

The Storage Function of Homeric Rhetoric

Homer's "heroes" do as much talking as fighting, as much arguing as acting. If so much of the epic narrative consists of rhetorical statement, this need not surprise us, for it conforms to the theoretic principle indicated earlier, that lively speech is a form of action performed by lively agents, and is therefore as memorizable as narrative itself; it responds to the mnemonic rules required of oral composition. But the sheer quantity of rhetoric in Homer can also be seen as a response to the need to maximize the amount of nomos-ethos which the narrative will requires us to memorize. Speeches tend to be protreptic and therefore suitable instruments for carrying the wisdom of the day's work. They may contain narrative explicitly directed toward didactic purpose, to teach a moral lesson, as in the tale told by Phoenix to Achilles when he is vainly admonishing him to relent. But this is exceptional.

Because Sarpedon's address is admittedly reflective, it may be thought to constitute a rather special sample. To demonstrate the contrary, one should select for examination any speech which appears highly personal and on the surface nonreflective. A suitable example can be found in a context already noted. Telemachus, at the opening of the second book of the *Odyssey*, calls an agora before which he may voice his complaint at the way in which his household is being abused by the suitors. As the agora meets, a leading elder opens the proceedings by inquiring who has called it and for what purposes. Telemachus gets up and makes a passionate reply. The elements out of which this rhetorical exchange is built can be disentangled as follows, beginning with the speech of the elder:

2.25	hearken now to me, men of Ithaca, whatsoever I may say	opening of proceedings requires audience to come to attention
26	never once has our agora been held nor council since Odysseus embarked on hollow ships	the agora and council should meet regularly
28	and now who has summoned the agora thus?	any citizen may request an agora
	on whom has such great need come?	to raise a matter of public concern
29	either of young men or those who are elder born	involving interests of either junior or senior citizens
30	has he heard news of an army approaching?	an agora is summoned on news of hostilities
31	news that he would declare clearly to us when he learned of it first	early warning depends upon reliable word from those who first get it
32	does he disclose and orate-in-agora some matter of the demos?	issues of public concern should be disclosed and discussed

33–34 I think this man is goodly; a blessing on him; may Zeus for him, yes him, accomplish good, whatever he purposes in his mind

to request an agora is a fine thing to do; let us hope that the proposals offered will be sound

Narrative then takes over briefly as Telemachus prepares to reply:

36–38 he purposed to speak-in-agora and stood up and the *kerux* Peisenor put the scepter in his hand, being a man of wise counsels

a herald (*kerux*) must have expertise; he is vested with authority to choose the order of speakers

40–41 Sir, you will at once learn who has summoned the *laos* to the agora; it is I

upon a meeting of the agora the author of the request for the meeting is to be identified

42–44 I have not heard any news of an army approaching

news that I would declare clearly to you when I learned of it first

nor do I disclose and speak-in-agora some matter of the demos

(to repeat) an agora is summoned on news of hostilities

early warning depends upon reliable word from those who first get it

issues of public concern should be disclosed and then discussed, but this is not so in the present case

45 the need is my own, that has fallen as an evil upon my house, etc.

a matter of purely personal interest can come before the agora

46–47 My father . . . he among you here was a *basileus* and as a father he was gentle

the rule of a magnate is paternal

50 suitors have beset my mother, who is unwilling

a suit should not be pressed against an unwilling woman

51 cherished sons of the men who are the top men [*aristoi*] here

any community has its leading men and their sons

52 who have recoiled from resorting to the house of her father

a suitor resorts to the house of the future bride's father

53 of Icarius, that he, even he, might dowry a daughter

a marriageable daughter is dowered by her father

54 he would give to whomsoever he would wish, even to him who should come welcome to him

the intended groom must be acceptable to the father

56–57 sacrificing oxen and sheep and goats, they revel and drink sparkling wine

for ceremonious entertainment one supplies meat of oxen, sheep, and goats and plentiful wine

58–62	most is being wasted away, for no man is at hand as Odysseus was to ward off from the house ruin; we are not such as can ward off; verily thereafter we will be in sorry case	it takes a strong adult male to safeguard the resources of a household
63	deeds no longer supportable are brought to pass nor rightly any longer is my house laid waste	some acts are definitely crimes
64	You, yes you, should be indignant, all of you	one should show indignation
65	have respect for others—men who dwell around	public opinion of the neighborhood should be respected
66–67	I bid you all tremble before the wrath of the gods lest they perchance turn around aghast at evil deeds	heaven's anger will turn against crimes
68	I invoke both Zeus Olympios and Themis	Zeus and Law are the suppliant's court of appeal
69	she who the agoras of men both dissolves and seats	the agora is the court of oral law
71–73	unless my father, goodly Odysseus, in enmity wrought evils on well-greaved Achaeans for which you, exacting payment, wreak evils in enmity on me	the sins of fathers are visited upon children (the parallelism and chiasmus of the Greek reflect the idiom of a saying)
76	If you should do the eating thereafter there would be recompense	a plundered victim is recompensed
77–78	we would go through town speaking and beseeching, asking back goods until such time as all were given back	a victim of robbery can appeal to the townsfolk for restoration of stolen property
79	as it is you cast in my spirit pains unmanageable	some wrongs are irremediable

Most of the wisdom in these addresses is heavily disguised; it is discernible only as implicit, a set of assumptions about what are normal acts and attitudes in the society in question. It can be described as a foundation upon which the narrative situation is built. This foundation describes behavior patterns but not principles. The Mycenaean fantasy intrudes only slightly in the formula "well-greaved Achaeans."

The sentiments are so stated as to be tightly included in the narrative, so that the subjects of statements are all persons speaking or acting and the verbs are all of actions occurring at a given moment of time; the only sentiments which in isolation are generic are the following:

54 he [a father] would give [a daughter] to whomsoever he would wish who would come welcome to him
63 deeds no more supportable are brought to pass
67 perchance they [the gods] may turn round aghast at evil deeds
69 [Themis] who the agoras of men both dissolves and seats

Even these avoid the idiom of a truly "generic" syntax: that is, they are not "is" statements of principles or laws abstracted from an activist situation. The subjects are agents or behave as such. Rhetoric of this kind is "storage rhetoric." The mnemonic requirement that even the saying itself be dynamic, and that it be incorporated incidentally within the dynamism of epic narrative, has been met.

7
The Justice of the *Iliad*

❀

As we have just viewed it, the Greek epic, so far from being an oral improvisation, is a compendium of social and personal conventions, as these become illustrated in an appropriate mythos—one that is told in a way and with a style that will continuously provoke their utterance. On the face of it, the culture that is being both reported and supported in this way by the enclave of contrived speech is self-regulating. No individual can stand outside it and criticize it on the basis of principles independent of the culture. Personal "alienation" from society is impossible because unthought of. What becomes law in a literate society remains custom and usage; morality is not easily definable except as conformity to custom.

Redress of Disorder

Yet conformity is surely not automatic. The behavior of the human being, as observed in Chapter 2, is not confined within the limits set by herd instinct. Whether his society is oral or literate, his individuation will interrupt and disrupt the web of custom and precedent by the self-motivated arrogance of personal decision or desire, anger or ambition, or even mere eccentricity. From time to time, the general rules will be broken: and very often their correct application in given cases will be doubtful, because of uncertainty created by competing claims. The nomos and ethos continually recalled and illustrated in Homeric narrative and rhetoric are normative. They state and restate the proprieties of behavior as these are assumed and followed. But the oral medium, in order to fulfill its complete function as the verbalized guide of the culture, will also be required to describe situations and frame statements which are corrective rather than merely normative, which, describing how the mores are abrogated, therewith describe also the means and manner whereby they are restored. The master symbol of this corrective process, which is also a procedure, is the Homeric *dikē* and its plural *dikai*, in which we encounter an oral prototype of what later was to become "justice" in the conceptual sense in which we now use the word.[1]

An epic mythos could not come into existence if it limited itself to reporting a culture that was self-regulating. The memorizable story must exploit the tensions of a conflict. Such a situation creates itself when the mores are subjected to disturbance or abrogation; they are defied in part or whole by at least some of the protagonists. A Sarpedon, a Diomede, an Aeneas, an Odysseus, a Nestor, a Priam, even a Hector are examples of characters whose roles as played in the *Iliad* are by and large normative and "normal." These roles could never of themselves create an *Iliad*. What the listening audience wants and expects from the singer is a story of a collision provoking the excitement of vigorous action and speech. This the mythos will supply, and then to fulfill its didactic function, it will proceed to narrate the corrective process which restores the proprieties. Both epics conform to this pattern, but it is particularly in the *Iliad* that restoration can be seen to depend upon the application of a set of rules recognized by the community present in the story, and recognizable by the modern reader, as a form of "justice."

The Psychology of Feud

The action of the plot grows out of a Greek raid on a neighboring town which is pillaged. The booty, in accordance with custom, is distributed through the army, Agamemnon receiving a captive girl, who turns out to be a priest's daughter. His rejection of her father's plea to return her involves the army in a disastrous plague, for which the required remedy is that he comply with the plea, which he does. But he then pulls rank on Achilles, and compensates himself by abstracting from him a substitute girl, hitherto Achilles' property. What have now been provoked as a central factor in the story are a contention and a feud (*eris* and *neikos*) between two powerful men. The preface to the epic carefully identifies these as the subject of the story, for their concomitant is a rage which, as it seizes on Achilles, has the effect of gravely damaging the Greek army. He expresses his feelings by withdrawing himself and his force totally from combat. The Greeks in due course confront a second crisis as they are pressed by superior opponents to the point of near defeat.

It did not take Agamemnon long to regret the "contentions and feuds" which he confesses he himself had initiated (2.375–378), and if resolution of the impasse had depended on him, it would have been resolved without critical consequences. As the Greek army suffers reverses, Nestor proposes that Achilles be conciliated and offered compensation. Agamemnon readily agrees, accepting the fact that he has erred. The burden he carries, and confesses to Nestor that he carries, is symbolized in the word "Disaster" (*Atē*), capitalized as a demon that afflicts mankind. She destroys both wits and fortunes; she infatuates and ruins. "You have accurately recounted my disasters. I have been disastered, no denying it" (9.115–116). "Disastered as I have been, through giving way to wits pestilential, I desire in return to conciliate and give enormous gifts" (9.119–120). Ten books later, after further prolongation of the crisis (for Achilles remains obdurate), as settlement of the feud is at last achieved, Agamemnon converts the occasion into a second opportunity to descant upon the operation of this demon. On that fatal day when he took Achilles' girl, "Zeus and Fate and Erinys cast into my wits savage Disaster" (19.88). "Eldest daughter of Zeus is Disaster, she who disasters all men . . . she passes over the heads of men disabling them . . . Yes, once on a time even Zeus was disastered" (19.91–94). Hera had tricked Zeus into giving her a solemn promise on false pretenses, "and then was he much disastered" (9.114). When he found out the truth, "straightaway he seized Disaster by the hair . . . and swore that never again would Olympus and starry heaven be entered by Disaster, she who disasters all men. So he threw her out of heaven and she descended on the works of men" (9.126–131). "So I too, when Hector began to slay the Greeks at their ships' sterns, could not evade Disaster, she by whom I first was disastered. But disastered as I have been, robbed of my wits by Zeus, I desire in return to conciliate and give gifts unlimited" (9.134–135). The reiteration within each context, and between two contexts so widely separated, is compulsively formulaic.

Agamemnon need not stand in the pillory alone. This demon can distribute her favors impartially. Earlier in the story, at the point where Achilles had declared his continued obduracy, he had received a solemn address from his tutor, Phoenix (*Il.* 9.502 ff.):

Supplications are daughters of great Zeus,
lame and wrinkled and blear-eyed,
moving cautiously on in the rear of Disaster;[2]
Disaster is strong and fleet-footed and so
she far outruns all of them and gets in front all over the earth,
disabling mankind; and they follow in the rear to heal.
If a man is gracious to the maids of Zeus as they draw near,
they greatly prosper him, and as he prays they listen;
if a man refuse and stubbornly say "No,"
then do they, even they, go to Kronian Zeus and supplicate
that Disaster go in that man's company, that he be disabled and pay back.

The predicted comes to pass. Achilles, still obdurate, makes only one small concession, which, precisely because of its niggardliness, proves his undoing. For when it is implemented by allowing Patroclus to go into battle to rescue the ships, Patroclus is killed. Achilles by his own action —or lack of action—has lost his best friend, and in a crisis of revulsion, aside from vowing vengeance on Hector, he formally pronounces against that Contention (Eris: she, like Disaster, is capitalized here) around which the plot to this point had been built (18.107 ff.):

O, that Contention from among gods and human beings might perish
and anger which sets even the prudent to make trouble—
(anger) which, sweeter far than honey spilled over,
in the hearts of men waxes as smoke.

This statement announces the beginning of the termination of the mythos announced in the opening lines of the poem: "which of the gods was it that set these two together in contention to fight"? Confronting the contrite Agamemnon, Achilles recalls the "contention spirit-devouring" (19.58) and, speaking for the poet, pronounces that the story of "this contention, mine and yours, will long be commemorated" (19.64). It is the poem's own definition of what the story has been all about and what its claim will be upon the memory of posterity.[3]

The Social Context of Feud

A perceptive critic noted over forty years ago that the *Iliad,* though of oral composition, is an epic with psychological overtones, exhibiting a sophistication uncommon in the genre.[4] The account so far summarized of the plot, to the conclusion of Book 19, confirms this judgment. The action is so described as to be explicitly governed by the passions and decisions of two men of power: the controlling symbols are those of feud and hatred, pride and blind anger, honor and arrogance, rash decision and rueful regret, pleas and reproaches, defiance and confession, as these distribute themselves on both sides of the argument. Even though the Homeric idiom can sometimes objectify these facts of psychology as forces external to man, we feel their operation within men as they speak and act. For the literate reader the epic is probably easiest to enjoy and sympathize with if understood in these terms.

But those in search of justice in the *Iliad* must take a different tack, focusing their inquiry on the political and social context. What precisely are the procedures that are followed in the story at those few occasions where the feud, its causes, its effects, and possible amendment are directly in question? Though the initial error was Agamemnon's, trouble first erupts when the aggrieved father appeals not just to him (and also his brother) but to the entire Greek company. He offers to buy his daughter back, a reasonable proposal, and the Greek audience shouts its approval, which is overridden by Agamemnon. To deal with the consequences, which fall on the Greeks as a body, they meet in an agora summoned by Achilles. This is not a casual event. The formulaic hexameters which describe the initial summons and the final dismissal, the succession of debaters as they get up and sit down, offering proposals or rebuttals, defiance or mediation, are carefully programed. We are watching a town meeting in session, and it is a fair inference that it was at a previous session that the priest had first appeared. As in the *Odyssey,* anyone can call a meeting (in this case Achilles), and when he speaks he holds the "scepter." The word *agora* can denote either a "speaking" or (in the plural) speeches, or an assembly where speaking occurs, or the place where the assembly is held (which later in Athens and perhaps elsewhere also became the marketplace). It is a "parliament" in the literal sense of that word. The Greeks for fantasy purposes are an army in the field besieging Troy. More realistically, they are behaving as the "parliament" of a polis, thereby furnishing a paradigm of civic procedure as an item of oral storage.

The Greeks in Assembly

The truth of this becomes clearer in the second book. Agamemnon has a dream which instructs him to marshal the troops: clearly a preparation for the catalogue of the ships. Unaccountably, he then instructs the heralds to announce an agora, which accordingly meets, as described in regulation formulas (2.51–52). Then it is left in suspense while Agamemnon "holds a session of the council of elders" (53), proposing to them to marshal the troops. They approve and the session then "rises" (85), and the scene reverts to "the people," now buzzing about like bees (86–89), but there are also "many nationalities drawn up in file on the foreshore" (91–92), who then proceed "en masse into agora" (93), an event which has already been stated. The next 306 lines are a narrative of the parliament and its proceedings. At one point it is interrupted, as the members leave their seats and make for the ships, but order is restored and the session resumed. Formulas appropriate to the occasion are reiterated (93, 95, 144, 149, 207, 264, 334, 337, 370). The assembly is seated in orderly fashion in rows of seats; heralds (whose duties are omitted in Book 1) have the task of arranging the seating, keeping order, calling for silence as a speaker rises (96, 99, 206, 211, 255, 398). The scepter, though described in antiquarian terms as the inherited property of Agamemnon, is at the realistic level appropriated by Odysseus (as previously by Achilles) when he wants to speak or use it to enforce discipline. The whole account, confused as it is (362–368 is a call to arms), to the point where the catalogue begins, is a blend of antique fantasy and contemporary political reality. It leaves the impression that for the transaction of public business and the formation of important decisions a parliament was essential,[5] assisted by a council which met separately, something which the narrative of Book 1 gives no opportunity to mention. Aristotle, in a later age, tacitly accepted the fact that such functions were indeed vested in the Homeric agora, when he remarks (*Pol.* III 14 1285a11), apropos of this same scene in Book 2 of the *Iliad*, that "Agamemnon (regularly) sustained verbal attacks in the meetings of the ecclesia," a term he would use only on the assumption that the agora was in fact the prototype of the parliamentary machinery employed in Athens. In drawing a sharp distinction between Agamemnon's role in the ecclesia and his power as a commander-in-chief on a campaign (1285a13), he appears to assume that the agoras of the *Iliad* were in fact not military but civilian, like those held in the *Odyssey*, where in Ithaca the agora at times seems to be in continual session, its proceedings being supplemented by a council who have reserved seats in it. There are several other agora sessions in the *Iliad*, on both Greek and Trojan sides, in one of which it is noted as an exception that the members are standing (18.246). Procedures are wholly oral. Aside from the debating process itself, all communications, motions, and decisions are framed and implemented by oral formula.

Legal Functions of Assembly

This does not mean that the agora is a legislative body. It can only accept or reject leadership supplied by the "top men" (*aristoi, basileis*). But acceptance or rejection can be decisive. Agamemnon by rejecting the priest's plea rejected a "vote" of the agora, and the results proved painful. The second meeting produces a debate in the face of which his reluctance is overcome. The pressure on him emanates not only from the speakers but from the silent listening audience. The plea he then makes to the agora discloses its powers. "You all are looking on as my prize is divested from me" (1.120). "So furnish me with a prize at once" (118). It is the prerogative of the assembly to do so, even as it controlled the original distribution of the loot, a fact which Achilles is quick to point out (125–126). Propriety (126) would be violated by opening up the process again. Agamemnon will have to wait for the army to seize more booty elsewhere. Yet the issue is dubious, precisely because it involves the commander-in-chief. Should not his superior rank take precedence? This is also a propriety (119): the two are discovered in collision. A personal decision to appropriate Achilles' girl as a substitute offers no solution; it only provokes a confrontation, which might be settled by direct action between the parties, murder, in fact. Such a solution lacks divine sanction, and it is abandoned (188–218). Achilles will wait for remedy and bring pressure by withdrawing himself and his men from battle.

Justice Mismanaged

It is as he announces this decision that the notion of Homeric "justice" enters into the debate. The decision takes the form of an oath and a vow sworn before the assembly and involving the audience and not just Agamemnon in the consequences. They had assigned Achilles Briseis; they are witnesses to the cancellation of that assignment; in effect, they are responsible for the act (299). Holding up the scepter before them, he describes how it was once a living tree, and is now become forever lifeless wood.

> Now just as surely the sons of the Achaeans
> carry and handle it, the managers-of-justices [*dikas-poloi*] who also the formularies
> under Zeus do conserve.[6] So shall this oath be great to you
>
> (237–239)

He then promises disaster for the Greeks, which Agamemnon will be powerless to avert. Having said which, he dashes the gold-studded club on the ground. *Dikai* in the plural are not principles of justice, but events involving justice which become procedures because they are subject to "management" by officials, who, however, do not manage the "formularies" but protect them.

But procedural justice in this case has not been put to work. Its task would have been to prevent the insult to a member of the army whose services were indispensable. The agora is a necessary partner in the procedure, for it has the responsibility for allotting not only spoils but the honors that accompany them. It has failed in the present case by acquiescing in Agamemnon's act of individuation. Achilles dramatizes the failure by dashing the club to the ground. The gold-studded scepter, honored in this case as the insignia of judicial rather than monarchical power, has been dishonored. The agora is so told, and is warned that it must share the consequences. The debate, however, continues with an attempt at mediation, appropriately undertaken by Nestor in the character of elder statesman, proposing the kind of solution that will in fact be followed in the end, but the case for the present is hopeless. The two parties are still contestants "fighting each other with counterviolent words" (1.304).[7] They rise and dismiss the agora.

Yet the meeting has achieved one positive result. Nomos and ethos, violated by the capture of a priest's daughter, are remedied by a decision taken in the course of the proceedings. The offender arranges for the girl to be ceremoniously restored to her father, and this ceremony as it is carried out is carefully and repetitively described, for it is required to complete the "legalities." One item of justice as orally managed has been implemented, though the poem does not use the term.

Redress Proposed

As already noted, Agamemnon's repentance is not long delayed, and it is noteworthy that it is stated in Book 2 before a fresh meeting of the agora. What he says is an expression of personal feeling which offers no legal solution. The business at this meeting is preparation for combat without Achilles. Only after the Greeks have suffered serious reverses is an agora summoned to deal formally with the crisis created by the fulfillment of his vow. It is formulaically convoked and seated (9.10–13). Addresses by Agamemnon and Diomede are followed by a speech by Nestor, who states in axiomatic form the communal danger created by the personal confrontation (9.63–64):

Out of clan, out of law, out of hearth stands [*estin*][8] that one
whose lust is for war internecine within the demos

This is a judgment upon both contestants. He then proposes that the
army recoup morale by eating a meal, and while they are doing so
Agamemnon can convoke the elders (70, 89–90) in his own quarters for
a meal. For practical purposes, this is a meeting of the council (cf. 75),
at which Nestor ceremoniously notes that in Agamemnon's hands "lie
scepter and formularies given by Zeus" to assist his leadership in counsel
(9.99);[9] it is therefore his duty both to speak and to listen to what
others have to say. This recollection of what happened in Book 1, or
rather did not happen, is continued as Nestor reviews his previous
abortive attempt at mediation (105–111). The remedy proposed at that
time being no longer applicable, he proposes instead adequate compensation from Agamemnon for injury inflicted. This suggestion, accepted
by Agamemnon, in effect emanates from the council, and it proves
ineffective. A final solution will require the renewed presence of the
agora which had witnessed the original rupture.

Justice Managed

If the *Iliad* were limited to being a psychological epic, Achilles'
revulsion at the news of his friend's death would be enough to cancel
the past without more ado. The epic itself, however, is well aware that
the functions of the story it is telling are not primarily psychological but
legal, social, and political. At the point where Achilles has become eager
to abandon the feud in order to join battle and kill Hector, his mother
admonishes him that he must first call an agora and formally renounce
his wrath (19.34–35). Formal and formulaic summons is then issued for
the meeting of all concerned; the attendance of noncombatants is specifically mentioned (19.41–54). Achilles as summoner gives the opening
address renouncing his wrath, and the assembly applaud. Agamemnon,
speaking from his seat, announces that he has something to say if the
agora will stop interrupting and give him a hearing (81–82). At the
beginning of the lengthy apology that follows,[10] he observes that the
savage demon which had destroyed his judgment was inflicted on him
"in agora" (88). The apology concluded, he signifies readiness to pay
lavish compensation, as already offered. The call to battle the enemy is
urgent, but wait, he says to Achilles, till the compensation is brought
here for your inspection (19.138–144). Achilles courteously declares his
indifference: he is impatient to begin fighting. Odysseus, assuming

Nestor's role as the voice of propriety, admonishes (as Nestor had done, 9.66) that the army should disperse and eat a meal if they are to fight. But first, a settlement between the two erstwhile antagonists should be ceremoniously performed (19.172–183). The goods constituting the compensation should be conveyed "into the middle of the agora so that all may view with their eyes," not just Achilles. Agamemnon must then "rise and give solemn oath" that he is able to restore Briseis in her original condition. He is also to play formal host to Achilles at a feast of reconciliation. Then Odysseus adds (180–183):

You [Achilles] will not be left holding anything that falls short of "justice," and you [Agamemnon] thereafter "more just" [*dikaioteros*] on any other ground as well
shall stand [*esseai*], since it is no matter of reproach
that a *basileus* should appease a man in a case where one has been the first to make trouble.

Agamemnon readily complies and prepares the formalities necessary to the completion of the negotiation: the intention to pronounce oaths is repeated three times (187, 188, 191); he will produce the gifts of compensation in full view. Achilles, still indifferent to the ceremony, will fast, he says, till he kills Hector; not so the army, says Odysseus. But before the meal is eaten, the ceremony is completed (238–275): the gifts are brought into full view, an animal is solemnly sacrificed, and a solemn oath is sworn, after which Achilles in brief but formal reply acknowledges for his part the disastrous effect of the demon of ruin upon Agamemnon personally and upon the body politic as well. So the agora is at last dissolved (276). It has been witness to, and, we may add, guarantor of, the termination of a *neikos,* achieved under the superintendence of an arbitrator who has functioned as a "manager of justices," though the narrative does not award him the title. The terms of Homeric justice, honored in the breach when the feud erupted, have emerged as decisive, pronounced in the settlement over which they may be said to preside as symbols of what has happened. Achilles receives an adequacy of justice, almost as though it were a quantity. His opponent also becomes "more just," so that his "justice" too may be said to be increased, in the sense that he is "justified" in apologizing (despite his superior rank) because (as he himself admitted in Book 2) he was the inciter of the *neikos.* Justice, whatever it is, can be seen as something exchanged beween two parties, or added to both, in the course of a settlement; or, alternatively, as symbolizing the process of exchange itself.[11] It is certainly not a principle which when applied excludes its opposite.

To achieve proper result, certain conditions have to be met. Though the feud which calls for such procedure occurs between two parties, justice can be applied only with the participation of the agora, functioning as a forum for rhetoric addressed to the issues that have arisen. The performance of judgment is also a function of rhetoric: the one is achieved through the other, so that the scepter is both a judge's symbol and a speaker's symbol. The settlement is likely to involve a reassignment of goods both material and moral, that is, of money and of honor. Since no documentary evidence of the settlement is available to be exchanged, the witness of a mass audience who will remember what they have heard and seen is vital. Equally, the procedure must include not only the material compensation placed on view but appropriate vows, promises, and confessions orally pronounced and heard.

Aside, therefore, from the substratum of nomos and ethos which is discovered incidentally as it lurks in Homer's verse, the mythos of the epic itself as announced in the preface and terminated in the nineteenth book is a paradigm of oral "justice," that is, of legal procedure as conducted in the early city-state. The didactic purpose of the storage epic emerges in the way the story is told. It may be objected that the *dikē* language actually present is scanty, and further that the epic after nineteen books has not completed itself. Action is transferred from the agora back to the battlefield, and the succeeding course of the story is dominated by the theme of Achillles' onslaught and its aftermath.

The Justice of Menelaus

In the twenty-third book, however, the scene once more becomes an assembly of the Greeks, in the form of an *agōn,* or race meeting, which, however, is "seated" (23.258, 448).

The chief sporting event is the chariot race. Homer's extended description includes an account of some cheating that occurred during the race. The poet narrates how the teams of Antilochus and Menelaus ran almost neck and neck till Antilochus by a trick got ahead, and how Menelaus at the prize-giving ceremonies then blocked the award to Antilochus. Neither was placed first, but they had conducted a private and fierce competition for second place. Antilochus, behind Menelaus, lashed his horses to overtake his rival and draw close to him; he observes that they are approaching a narrow point in the course, where there is not room for two chariots to pass; he is just behind Menelaus; he swerves his team off the course to bypass him. Menelaus exclaims: "You fool! Wait! The way is narrow here, it will soon widen to allow your team to pass; otherwise, you will smash up both of us." Antilochus ignores the warning, Menelaus slackens pace to avoid the collision, Antilochus gets ahead, followed by the curses of Menelaus: "You dastard, damn you, you haven't any sense, as we Achaeans said; but don't think that you can carry off the prize (he means for second place) without swearing oath" (23.441). Seventy-five lines later, the race ends, with Menelaus closing in on Antilochus; if the course had lasted longer, says Homer, "he would have bypassed him."

Diomede was first. The rest of the field in order of arrival are Antilochus, Menelaus, Meriones, and Eumelus. Achilles awards the prizes; there is no dispute over the winner, but Eumelus, who came in last, is judged by Achilles to have deserved second place, which an accident had prevented him from winning. Antilochus protests, and proposes instead a consolation prize for Eumelus, himself taking the second, to which Achilles accedes; whereupon Menelaus gets up in anger and presents a formal accusation against Antilochus of cheating, in support of his own claim to second place.

"Before them Menelaus stood up . . . and the herald placed the staff in his hand, and commanded silence upon the Argives. And Menelaus then addressed them" (23.566 ff.). "You disabled my horses by casting yours in front" (571–572); this is his accusation. Then, turning to the audience and addressing them formally as "lords and leaders of the Achaeans," he invites them to intervene: "Apply justice to this," he says to them, using the verb *dikazō*,[12] "in between both parties without favor"; he adds that he does not want any Greek to be able to say that Menelaus, pulling rank on Antilochus, used false statements to take the mare from him. Then he substitutes a second method (579–585): "No, I will do the justicing [*dikasō*] myself, without, I think, any risk of criticism; the justice [*dikē*] will be straight. Come here, Antilochus; take your stand as the formulary has it [*themis esti*]; stand in front of your horses, take the whip in your hand, touch the horses, and swear oath by Poseidon that you did not deliberately use guile to cripple my team."

Antilochus promptly gives in quite gracefully, saying in effect (587–595): yes, I did; I admit I was ignorant and rash, and I could not swear such an oath. Whereupon not only are the two reconciled, but Menelaus replies in effect: I forgive you, your youth prevailed over your senses; and he invokes the testimony of those present: "I am a man of kind heart, never arrogant" (611).

The episode conspicuously dramatizes the settlement of a dispute carried out orally in public and rendered effective because it is witnessed by the community acting as a body. Its "legality" depends upon an oath uttered by one party (or in this case declined) and heard by the other, in public, before witnesses. Equally, the episode illustrates how the procedure can be taken over by one of the litigants who himself becomes the utterer of a "justice" which is not less so because he speaks it. He does not pronounce a verdict, he demands one. The equity of his management is guaranteed in this case not only by the agreement of the opposite party but by the assent of the audience who would otherwise protest. Both parties know that what they say and do is "public."

The Orality of Homeric Justice

A "justice," singular or plural (*dikē, dikai*), is something spoken aloud.[13] This can be seen from an episode familiar to historians who have explored the origins of Greek law. The life-style of the city at peace as described on Achilles' shield is symbolized by two civic situations, a wedding ceremony and also a legal trial described as follows (18.497 ff):

The people were assembled en masse in agora. There a feud [*neikos*]
had arisen; two men were feuding over penalty
for a man killed. One claimed to have paid all of it,
explaining to the demos; and the other said, no, he had taken nothing.
Both parties were eager for a "knower" [*histōr*] to make a determination
[*peirar*];
the people were shouting for both, supporting this side and that;
heralds were seating the people; and the elders
sat upon polished stones in a sacred circle;
and the staff of the heralds clear voiced they held in hands.
They then rushed up to them and alternately argued the justice of it
[*dikazon*];
there were placed in the midst of them two gold talents
to give to him who among them should speak justice most straightly.

Oral law (themis) had forbidden Achilles to murder Agamemnon. Here too the same rule holds. Causing the death of a man in civil life can be redressed by payment of compensation in money, probably to a surviving relative. But there is no written record to attest such an act; the memories of the two parties concerned are the sole source of knowledge, and this situation can give rise to doubtful claims on one side or the other. A feud (*neikos*) is the result, to be settled by a comparison of oral statements, for which there is a proper procedure. For guidance, both parties resort to the "knower"; what he "knows" are "justices and formularies" (*Od.* 9.215): his memory is stored with relevant information to guide the parties in their argument. The case, however, has to go before the seated agora of the "demos," where the oral machinery for settlement consists of two parts: the agora itself and the committee of elders, who have special seats (in front?). Their duty is that of regulating the order of speakers and listening to them. Do they vote, or simply preside over an agreement reached by the agora as to which side of the case wins, that is, is preferred? The "justice of it" is pleaded by the litigants in person, as it was by Menelaus; the decision will go to the rhetorician who can "state his justice most directly." The audience, previously divided, will be supposed to acclaim the winner; perhaps the elders address them before this happens.[14] The award is placed on view, to be witnessed by the agora. Court discipline, if that is the best word, is regulated by heralds in charge of the seating and by the sight of the staff held in the hand held up to command silence; what is not stated, but may be inferable, is that the litigants receive the staff alternately from the elders before speaking. This kind of justice is not a set of preexistent princples or a set of rulings imposed by judges in the light of such principles. It is a symbol or a process achieved through oral persuasion and oral conviction.

One might expect that such legal proprieties might occasionally be encapsulated more explicitly in aphoristic or proverbial form. The *Iliad* contains one such example. Characteristically, it is occasioned by a simile. Describing the headlong rush of Hector's horses as they carry their owner away from Patroclus' onslaught (16.383), the poem compares it to a cloudburst resulting in a destructive flood which carries away the works of men; it is a hazard typical of valley settlements in mountainous country and therefore typically Greek. A cloudburst, however, is the work of Zeus, and so the verse supplies a motive for his intervention. The god acts in this way (16.386–388)

when in anger with men he inflicts severities upon them
who by violence [*bia*] in agora adjudicate formularies [*themistas*] crookedly
and drive out justice, regarding not awe of gods

The latter two lines propound the rule which nomos requires by describing its negation. In oral citation the formulas of the tradition guarded in memory can be twisted or bent "crooked," that is, misquoted, or misapplied, to suit the interest of one party or the other. This is the error which in Homer's formula is stigmatized as "adjudicating" or perhaps "selecting" them "crookedly."[15] The legal situation places the litigant before the agora where he and presumably his opponent have pleaded the case; he receives an adverse ruling based on precedents incorrectly used. He insists on arguing against it; his argument has "the justice of it" on its side; he has to be physically removed by force so that his "justice" is "expelled" from the agora; this is the concrete sense of the language employed. Nothing in the formula is inconsistent with the way *dikē* has operated elsewhere in the epic. There is no need to look for a late or post-Homeric source; the only difference is that elsewhere the procedure is memorialized by describing how it is applied, whereas here it is recommended by describing what happens when it is not applied. Both types of definition are conveyed by indirection, but less so in this negative example.

Procedure in Place of Principle

In sum, the "justice" of the *Iliad* is a procedure, not a principle or any set of principles. It is arrived at by a process of negotiation between contending parties carried out rhetorically. As such, it is particular, not general, in its references, and can be thought of either in the singular or in the plural—the "right of it" in a given case or "the rights" as argued and settled in one or more cases. There is no judiciary conceived as an independent state authority, but there are experts on oral "law"—men with specially equipped memories, one would guess. Judicial functions are mainly confined to presiding, listening, speaking, and sensing a consensus in the audience; they are shared or passed around indifferently between the experts, acting as "managers of justices," the elders or the contestants themselves, according to circumstance. The procedure takes place in public, because in a preliterate society the memory of the public is the only available attestation as to what is promised or agreed to. However loose or vague the procedure may appear from the standpoint of literate practice, it worked effectively to preserve "law and order" (*eunomia*) in the city-states of early Hellenism. It supplied those directive formulas which were also corrective, a necessary supplement to the nomos and ethos as normatively taught and accepted. Such procedures may have been of immemorial origin, invented to control the impact of individuation upon nascent human communities.

But for disputes between competing city-states, the procedure was not available, because no common agora was available to allow it to function. Between Greeks and Trojans, "justice" cannot exist, only the inaction of peace or the activity of war. So *dikē* vanishes from the epic when Achilles takes the field, returning only when confrontation with the enemy is replaced by a fresh assembly and a fresh dispute between the Greeks themselves. For any attempt to suggest a paradigm of international behavior which might also be "just," we have to look to the *Odyssey*.

8

The Legalities of the *Odyssey*

❦

The tale of the *Odyssey* as it is told is only in part a narrative of adventure and travel. The larger portion concerns itself with confrontation between domestic adversaries, and in this respect reuses the type of framework round which the mythos told in the *Iliad* was built. For Achilles versus Agamemnon are substituted Odysseus and his household versus the suitors. The quality of the confrontation is different and the manner of its resolution will be different, but it is a confrontation.

On Olympus, as the story opens, a full council of the gods (1.27; compare the divine councils in the *Iliad*) is being held with one absentee; Poseidon is not among those present and this fact removes his veto, enabling the council to take action. Zeus invites proposals dealing with Odysseus: "Come then, let all of us present take under consideration the problem of Odysseus' homecoming" (1.76). Athene, Odysseus' partisan, promptly rises to the opportunity; she moves that Hermes be sent to release Odysseus from Calypso; she herself will despatch the son, Telemachus, in search of news.

Due Process

But first, Athene says, she will give him what might be called legal instructions. First, he is to summon a full agora (1.90), before which "he must then give suitors formal notice to cease and desist" (91)—the suitors being here introduced into the narrative without further explanation. Appearing then to Telemachus, and after conversation with him, she conveys the directive with due ceremony and emphasis (269–271) and amplifies it: (1) his formal statement is to be made before the full agora, (2) he is to invoke divine witness also, (3) he must invite the suitors to scatter to their houses, (4) he must invite his mother to return to his father's house, and (5) she is to be given to a fresh husband with due ceremony should marriage be her inclination (274–278). It will be observed that these steps, if taken, have the effect of replacing Odysseus by his son as the source of authority. This at least is an alternative in the legal dilemma now confronting the house of Odysseus. Athene makes this clear by adding three more instructions: (6) if in the search for news he ascertains that his father is dead, he should on returning carry out a ceremonial funeral for him, (7) and give his widow away in marriage, (8) then and only then (293) taking steps to kill the suitors. It is possible that in the poetic formulation steps 7 and 8 have been reversed.

Telemachus before summoning the agora announces his intention to the suitors gathered in his house: they are ceremoniously and pejoratively addressed (368) and invited to attend a "session" (372) of the agora to hear a formal statement from himself requesting them "to cease and desist"; they may refuse and continue to devour his substance; he will then invoke divine witness to what he has said, inviting retribution upon them. This summary naturally does not include all the steps to be taken as proposed by Athene, but it pinpoints the intention to obtain a legal determination of what has become a critical situation between two adversary parties.

The agora being duly convoked, an elder statesman rises to ask what is the business before it. This gives Telemachus his clue. He gets up, the herald places the club (*skēptron*) in his hand, he identifies himself as the convoker of the session, and launches into a very personal, not to say emotional, harangue dramatizing his dilemma and appealing for popular sympathy. (Its substance was analyzed in Chapter 6). His oration, a prelude to the following debate, is directed toward the agora as a whole. His audience, we learn, includes the "great men"[1] (*aristoi*) who are the parents of the suitors (2.51), and he asks them to put a stop to what is going on (70), so that his house can be left in peace and not pillaged by consumption of the domestic stores; he needs protection in the absence of the senior member of the household. Concluding this emotional outburst, he dashes the club on the ground.

The debate then opens and is continued by a response from the side of the suitors. Their case is presented. It rests upon the postponement and deceit practiced by Penelope: she carries the responsibility for a decision which could end the impasse; until she acts they will keep up the pressure by continuing their present policy. Telemachus offers a rebuttal, alleging the impropriety, nay, the impiety of a son's ejecting a mother from her house preparatory to another marriage against her will; her Erinys (does this recall the case of Clytemnestra?) will harm him if he does such a thing. He then gives formal notice: (1) leave my house and eat elsewhere at your own mutual expense; (2) if you refuse, I invoke divine witness of what I have said, inviting retribution upon you (2.139 ff. = 1.374 ff.). The reiteration heavily underlines the formulaic and legal character of what he is saying. Two eagles then enter the sky directly above the debating agora (2.150), and their behavior as they circle is interpreted by a prophet as predicting that Odysseus is not far away and that his imminent arrival menaces all the suitors; they should take this as a warning. A second spokesman for them contemptuously dismisses such prophecy as a futile exercise prompted by bribery and then proceeds to make a formal counter-declaration before the full agora (194): order your mother to retire to her father's house to be given to a fresh husband with due ceremony (2.195–196 = 1.276–278). This repeats part of the terms included in Athene's original instruction to Telemachus, underlining the fact that the demand has a formal propriety on its side. Two parties to a disputed case have now put forward their contending positions. The spokesman then adds a repetition of the sanction, which from their side the suitors are prepared to impose to achieve enforcement of their demand: they will keep up the pressure by continuing to eat at the expense of the house. Telemachus, still following previous instructions, responds by accepting the fact of continued pressure as inevitable—he lacks the means to oppose it. But, recalling the procedure before the agora which he had so carefully followed, he solemnly notes again that his appeal has been made before the gods and the entire community (211).

So he now requests a ship to allow him to travel for news of his father. If it is learned that he is dead: I will return and (1) carry out a ceremonial burial for him and (2) give my mother away in marriage. In this way he verbally repeats items 6 and 7 of Athene's advice, but naturally suppresses the eighth. The request for a ship brings the issue round to a problem posed by the status of Odysseus himself: is he dead or alive? This is a question which so far in the course of the debate has not been directly faced. An aged deputy of the absent chief, left in charge when he departed for the wars, takes the occasion to get up and pay the first formal tribute offered to his memory, to which he appends an attack on the demos for failing to protect the interests of Odysseus' household (*oikos*); after all, they constitute the majority (241). Replying, in part on behalf of the agora, the third spokesman for the suitors reminds the protester that even if Odysseus returned he would be hopelessly outnumbered by his opponents and killed. These aggressive words carry a threat which is openly illegal. So he continues, turning to the audience, "you people break it up; go each to your own fields" (252); as for Telemachus, he adds contemptuously, he can have his ship for all the good it will do; and then: "thus he spoke and hastily dismissed the agora" (257).

The proceedings are over. What has Telemachus accomplished? He resorts to the seashore to call on Athene and protest his helplessness. Although appearing in the guise of Mentor, the deputy of Odysseus, she in effect mothers him: she is sure he will not be like most sons, inferior to his father; and she adds reassurance by offering a formal prophecy: the suitors, already damned by their own conduct, are all doomed to die on the same day (282–284). She will make arrangements to procure a ship if he looks after the stores required for the voyage. Restored by her words, he returns to the house and is contemptuously invited by the leading suitor to rejoin the company so that he can get his ship. He spurns this patronizing offer; he will get his own ship; and he vows vengeance upon them all. They remain unaffected, careless and contemptuous. The ship and stores are procured and a crew is recruited, and while the suitors are asleep, Telemachus, accompanied by Athene in disguise, sets sail and leaves the island.

Resemblances to the *Iliad*

Much of the substance of these first two books of the *Odyssey* recalls what takes place in the first book of the *Iliad*. Athene, the earnest advocate of Odysseus' interests on Olympus, resembles Thetis in her partisanship before Zeus on behalf of her son Achilles. When Telemachus in despair goes to the beach to complain to his patroness and is comforted, we think both of the priest Chryses resorting to the shore to appeal to his god and of Achilles doing the same thing to appeal to his

mother, and receiving similar support from her (*Od.* 2.260–262 has
correspondences with *Il.* 1.34–35 and 351). When the suitors' spokesman dismisses the prophet's credentials, he recalls Agamemnon's attack
upon Chalcas. Telemachus dashes the club on the ground in the manner of Achilles after a similar emotional outburst. These and other
details are not properly to be explained as one "author" imitating or
echoing another. They occur in and around a narrative context which is
common to both poems because fundamental to the mores of the society
which is being reported. The mythos is going to turn on a contest
between opponents, both parties being members of the same polis.
However, the terms of the contest and its conclusion are going to be
different: not a final adjustment of claims between two sides where
compensation is rendered and publicly witnessed, but a duel to the
death between enemies who are irreconcilable.

Formally speaking, the agora's role in both poems is identical. It is
to provide a forum which will (1) listen to the terms of a dispute as
these are made the subject of harangue by contending parties and (2)
attest as listeners statements made on oath by either party, attestations in
which the gods are to be included. In the *Iliad* the agora also performs
the function of witnessing an agreement finally achieved with attestation of the terms of the agreement. In the *Odyssey* this function will be
denied it. It is perhaps significant that the formula with which in the
Iliad the last prolonged and successful session of the agora is swiftly and
thankfully dismissed (*Il.* 19.276–277) is used in the second book of the
Odyssey to signify the hasty dismissal of an agora which has failed (*Od.*
2.256–257).

Dubiety of Issues

The proceedings so far carried out reveal a dispute which, again as
in the *Iliad,* turns on a genuine difference of interest and opinion; the
suitors have a case:[2] a widow is a woman available for remarriage if she
be of suitable age, and in a male-dominated society, if her hand is
sought, she is expected in her own interest to accept a fresh partner.
This is what Athene originally proposed and what the suitors assert to be
the proper course to take. When in the nineteenth book of the epic
Penelope is brought at last into converse with a disguised husband
whom she does not recognize, she acknowledges that her parents have
been urging her to remarry and even admits that her son, while accepting her opposition to marriage when he was a boy, is now impatient

with her for letting the household suffer by her procrastination (19.158 ff. and 524 ff.). Her device of the web constantly woven and unraveled is a deceit which has now been exposed; the initial responsibility for what has become a crisis rests upon her. The pressure now exerted by the suitors' policy of eating at the expense of the household is too extreme to be socially acceptable, but it is a response to a dilemma created by her and her situation. As the story opens, she nourishes a diminishing hope, a lingering expectation, that Odysseus may be alive. Neither her son, nor her servants, nor the suitors believe that he is. If he is, then the legal situation of the suitors becomes impossible.

But is he? The confrontation and clash as arranged by the story thus arise in a case which, as in the *Iliad*, presents some dubiety, and that is why the convoking of an agora to air it, and if possible to seek to resolve it, becomes an essential procedure. In that agora the "top men" are always in a position of leadership; it is to them that Telemachus initially appeals for support. They are the elders, the fathers of the young bachelors who seek Penelope's hand. A situation in which a debutante is put up for auction, so to speak, before a company of wooers is a commonplace of Greek mythology and perhaps reproduces a not uncommon practice in the early Greek polis. The usual patron of such a procedure is the father. What do you do in the case of a widow except return her to the status of the debutante in her father's house? But what then of the property of the dead husband? This should remain in his own family, protected and inherited by his sons. But in this case there is only one son, and he is the only child of a man who was himself an only child and his father likewise before him. Such is the lineage that Telemachus, for the benefit of the bard's audience, later spells out to his own father, still disguised and unrecognized (16.117 ff.). He gives it by way of reply to the natural question: why, when beset by the suitors, cannot you rely on your brothers to rally to your support? That is the expected resource in a feud (*neikos*) of this sort (16.97–98). In Telemachus' case protection normally afforded by the family apparatus cannot be brought into play, and the agora is resorted to as a court of appeal. But like all assemblies it relies on the powerful to lead it, and the powerful remain silent except for one elder, while the younger elements take over (the *neoi andres*, 2.29).

The function which the agora fails to perform is one which would normally be expected of it. When Telemachus acquaints his host, Nestor, with the impossible situation that he had left behind him in Ithaca, Nestor asks the natural question (3.214–215):

Are you giving up voluntarily or is it that the people
through the township [*demos*] repudiate you, being influenced by a god's
oracle?

Telemachus avoids replying. When the disguised Odysseus asks him the
same question, he replies (16.114–115): "the whole demos are not
hostile but I have no brothers."

Sessions of the Assembly

As events march toward their climax in Ithaca, the narrative appears to assume that the agora of the city is in daily session and that its
proceedings cannot be ignored by the protagonists in the drama. Thus at
16.361 the suitors "proceed in a body [*kion athrooi*] to the agora"; they
have learned that their attempt to waylay Telemachus on his homeward
voyage has failed. They sit down, "but allowed no one else of the young
or the elders to sit with them." Antinous, who had commanded the ship
despatched to intercept Telemachus, "spoke among them saying . . ."
This would be the normal formula for addressing the agora, but clearly
he is here conferring within his group in a whispered conference while
they remain seated in the meeting; for he says: the people are starting to
withdraw support from us (16.375); we have to act before Telemachus
"calls a pan-assembly of the Achaeans into the agora" (376); he will
then "get up among all and report" how we have plotted his murder,
and they will not approve evil deeds when they are told of them (380);
they may perform some evil and expel us from our land so that we have
to go to the demos of others." So, he concludes, "let us anticipate such a
popular decision by catching him in field or road and killing him at
once, and then we can possess his livelihood and possessions, distributing
them share by share among ourselves; and the homestead [*oikia*] we can
let his mother have and anyone she marries." This proposal once more
carries the suitors' policy far outside any possible legal framework; it also
reveals that the agora need not remain ineffective; it can be a court of
last appeal for the victim of injustice, and indeed it can in an extreme
case take action, essentially judicial, to remedy a wrong and penalize
offenders by exile.

Or else, he continues, we can give up our present policy, return to
our respective houses, and woo the lady in orderly fashion. A second
suitor proposes that they postpone decision about the murder, which
would be an extreme and dangerous step to take; if the oracles of Zeus
prove propitious, then the speaker will kill Telemachus himself. They
agree and move back again into the house of Odysseus.

The next morning Telemachus, leaving the swineherd's hut, first goes home to be welcomed with relief by his mother. Rather peremptorily, he tells her to withdraw to her quarters; he has business of his own (17.52–53):

I will go and enter the agora in order to introduce [*kalessō*]
the stranger-guest [*xeinos*] who accompanied me thence and hither

This guest friend, he explains, is temporarily housed with one of his crew. So he "proceeds out through the hall" (17.61), and "all the people gazed on him as he came on." The suitors would wish to throng about him in pretended friendliness, but "he went and sat where Mentor was seated and Antiphos and Halitherses, who from the beginning were constituted [*esan*]³ his family friends [*patroioi hetairoi*]." They proceed to question him in detail (70). It seems evident that at this session of the agora Telemachus is holding a private conference with his party, just as the suitors had done the day before with theirs. The crewman arrives (73),

conducting the *xeinos* agoraward through the city, nor for a moment
did Telemachus turn aloof from the *xeinos* but stood by his side

The crewman wants to produce the gifts, the presents given to Telemachus by Menelaus in Sparta. No, wait, says Telemachus: the suitors "might kill me secretly and distribute all of my family property [*patrōia panta*] among themselves" (17.79–80).

Why should these proceedings and conversations have to take place in the agora unless propriety demanded that a guest friend from abroad, though accepted by a private household, had to be introduced to the assembly? Were the gifts receivable from donors abroad also normally to be reported to the agora and displayed before them, as was the case when the compensation was displayed in the agora held in the *Iliad*? This is not altogether clear. What is clear is that as the domestic crisis gathers momentum various decisions and actions of the suitors, of Odysseus, and of Telemachus are not being made in a social vacuum. In the background there is the city assembly constantly in session (even though in Book 2 the complaint was made that it had not been called for twenty years—part of the fantasy of the story). It is a body with some jurisdiction over anything that may take place.

On the very morning of the day which will witness the last feast of the suitors and their destruction, Telemachus gets up, and after inquiring of the nurse how his house guest, the disguised Odysseus, has slept, he "proceeded out through the hall" and "proceeded to go to the agora among the well-greaved Achaeans" (20.144, 146). The formulas are parallel to those applied to his previous entry into the assembly (17.61–62). To attend the agora was the normal business of a morning. What, if anything, took place at this meeting we are not told, unless a fresh conspiracy to kill Telemachus, averted by an omen, was supposed to be plotted there (20.241–246).

An Extralegal Solution

However, the agora as a vehicle for the resolution of the dispute proves inoperative. The remedy to be applied will be one carried out in the manner of a private blood feud, by killing.

This is forced upon the plot by the extreme policy of the suitors; they overdo their case, they are the guilty. It is a characteristic stamped upon them from the beginning, and the poem also seems to hint that they have succumbed to physical greed; they eat, drink, and play; have they ceased to be hardy men worthy of their community—a status which they had previously enjoyed? Moreover, before the agora is dissolved, one of their spokesmen takes the fatal step of arguing that if Odysseus should return (though he does not believe he will) he could easily be murdered. This puts their case wholly out of court, and they subsequently compound their felonious intention by discussing plans, never implemented, to murder the son and appropriate his property. No doubt such illegalities were not unknown in the early city-state and if successful had to be tolerated, but civic order (*eunomia*) demanded otherwise.

Yet the killing was not a matter that could easily be accommodated within the rules of the community. It violated the nomos and ethos of the city-state as these were commemorated in the *Iliad*. Murder takes the place of a "justice" negotiated between parties. So, at the end of the story, the agora resumes its function as a forum in which a feud and its consequences are debated.

Reassertion of Legality

The people "moved en masse into agora" (24.420); they had already heard the news of the slaughter, had gone to Odysseus' house and recovered and buried some of the bodies, dispatching others by ship abroad to their respective cities (24.418). Their grief and consternation is apparent, and as the debate now begins, the father of the leading suitor calls for redress (*tisesthai*, 435, 470) from the killers of their children and relatives, whose leader has already been responsible for taking part in the expedition to Troy, with disastrous results to his fleet and company. He would have them attack before the miscreants can get away. But the party of Odysseus have their case to state: Medon arrives from the house, announcing that the slaughter was divinely sanctioned; he had seen the god in action in front of Odysseus. This appeal to the authority of the supernatural is then reinforced by a second member of Odysseus' party: what has occurred is the result of inferior performance (*kakotēs*) by the agora itself; they would not listen earlier to the speaker or to Mentor (24.456), who had admonished them to restrain their children's folly and wickedness; so they should refrain from going on the offensive. However, the first speaker in the debate prevails, and "they were gathered together before the city" (as though to meet an advancing army).

Olympus has to intervene to settle what has become a civic impasse involving a choice between internecine war and civic accommodation (*philotēs*). Zeus has to remind Athene that the plot to this point is the result of her engineering (479–481), but proposes a procedure for reconciliation (481 ff.). Fighting, however, erupts in which one father, the parent of Odysseus, kills another, the parent of Antinous. Odysseus and his party are ready to launch a war, but at this point the Ithacesians desist on Athene's command; and when Odysseus would advance, Zeus arrests the action by a thunderbolt,[4] and Athene orders him to "put an end to the feud [*neikos*] of war" (543). So oaths are exchanged between the two sides (the equivalent of signatures attached to a treaty), ending the story with what is assumed to be political concord.

There is common agreement that the poetics of this book are slovenly; it has the air of an appendix composed on routine lines.[5] This, however, does not invalidate the necessary connection with the plot of the epic. The excitement of the narrative had been exhausted by Odysseus' victory; lesser composers may have completed the story. But the legal formalities established in the second book have to be completed in the twenty-fourth, just as the legal situation enacted in the first book of the *Iliad* had to be completed in the nineteenth. Only this would satisfy the expectations of a contemporary audience.[6]

The story of the *Iliad* makes perceptible a "justice" operating as a method for resolving disputes or as a symbol for such a method; it replaces physical conflict by a form of negotiation under the aegis of a popular assembly. There is no such "justice" operative in the *Odyssey*. The main action is extralegal; that is the way the story is told. In this respect the *Odyssey* reflects a level of behavior in early Hellenism more primitive than the procedures followed in the *Iliad,* one which it is reasonable to suppose existed for a long time alongside the more peaceful methods of settlement. These latter, though orally administered, embodied the application of a legality sanctioned by the city as a whole, in contrast to the method of direct revenge available to families. The *Oresteia* of Aeschylus in effect is a replay of the competition between the two methods; a replay of feud as pursued in the *Odyssey* completed by the resolution of feud as achieved in the *Iliad.* If there is a notion of Homeric "justice" perceptibly at work in the *Odyssey,* indirectly recommended in the way the story is told—as indeed there is—the plainest evidence of its presence is not likely to emerge in Odysseus' battle with his enemies, but must be sought elsewhere.

9

The Moralities of the *Odyssey*

✤

In the confrontation between Agamemnon and Achilles, the mythos pits
a man of rank and power against a man of dynamic personal energy.
The collision is not between virtue and vice, right and wrong, and the
resultant feud (the *eris*, or *neikos*) is therefore resolvable. Nor is there
any discernible moral difference between Achilles and Hector, even
though confrontation in their case is not soluble except by the extinction
of one party. The *Iliad* may intend to suggest that the Achaeans have
some moral advantage over the Trojans,[1] but the listener has difficulty
remembering this as the two sides maneuver, negotiate, or do battle.

Moral Polarization

The *Odyssey* in this respect is markedly different. The legalities of
the poem, described in the previous chapter, prove ineffective precisely
because the party of the first part is upright, and the party of the second
part is not, and between two such no procedure of adjustment is possible. The characters grouped round the house of Odysseus (aside from
traitors), consisting of wife, son, and servants, political supporters, and
finally Odysseus himself, are consistently represented or represent themselves as protesting against wrongs which are inflicted upon them. Their
opponents, the suitors, with equal consistency are represented as the

inflicters of wrong, not just as enemies, and they are continually labeled
with formulas which are morally pejorative. There is nothing like this
in the *Iliad*.

The introductory paragraph offers a preliminary sketch of its hero's
character: he is a man of many parts, a knowledgeable traveler and
observer who has survived hardships in his endeavors to get both himself
and his company and crew safely home. In contrast, the poet says of the
latter: "their own abominable deeds [*atasthaliai*] did destroy them"—a
rather extravagant characterization of the results of their fatal impiety in
eating the Cattle of the Sun, but one which polarizes them over against
the hero.

It is his intelligence and ingenuity, along with his afflictions,
which remain in focus as Zeus and Athene debate his fate (1.48 ff.,
1.65) and also his piety (1.65), and Athene, now disguised, recalls his
ingenuity in the reassurances she gives Telemachus (1.205).

As Penelope enters the scene, the portrait begins to enlarge a little.
She asks the bard who is entertaining the suitors with a song of the
homecoming of the Achaeans to choose some other theme (1.343–344):

So dear a head I desire ever in memory
of a man whose broad fame runs through Hellas and mid-Argos

These are the expected sentiments of a faithful wife, but they are
recalled when, hearing of the threat to the life of Telemachus, she
laments to her maids (4.724–726):

I who once lost a goodly husband lion hearted
with excellences [*aretai*] of every sort equipped among the Greeks,
goodly indeed whose broad fame runs through Hellas and mid-Argos

These three lines are repeated once more in reply to the consolation
offered in a dream by Athene at 4.814–816.

When the house of Odysseus at last begins to receive political
support in the agora, the dimensions of the hero's portrait expand further (2.230 ff.):

Why should one any more with ready heart be mild and gentle,
even a scepter-holding prince? Why have a mind that thinks of the rules
[*aisima*]?
No, let him be ever harsh, whose acts flout the rules [*aisula rhezoi*],[2]
since no one has memory of divine Odysseus,
none of the people for whom he was lord and as a father was ever gentle.

We suddenly see the hero not as an individual adventurer but as the source of authority in a community. This authority is responsible; it keeps within the proprieties set by precedent; it is also affectionate and mild like a father's care for his children. But the people who have benefited from it have forgotten it.

The news of his father that Telemachus gathers on his journey is meager, but the tributes to his memory continue. Nestor recalls his intelligence, his guile, and his prudent policies (3.120, 122, 163). The two of them never differed in agora or council (3.128). This portrait accords with the account given in the *Iliad*. In Sparta the reminiscences of Menelaus and Helen revert to Odysseus' hardihood and levelheadedness under stress (*emogēsen*, 4.106; *aethloi*, 241; *talasiphrōn*, 241; *etlē karteros anēr*, 242—cf. 270–271, a repeated formula). In Ithaca meanwhile, before the fourth book ends, an orderly (*kērux*) arrives to acquaint Penelope with news of fresh disaster: the suitors are plotting to waylay her son on his return. But before he has a chance to speak he is met with her reproaches (4.688 ff.):

You all did not listen to your fathers of former time when you existed as children
(when they told) what manner of man Odysseus was-proved-to-be among your parents,
neither doing nor saying to any man anything out of rule
in the demos, which is the right of divine lords [*basileis*] to do—
that one should hate this one of mortals and love that one—
but as for him he never once at all did any abominable thing [*atasthalon*] to a man;
behold, of all of you the spirit and unseemly works
are manifest nor is there any thanks afterward for benefactions [*euergeōn*]

Her bitter complaint, unjustified so far as the servitor is concerned, enlarges the portrait previously supplied by Mentor: Odysseus was a just ruler; magistrates who hold power are arbitrary in their favors and often disregard justice;[3] this is what you expect of them; but not so Odysseus; the authority he exercised was, we might say, "constitutional," and significantly he can be remembered as one of the "benefactors" of men.

The logic of the characterization thus far pursued is continued into the fifth book. Athene, present in a reconvened council of the gods and demanding action to release Odysseus, repeats the terms of the tribute given by Mentor in the agora in Ithaca, which at the same time recall the tribute given by Penelope (5.8–12):

Why should one any more with ready heart be mild and gentle
even a scepter-holding prince? Why have a mind that thinks of the rules?
No, let him be ever harsh, whose acts flout the rules,
since no one has memory of divine Odysseus,
none of the people for whom he was lord and as a father was ever gentle.

In this way a definition first placed in the mouth of Odysseus' peers is restated on Olympus.

The adventures of Odysseus that are narrated in the following books, 5 to 12, carry him far away from the Ithaca where these virtues had once been exercised. When at last he reaches home territory, the role of the just and beneficent ruler has to be laid aside. But it is not forgotten. The swineherd whose cottage provides the mise-en-scène for events occurring in Books 14 to 16 adds a personal and moving testimony; lamenting the loss of his master, whom he misses more than his own parents, he recalls him as gentle, protectively affectionate, and "civilized" (*ētheios;* 14.139–147).[4] A retainer's personal tribute is not political. But the role of Odysseus as a ruler, commemorated by his wife in the second book, is in the nineteenth transferred by way of compliment to herself. The speaker who does this is her own husband disguised (19.107 ff.):

Lady, none of mortals over the boundless earth
could fault you. Your fame indeed reaches to broad heaven
even as of some man—a blameless lord perhaps who, god fearing
among many men and mighty holding sway,
sustains procedures-of-justice-that-are-good [*eudikias*], and the black earth
bears
wheat and barley grain, and trees are loaded with fruit,
the sheep bear sturdy young, the sea provides fish
because of his beneficent leadership [*euēgesiē*], and the people under him
wax excellent.

The syntax of this paragraph makes no concession to Penelope's sex; the *basileus* remains masculine, and it is scarcely possible to doubt that Odysseus (by a nice stroke of irony) is in fact complimenting himself through his wife. The passage is an extended aphorism.

The suitors are first mentioned as the parties of the second part in a casual reference by Athene at the end of her second reply to Zeus on Olympus (1.91). Telemachus, welcoming his guest, the disguised Athene, takes care to segregate her from their company to give protection from their noisy arrogance (134). The poet's narrative then formally introduces them, describing them as they take their seats preparatory to eating and entertainment (144–145). They are described as "overweening" (*hyperphialoi*) by the poet (134) and by Athene as "shameless" (*anaideis*, 254), epithets which will recur but are in themselves routine. So far, while their conduct is obviously hostile to the interests of the house of Odysseus, their role as the villains of a morality play has not been made clear. Even Athene's advice to get rid of them (270) or kill them (295–296) treats them as natural enemies rather than as criminals.

The process of moral identification begins when Telemachus sets out to apply the encouragement and instruction that he has received from her. Requesting his opponents to leave, he addresses them with the words (1.368):

Suitors of my mother possessed of overwhelming outrage [*hubris*]

This is not a realistic way of opening negotiations. Rather, through Telemachus' mouth the poet has applied a formalized category to this party of the second part. After Telemachus' attempt to achieve remedy before the agora has failed, Athene, instructing him to get started on his voyage, bids him dismiss the suitors temporarily from his mind (2.281):

For they are not men of mind [*noēmones*] nor "just" [*dikaioi*]

And he himself supplies a further definition of their villainy when he visits Nestor (3.206–208):

Would to God I could be equipped with power as great [as that of Orestes] to take redress [*tisasthai*] upon the suitors for their inflictive transgression, who inflicting outrage [*hubrizontes*] upon me contrive abominable things [*atasthala*]

Proceeding on to Menelaus, he repeats in the third person the formula he had previously used in the second person (4.321):

Suitors of my mother possessed of overwhelming outrage

Odysseus in person does not enter the story till Book 5. Before narrating his adventures by land and sea, the epic has effectively placed him in a moral polarization by investing him and his future opponents with antithetical attributes. A foundation is being laid for a future moral confrontation between the parties which will occupy the last half of the epic. The way it is done illustrates several features of the laws of oral composition as these are applied to the task of storage. It is the agents in the story and their acts which are polarized, not concepts of right and wrong. Polarization is achieved through the use of moral formulas, the significance of which is betrayed by repetitions which the listener to the recital is expected to pick up. Only an overliterate critic would mistake them for later insertions. This is an echo system[5] which, as will be seen, is continued beyond the first five books and pervades the entire epic. Although such statements have the effect of programing the future development of the story, they occur incidentally as the narrative context suggests or invokes their utterance: the polarity is implicit, the didacticism is indirect. The nearest approach to direct statement occurs much later, precisely at that point in the story where Odysseus and the suitors are at last to be brought into personal contact with each other. At Athene's prompting, he is to go among them and collect alms (17.362):

to discover who keep the rules [*enaisimoi*] and who are outside-the-formularies [*athemistoi*].

Xeinos: The Stranger-Guest

But it is not as the wise ruler, the gentle protector, or even the ingenious plotter that Odysseus fulfills the role, the most complete and significant, which the epic has prepared for him and for which he must be prepared. What that is to be is anticipated, before he personally enters the story, in the roles assigned to two other persons, Athene and Telemachus.

At the opening of the narrative Athene in disguise appears before the house of Telemachus as a foreign visitor (*xeinos*).[6] Her presence in this role is reiterated (1.105, 119–120, 123, 133, 307). Telemachus on his side conforms to the other half of the model. He is friend to the stranger (*philoxeinos*, 1.123); he shows consistent courtesy and consideration for his visitor's material needs and nurture. When she leaves he presses upon her the appropriate refreshment and the gifts of hospitality. Her real identity when she arrives is unknown; this is important too. In an oral culture the foreign visitor does not carry a passport or documents proving identity. A host cannot even be sure of his name, for he has had no oral commerce with him as a neighbor. It is therefore incumbent on the host to err on the side of hospitality.

Telemachus then reverses his own role as he progresses through the Peloponnese (Books 3 and 4). When with his companion he approaches the palace at Pylos, Nestor and his sons recognize them as *xeinoi* and without further ado welcome them with food and drink. Pisistratus hands the wine cup to the disguised Athene as the elder of the two visitors. She is gratified: here is a "just man," that is, he does the right thing. Only after these preliminaries does Nestor inquire their identities, noting that the occasion, after due ceremonial, has now arisen (3.69) to ask

of stranger-guests who they are, they having taken pleasure of eating.
O stranger-guests, who are you? . . .

The noun is repeated formulaically to mark the role in which they have appeared, and he adds: are you perhaps pirates? This, if true, would not apparently qualify the law of hospitality. It is of course not true. Telemachus identifies himself—the time has come for this—and explains his mission, receiving in return what information and advice Nestor can give him. The whole exchange is ceremoniously handled. Athene vanishes. Her previous presence is recognized, and offering is duly made to her. Nestor's son replaces her as Telemachus' traveling companion, and the departure for Sparta is marked by the same careful courtesies that had graced their first appearance.

At Sparta, the story goes out of its way to accent the duty of proper reception of stranger-guests. A servant announces to Menelaus that *xeinoi* are at the gate: should they be received or sent on their way? His hesitation only angers the host (4.33–36):

You and I have eaten often enough of guest hospitality [*xeinēia*]
from others of mankind in our coming hither—if Zeus some day
late but at last give surcease from hardship. Nay, loose the horses
of the stranger-guests, and bring their persons forward to be entertained.

After two days when memories have been shared, and stories told, and some precious information imparted, the host heaps gifts upon his guests preparatory to departure: one of them is a guest-gift that he had previously received himself which he now passes on to his own guest (4.615–619).[7]

The time has arrived for the entry of Odysseus. The role of stranger-guest played by the son is to be transferred to the father, but under very different conditions. When first discovered, he is in a rather pitiable situation, the prisoner of a woman. Odyssean energy and resource is aroused sufficiently for him to get away from Calypso's island and to survive the storm which demolishes his boat, but survival is all he can manage. Washed into the mouth of a small river, he has strength to offer a suppliant's prayer (*hiketēs*) for rescue before sinking insensible upon the beach. He has become almost a nonperson (5.456). He revives sufficiently to find shelter in a thicket and sleeps the sleep of utter exhaustion. In the light of day, naked and resourceless, he wakes at last to the sound of human cries. "Who are these people?" he exclaims (6.121):

Could they be friend to the stranger-guest [*philoxeinoi*] and the mind within them be god fearing?

This *xeinos* is not like Athene or Telemachus, clothed and competent. He is not his own master but a victim of the pressures of dire need (6.136). Facing the girl who stands her ground as he emerges, he loses neither courage nor cunning (130, 148). But for all that, he has become a suppliant who requires compassion and protection, and he says so (173–176). As will appear, he needs the protection both of Zeus *xenios* and Zeus *hiketēsios*. Her reply to him makes formal acknowledgement of his double role. Greeting him as "stranger-guest" (187), she recognizes him as also a suppliant owed the proprieties due to such: (191–193). Rallying her maids, who have panicked, she reminds them (207–208)

under Zeus are all
stranger-guests and beggars; what is given is little and welcome

This aphorism on her lips assigns to Odysseus the role into which he has fallen: not just a visiting stranger but a *ptōchos*—a man impoverished.

But is it also his character? What is the natural man embodied in him? Washed and dressed, he resumes by transformation the appearance of a nobleman, an object of maidenly admiration, fit to be conducted to her home (255):

Bestir yourself, stranger-guest, to go cityward

But he must not accompany her; the bystanders would remark (276–277):

Who is this man with Nausicaa, handsome and tall,
this stranger-guest? Where did she pick him up . . . ?

She would be accused of looking for a husband among foreigners (*tēledapoi*) in preference to suitors at home "among the people" (279,

283). The comment vividly illustrates the parochialism that was the price of autonomy in the early Hellenic city. So, addressing him once more as "stranger-guest," she gives instructions: he is to follow later and present his plea to her mother.

Left alone, he prays to Athene (6.327)

that I come among the Phaeacians with welcome and compassion

Shrouded by a protecting cloud, he is able to penetrate the city unseen. When he meets his own goddess, disguised this time as a young girl, she twice greets him with the salutation "stranger-guest and father" (7.28 and 48) and warns him that the inhabitants are not fond of "stranger-guests"; their isolation had made them so, as Nausicaa had implied (6.204–205). He will find Arete in Alcinous' house; she is the mistress (*despoina*); she is the one to approach.

Entering, he falls before her knees and pleads as a suppliant in distress (7.147). His plea spoken, he sits down in the ashes by the hearth. An elder among the company present breaks the silence, addressing Alcinous (159–165):

It is neither fair nor proper
that a stranger-guest sit on the ground in the ashes by the hearth;
but come lift up this stranger-guest and upon a chair silver studded
set him and do thou command orderlies
to mix wine that even to Zeus the thunderer
we shall make libation who upon suppliants revered does attend;
supper for the stranger-guest let the housekeeper give from her store.

Alcinous complies, and in response repeats the formula which recognizes Zeus as the god of suppliants (180–181).[8]

The role of Odysseus in this story is now set: whether his guise be that of penniless vagrant or distinguished nobleman, he is the *xeinos*, the foreign visitor whose arrival tests the intentions of his hosts: will he be received or rejected? His title of *xeinos* is obsessively repeated; there is no need to recapitulate further details except to note the moral formula employed at 8.542–547:

that we may all enjoy ourselves alike;
stranger-guests and guest-receivers, for it is far better thus;
it is for the stranger-guest revered these things have been assigned,
escort and welcome gifts which we gave him in our welcome;
in a brother's place the stranger-guest and suppliant stands assigned
in the eyes of a man who reaches even a short way in wits.

Having stated it, the king at last asks the name of the unknown
He would also like to know what men and cities he has encountered,
including (8.576):

those that are friend to the stranger-guest and the mind within them is god
fearing.

The formulaic address by Odysseus to the unknown island on which he
had been cast is now in turn, with slight variation, put to him. The
Phaeacians for their part have fulfilled the formula. What of the other
peoples encountered by the traveler over the earth?

Of the travels now to be narrated by the protagonist, the most dramatic is surely the adventure undertaken in the land of the Cyclops.[9]
Encamped on an island, Odysseus and his fleet notice smoke, the sign
of habitation on the mainland. At dawn the commander proposes to
leave most of his crews behind while he takes his own ship and crew
over (9.174) to find out who these people are. Perhaps (176):

they are friend to the stranger-guest and the mind within them is god
fearing.

The echo principle is at work. Confronting alien territory, Odysseus
again is given the role of *xeinos*. But its assumption is now deliberate; he
gives it to himself, for he need not go to the mainland. If he does, it is to
impose a test (174) of attitude and behavior. Having sailed across, they
spy the Cyclop's cave; its resident is a monstrous thing, not really
human (188–189). Odysseus makes a further selection of twelve men
from his crew, leaving the rest with the ship on the shore, and starts for
the cave. It is empty, but he expects the arrival of a savage creature
(215). To enter such a place is a willful act of exposure; there is no
practical purpose to be served. And the men want to leave:

but I myself would not listen to them; indeed, far more profitable would it
prove
that I might see him and find if he would give me the gifts due stranger-
guests [*xeinia*];
he was not, however, likely to be beloved of my comrades on his appearance.
(228–230)

The giant on arrival duly hails his visitors as "stranger-guests," and
in reply to his query their leader correctly supplies their group identity: they are Greeks from Troy. Odysseus then proceeds to impose the
test in the following formula (266–271):

We come as suppliants to your knees
to see if haply you might furnish that which host gives guest [*xeinēion*] and in general
bestow the bestowal [*doiēs dōtinēn*] as stands the formulary [*themis*] of stranger-guests;
yes, respect the gods, your excellency, we are here as suppliants;
Zeus is the guarantor of suppliants and stranger-guests,
Zeus god of the stranger-guest who upon stranger-guests revered does attend.

The title *xeinos* and its derivatives occur five times in five lines, *hiketēs* and *hikōmetha* (the suppliant) three times. The refrain is unmistakable. The last two lines express a formula previously uttered by an elder at Alcinous' court. The echo principle persists.

The giant's only reply is to affirm his atheism: the Cyclops reck not of gods or Zeus. The implicit moral is that to repulse a stranger one has to be impious. The test (281) that the giant would like to impose in his turn is merely to ascertain where their ship is. Human cunning prevents him from finding out, and he then resorts to cannibalism, eating the crew, two at a time. A further exercise of human skill extricates Odysseus and the survivors: the Cyclops, compared with a Hellene, is not only a savage outside society and law but stupid. The lesson is driven home after they escape, by a second willful act. Having embarked but being still within earshot, the triumphant protagonist hurls his accusation and taunt at the giant (477):

only too soon were evil deeds bound to find you out,
dastard [*schetlie*]. For stranger-guests you did not hesitate in your house
to eat. Therefore, Zeus has penalized you—and the other gods besides

Once uttered, the words prove rash in the extreme, the giant hurls a rock that nearly swamps the ship; the survivors protest again against this unnecessary hazard. But the words have to be spoken to satisfy the moral of the tale. If the protagonist had stopped even there, the story might have been different. But he now flings a personal challenge "from Odysseus waster of cities"; his identity is at last revealed,[10] and Poseidon, the parent god of the monster, is then invoked by his gaint progeny to retaliate upon the protagonist, which in due course he does.

The cost of that retaliation was to prove heavy: detention on Calypso's isle and shipwreck in sight of land. Even the kindly mariners who convey Odysseus at last to his native shore are struck dead for this service. He himself awakes to a new day deserted, forlorn, and confused. For the land seems as strange to him as any other. Once more he places

himself in the position of a *xeinos* on foreign soil, once more furnished
with occasion to utter the anxious question (13.202):

Could they be friend to the stranger-guest and the mind within them be
god fearing?

Overcome by what appears to him to be the realities of the situation, he
turns on his erstwhile hosts, invoking upon them divine retribution:

May Zeus, the suppliant's god, penalize them, even he who all
mankind oversees and penalizes whosoever errs

It is a fine irony that this undeserved apostrophe recalls a sentiment
twice affirmed in the palace of Alcinous himself (7.165, 181): the echo
is compulsive.

Ptōchos: The Beggar-Man

But these are not the realities; Athene, rather than the romantic
hosts of Phaeacia, has to take over at this point. Concealing her own
identity, she engages in a colloquy in which her protégé also conceals
his. There is a moment of semicomic relief as they match wits. Then the
pretense is dropped, and speaking as his patron and protector, she announces a new ordeal for him and a new role that he must play
(13.306–310):

I declare what measure of trouble your lot decrees must in your builded
house
be by you fulfilled. You must endure even of necessity
nor speak out to any of man or woman at all
how that you have arrived a wanderer. Instead in silence
must you endure pains in plenty, submitting to the violence of men.

Hitherto, in the role of a visiting foreigner, he has either received what
is due to such status or vindicated his right to receive it by punishing the
failure to provide it. Tomorrow in his own homeland not only will
civilities be denied him, as they were by the Cyclops, but he must
endure this treatment as a patient victim. The moral formulas which
begin to accumulate round this role as the story proceeds show that it is
thematic, and not a mere stratagem designed to overcome his opponents
by surprise. The surrounding mist is dissolved and he recognizes he is
indeed home, and yet not really home. Fresh and dangerous obstacles
have to be overcome, in the presence of the suitors in his house, and

Odysseus at once thinks of how Agamemnon, home from the wars, was betrayed and murdered. Only his skill combined with Athene's help will avail, as he passionately tells her, recalling how she had stood by him at Troy (13.383–391). She comforts him with the required assurances. But what of the ordeal he must undergo? It now transpires that this will be unlike anything previously endured and overcome; it will involve not only his own humiliation; he himself must change, must become other than he is (13.397–402):

But let me tell you: a man unknown to all mortals shall I make of you,
I shall shrivel your fair flesh upon limbs that are bent,
the fair hair of your head I will destroy, and in rags
shall I clothe you which will make you repugnant to any human beings
who see them on you,
I shall blear those brilliant eyes of yours to give you a disreputable
appearance before all the suitors
and before your wife and son that you left behind in the halls

The listener to the story need not have been surprised at this promised transformation, if he remembered how he had been prepared for it at an earlier stage in the epic. Helen, home in Sparta, had recalled in what guise she encountered Odysseus in Troy during the war (4.244 ff.):

He subdued his body with sorry stripes,
cast a miserable covering about his shoulders like a servant,
concealing what he was, he likened himself to another man,
even to a beggar . . .

Athene gives Odysseus brief instructions for himself, while she will go and fetch Telemachus from Sparta. He thus learns of his son and is ready to conclude that he too, now far from home, will share his father's fate. But she reassures him again, and touching him with her magic wand, turns him from prince to beggar. The promised details of the change are repeated with the significant addition of a staff and a ragged wallet to hold alms (13.430–438).

Reception by Eumaeus

In accordance with instructions Odysseus makes for the cottage of Eumaeus, the swineherd on the estate. It is remotely located in the country. He has been told that this man "knows gentleness" and is loyal to the house. In conformity with the guise which he now wears, he is greeted as an "old man" (14.37, 45) and invited to enter and to eat and drink preparatory to identifying himself (45–47). Odysseus notes the kindly reception and expresses his pleasure at it, adding (53–54):

May Zeus, O stranger-host [*xeine*], and all immortal gods besides
grant you your heart's desire for that you with ready mind received me.

Eumaeus, named here by the poet for the first time, with equal ceremony reciprocates (56 ff.):

Stranger-guest [*xeine*], not for me does the law stand, not even if one in
worse shape than you should come,
that I a stranger-guest should disdain; for under Zeus are all
stranger-guests and beggars; little the gift and welcome
even the one we give

The brief dialogue is so structured that the title *xeinos* is exchanged between the participants. A five-line definition of a nomos of reciprocal behavior has been furnished by indirection. The last two lines repeat the definition uttered by Nausicaa as she arranged hospitality for the ship-wrecked mariner (6.207–208). But the addition of the word "beggar" to the formula significantly extends the moral dimension and accords with the role that Odysseus is now going to play. It is a double one: the "stranger within the gates" is also an afflicted member of the human species, poor and in need of compassionate alms.

Food is duly offered, which the beggar eats greedily. After he has drunk, and in reply to his question, the host names his absent master: he is Odysseus (14.144), who must now be dead; his servant has given up all hope. The guest would contradict this despair and does so by swearing a solemn formula (158–159):

Let Zeus now be witness [*istō*] first among the gods and the table spread
for stranger-guest
and the hearth of blameless Odysseus to which I am come . . .

It is in effect the house of Odysseus that has given proper reception to the speaker, the *xeinos*. Having fulfilled this solemn role, the house becomes a fitting guarantor of the prophetic truth (161):

Verily in this same hour will Odysseus hither come

—as indeed he already has.

It is time to inquire the stranger's identity, and it is purportedly supplied by him in a fiction which also claims to report some news of

Odysseus. Eumaeus refuses to believe it: there are too many liars around ready to supply such inventions (14.387–389):

Do not try and please me or comfort me with lies;
I will not for that respect you or welcome you,
but only in awe of Zeus the god of stranger-guests and in compassion for yourself.

With these words he accents his own role as host. His guest, responding, caps the oath previously given with a further promise: if your lord returns, then clothe me with raiment and send me on my way; but if not, have me killed (400)

that every other beggar may beware of using deception

This challenge to Eumaeus' hospitality is at once met by him and ironically repudiated (402–405):

Stranger-guest, that would indeed be the way for me to gain fame and virtue among mankind, both now and hereafter,
if when I had brought you into my hut and given you guest gifts straightaway I killed you.

To further underline the hospitality that has become the theme of their conversation, Eumaeus holds a ceremonial feast, sacrifices a boar "for the stranger-guest-from afar" (414–415), and gives to the guest a preferred portion, upon which Odysseus formally blesses him in the name of Zeus for this privilege (441). "My marvellous guest!" is Eumaeus' response.

Implicit in the stages of the encounter between swineherd and beggar is a moralizing lesson: a test is being set up to demonstrate the centrality in the culture of the rule governing the host-guest relationship when the guest is (1) a foreigner visiting alien soil and townspeople (2) an impoverished individual requiring protection from the more fortunate. The testing process becomes explicit in the next book, all the more strikingly so because by the standards of narrative realism it is unnecessary. Athene had assured Odysseus of Eumaeus' loyalty and sincerity, and he has now learned of these himself. But the night comes on and it is cold and the beggar needs a coverlet. Will his host lend him one? Instead of asking him forthrightly, he proceeds to "test" (*peirētizōn*, 14.459) his readiness to do this (as he had "tested" the Cyclops), telling a contrived tale to convey a hint as to what he wants. Eumaeus readily meets the test, giving him his own overcoat. Not content with this proof, the beggar imposes a second test (*peirētizōn* again, 15.304). The formality, not to say artificiality, of this procedure is indicated by the formula used in the line. Odysseus "spoke among them testing the swineherd," as though he were addressing an audience (the rather careless use of this idiom recurs in the *Odyssey,* a symptom of the didactic purpose lurking in the epic). This time he proposes to go down to the city and beg to avoid burdening his host; perhaps he can offer to work for the suitors. Will his host press him to stay or get rid of him? It is only a test of intentions, for he is going to go to the city anyway. Eumaeus once more passes easily; he is horrified at the exposure to the suitors that this will mean and warns Odysseus of the treatment he is likely to get. As for the beggar offering his services to the suitors, considering what he is wearing and what he looks like, he is no fit competitor for the elegant youths who are doing the waiting (15.325–336). This response elicits a second and solemn blessing upon him from the beggar (342–345):

For that you have made a ceasing of me from my wandering and dread woe—
for than vagabond straying nothing other exists that is worse for mortals—
yes, for a devouring belly's sake they have sore troubles,
even men on whomsoever comes wandering and pain and affliction

These are strong words; they identify a fact of life as life was lived in early Hellenic society.

The Beggar-Man's Mission

Mutual converse between Odysseus and Eumaeus is now over. The drama of the first reception scene in Ithaca is completed satisfactorily. The second one is about to open, critical and climactic. The plot first requires that son and father collaborate; so when they meet in the absence of the swineherd, Odysseus is temporarily restored by transformation into his heroic guise to be recognized by Telemachus. But their joyous and tearful reunion is only a prelude to the stern instruction which the father must now solemnly lay upon the son, as also upon himself (16.270–280):

You on the one hand must now go at opening of dawn
to the house and join the company of the overweening suitors;
I on the other hand will by the swineherd be conducted to town later
in likeness of a beggar miserable and old,

and if they do me dishonor in the house your very heart
must endure steadfast in your breast as I suffer,
even if through the house they drag me by the feet to the door
or assail me with missiles. Your part is to look on and put up with it,
but alternatively you must bid them cease from follies
with soft words seeking to divert them. But they not at all
will listen, for surely there now stands beside them the day of doom.

The ordeal of patience that Athene had promised to Odysseus is by Odysseus also laid upon his son.

A "test" (*peirētheimen*, 16.305) will also be applied to the working force to distinguish between the loyal and the disloyal. Telemachus advises that this "testing" (*peirētizōn*, 313) must not be pressed too far at present; to conduct a test (*peirazein*, 319) covering all the people on the property will waste valuable time. But the maidservants are a different matter.

The moment has come for Athene to change Odysseus' appearance once more; Eumaeus is about to return to the cottage and must not recognize him. But the determining reason for the reconversion lies in the role which Odysseus is once more required to enter into. As Telemachus leaves the cottage to visit his mother, his formal instruction (17.9) to the swineherd is as follows (10–12):

The hapless stranger-guest conduct toward the city that there
he may beg a dinner. Any who wants to will give him
crust and cup . . .

And he continues by pretending that his hospitality has lasted long enough, upon which the *xeinos* himself comments by repeating what has already been said (18–19, 22):

Better for a beggar in city or countryside
to beg a dinner. Any who wants to will give one . . .
As for me, this man whom you command will lead me.

Reception of a Prophet

The moral mission of Odysseus—for such it is—is postponed by an interlude, but an interlude pertinent to the theme that is being pursued. Telemachus, visiting his mother and welcomed back by her with thankfulness, loses no time in telling her that he has a duty to perform: he has to enter the agora to "invite a stranger-guest" (17.53) of his own. This duly occurs. The "stranger-guest" (72) is conducted to the agora by the man with whom he has been temporarily lodged. Telemachus is careful (73)

not to avoid the presence of the stranger-guest but stood there at his side.

He then conducts the travel-worn "stranger-guest" (84) to the house, and only at this point acquaints his mother with the news of Odysseus which he had heard at Sparta. The choice of this moment for telling her becomes apparent. It affords occasion for the "stranger-guest" to utter a solemn asseveration. It is in character for him to do so, for he is a prophet who has joined Telemachus' ship on the homeward voyage (17.155–156):

Let Zeus now be witness first among the gods and the table spread for stranger-guest
and the hearth of blameless Odysseus to which I am come . . .

With this oath he attests the prediction that Odysseus is already home. It is precisely the formula that Odysseus had used when he was guest at the table of Eumaeus. Here its use is a reminder that the prophet has been received with equal propriety into the city and the house of Telemachus. The design of this interlude is to furnish one more example of the law of reception for the foreigner fulfilled rather than broken.

First Rejection and Warning

Swineherd and beggar-man prepare to leave for the city: the mission appointed by Athene in Book 13 and affirmed by Odysseus for himself and his son in Book 15 is now in Book 17 to be undertaken. The poet marks the event by himself repeating and enlarging the formula which defines the role of Odysseus (17.202–203):

in likeness of a beggar miserable and old
leaning on a staff, and miserable the rags that clothed his flesh.

The first rejection of the *xeinos* begins at the town spring. The goatherd on the property, meeting him, reviles his poverty: he is a shiftless mendicant to be beaten up if he gets to Odysseus' house; for good measure he kicks him. Arriving at the door, the beggar tells Eumaeus to go in first: he will wait outside; he is used to ill-treatment and must put up with it (17.283–287; cf. 13.307). Beside him while he waits lies his old dog, dirty, flea-ridden, neglected, like his master. But the animal can do what men cannot do, recognize his fellowship with his master; and so dies.

At last the beggar ventures across the threshold—his own threshold. It is a decisive moment, marked by a third repetition from the poet's own lips of the role assigned to Odysseus (17.337–338):

in likeness of a beggar miserable and old
leaning on a staff, and miserable the rags that clothed his flesh.

He is only just inside (339). Telemachus within has taken charge and his first words ring out (345):

Take this and give it to the stranger-guest.

The swineherd approaches with the food and repeats the injunction (350):

Telemachus to you, O stranger-guest, gives these.

Xeinos is to be his title, reiterated throughout the narrative that follows till his identity is revealed. The beggar utters a beggar's blessing upon Telemachus for what he has been given, as on the previous occasion he had blessed Eumaeus (17.354; cf. 15.341).

And now, the house of Odysseus in the person of the son of the house having ceremoniously fulfilled the law of hospitality, the test of the suitors is about to begin (17.362 ff.). Like the Cyclops and Eumaeus, they will be tested as hosts of a stranger-guest, but Athene, who takes over direction at this point and prompts the beggar (362) to go among them and collect alms, places the test in the context of the moral polarization established early in the epic (363):

to discover who keep the rules and who are lawless

The test proposed is one they are in the end going to fail (364). For this first time it is met; they do give alms, but with one vital exception. Antinous, their leader, demands to know why this fellow has been brought to the city. Telemachus takes up the challenge and requests Antinous to give alms personally. He refuses; whereupon the beggar undertakes the test himself, deliberately approaches Antinous, pays him a compliment, and describes his own ill-fortune: "I have come down in the world." This provokes a contemptuous rejection. Odysseus, instead of withdrawing, carries the test a step further, sternly upbraiding Antinous for his behavior. This further provocation is too much. The suitor throws a stool at him; whereupon the beggar, retreating to his corner, curses the man who has refused him, calling down on him "the gods and avenging spirits [*erinues*] of beggars" (475). The curse is solemnly invoked with the other suitors as witnesses (468). Antinous is temporarily cowed, but threatens that the servants will drag the offender outside if this goes on. The rest of the company are afraid. The circumstances of the uttered curse recall to their wavering minds the popular belief that the gods sometimes mingle among men in disguise to observe and judge their behavior—"in the likeness of stranger-guests that are foreign, changing themselves manifold" (17.485–486). Might the beggar be such a one? In the ears of the audience listening to the tale, the sentiment voices the theme of the epic and is prophetic of doom to come. But for the suitors it is a passing thought, soon forgotten.

Penelope in her chamber overhears and voices her consternation (17.501–504):

Some stranger-guest hapless is abroad in the house
begging alms of men; his dire want so bids him.
Thereat all the others filled his bag and gave to him,
but Antinous struck him with a stool on the right shoulder.

However, the beggar's status temporarily improves. He takes on another mendicant in the hall, a hanger-on, fights him and thrashes him. Though a beggar, Odysseus is a real man, the genuine article; his opponent is not. The suitors congratulate and feed him. In response to this interval of kindly treatment, Odysseus favors one of them, Amphinomus, with advice and warning (18.125): human life is uncertain, our attitudes fluctuate with our circumstances, sometimes arrogant, sometimes reduced to humility; I recall I was once a violent lawless man, my deeds were abominable; but it is better to accept good fortune with sobriety and not behave as these suitors behave; they are consuming the property and dishonoring the wife of a man who will return. And he advises Amphinomus to leave before vengeance overtakes them.

The suitor listens but he does not leave. He has been tested and given the chance, and he has failed to measure up. His doom is decreed by Athene's will (18.155). The beggar has been made the mouthpiece of her warning voice.

Penelope protests to her son the mistreatment of the stranger-guest which had earlier attracted her attention (18.215–225): her house, she says, is responsible and Telemachus will suffer disgrace if this continues. Her son reassures her; but he has to be careful.

Second Rejection and Warning

The maidservants now enter the picture. Melantho, who has been seduced by a suitor and has become disloyal to the house and to her mistress, turns on the "stranger-guest" and threatens him with expulsion (18.336). She and her companions are intimidated by his reply but not converted.

The testing of the suitors is resumed, and this time they will all become entangled in corruption (18.346–348):

The lordly suitors not at all did Athene suffer
to refrain themselves from insult and affliction of spirit that even yet more
the pangs might sink into the heart of Odysseus son of Laertes

Like the pharaoh of the Old Testament their hearts are to be hardened. So Eurymachus, another of their leaders, contemptuously offers the beggar a job as farm laborer; but he is sure he is too lazy to take it. The beggar replies that he can be plowman or fighter as the occasion requires, and adds that if Odysseus should show up Eurymachus would run away. This deliberate taunt provokes a second assault, but this time the missile, another stool, misses its mark and hits the cupbearer, who collapses. The rest of the company now begin to turn on the "stranger-guest." He is becoming a nuisance. Why has he intruded to disturb their meal? Telemachus tells them they must be drunk and truly observes that some god must be at work on them. This prompts a proper response from Amphinomus, who exhorts the company not to "abuse the stranger-guest" or the servants (18.416). The warning is heeded to the extent that they eat and go home, leaving the beggar in the house; he is after all the *xeinos* of the house.

Nightfall provides occasion for a fresh encounter with the maidservants (19.65–66, 68–69):

She addressed Odysseus, even Melantho, for the second time again.
Stranger-guest, are you even still making yourself a nuisance . . . ?
There is the door; get out, you wretch, and be glad of your supper
or else pretty soon a torch will be flung at you to get you out of doors

He can only address to her too a ceremonial warning, the terms of which offer a variant version of the warning that he had spoken to the men (73–77, 80–86):

I go a beggar among the demos; necessity constrains me;
that is how beggars are, and vagrant men.
Once I too dwelt among men a householder
prosperous and rich, and often gave alms to the vagrant
according to his condition and need . . .
But Zeus the Kronian plundered me; such I suppose was his will.
Maybe therefore you too, woman, might one day utterly lose all
that bright vanity that gives you quality among the serving girls—
maybe your mistress will turn malicious and deal harshly with you—
maybe Odysseus will come; there is still a portion of hope for that,
and if so be it he is perished and is to come no more returning home,
surely there is now his son, grown such a man by grace of Apollo . . .

But the warning again is of no avail.

Reception by Penelope

An interview with Penelope (19.103–352), Odysseus' first, in which they exchange reports of their experiences, hers being truthful and his a fiction, reinforces her acceptance of his presence in her house (253–254):

Now indeed, O stranger-guest, though before you were pitiable
in my halls, you will become a respected friend

His response is to promise her that her husband's arrival is imminent (303–304, 306):

Be Zeus now witness first of gods, supreme and most excellent,
and the hearth of blameless Odysseus to which I am come . . .
in this same hour Odysseus shall come hither

This is the third occasion for the employment of this formula (cf. 14.158 and 17.155), and as on both previous occasions, assurance that the prediction is true is based upon the fact of hospitality received.

This oath fails to console her: Odysseus will not come home, she says, and if he does not her stranger-friend will not meet with the "home-sending" (*pompē*, 19.313) appropriate to the entertaiment given to foreign visitors. No one like Odysseus is around (315–316):

as he used to be among men—if indeed it was once true of old—
a man that would manage a home-sending [*apopempemen*] for stranger-
guests revered and would welcome them too

The description is thematic. It places upon Odysseus a trademark which identifies the virtue celebrated in the epic in contrast to the vice practiced by his enemies. In accordance with it, Penelope at once offers to bathe and reclothe her *xeinos* (as Helen had done in Troy, as Alcinous in Scheria); these are the proprieties appropriate to the reception of a foreigner who arrives travel stained (19.325–327):

What shall be your acquaintance of me, stranger-guest . . .
if unkempt and evilly clad in my halls
you dine . . .

and then she adds (332–334):

whosoever himself be blameless and knows blameless things at heart,
even of him wide fame do stranger-guests report
over all mankind, and many declare him noble.

The aphorism supports the duty of obeying the nomos which governs the reception of foreigners by asserting the reward that ensues through reputation gained over all mankind, not just among one's own citizens. Odysseus must decline the service offered this time (though the nurse is allowed to wash his feet), less to avoid discovery than because his role must be sustained to the last encounter with the suitors. Penelope then replies to him as follows:

Dear stranger-guest—for indeed no other man so discreet
of stranger-guests from foreign lands dearer than you has yet come to my
house

She is of course becoming obscurely aware, or semiaware, that she is really listening to the beloved voice of her long-missing husband. But it is as her *xeinos* that she views him and woos him, and as *xeinos* she repeatedly identifies him.

During a second conference between them she finally decides to propose an ordeal (*athlos*) which will settle her destiny—the ordeal of the bow and the axheads; the winner who shoots through them using her husband's bow will marry her. He encourages her to make the arrangement at once,[11] and as night falls she retires to her bedchamber while he beds down in the hall. He observes the shameless conduct of the maidservants again and can scarcely endure it, but he thinks of a previous occasion when he had to wait and endure; significantly, it was in the cave of the Cyclops (20.19). But his memory does not refer merely to the fact of endurance: that also was an hour in his life when a test was being imposed upon hospitality, a test which was not met.

Reception by a Stockman

So a new day dawns, the suitors' last. It is a holiday, celebrated in the city as well as in the house. A special dinner is in order, and the servants enter the hall to make preparations. Eumaeus inquires in kindly fashion of the "stranger-guest" how he has been treated. Melantho with hostility bids the "stranger-guest" get outside. A new member of the working force arrives, the stockman, and his greeting is friendly (20.199–200):

Welcome, stranger-guest and father, may you hereafter
be prosperous as now there are many evils upon you . . .

And he invokes Zeus to have compassion on the unfortunate among mankind (203),

mingled as they are in distress and miserable pain.

His words restore Odysseus to his role of miserable penury. During his reception by Penelope we have been tempted to forget it. The stockman continues by recalling his absent master, to whose memory he still remains firm, upon which the *xeinos* seizes the occasion to pronounce for the fourth time (20.230–232):

Be Zeus now witness first of gods and the table spread for stranger-guest
and the hearth of blameless Odysseus to which I am come;
while you are still here Odysseus will come home

It is the welcome given by this working man that prompts this last attestation, made in the name of hospitality duly offered and accepted.

Third Rejection and Warning

The suitors enter, bloody-minded, but their intention to kill Telemachus and take over is averted by an omen. The feast begins with the beggar seated at a separate table near the door. Once more, by Athene's determination, the suitors must willfully commit folly and willfully inflict pain upon the stranger; the previous formula asserting this is reused: (20.284–286 = 18.346–348). Ktesippus, a third offender, is moved to make the following formal announcement (20.292–298):

Attend me lordly suitors that I may speak and say:
his portion the stranger-guest has been enjoying as is seemly . . .
But look here let me too give him a stranger-guest's gift—

whereupon he hurls an ox foot at him but misses. This cynical misuse of the formula for entertainment is a fatal step to take. Telemachus bursts into anger and threatens death to him: in me you are dealing with a grown man; better for me to be killed by all of you than to have to witness (318–319):

stranger-guests abused while the serving maids
you debauch . . . in my house

Another suitor voices agreement (20.322–325), and concludes with an appeal to Telemachus to instruct his mother to pick a husband and end the impasse.[12] The effect, as before, is only transient; the protesting voice is not strong enough to negate the collective folly.

When Telemachus replies by asking how he can drive his own mother out of her house, they respond with witless laughter; their thoughts become distraught; they begin to babble unintelligibly; the meat they eat becomes covered with blood; their eyes are filled with maudlin tears as they sob in self-pity. Athene has intervened again (345) to bemuse them and destroy them.

At which Theoclymenus, the prophet who had been brought home as Telemachus' "stranger-guest," rouses from his seat to tell them what he now sees: shrouded in night are their heads . . . kindled is the cry of wailing . . . walls and roof all sprinkled with blood . . . porch and court full of ghosts hastening hellward . . . the sun has perished from the heaven . . . dire fog spreads over all. We hear the cries of a Cassandra, discerning the doom of the house of Atreus. What is their reckless reply? To applauding laughter, Eurymachus pronounces as follows (20.360–363):

This stranger-guest is crazy, having just arrived from elsewhere;
you fellows [to the servants], please escort him a homecoming
[*ekpempsasthe*] forthwith through the doors
to go to the agora, since he finds it like night here.

The prophet responds to this taunt in kind (20.364):

I have not asked for escort to accompany me

and so gets up and leaves them. All they can do in their desperate folly is to keep on laughing at the expense of "stranger-guests" (376–383):

Telemachus, no host can be unluckier in his stranger-guests than you;
here's one that you have, a filthy wanderer

desperate for food and wine and no good for work
or for violent fighting but just a burden on the earth;
and here's another that has got on his feet to prophesy;
take my advice—it will be much more profitable—
our stranger-guests let us throw into a ship
and send off to Sicily—which would bring a good price.

The cup of their folly is nearly full. The prophet previously received by the house of Odysseus now joins the company of the beggar; both *xeinoi* are to be derisively rejected. The derision is at the expense of one of the custom-laws of early Hellenism, and its utterance dooms the suitors by their own mouths; the sentiment assigned to them in their role as nonhosts seems to owe as much to the moral design of the epic as to their own characters.

Victory and Vindication

But we are not yet quite finished with this theme. The contest being set up, the axes planted, three suitors try the bow and fail to bend it. The beggar offers to try himself; Antinous threatens to throw him out for his impertinence. Penelope intervenes: the beggar is a "stranger-guest of Telemachus" and should be respected as such. A suitor complains with some show of reason that they cannot afford to be outfaced by a nameless wanderer. Penelope replies: this "stranger-guest" is well built and of good family.[13] Telemachus speaks up and bids his mother retire: I am the one here with authority; give the "stranger-guest" the bow. When Eumaeus hesitates to give it, Telemachus reiterates his order. The doors are locked, and Odysseus shoots. It is as the impoverished and pitiable "stranger-guest" who has been formally rejected by the suitors but accepted by his own people that he performs the final act.

When the suitors are all slain, he pronounces an epitaph over their dead bodies. Addressing himself to the nurse, who has greeted the spectacle with cries of relief and triumph, he speaks in the following terms (22.411–416):

Aged dame, rejoice in spirit but restrain yourself nor cry aloud;
it is not piety over men slain to boast;
them lying here did their doom overcome and their vicious deeds,
for none did they respect of mankind upon the earth,
neither base nor noble, whoso might come to visit them;
therefore by their own abominations an unseemly fate have they
encountered.

His words have an unmistakable formality: a commentary and a conclusion upon the epic tale. The terms "vicious deeds" (*schetlia erga*) and "abominable behavior" (*atasthaliai*) are commonplaces of epic malediction.[14] What we need to know is precisely what type of behavior is meant. The fourth and fifth lines of the epitaph supply the answer: it is the refusal of a decent reception to the visitor, be he base or noble. "Base" (*kakos*) refers here to a man's condition, not his character, though to our way of thinking an archaic Greek might confuse the two. Odysseus himself has played both roles and been rejected in both. A little earlier, speaking to one man he had spared, he had used a more general formula (22.373 ff.):

Courage; my son's words have saved you
that you may learn in your spirit and likewise tell to another
how that benefaction [*euergesiē*] is preferable to malefaction [*kakoergiē*]

The phrasing of the sentiment, recalling as it does the tribute paid to Odysseus' benefaction by Penelope in Book 4, indicates that it is intended to enunciate a doctrine to be taught to others. By both these pronouncements, the moral structure of the *Odyssey* is completed.

Didacticism by Indirection

The dangerous journey and the conflict between enemies represent the two forms of mythos most amenable to memorization. The *Odyssey* exploits and interweaves them both, in the interest of creating a moral polarization, determined by applying the criterion of hospitality offered or refused to a journeying stranger. Superimposed upon this role is that of the beggar, whose poverty and helplessness call for assistance and a degree of compassion. Its thematic significance for the story is underlined by the fact that it is artificially introduced by an act of divine transformation. The first half of the epic devotes itself to illustrating the law of hospitality to strangers; this is done through numerous recurrent episodes which exploit the situation of such a stranger in varying situations. The second half commits itself to exploiting the double role of the stranger turned beggar, the traveler who is also destitute. These thematic effects are achieved in the first instance by contriving the narrative situations so as continually to place the characters in host-guest relationships to which they have to respond by word and deed, relationships between Athene and Telemachus, Telemachus and Nestor, Odysseus and the Phaeacians, Odysseus and the Cyclops, Odysseus and Eumaeus, Odysseus and Penelope, Odysseus and Telemachus, and, finally, Odysseus and the suitors. To reinforce the effect of this structuration, we hear the insistent hammer beat in the verse of the title "stranger-guest" and its correlatives and the title "beggar" with accompanying description. Such effects register on the ear of the listener more readily than on the eye of the reader. Homer did not have readers. He is practicing the echo technique which acoustic laws of memorization require, and the same should be said of the moral formulas which have been quoted here, commemorating the rules of reception or the danger of their abrogation. These occur, usually as utterances, as the narrative context calls for them; they do not intrude a conscious didactic lesson. The didacticism of the story, conformable to the rules of contrived speech in an oral culture, remains indirect.

The moralities are not an artificial invention of the poet. They constitute an example of cultural storage of nomos-ethos central to the society in which the poems were sung.

Two Required Codes of Behavior

The *Odyssey* is par excellence the oral encyclopedia of the maritime complex, encoding and reporting and recommending those patterns of pan-Hellenic behavior which also could protect interpolis traffic and enable the complex to work.

The mythos devotes itself to describing and recommending "international" or "intercity" propriety. The legal procedures applied in the *Iliad* and abrogated in the *Odyssey* concern themselves with "intracity" propriety: they regulate dealings within the citizen body. Strictly speaking, there were no legalities between cities. The Hellene who crossed city boundaries, to trade, travel, or explore, could be protected only by what we would style a "moral" feeling sanctioned and protected by religion. He was "the stranger within the gates." No international authority or court of appeal existed, corresponding to that provided within the city by the agora, which could guarantee proper reception and treatment of the Hellenic *xeinos*—not in early Hellenism. That is why the "moralities" of the *Odyssey* are more significant than its legalities.

Yet the poem does not stop there. When upon Odysseus the stranger-guest there is superimposed Odysseus the impoverished beggar, the moralities of the story take us back within the walls of the polis. A second lesson is to be learned, aside from the international one. Any polis society contained both its rich and its poor. The poor need sustenance, and it should be given them when they ask for it. They also are free men and should be guarded against insult. This too is part of the nomos of the Greek polis, for without it community is threatened and the society may cease to be viable. Need we wonder that an Athens educated on the poetry of Homer from the time of Solon onward made more than one attempt to preserve or restore this rule of propriety between the classes?

10

The Justice of the *Odyssey*

❦

Several of the moral formulas translated in the previous chapter furnish the word "just" (*dikaios*) as an epithet applicable to certain kinds of human beings. The adjective may seem commonplace enough, but it is in the *Odyssey* that it seems to come into its own. Occurrences in the *Iliad* are rare. It will be recalled that there the noun *dikē* operated in the plural to signify "procedures of justice," whether viewed as verbal pronouncements (decisions) or as transactions ("cases"), and more usually in the singular to indicate the "justice" effected by a given plea or transaction, something which almost became the property of a litigant, to be recovered through redress of honor or goods previously abstracted.

Dikē as Propriety

The *Odyssey* is familiar with this kind of "justice." It mentions, as does the *Iliad*, the "manager of just procedures" (*dikas-polos*), designating him as an official who is paid in kind for his services. The same function in an archaizing context is assigned to the "blameless prince" (*basileus*) who "sustains procedures-of-justice-that-are-good" (*eu-dikias*),[1] and in Hades Odysseus views King Minos (*Od.* 11.569–571)

holding the golden scepter, pronouncing formularies [*themisteuonta*] to the dead
seated. They surrounding him asked justices [*dikai*] of their lord
sitting and standing up, filling the wide-gated house of Hades.

In similar vein, at a more realistic level (discarding the Mycenean-Minoan fantasy), Eumaeus the swineherd comments on the suitors (14.82–84):

unmindful in their minds of awe and of compassion—
not ruthless [*schetlia*] deeds do the blessed gods embrace;
nay, it is justice [*dikē*] they esteem and the deeds of men done-within-the-rules [*aisima*]

In this saying, acts of unfeeling recklessness and acts of propriety are balanced against each other. The gods prefer the latter, and the *dikē* they also prefer is that procedure which preserves or restores propriety by peaceful adjustment of claims rather than indulging in ruthless or extravagant behavior. Odysseus is aware that the Cyclopes are in effect a peculiar species of being because (9.112)

they have no agoras-of-counsel nor formularies

The specimen he encounters (9.189)

did not consort
with others; but living apart was a nonknower of formularies

In fact, he was (9.215)

a savage, not well knowing procedures of justice [*dikai*] or formularies

As in the *Iliad*, a distinction is implied between the precedents or formularies on which oral memory must draw and their administrative application in a given procedure or an oral judgment (*dikē*) of what the just thing in a given case requires. It is to be remarked that the epic voices an awareness that there is a connection between the existence of such procedures and the existence of human society as such—or more particularly, the agora society. The Cyclopes are not members of that kind of city-state.

Both epics, however, are very far from identifying "justice" as a principle with a priori foundations, whether conceived as the necessary "rule of law" or as a moral sense in man. These "justices" administered in the plural by kings (archaistically) or by magistrates (realistically)

are processes not principles, solving specifics, not applying general laws; they express themselves in negotiated settlement of rival claims. They operate to restore proprieties in human relationships. They are, in fact, "proprieties" administered in given contexts. This kind of "justice" is simply the rule of conservation of existing mores, or the correction of a violation. It does not prescribe what in general the mores "ought" to be. The noun in the singular therefore comes close to indexing that "rule of propriety" which in the plural becomes the acts of restoration of given proprieties. This significance of the singular offers a bridge to the understanding of a usage of *dikē* in the *Odyssey* which has often been needlessly severed from that of "justice," almost as though we were dealing with two different words with perhaps common etymology but separate references.[2] Seven examples of this usage can be pertinently reviewed, the first of which has occurred in a previous citation.

1. Penelope is protesting the attitude of the Ithacans; they have forgotten what their fathers used to say about Odysseus and the kind of man he was (4.690 ff.):

neither doing or saying to any man anything out of rule [*ex-aisimon*]
in the demos; the "justice" of divine lords stands so [*esti*]
that one should hate this one of mortals and love that one—
but he never once at all did any abominable thing [*atasthalon*] to a man.

2. Odysseus complains to his mother's shade that Persephone has raised up a mere phantom which he cannot embrace; she replies (11.217 ff.):

No, Persephone is not cheating you. The "justice" of mortals stands so
[*esti*]: they lose flesh and bones, which the fire consumes, and the
psyche takes wing and flies away.

3. Eumaeus, offering the beggar hospitality, apologizes for its meagerness (14.59 ff.):

tiny and precious is the giving I can give; so stands [*esti*] the "justice"
of servants who are continually afraid, when ruled by youthful masters

4. Penelope complains to the suitors that their conduct as suitors has reversed the normal rule (18.275 ff.):

this has not been the "justice" of suitors as hitherto arranged, who want
to court a noblewoman in competition; it is they who bring the oxen
and sheep . . . and give gifts . . .

5. Telemachus, preparing with his father a confrontation with the enemy, observes a magical light on the roof beams of the hall (19.36 ff.):

there must be a god inside—those who hold high heaven!
Hush! (replies his father) control your wits and do not ask questions;
this that you see is the present [*esti*] "justice" of the gods who hold
Olympus

6. Odysseus begs Penelope to stop questioning him (19.167 ff.):

you will endow me with sorrows even greater than possess me; (so is)
the"justice" whenever from his native land a man has been severed a long
time as I (have) now

7. Odysseus, meeting his father, observes his neglected condition (24.253–255):

you have the likeness of a lordly man,
yet, a likeness to such a one as would bathe and eat
and sleep soft; for the "justice" of the aged so stands [*esti*]

The usage of the verb "to be" in these formulas will be noticed in a later chapter. Homer's intention is not to give a series of definitions; the various samples of *dikē* are not properties belonging to persons but standing procedures or behavior patterns which are accepted or expected. The reference is not to a characteristic, but to what one is supposed to do or feel or what is supposed to happen "in the case of lords, gods," and so forth; the genitive is one of reference, not of possession. *Dikē* indicates a code which is followed: mortals lose their bodies at death, suitors ought to bring gifts, gods can throw magic light, old men should sleep soft. Such codes can be regarded either as "expected customs" (*nomoi*), or as "expected habits" (*ēthē*) (as in the case of the exile in example 6), or as a combination of the two. It is significant that in most instances the code is stated by way of protest: it has been abrogated or challenged; it is being defended as the proper thing to expect. The sense lingers on in the later adverbial use of *dikēn* in the accusative: "in the (expected) manner of . . ."

All this amounts to saying that it is "right" or "just" for gods or mortals or suitors or exiles to do so and so. One can perhaps foresee how some centuries later the first philosopher of justice, Plato, might convert this idiom of behavior into the formula "doing one's own thing" (*to ta heautou prattein*) and designate it as a principle,[3] defining a justice (*dikaiosunē*) which should be universal. Homeric *dikē* remains faithful to that sense of social propriety which surrounds its legal usages. It symbolizes what one has a "right" to expect, what it is "just" to expect, of given persons in given situations. The expectation, in order to be "just," must fit with the kind of behavior that pragmatic common sense would view as normal in specific cases, and therefore as normative, in the sense that the crazy-quilt variety of behavior patterns adds up to a total for the society which is socially cohesive and "works." It is not the index of a general rule of justice governing all human relations uniformly. This is shown quite strikingly in the first example, where the "justice" that belongs to autocrats is contrasted with the evenhanded methods of Odysseus. In a preliterate society, as noted above in Chapter 2, the effective expression of a general rule would be very difficult, given the tendency of orally preserved speech to eschew universals. The *dikai* and the *dikē* of both epics, as so far surveyed, as they reflect oral transactions, also conform in their idiom to the narrative syntax of the particular and the concrete which the preserved speech of preliterate society requires.

Though the mythos of the *Odyssey* is built round what I have called a moral polarization, the antithesis that is drawn lies between persons whose acts and interests are adverse, rather than between persons who on moral principles are in the right, opposing villains who are wrong. The "moral" difference between them, as the epic describes it, lies in a willingness to keep within the rules versus a reckless disregard of them. This purely conservative conception of morality betrays itself in two epithets constantly employed in both epics to indicate moral disapproval. They are *schetlios* and *atasthalos,* to which it is difficult to attach any consistent meaning more precise than "excessive" or "extravagant," "wanton" or "reckless," or, as we say, "shocking," a term which lacks reference to any objective standard. They denote persons or actions which exceed the bounds of what is allowable. But what precisely is the allowable if it is not what is deemed seemly or appropriate, this being determined by the regular and recurrent patterns of behavior in the culture, whatever these may happen to be? The same rule of conservatism is shown in the words *aisimos* and *enaisimos* as epithets of approved action, meaning action which conforms to the *aisa,* the due portion, and also in *exaisimos* or *aisulos,* action which exceeds the portion (I have translated them, respectively, as "keeping" or "breaking" "the rules"). The first words of the *Odyssey* are spoken by Zeus, and are often cited as evidence that there is a sense of morality in the epic which goes beyond anything in the *Iliad*. But all Zeus says of mankind is that "they have afflictions beyond due portion because of their reckless excesses" (*atasthaliai*, 1.34). The particular example is Aegisthus, who not only killed Agamemnon but was rash enough to marry the widow. These actions (and Zeus seems to imply particularly the latter) went "beyond due portion" (35) and incurred the wrath and vengeance of the son. And Aegisthus knew it (37) because Zeus had tried to warn him against such action because of its inevitable consequences (40–41). Whether or not it was "morally wrong" is not stated. It was just that the accepted norms governing a given relation in the society were being exceeded.

The "Just" Person

The root *dikē* supplies the adjectival form *dikaios*, the man of justice, which, following the sense of the noun as "due process," need mean no more than "a man of propriety" or "a man who does the appropriate thing," as in one of the rare occurrences in the *Iliad*. Agamemnon, making restitution to Achilles, his inferior in rank (which might violate propriety), will nevertheless "stand more just on another ground," for if it is the king who has initiated the quarrel with an inferior, he can offer reconciliation without fear of criticism.[4] Similarly, when Nestor hands the cup of ceremony to Athene (disguised as the elderly Mentor) before it is passed to the younger Telemachus, she approves his good manners: he is "a just man." When the suitors are described as wooing Penelope "not justly," it is not because they are morally wrong to do so, but because their manner of doing it violates the rules in such cases (*Od.* 14.90; 18.275).

Yet, so far as the *Odyssey* is concerned, this is not the last word. Justice, as the name of a social principle of universal dimensions, or of a moral sense fundamental to our human nature, may be wholly absent. But in the adjectival extensions, which make *dikē* an attribute of a person, the seeds are sown of a moral criterion which to a degree transcends the criterion of mere propriety.

A Table of Formulas

There is one series of moral formulas permeating the epic, pronounced by participants in the action at critical points and forming an echo pattern in which the adjective *dikaios* frequently recurs. Cross-comparison can also establish that where the word does not appear, its presence can still be felt implicitly. This fact becomes perceptible when the formulas are traced together in their successive contexts as the mythos unfolds; corresponding formulas are designated by corresponding capital letters. In some cases (as especially in the C examples), Homer's symmetries and the ways he has manipulated them can be rendered and exposed only by manipulating English prose.

1. Telemachus opens negotiations with the suitors (1.368):

A   Suitors of my mother possessed of overwhelming outrage [*hubris*]

2. Athene to Telemachus: bids him disregard what the suitors may intend (2.281):

B   They (are) not intelligent [*noēmones*] or just

3. Nestor to Telemachus: describes the disasters that befell the Greeks returning from Troy after incurring the wrath of Athene (3.133):

B   They all of them were proved neither intelligent nor just

4. Telemachus to Nestor: voices his fervent wish (3.205–207)

C   to take vengeance upon suitors for grievous transgression
    who inflicting outrage [*hubrizontes*] against me contrive abominable
    things [*atasthala*]

5. Telemachus to Menelaus: describes the enemies consuming his house as (4.321)

A   suitors of my mother possessed of overwhelming outrage

The plot to this point has focused attention on domestic events in Ithaca, so that it is the suitors' presence which provides relevant contexts for such pronouncements. But now the adventures of Odysseus take over (Books 5–13), and his role of stranger-guest, as it is played out in this part of the epic four times over, at four crises of confrontation, elicits the pronouncement of a moral formula more elaborate than any other in the poem:

6. Cast ashore naked and exhausted, he awakes on the island of Scheria to the sound of voices (6.119–121):

D   What (is to become) of me? Who (are) the mortals to whose land I
    am come?
    Indeed, they (may be) outrageous [*hubristai*] and savage [*agrioi*] and
    not just [*dikaioi*],
    or perhaps (they are) friends-to-the-stranger-guest, and the mind
    within them is god fearing?

7. His anxious question is answered by the hospitality of the
Phaeacians, who entertain him with prolonged festivities. He is moved
to tears by the epic of Troy, but his own identity remains unrevealed
until the king, seeking to ascertain it as propriety required, puts to the
guest with adaptations the question which the guest had originally
asked (8.572–576):

D   But pray tell me this and recount in order precisely
    how-and-where you were cast away and to what lands you came
    of mankind: tell of them and their cities established-and-inhabited,
    both all those (that are) harsh [*chalepoi*] and savage and not just
    and they (that are) friend-to-the-stranger-guest and the mind within
    them is god fearing

8. By appending the formula to his request for information, the
king, in effect, asks the wanderer not only to relate his adventures, but
to report also the peoples he has encountered in terms of a general
classification. Replying, Odysseus does this only in the Cyclops story,
describing how he told his men his intention (9.174–176)

D   to make test of these men who indeed they prove to be.
    Indeed, they (may be) outrageous and savage and not just,
    or perhaps (they are) friends-to-the-stranger-guest, and the mind
    within them is god fearing

This he says despite the fact that his narrative has already fully described their precivilized condition. Two of the three lines revert to the
wording originally used.

9. None of the remaining adventures offers occasion for the
formula until Odysseus' last landing. Awaking alone on an Ithaca he
does not recognize, he repeats the cry word for word that he had first
uttered as he awoke on Scheria (13.201–203):

D   What (is to become) of me? Who (are) the mortals to whose land I
    am come?
    Indeed, they (may be) outrageous and savage and not just,
    or perhaps (they are) friends-to-the-stranger-guest, and the mind
    within them is god fearing?

10. In his deserted condition (as he deems it), he even turns upon his erstwhile hosts, fastening on them with slight adaptation the phraseology applied early in the story to reckless suitors and reckless Greeks alike (13.209–210):

B   alas not in all (things) intelligent or just
     were-they-proved, even the leaders of the Phaeacians . . .

11. However, as Athene takes charge, the true enemy, as defined in the first four books, reemerges, first in dialogue within the swineherd's cottage. This loyal servitor fastens on the suitors a pregnant formula (15.329):

E   Their outrage and violence [*hubris, bia*] reach to heaven's iron dome.

This is said to the disguised Odysseus. Telemachus, returning home from his voyage and discovering that his swineherd has a guest, exclaims that he cannot entertain him properly in light of the "abominable outrage" of the suitors, upon which the beggar comments that it grieves him to hear of their "abominable contrivance." Each speaker furnishes a partial echo of formulas A and C (16.86 and 93).

12. Such are the men whose behavior, as the action moves into Odysseus' house, is to be tempted and tested by the beggar-man. The procedure, as it steers the epic toward its crisis, furnishes occasion for eight successive moral formulas pronounced at the suitors' expense between Books 17 and 21. At his first rebuff, Odysseus curses their leader with a solemnity that for a moment makes them afraid. For all his rags, he is a man of mystery. Does he possess mysterious powers? The thought as it occurs prompts the utterance of a popular belief in the magical power of spirits to walk the earth, performing functions not magical but moral (17.483–487):

F   Antinous, you are wrong to strike the hapless wanderer.
     Death to you! Suppose it be some god from heaven present here.
     Yes, indeed, gods in the likeness of stranger-guests (that are) foreign,
     changing themselves (in) manifold (ways), do go to and fro over cities,
     overseeing both the outrage and the lawfulness of mankind.

As phrased here, the sentiment is for Homer unique, but we shall encounter it again.

13. Because Penelope has overheard what is going on, she would like an introduction to the stranger from the swineherd, but the stranger

declines for the moment on grounds of prudence; better wait till night-fall; the suitors are in a dangerous mood (17.565):

E   Their outrage and violence reach to heaven's iron dome

14. Receiving this message, she agrees (17.588–589):

C   Never yet in this fashion do any of mortal mankind—
(as) men inflicting outrage contrive abominable things

15. For a second and a third time the beggar is instructed and the suitors warned of the consequences. The second occasion elicits a protest from one less infatuated than his fellows (18.414–415):

G   My friends, one should not upon a just thing uttered
with counter-violent words assail (the speaker) with harsh objection

16. The third occasion falls on a civic holiday, with a special dinner for the suitors: it is to be their last. As the servants bustle to prepare, Eumaeus warns the beggar to expect fresh insults, to which the beggar makes formal reply (20.169–171):

C   May gods, I pray, Eumaeus, avenge mistreatment
which these men here inflicting (as) outrage contrive abominable things
in the house of another, nor have they due portion of respect.

17. The prayer is a preface to what follows. They cannot "refrain from mistreatment" (285); Athene has seen to that. One more reckless than the others goes so far as to show contempt for the law of entertainment by parodying it. Before conferring on the stranger-guest a mock present by way of throwing a missile at him, he utters the appropriate formula, applying it with mock seriousness to the present case (20.294–295):

H   Neither good nor just (is it) to mistreat
the stranger-guests of Telemachus, whosoever may come traveling to
these halls

18. His cynicism provokes not only an angry outburst from Telemachus, but a repetition from another suitor of the protest uttered on the previous occasion (20.322–323):

G   My friends, one should not upon a just thing uttered
with counterviolent words assail (the speaker) with harsh objection

The formula does no more than call for propriety in oral procedure: "just" (meaning temperate) proposals should be met by counter-proposals equally "just." Opprobrium of the suitors' behavior is avoided since the speaker is a suitor himself.

19. But as the prophet, temporarily a guest of the house, gets up to leave, pronouncing upon the company their impending doom, he fastens on them the fatal formula (20.367–370):

C   I sense the evil approaching
    upon you, which not one may escape or evade
    of suitors—(you), who in the divine house of Odysseus
    (on) men inflicting outrage contrive abominable things.

20. Finally, as the contest of archery gets under way and the beggar offers to try the bow, one last attempt is made to get rid of him, upon which Penelope herself pronounces the formula of hospitality previously derided (21.312–313):

H   Neither good nor just (is it) to mistreat
    the stranger-guests of Telemachus, whosoever may come traveling to
    these halls

A Pattern of Echoes

This tabulation uncovers a stratum of statement in the epic which is predictive of things to come. Readers of Plato and Aristotle who revert to the Homeric poems can see foreshadowed there, as in a glass darkly, the provenance of justice in later Greek thought. But first a word on some technical aspects. Echo pattern[5] has already become familiar in the deployment of aphorisms, clustered round the stories of reception or rejection of travelers and indigents. The list above segregates from the story those that make connection with the adjectives *dikaios* and *dikaion*, the "just man" and "the just thing," and their opposites. They are classifiable in eight types or versions (A to H), occurring twenty times overall. Only one (F) is unique. Types A, E, G, and H are each used twice, B three times, C and D four times. Their distribution is governed by the way the story is told, as indeed the rules of oral storage require. Since Part One of the epic (roughly Books 1–4) either delineates or reports, through the mouth of Telemachus, the domestic scene, with the suitors as villains of the piece, it is not surprising that A, B, and C, being essentially pejorative definitions, occupy this area. Part Two, roughly Books 5–13, is committed to the encounters which befall

Odysseus in the role of a foreigner on strange soil. Within this area type D, a formula of some complexity, is uttered four times, thrice to express anxious anticipation after making landfall, and once in the course of a challenge to disclose his identity and history. The final landfall also provokes a repetition of B. Part Three resumes the domestic scene, divided roughly and unevenly between the swineherd's cottage and Odysseus' house. In the cottage, Eumaeus is chosen as the mouthpiece to introduce E, another pejorative formula. After the house is entered and the behavior of the suitors increasingly laid bare, example C, the most intensely pejorative of the formulas, recurs three times. Examples G and H, on the other hand, introduced by way of protest to affirm the proprieties that are being broken, are more positive in expression. F, the unique one, resembles D in its greater complexity. Though prompted by the exigencies of the moment—it is a response to Odysseus' curse—it addresses itself, like D, to a situation in which all men find themselves.

This tabulation has been applied to an oral-acoustic flow of contrived and remembered speech. It employs methods of visual selection and apprehension which are characteristic of the literate reader (below, Chapter 12), not the listener. The formulas have to be isolated in this way to see what is happening, but care must be taken not to conceive of them in separation from the narrative contexts which have stimulated their expression. Viewed in the light of a literate aesthetic, they may seem intrusive, routine additions to a narrative which for its dramatic effects does not need them. It should be remembered that the group, selected for its relevance to the term or topic of "justice," is a tiny fraction of the stock of moral formulas woven into the verse, usually concealed in ways described in Chapter 6. The members of this particular group are more overt than most, but they still illustrate the rule of instruction by indirection characteristic of preserved storage in an oral culture. They do indeed belong to the story as it is told, the episodes of which are of that particular kind that makes them relevant. In accordance with this rule of relevance, the grammar of the "saying" is in each case adapted to the syntactical or metrical situation in which it occurs, occasionally with some awkwardness.

The Just and the Violent: A Moral Polarity

We turn finally to the symbols employed, and their possible "meanings," as they may point to the future. The significance of A on the face of it may seem minimal. It merely identifies the suitors pejoratively as committing *hubris*, an untranslatable word, "outrage" being only one possible rendering, though perhaps the least unsatisfactory.[6] B, though equally pejorative, introduces the affirmative adjective "just" (*dikaios*), assimilating it to a form of "intelligence." C more significantly connects the commission of outrage with deliberate intention, giving it a psychological dimension, reiterated four times over. D brings the outrageous and the just together in a formal antithesis, the "outrageous" man being equated with the "savage." The antithesis is implicitly given a universal application, and the successive reiteration adds resonance to the echo. E returns to purely pejorative idioms, linking *hubris* with *bia*, outrage with violence or physical aggression. F, like D, proposes a universal antithesis, but the opponents this time are abstractions instead of people. *Hubris* is retained as the negative term, but it is interesting that *dikē* will not do as the positive one. A metrical means for using it could have been devised if required. Instead, the term "orderliness" (*eunomia*)[7] is substituted. Is this because, while *hubris* is "personal," *dikē* is not? G opposes the "just thing" to violence (cf. *Il.* 1.304), as each is embodied in speech. H observes simply that "the just thing" is opposed to maltreatment of guests.

Earlier in this chapter I observed that the "moralities" of the *Odyssey*, meaning the epithets of approval and disapproval employed in the epic verse, do not do more than identify conservatism and propriety as good things, and excess or extravagance as bad, and that this reflects the fact that a sense of "justice" is what one has a "right" to expect of human behavior in given cases from given types of people. It is a sense which has correspondence to *dikē* viewed as a legal procedure for the redress of grievance and the adjustment of claims. In the present series of formulas, a larger dimension of meaning is perceptible. Regarding the series as interconnected, and the symbols as associatively linked together, we begin to see that "the just man" at least does more than merely conform to the mores or conserve them. He eschews aggressive action and attitude (*hubris* can imply either) and the physical violence which is its concomitant. I have argued that confrontation of some sort is an eessential element of the memorizable tale. Yet the "moral" of the tale, so to speak, is that one should prefer compromise above confrontation. This is the social ethos which the tale is indirectly conserving and also recommending; it seems also to be the lesson of the *Iliad*. The just man, if he prefers orderliness above outrage, may be said also to prefer peace above war, for orderliness is not only a personal but a social condition.[8]

The narrative contexts in which these moral formulas are placed suggest a further dimension. The confrontations that occur are not between opponents of roughly equal strength, as in the *Iliad,* but between the strong and the weak. The *Iliad* is briefly aware of the part played by outrage in human affairs. Characteristically, it is when Athene appears that Achilles is prompted to say to her, "Have you come to contemplate Agamemnon's *hubris?*" She imposes her own formula for handling the confrontation, but assures him: "You will be recompensed three times over for this outrage of his." In subsequent dealings between the two antagonists, to the point of their reconciliation, the term does not recur. In the *Odyssey,* the antithesis between the outrageous and the just man is continually offered in juxtaposition with confrontations between patron and suppliant, native and stranger, and finally between men prospering and men in want. The last is indeed surprising, placed as it is, by a kind of tour de force, within an epic of heroic fantasy. The character of Odysseus as the "hero" of the story (in modern terms) is in fact defined by his paternal protectiveness, his gentleness, his civility, and his benefactions to those under him. These are themselves moral formulas. They do not verbally overlap with those bearing on the antithesis between the just man and his opposite number; their immediate contexts do not call for this. But the way the story is told brings home the lesson that this kind of man may be also the just man, the recommended model. In this role Odysseus becomes the appropriate mouthpiece to pronounce over the corpses of his enemies a lesson not of triumph but of morality as understood by the society of the day. The justice rendered to the noncitizen, the stranger within the gates, has its counterpart in that rendered to the impoverished portion of the citizen body by the more privileged. Such was the rule applied by Solon the lawgiver to his own city.

Yet the epic does not quite say that, and one must beware of overconceptualizing what it does say. To speak of the "justice" of the *Odyssey* is perhaps allowable if the word is placed in quotation marks. There is no concept of justice in Greek epic, in our sense of that word. What we have been observing are commentaries upon the actions of just men and their opponents, and how the "just thing" operates in a given case. The "thinking" of the epic on these matters is conducted through the way the story is told. The agent with his actions and words prevails over the idea, which only from our standpoint may be said to reside implicitly in the diction of the story, but which would demand a syntax of expression as yet unavailable, for it would be alien to the genius of a speech orally preserved in the mouths of men who in early Hellenism remembered but did not read.

11

The Justice of Hesiod

An Essay in Detection

The prevailing style of the poetry ascribed to Hesiod is oral. Taking it verse by verse, the reader observes a recurrence of the hexametric formulas—or types of formulas—characteristic of Homeric epic.[1] Yet when the overall composition of both the *Theogony* and the *Works and Days* is considered, the way statements are made and the way paragraphs are put together, we become aware of a difference: the verse is no longer controlled by narrative flow; mythos is no longer dominant. It is present, but only fitfully. Compositional structure seems to address itself to topics rather than to a narrative.[2] Is it possible that Hesiod, as against Homer, is one who not only sings but writes, not only remembers but sees what he is remembering? Does he deserve the literate title of "author," as one who is uniquely responsible for a work which draws its diction from the oral reservoir, but has been put together with the aid of the written word?[3] Is this why both poems are comparatively short, somewhere between a tenth and a twelfth of epic length, and why their content is so concentrated compared with the diffuse and leisurely progress of epic? Is this why each poem contains a kind of signature, giving to its composer a shadowy personality which bards of the previous nonliterate tradition did not think to claim?

A Concentrate of *Dikē*

It is appropriate to ask such questions, even if they are not at once answered, by way of preface to coming to terms with a phenomenon of some importance for the history of Greek moral theory. One of the component parts of the *Works and Days,* itself a poem of over eight hundred lines in the form in which it has been transmitted to us, is a discourse of less than a hundred lines, a poem within a poem, which possesses an identity of its own, for it addresses itself with considerable concentration to a single topic, namely, justice. There is nothing like it in Homer, and yet without the help of what Homer has said about justice and just men, it is unlikely it would ever have been written. The Homeric term *dikē* ("justice") within a total of seventy-three hexameters (11.213–285) occurs twelve times in the singular and eight times in the plural. The Homeric *dikaios* ("just") occurs five times and *adikos* ("nonjust," which is not Homeric) twice, and there is also one occurrence of the compound adjective *ithu-dikēs,* a person "of straight justice," which Hesiod possibly made up himself. This amounts to a total of twenty-eight instances, an average of once for every two and a half hexameters. Actually, the poem contains one paragraph of twenty-three hexameters (225–247) in which *dikē* and its derivatives occur only four times; so the concentration in the rest of the poem is all the heavier.

There is nothing to match this elsewhere in the *Works and Days.* Hesiod's verse can be seen in many instances to follow the lead supplied by certain key words, like *eris* ("contention"), *ergon* ("work"), *genos* ("family"), which repeat themselves within given portions, but these sequences are much shorter, or else the recurrence is much less frequent. The sheer density of *dikē* within the poem is unique. The word, to be sure, has intruded occasionally in the earlier parts of the *Works and Days,* at lines 9, 36, 39, 124, 158 (the adjective), 189 (a compound), 190 (the adjective), and 192. Perhaps in the last group of three, occurring within four lines, we detect a build-up in the poet's mind toward a point where he will wish to fasten on *dikē* as a topic with its own claims to treatment. When that treatment terminates (at line 285), the topic vanishes from the verse. There are still 604 hexameters to follow, but with one irrelevant exception the word is heard no more. In Homeric fashion, but at greater than Homeric length, the entire work begins with an invocation to the Muses, this time in the plural. But a second object of address is a certain Perses, apparently a brother, who from time to time is the recipient of admonitory formulas. The name of a relative serves in an indirect way as Hesiod's own signature of authorship. Whether its significance is also more personal is a debated matter.[4]

The poem within the poem makes a series of statements about both "justice" and "justices," of a variety which borders on the bizarre, and calls for explanation. It is true that the discontinuity which appears to result can be partly evaded if the symbol *dikē*, singular and plural, is altered in translation to suit alteration of context. This paraphrase method destroys the identity of what in the Greek is a single symbol persistently and compulsively pursued. As in the case of Homer, it is better to stay with "justice" as conferring a similar identity, however awkward the plural may sound. The variety of roles which it is called upon to play is best exposed when the poem is dissected in a series of paragraphs.

Hubris and Its Two Victims

213 O Perses, I pray you: hearken to (the voice of) justice nor magnify outrage;
214 outrage (is) evil for a lowly mortal, nor can the noble
215 easily carry it, but is weighed down under it,
216a having met with ruinations.

The opening offers a stark antithesis between justice (*dikē*) and outrage (*hubris*), one which we might say equates justice with non-aggression. *Hubris* became a commonplace in Greek moral discourse after Hesiod, its significance being summed up in the maxim: Pride goes before a fall. But we should beware of taking it for granted here, as though Hesiod were merely exploiting a moral postulate that already existed, rather than perhaps inventing one. Has he found it in the mythos of the *Odyssey*? Is he recalling and rationalizing the contrast between the "just" and the "hubristic" which runs like a continuous thread through all Odysseus' adventures, to the point where his character and cause become polarized over against the actions of the suitors, and overweening outrage meets its just penalty? Is it from this paradigm that Hesiod constructs something that borders on a definition, allowing it equal control over his own poem? The suggestion acquires some pertinence when we observe that instead of continuing the commendation of justice, the two and a half hexameters that succeed dwell upon the effects of outrage. Its moral quality is not in question—only the fact that it can be exercised at the expense of two types at opposite ends of the social spectrum, the "down and out" (*deilos*) and the "noble" or "distinguished" (*esthlos*). The latter carries it, but only with difficulty; the weight is too much for him after he has encountered disaster. Is it possible that Hesiod, starting with an antithesis suggested to him by the theme of the *Odyssey*, has conjoined memories of both epics, that of the beggar-man enduring the outrage of the suitors, and that of Agamemnon, who as he surrenders to an act of *hubris* becomes the victim of the demon of disaster, so that he has to carry the burden and its consequences for a prolonged period? Such an explanation proposes that in composing an encomium of justice Hesiod would look for its materials in the justice of the *Iliad* and of the *Odyssey*.

The Runners in a Race

216b The road (taken) to bypass on the other side
217a (is) superior to (reach) just (things);
217b justice over outrage prevails,
218a having gotten through to the goal;
218b even the fool learns from experience;
219 for look! oath is running alongside crooked justices.

So far, justice has been introduced as a voice to be heard, versus outrage as a human affliction. These general sentiments are abruptly succeeded by a series of short statements describing a scenario in which various persons are either traveling to some destination or running in a race. It is arranged in sequences which are themselves rather bewildering: a traveler on a road (*hodos*) is able to bypass either a presumed obstacle or another traveler in order to reach an objective (216b–217a); two competitors are racing toward a goal, with one winning in the last lap (217b–218a); a young fool learns a lesson (218b); a single competitor is running neck and neck with a pack (219). If these are the actions performed, who are the actors? The pair of individual competitors (217b) are presented without dubiety: they are justice versus outrage arranged in antithesis, which is how they had been introduced. But in line 217a justice, instead of being a competitor, becomes the objective; in line 219, justice and outrage are replaced as competitors by oath and a pack of justices that are crooked. As for the young fool, his intrusion remains unexplained.

Disconnection has become disjunction; the competitors in the scenario are also competing for attention in the poet's mind; they are linked by association but not by logic. Where could they have come from?

The Homeric justice of Menelaus supplies the possible answer. In that episode of cheating in a chariot race, the operative term governing the proceedings was "justice," the "right of it." Has Hesiod, composing material for his own hymn to "justice," remembered this example of its application? It had been a race in whch Antilochus at a narrow point in the "road" (*hodos*) had unfairly "bypassed" his opponent, who to avoid collision was forced to give way, so that Antilochus got ahead. In the end, Menelaus was judged the winner and given the "justice" due to him, in a procedure which required sworn testimony on oath from Antilochus. Menelaus graciously accepted his apology, remarking: "Your youth prevailed over your senses."

In Hesiod's vision of the episode, justice has been translated into the personality of Menelaus, who won in the end, but "she" wins because "oath" is there to assist her, so oath is doing the running too; in the outcome, youthful presumption, that of Antilochus, learned a lesson. But Hesiod also remembers with clarity Antilochus' success in "bypassing" his competitor in a narrow part of the *hodos* (it is the most vivid portion of the epic description) and Homer's concluding statement that Menelaus would have caught up and "bypassed" Antilochus if the race had lasted a bit longer. So he cannot resist indulging in a brief image of the winner attaining what is right by similar action. Some of his own verbal choices in arranging his vignette—the bypassing, the youthful ignorance, the oath—are assisted by Homer's language, for all three are items which Homer keeps repeating as his description of the race and its result moves forward ("bypassing": *Il.* 23.416, 423, 424, 427, 527; "ignorance": 426, 440, 570, 589, 590, 604; "oath": 441, 585). The naming of "outrage" as the opponent of justice in the race maintains the antithesis proposed in the opening hexameter. The pack of crooked justices has a different inspiration, still to be explained.

The Woman Abused

220 Uproar of justice being dragged away where men may take her—
221 fee-eaters, and with crooked justices they adjudicate formularies—
222 she follows on, weeping, to city and dwelling places of people
223 clothed in mist, carrying evil to mankind,
224a such as drive her out,
224b and they have not meted her [*eneiman*] straight.

In these five hexameters Hesiod's composition has suffered an abrupt shift in perspective. The confident runner commanding victory in a race is summarily replaced by a helpless victim seized and dragged screaming away. The hexameter thrusts itself into the verse with sudden poignancy. Justice has become a woman, who in this particular role does not reappear, for two lines later she is discovered, still weeping to be sure, but now autonomous, proceeding on her way to a destination which may be of her own choosing. Who is she?

The story of the justice of the *Iliad*, its abrogation and restoration, was set in motion by the unlawful appropriation of a woman, Chryseis a priest's daughter. Replying to her father's protest, which the agora has approved, Agamemnon angrily retorts (*Il.* 1.29–31):

her will I not set free; ere that will old age come upon her
in my house in Argos far from her country,
going to and fro before the loom and serving my bed.

In fact, she is rendered back. But some of the compulsions of her case are formulaically repeated when Hector in a later instance addresses his wife Andromache: his grief, he tells her, for his people, his father and mother and brothers fallen before the enemy, cannot match his grief for her (6.454 ff.):

in the hour when some man of the Achaeans
shall take you away weeping, robbing you of your freedom day;
set down in Argos, you will weave maybe at the loom of an alien mistress
and carry water from Messeis' spring or Hypereia
sore afflicted, carrying the burden of overpowering necessity . . .
May the heaped earth cover me in my grave
before the screaming of you and the dragging of you reaches my ears.

The lines have had their effect on literature and on art; Homer's posterity has not ceased to be moved by them. Is it possible that they also moved Hesiod to indulge in a chain of association which produced this echo in his own poem? The original violation was on the person of a woman, and when this was remedied, retaliation was exercised at the expense of a second woman, Briseis. When the dispute was formally ended, the ceremony was validated by the reliability of a sworn oath, publicly witnessed, that the integrity of the second woman had been protected. If Hesiod imagines justice placed in a similar situation, it could be because both women symbolize in one person justice violated and justice restored. But in the meantime Homer had shifted his scene to Troy, and reproduced in the person of Andromache the situation that had confronted Chryseis: she too will "ply a foreign loom in Argos." But with added poignancy the husband describes how she will be "taken away by some man," how she will "weep"; he imagines her "outcry" as she is "dragged away." The situations of the women have coalesced in Hesiod's mind, to produce a sudden, vivid but isolated, image of justice herself led off "crying aloud," "dragged along," "weeping."[5]

The intrusion lasts only one line (220, with the addition of *klaiousa*, the "weeping woman," in l. 222). The next hexameter with equal abruptness opens with the word "fee-eaters." To be sure, these are grammatically connected with the "men" who have been raping the woman in the previous line, but this is only a syntactical convenience. We have moved into a quite different situation, for the single victim has been replaced by "justices" in the plural, and these are now "crooked." They have previously intruded as the runners alongside oath; now they become instruments employed by judges. Then (222–223) justice in the singular reemerges as a personal subject performing certain actions; then (224a) yields place to certain persons who act on her, first by "expelling" her from some location unspecified (224a), next by "meting her out crookedly" (or "apportioning," 224b).

Such disjunction calls for sorting out. What are these judges doing here? They are important, for they adjudicate the traditional formularies. Again, when the poet introduces justices in the plural into his composition, why (as will appear later) is he so frequently preoccupied with their crookedness? Are the unspecified persons who expel justice in line 224 supposed to be identical with the judges of line 221? One recollection is evident, that of Homer's simile of the cloudburst in the sixteenth book of the *Iliad*. It was the more congenial in that it stated a paramount connection between "Zeus," "justice," and the "works" of men, a connection which is very much in Hesiod's mind as he composes the *Works and Days*. The offenders in the Homeric context (above, Chapter 7) are men

who by violence in agora adjudicate formularies crooked
and drive out justice, regarding not the awful word of gods.

Clearly this is the source of lines 220, 224a in Hesiod. The formulaic components of the Homeric original have been improved upon. For "crooked formularies" Hesiod substitutes "crooked justices," that is, the procedures employed in applying the traditions rather than the traditions themselves;[6] the same point is made when he complains that "justice is meted not straight." But since Homer had also realistically spoken of justice expelled like a litigant from a hearing, Hesiod retains this metaphor, though it assigns justice a role inconsistent with her "crookedness."

Why does he interrupt this Homeric memory by inserting the quite different image of a justice proceeding down a road to a destination (222)? Clues may lie in the verbal niceties of his description. Who, or what, was it in Homer that proceeded clothed in mist toward a "city," and its inhabitants, and its dwelling places? The prototype who fits was of a different gender, but had female company. It was Odysseus approaching the city of the Phaeacians. "Bestir yourself to go cityward," says Nausicaa to him (*Od.* 6.255); when they reach "the fields and works of men" (259), he is to wait behind. With naive pride she describes what he will see when he arrives—the walls, the harbor, the agora. But the inhabitants are stiff-necked; the demos will feel slighted if she arrives with an unknown man in company (6.283). So he waits in the grove of Athene, praying to her for protection, and then "bestirs himself to go cityward" (7.14), whereupon the goddess pours mist around him and then in the guise of a young girl meets him to guide him as he goes. He tells her, "I do not know the men who 'mete-and-manage' [*nemontai*] this city and these works" (7.26). She warns him they are not tolerant of stranger-guests (7.32), so she continues to surround him with mist (7.41–42), and he arrives, marveling at the "harbors, ships, agoras, walls" that he sees before him. The inference that these are the "dwelling places of people" which are approached by justice in Hesiod's text may seem frail, but it will receive strength below, when the next paragraph is examined. The transfer of gender is the less artificial because both Nausicaa and Athene are company for Odysseus on his journey.

Why is Odysseus chosen for recollection in this particular episode of his career? Surely because it is concerning the people whom he is now approaching that he has asked the question: "Are they outrageous men, or men of justice [*dikaioi*]?" (*Od.* 6.120). The answer temporarily supplied by Homer is that they are not likely to be *dikaioi*, unless precautions are taken; the outlook is uncertain, and Hesiod's text makes us feel that it may be uncertain for justice also. In this way the Odysseus of line 214 reenters at lines 222–223.

In the *Odyssey*, the reception of Odysseus by the Phaeacians had its contrasting counterpart in the reception accorded him in Ithaca, after he had left the swineherd's home. Both became tests of hospitality; in Ithaca, as in Phaeacia, he "bestirs himself to go cityward"; in both cases he was required to follow a guide (16.272; 17.10, 22, 201). The two Homeric situations were, thematically speaking, replicas of each other. But in Ithaca the test was not met. Odysseus in Phaeacia was a genuine suppliant; in Ithaca he was an avenger in disguise whose mission was to "plant a crop of evil for the suitors" (*Od.* 14.110; 17.27, 82, 159): Hesiod's phrase "carrying evil to mankind" (223) is a formulaic equivalent (cf. also *Od.* 16.103; 20.367–368). He has remembered both these roles and amalgamated them.

Justice in Utopia

225 They who to stranger-guests and demos-dwellers give justices
226 (that are) straight and do not step across out of justice at all—
227 for them the city flourishes merry and the people in it blossom
228 and peace over the land (is) nourisher-of-*kouroi*; nor for them
229 travailing war does wide-viewing Zeus betoken;
230 nor ever among men-of-straight-justice does famine keep company
231 nor ruin, but with merriments they mete-and-manage their given works;
232 for them the earth bears much livelihood, the oak tree on the hills
233 bears acorns at the top and bees in the middle
234 and shaggy sheep with fleeces are weighed down;
235 the women bear children in likeness of their begetters;
236 they flourish merrily with goods continually; nor upon ships
237 do they fare forth; and the grain-giving ploughland bears fruit.

The just inhabit utopia; it is a vision in which Hesiod indulges himself. Is it entirely his own? He had only to turn to the *Odyssey* for his model, finding there that earthly paradise of the Phaeacians in which Odysseus was entertained. There are correlations. The inhabitants of Scheria, that magic place set apart in the waves, had once lived proximate to the threat of "violence" from the Cyclops, which was too much for them, but, says the poet, they were transferred to a site remote from mankind (*Od.* 6.4–8). Nausicaa, reassuring her maids as Odysseus appears, reminded them (6.201 ff.):

that mortal man breathes not nor ever will be born
who may come to the land of the Phaeacian men
bearing battle-din; for very dear to the immortals are we . . .
and we live far apart in the wave-swept deep
on the edge of the world, nor does any mortal else mingle with us.

The accent is on peace, and a sense of security which is complete, and it is repeated when their king later arranges for a crew to despatch the hero homeward (8.562):

no fear is upon them that they should suffer privation or perish

In Hesiod's vision, "peace is the nourisher of *kouroi*" (228); the youth of military age are spared military casualties. Is he remembering the handsome *kouroi* who were in evidence among the Phaeacian population? (8.34 ff., 40, 48, 262; and cf. 8.250). His city "flourishes merrily," its people "bloom" like flowers, they pursue their tasks "with merry enjoyments." The life of the Phaeacians, as exposed to the eyes of the visitor, was equally relaxed; it was devoted to pleasure (cf. *Od.* 13.44 ff.) and seemed to consist of one long holiday, of sports, dancing, singing. Hesiod's description of agricultural fertility is notably fantastic: acorns at the top, bees in the middle, the sheep overcome by the burden of their own fleeces, the produce of the earth proliferating. Equally fantastic were the fruits grown in the gardens and grounds of Alcinous: "pear upon pear, apple on apple" (*Od.* 7.112–128).

This paragraph of Hesiod's poem moves easily forward in free composition, because the poet is freely indulging a vision of his own. Recollection of Phaeacia is vividly there, without being closely copied. That it is there is surely indicated by the opening: these utopian rewards are earned by

those who to stranger-guests and demos-dwellers give justices
that are straight

This constitutes Hesiod's sole reference (in this hymn) to the rules of intercity behavior which were central to the "justice" of the *Odyssey*. But the wording of the sentiment at this precise place is scarcely accidental. Who were the prototypes of such hospitality in the *Odyssey*, if not the Phaeacians? Their presence we have already detected, near the conclusion of the previous paragraph (above, ll. 222–223). Each echo confirms the other. From a memory of Odysseus' route to the earthly paradise the poet switches to a memory of the paradise itself. This also explains that curious addition in the Hesiodic version: "they do not fare forth on ships" (236–237). No doubt this reflects the indifference to the sea voiced by Hesiod elsewhere in the *Works and Days* (though indifference does not prevent him from including a navigator's almanac). But why the sudden intrusion of the prejudice unless to distinguish his paradise from that of the original? His vision, he seems to be saying, is his own, not Homer's. Having recalled so many features of Phaeacian life, he was left with the most prominent of all—their exclusive devotion to seafaring, which Homer is at pains to reiterate (*Od.* 6.270; 7.34,

108; 8.247). This will not do, but here again Hesiod has help from Homer. The last voyage they undertook proved unexpectedly disastrous (*Od.* 13.149–164). Their king drew the moral, and enjoined them to discontinue their previous carefree practice (*Od.* 13.179–181):

Hearken all of you to me and let us consent thereto:
Cease from conveyance of mortal men whosoever may make visit
to our city . . .

The Homeric admonition is translated by Hesiod into a renunciation of all voyaging.

Though memory of the Phaeacian paradise pervades the whole paragraph, it is possible to perceive a juncture, as though to one version of utopia has been added a supplement. The "givers of justices" and their rewards are presented in lines 225–229, "those-of-straight-justice" and their rewards in lines 230–237. The two are not exclusive of each other, but in presenting the second the poet seems to be making a fresh start, switching from the blessings of peace to the theme of material plenty. This has been connected by critics to another utopian reference in the *Odyssey*, where Odysseus paid compliment to Penelope, and indirectly to himself, likening her to the lord whose rule is prosperous because "he sustains procedures-of-justice-that-are-good." For the lord's people as for the Phaeacians, nature was bountiful, but the details were a little different: "trees are loaded with fruit," but "the earth bears wheat and barley," and "the sheep bear sturdy young" (*Od.* 19.109–114). This last trait is transferred by Hesiod to the women (235). It is even possible that in coining the adjective "of-straight-justice" and placing it where he does, in the initial colon of the hexameter (*oude pot' ithudikēisi*), he constructs an acoustic echo of the corresponding Homeric colon *eudikias anechēisi* (*W.D.* 230 = *Od.* 19.111).

The common factor which links the two versions is their joint relevance to the practice of "justice," implicit in the Phaeacian case, where Odysseus' hope that the inhabitants would prove "just" was fulfilled, explicit in the case of the ideal king whose decisions upheld "justices that are good." The poet is overlaying one memory with another, melding them together; their capacity for cohesion is furnished by the topical purpose and format of his composition.

Hubris and Its Misfortunes

238 But they who are given to evil outrage and ruthless works—
239 for them justice does the Kronian betoken, even wide-viewing Zeus;

240　often even a city entire enjoys the fruit of[7] an evil man,
241　whosoever may offend and contrive abominations;
242　upon them from heaven does the Kronian deliver great misery,
243　famine and plague together, and the people perish away,
244　the women do not bear, the homes are diminished
245a　by the considerations of Olympian Zeus;
245b　again at other occasions
246　he destroys a wide army of them, yea, or their wall
247　or ships on the deep does the Kronian remove from them.

To the utopia is appended a companion piece describing the lot of the wicked, each grammatically balanced against the other by the generic pronouns which respectively introduce the lines (225 plus 227 equals 238 plus 239). The damned are the devotees of *hubris,* a definition which carries out the terms of the original polarization between *dikē* and *hubris* that continues to control the poem. But what "outrage" consists of exactly is not otherwise explained, except that it seems to be equivalent to "dastard" or "ruthless" deeds (*schetlia*) and to "abominations" (*atasthala*). Hesiod reuses the two symbols, which are commonplaces of epic but not susceptible to precise ethical definition (Chapter 10). Justice on the other hand now appears to be assigned the role of a redress which involves a punishment rather than a compensation; to be visited on the hubristic by Zeus's decree (238–239). The two hexameters constitute a moral maxim, unexceptionable if the basic antithesis is to be upheld; obviously if the utopians enjoy the favor of Zeus, their opposite number do not; the contrast between Zeus's favor and his hostility is expressed in verbal and metrical parallelism (between ll. 229 and 239).

But why do the next two hexameters (240–241), in place of transgressors as a class, substitute a single transgressor, an "evil man," for whose wickedness "a whole city," presumably innocent, has to pay? Why, again, do the next four take us back to the plural in order to describe the impact of famine and plague on whole populations? Are these being directly punished for *hubris,* or still suffering for the sins of a single individual? Any why finally switch to "other occasions" (*allote*) involving only military disasters: an army destroyed, fortifications stormed, a fleet cast away?

There is some discontinuity here. Does it reflect a variety of epic prototypes? If a model is to be sought for those "who make outrage their business," it lies with the suitors of the *Odyssey.* The formula "who devise abominations" was employed with frequency in the epic to characterize their actions; here it is applied to a single culprit. In this person, whose transgression brings disaster on an entire city, it is tempting to see a portrait of Oedipus, drawn presumably from the Theban cycle of epic, except that it is very doubtful whether Hesiod could have been acquainted with that version of the legend employed by Sophocles two centuries later. The *Iliad* can furnish two candidates: Agamemnon again, whose rape of Chryseis, being sacrilegious, brought plague on the whole army (but not on a city; and the offended god is Apollo, not Zeus); and, more probably, Pandarus, whose treacherous arrow, by violating the solemn oaths of agreement exchanged between the two armies, doomed Troy's city, "its king, its king's people" (*Il.* 4.164–165), "its wives and children" (4.162) to destruction. The moment was marked solemnly when it occurred, and Hector repeated the sentiment to Andromache, a passage already present in Hesiod's mind (*Il.* 4.163–165 = 6.447–449). The pronouncement of Troy's fate, essentially a penalty for breaking a sworn agreement, the kind of act which Hesiod will later link so closely with violation of justice (cf. comments on 282, below), was preceded and followed by two solemn assertions of the inevitable vengeance of Zeus (*Il.* 4.160–161 = 166–168). Was it this passage above all, with its unique emphasis on Zeus, which kindled the imagination of a compiler of moralities committed to the principle that justice is uniquely Zeus's province? The god's presence in Hesiod's ten hexameters is reiterated four times (239, 242, 245, 247).

The "other occasions" of his wrath with which the passage concludes are equally germane to epic. Armies destroyed and fortifications stormed recall the *Iliad,* and the fleet lost after military operations are concluded is that of the Achaeans, a disaster ascribed by Nestor in the *Odyssey* to their own wrong-doing:

they had no sense nor were they just.

It could, of course, be argued that the various disasters in this catalogue are merely drawn from the common catalogue of human misfortunes. But it is a little difficult to see why a Greek poet would wish to warn that disastrous wars in general are always due to previous moral failure. The conception is common in the Old Testament, but Hesiod is not a Hebrew prophet, nor is Troy a Homeric Jerusalem.

The Guardians

248 O lords, I pray you: do you, even you, consider deeply
249a this justice;

249b near at hand, among mankind being present,
250a the immortals consider
250b all who with crooked justices
251   inflict attrition on each other regarding not the awful word of gods.
252   Present are thrice ten thousand upon the much-nourishing earth,
253   immortal guards of Zeus (and) of mortal men
254   who keep guard over justices and ruthless works
255   clothed in mist going to and fro all over the earth.

Who are these "lords" (*basileis*)? The title intrudes only in this and the succeeding paragraph of the justice poem. Elsewhere in the *Works and Days* it was used in the opening sequence to indicate judges who had apparently rendered a dubious decision in a case involving Hesiod and Perses. Are the persons of this context the same, that is, Hesiod's contemporaries? I say the title "intrudes," because the vocative formula reproduces that previously used to Perses (l. 213). The format seems rhetorical, with one addressee replaced by another (cf. also l. 27).

The puzzle of their presence is not mitigated by the nature of the admonition addressed to them: they are invited to "give consideration to this justice." What "justice" is the poet contemplating at the moment when he composes these lines? The phrase seems specific (as also below, in l. 269). But whereas at line 221 it was the injury done to the litigant that had provoked the wrath of Zeus, in the present context the adverse result is a mutual injury inflicted by the lords on each other. Who can these be if not Agamemnon and Achilles? Is Hesiod pointing the moral of the *Iliad*'s story—justice abrogated and wrath pursued alike recoil upon the heads of both parties? Then, turning to the *Odyssey*, he addresses the suitors (who are also "lords") and repeats the warning that in the *Odyssey* they had heard from one of their own number (17.484–487). The warning was very apposite to Hesiod's purpose, for it had voiced in solemn terms a moral polarization between outrage and lawfulness; these were what the gods were watching for. Hesiod, replacing lawfulness (*eunomia*) with justice (*dikē*), in accordance with his poem's subject, produces an alternative to Homer, replacing oversight and outrage with guardianship and ruthlessness (*W.D.* 254 = *Od.* 17.487).

The Goddess

256 Present is maiden justice, of Zeus the offspring born,
257 both renowned and revered of the gods who tenant Olympus,

258 and should one at any time disable her, crookedly castigating,
259 straightway sitting beside father Zeus the Kronian,
260 she sings the nonjust [*a-dikos*] intention of men till it pay back
  [*apotisēi*]

The scene is transferred to Olympus; "justices" in the plural protected on earth are replaced by the goddess "Justice" in the singular, Zeus's virgin daughter. That "she" might assume divine powers has already been indicated (223). She now becomes clothed with a majesty which is unique (257). As a female divinity with special powers, Justice reappears in the speculations of some of the early Greek philosophers. The role seems to have been Hesiod's invention. (In his *Theogony* she appears among Zeus's progeny.) Its introduction marks an alteration in the vision of what justice is: not just a procedure, but also a power. Is the symbol acquiring some absolute significance? Her (or its) opponent becomes not a particular outrage or violence, but the "nonjust" intention in general. The negative is not Homeric. But did Hesiod have Homeric inspiration for "her" role? The immediately preceding paragraph had drawn on the *Odyssey*. In that epic Zeus's virgin daughter was Athene, guide, counsel, and defender of father and son. As they face a conflict apparently so unequal, Odysseus reassures Telemachus: with Zeus and Athene as allies they cannot be overcome (*Od.* 16.260–261). She proceeds to impose control over the confrontation in Odysseus' house, imposing a moral test on the suitors which is to doom them. At Zeus's side, in council of the gods, she had originally protested the way Odysseus and his memory were being treated by his own people. How easy for Hesiod to amalgamate her image with that of justice protesting "the unjust intention of men." Then Hesiod adds "till it pay back" and the "men" become the suitors.

But line 258 complicates the image. How can a divinity be "disabled" by crooked (that is, unjust) verbal means? The inhabitants of Homeric Olympus, often cruel, cowardly, or capricious, are always immune and carefree (with occasional comic exceptions). "Disable" (*blaptō*) is a strong word denoting the effects of being crippled or blinded physically or psychologically (archaic Greek drew no distinction). How can justice be not only attacked but impaired? The use of the verb supplies the clue. Hesiod is still melding memories of the *Iliad* and the *Odyssey* together. In the former, the demon goddess, also named the elder daughter of Zeus, whose power is formidable in Olympus and among men, was Disaster. She is eloquently described as the penalty that will inflict itself till a man "pay back" (*apotisēi*). The act of "disabling" was her hallmark (*Il.* 9.507, 512; 19.94). With the perverse logic of associative imagery, Hesiod remembers Disaster and her role, but has room in his mind for only one female divinity, so disaster becomes that impairment which men by their abrogation of justice inflict upon justice, and they do it by resorting to the same "crooked" pronouncements previously cited in the poem.

Lords and Demos

260 She sings the unjust intention of men till it pay back—
261 even the demos, for the abomination of lords who with dismal intention
262 divert justices aside, pronouncing crookedly.
263 Keeping guard against these (things), O lords, make straight your speech
264 fee-eaters, and let crooked justices be hidden-and-put-away from you.
265 For himself a man prepares evil who prepares evil for another.
266 Evil counseling (is) most evil for the counselor.

The syntax of the previous paragraph allowed it to terminate at line 260. The guilty parties are the nonjust who pay directly for their own error, a reminiscence of the *Odyssey*. The next hexameter appends an alternative subject, the demos, a body which is paying not for its own errors but for those of the lords here reintroduced. Hesiod's memory, or attention, has switched back to the *Iliad,* in order to moralize over what happened to the army (functioning as a demos, above, Chapter 4) as the result of the quarrel between lords. He fastens on them the epithet "fee-eaters," which makes them contemporary (he has used it earlier in the *Works and Days*), but his reminiscence is of the equally unique epithet "people-eater" (with metrical and phonetic equivalence) hurled at Agamemnon by Achilles (*Il.* 1.231). He then adds two aphorisms (265, 266) which delineate Agamemnon's self-imposed predicament: the second of these echoes the terms in which he had ruefully expressed his early regret for his actions (*Il.* 2.375-380).

Zeus and the City

267 The eye of Zeus having seen all and noted all intently,
268 even these (things) should he so wish he is looking at, nor is it hidden from him
269 what kind of justice indeed (is) this (that) a city confines inside;
270 as things are, neither I myself among mankind a just man
271 would remain, nor son of mine either, since (it is) evil for a man
272 just to remain, if larger justice the more unjust shall have;

273 however, these (things) not yet do I anticipate Zeus the counselor to
accomplish.

Zeus himself makes a fresh entrance (as above, in ll. 238 ff.). The
entire *Works and Days* can be viewed as a "Zeus-poem," insofar as it
continually presents the lives and deeds of mankind as taking place
under his superintendence and subject to his superior purpose.[8] If,
however, justice in the present context becomes his protégé, may this
reflect not merely a general preference for a monistic theology, but more
specifically a model furnished by the *Odyssey?* Lines 267–268 constitute
a pair of aphorisms, the subject of the first being Zeus's eye, the verb
converted to the participial construction; of the second, Zeus himself,
the eye and its owner being in loose apposition. They express a sentiment already voiced in a postscript to the story of Prometheus (*W.D.*
105). These variant versions of a moral formula have been drawn from
the common oral reservoir of such. There is an apposite Homeric example. Though Athene was Odysseus' patron and protector, Zeus alone,
overriding Poseidon in his absence, had authority to pronounce the
decision that would free Odysseus from Calypso's isle in order to come
home. Calypso was reluctant, but Hermes reminded her that he, like
her, had to obey orders (*Od.* 5.103–104):

not anyway is it possible that the purpose of Zeus aegis bearing
be either got around or evaded by any other god

Bitterly protesting, she nevertheless gives in, and, responding, repeats
the aphorism back to Hermes, adding:

let Odysseus be gone, since so does Zeus insist and command.

Characteristically the aphorism as placed in epic storage is stated as it
applies to specific agents in the action—in this case Hermes and
Calypso. In Hesiod it emerges converted to a generalization. But Hesiod
himself reverts to particularity; what are "these things" that Zeus might
look at, and what is "this justice" that is "hemmed up" inside a city, and
what city hems it up? The idiom "what . . . indeed" (269), as used
elsewhere in epic, is indignant.[9] Is the justice that Zeus is looking at
something objectionable in his sight? These are puzzles not to be evaded
by paraphrase, and their effect is compounded by the cynical outburst
that follows, which abjures any attempt to be just in an unjust world,
thus denying at least temporarily the whole burden of the poem. Ex-

planations may lie once more in the *Odyssey;* the pieces fall into place if
we suppose that Hesiod continues in the vein of reminiscence of that
epic, which from the first book to the last placed the career and affairs of
Odysseus under the guidance of Zeus's purposes. What "justice" can the
god be indignantly contemplating within a city, if not the tolerance
extended to the suitors by the agora of Ithaca (above, Chapter 5),
which had provoked an elder statesman to exclaim that Odysseus'
paternal protection had been forgotten by his own people; why then
should anyone seek to emulate such virtue in the future? The protest
was angrily repeated in identical terms by Athene on Olympus. Hesiod,
recalling this civic defection and the reproach it earned, places them in
the context of the justice to which the poem is committed: if the
"nonjust" are awarded "greater justice" by being allowed to press their
suit in this way, then the justice of Hesiod is being repudiated: "Not I
nor my son need try to be just." What son does he have in mind? Why
this intrusion of a blood relative not otherwise mentioned? Is the phrase
merely conventional, an equivalent for "my whole family"? Or has it
suggested itself because Hesiod is looking at that father-son team whose
treatment in the *Odyssey* would justifiably provoke such an exclamation
on their behalf?

Hesiod on this view is in this paragraph placing justice in quotation
marks: it represents a virtual decision on the part of a city given by
default concerning a dispute between the household of Odysseus and
the suitors over an issue which had been argued both ways. This is the
justice that is "confined inside" a city. The expression is precise and
peculiar (cf. *Theog.* 751); why confined? Is there also a clue for this in
the *Odyssey?* Dawn was breaking on the last day when Odysseus,
formally acknowledging that Zeus's designs have controlled his career to
this point in the epic, invoked his aid and favor in the crucial hour
(20.98–101):

> now that over dry and over wet
> you have brought me to my land, after afflicting me sore,
> let a voice of someone waking be raised
> inside, and outside let a sign of Zeus appear.

On these words Zeus thunders, while inside a kitchen maid busy preparing the dinner simultaneously is heard cursing the suitors: "May this
feast day be their last! They are making me work so hard!" The hero
hears both the exclamation within and the clap without: "for him it
meant vengeance upon the guilty" (20.121). The time comes for him to

reveal himself to the two retainers. All three go outside; the action is described three times over, as if to mark off the outside from the inside (21.188, 190, 191). Having first listened to Eumaeus invoking the name of Zeus to bring Odysseus back home (21.200), the hero identifies himself with these words: "Inside [*endon*] here am I!" (207). The expression, though graphic, seems illogical; its logic is revealed in the careful instructions now to be given and then carried out preparatory to the execution. Eumaeus is directed to instruct the women (236):

to shut tight the fitted doors of the hall

Orders are given to Philoetius (240–241):

I lay this charge on you: the doors of the court
to lock and bar with bar and bolt and double lock as well with speed

They return within. At Telemachus' command the bow finally passes into the beggar's hands. The point has been reached where the instructions previously given must be carried out. Eumaeus passes word to the women (382):

to bar close the doors of the hall well fitted

and adds (383–384; cf. 237–238):

if any of you hear sounds of screams or blows inside [*endon*]
of men within our enclosures [*herkē*], don't go outside

So the doors are "shut close" (387). Philoetius swiftly and silently steps outside to (389)

bolt the doors of the well-enclosed [*euerkēs*] court

and makes assurance doubly sure by using a ship's cable (391)

to tie a knot upon the doors

The beggar, holding the bow, does what nobody else has managed to do. He bends it and strings it and strums the cord with his fingers. The suitors had not expected this; pallor spreads over their faces. Then Zeus interposes a thunderclap, a manifest sign (413):

and thereat the much-enduring goodly Odysseus rejoiced
for that the son of Kronos of crafty counsel had sent him a portent.

Odysseus had asked for two omens, one inside, one outside. Hearing them both, he assumes the hour of vengeance has struck. When the third is announced, in the form of a second thunderclap from Zeus, all participants in the crisis have been brought inside an enclosure which has been carefully barred and bolted. The execution is to take place within a confined space, as though this were a formality to be complied with, a required ritual. When Odysseus speaks of being "inside" when he is outside, when Eumaeus warns the women to ignore what goes on in "our enclosures," these expressions sever the suitors from contact with the outside world; the last thunderclap completes and seals the separation. In their extremity they would try to make contact with the city and its people and summon help. They had every reason to expect it, since the city had allowed itself to become involved in their cause. When the citizens learn of the execution, their first thought is to massacre those who have carried it out, and Zeus has to intervene again to impose a treaty of peace (perhaps recalled in l. 273 of Hesiod's poem). But for the time being, it is the chief offenders who have to be dealt with. They are formally isolated and enclosed; the space reserved for their execution will be polluted by the act, and will have to be ceremoniously cleansed (22.481–482).

Is this the scenario present before Hesiod's eye when he asserts that Zeus is actually "looking down at *these* things" and "has not failed to notice what kind of justice *this* is, that is being confined inside the city"? Are the demonstrative adjectives pointing to the scene?

Divine Gift but Public Process

274 O Perses, I pray you: cast these (things) up in your thoughts:
275 hearken to (the voice of) justice, and let violence be hidden from your sight;
276 this usage [*nomos*] for mankind the Kronian has severally ordained,
277 for fish and beasts and winged fowl
278 to eat each other, since justice is not present among them;
279 but to mankind he gave justice, which most excellent by far
280a comes-to-be.
280b If (it be) a man's wish to declare-in-assembly (what is) just,
281 discerning (what it is), on him prosperity does wide-viewing Zeus endow;
282 whoever in testimony having wittingly sworn false oath
283 shall deceive, and therein having disabled justice shall immediately be disastered—
284 verily of him the generation after is left more shadowy;
285 of the man of true oath the generation after does wax stronger.

The last paragraph of the poem is marked by a return to the original formula of rhetorical address to Perses and a reassertion of the formal antithesis between justice and its opposite. This time violence (*bia*) replaces outrage (*hubris*), an equivalence which had appeared in the moral formulas of the *Odyssey*. The paragraph, as it winds up the poem, attempts a summation, a completed portrait of what the poem has been trying to say. Justice becomes the symbol of a usage specifically human, as opposed to the behavior of animals. It is still being identified not as a principle, but as a procedure, a legal process, one which is the hallmark of human society and necessary for its existence. So Hesiod implies rather than states, but the inference that this is his meaning is justified by the realization that he is still looking to the *Odyssey* for his model. What could have inspired him to pick on abstention from cannibalism as the decisive trait which marks off man as a species? The choice, not an obvious one, becomes explicable if he is recalling the Cyclops story, in which Odysseus encounters not just other individuals but a whole species who "do not have agoras-of-counsel or formularies," who will prove to be "outrageous and savage nor just," and whose representative is "not well knowing justices or formularies" (Chapter 10). The Cyclops is precivilized, precommunal, a "monster" who commits violence upon the men who visit him by eating them.[10] For this inhuman crime he was destined to be punished by Zeus himself. Odysseus in the last words he hurls at him declares that this is so. Later in the story, when Odysseus needs inner support to sustain his patience in the long ordeal awaiting him in his own house, he finds it in a recollection of how he had faced down the Cyclops (20. 19–20).

Cannibalism is murder carried to its ultimate. The justice among men which prevents it is not imagined as a human device, but as a gift conferred by Zeus. Yet when it comes down to it, what is this divine gift if not the procedure that men follow in the agora in resolving disputes (280–285)? The scenario reverts to the *Iliad*, with Hesiod pronouncing a judgmental addition to the story. The test of justice comes in what is spoken aloud in assembly; Zeus rewards the word justly spoken. The test involves oaths publicly pronounced in the presence of witnesses: asseverations and promises that are not intended to deceive. To swear falsely is not only to cripple the procedures of justice, but also to incur the sanction imposed by the demon of disaster. That sanction, whether or not it is effective upon the culprit, will blast his descendants. So it is affirmed in a concluding aphorism. The oath that was the concomitant of justice and of justice perverted, at the beginning of the poem, is still in the same company at the end.[11]

A text of seventy-three hexameters has been scrutinized for peculiarities of expression and idiom which a literate reader is disposed to gloss over. These, being uncovered, have tended to group themselves in paragraphs offering a series of shifting perspectives upon the subject of justice. The whole effect has been traced to a persistent cause, namely, a method of composition which proceeds by extracting and remolding a series of passages from the *Iliad* and the *Odyssey* relevant directly or indirectly to the subject. How strong are these Homeric connections, how firmly demonstrated? Sometimes they are philologically "tight," in that specific verbal expressions can be matched closely. Previous scholarship has acknowledged this in at least three instances (221 and 224, 230–237, 252–255); the list is extendable. In many cases the connection is more tenuous, dependent upon what appears to be a recollection of general Homeric contexts or an associative melding of remembered personalities and images, which fall short of philological proof. It is in the constancy of presence of such a variety of Homeric echoes, some strong, some weak, that an overall impression of what Hesiod is doing becomes irresistible. This is not a chain dependent for its strength upon the weakest link, but a compound of ingredients in some of which the flavor present is strong, in others weak; but it is always the same flavor.

The Priority of Homer

Such a compositional procedure would require that Homer (in whatever sense the name is used) be chronologically the prior poet. Scholars have occasionally supposed otherwise,[12] at least so far as concerns the Homeric text we now have, so that *Iliad* 16.387–8 (in cloudburst context) would be a Hesiodic "interpolation," or that Hesiod's utopian passages were imitated by the poet of the *Odyssey*. A comparison of the logic of Homer's composition with Hesiod's logic, or lack of logic, makes this seem very unlikely. For example, In Homer's cloudburst example, catastrophe due to storm is logically ascribed to the sky god. Why did he send it? To judge from the communal effects, the offense committed must have been communal, of which a typical example is misuse of legal process, involving misuse of the formularies, which are under the god's protection. When the protesting litigant is thrown out of the agora, the listening audience might well infer that he then appealed to Zeus for remedy, who accordingly sends the storm in answer, though the story does not say so. The whole incident is a typical piece of early Hellenic nomos placed in storage within the narrative and with its own narrative logic. In Hesiod's adaptation, this is disrupted. The crooked judgments are placed in line 221, their appearance in this place being triggered by their previous appearance (219), also drawn from Homer, but from a disparate context. The expulsion of the litigant is deferred till line 224, disconnected from its companion hexameter by two intervening lines drawn from a third Homeric context equally disparate. Or take the two utopian passages (225–237). Phaeacia might be an ideal state, but the royal garden was a real garden, growing a variety of fruit trees carefully planted and assisted by an unusually favorable climate; the ideal king to whom Penelope is compared was ideal because his government was effective, that is, fair and just enough to command the support of the citizenry, an usually vigorous people who might otherwise have given trouble. Under such administration agriculture and fisheries, the two industries vital to the food supply of a maritime polis, flourish. In Hesiod's amalgamated version, communities enjoying specific material conditions, which though fortunate are the result of good management, are translated into idealized persons whose location is nowhere, whose society resembles no other society on earth, and whose material conditions are miraculous and fantastic. As for the ten thousand guardian spirits (252–255), their Homeric original has become almost unrecognizable through the distortions imposed upon it. The cursing stranger had aroused superstitious fears: such apparitions with strange dress and speech are always turning up in the maritime cities; you have to be careful of them; they may be on the lookout for violations of public order (*eunomia*); better treat this one civilly. Hesiod's version fractures the effect of this passage into two parts. First, there is the Homeric image of "some god present in visitation from heaven" (*Od.* 17.484); this is recollected as "immortals present and near," who are appended to reinforce a warning addressed to the "lords" of the *Iliad* who are injuring each other. Then the poet starts again: he picks up the gods disguised as strangers, and transforms them into an army of ten thousand spirits, derived from his own previous description of a golden age of human beings now defunct (*W.D.* 121–125).[13] These are assigned the general role of roaming the earth instead of the specific one of visiting various Greek cities on circuit; Homeric naturalism and coherence have been lost in the course of an effort to replace narrative logic by a general concept, the terms of which become disconnected and fanciful.[14] The poem is pervaded by similar disparities; the reasonable conclusion is that Hesiod is using Homer and not vice versa.

Process not Principle

I have touched on the possibility that Hesiod, though an oral stylist, was also a reader and writer. The possibility has become a probability to be explored in the next chapter. However, the justice which Hesiod is attempting to rationalize out of Homer is still justice or justices as practiced in a preliterate society. It or they are something which is spoken aloud, pronounced, proclaimed, declared, or else listened to, heard and remembered. Twice Perses is adjured to hearken to justice as to a voice: the idiom is not a metaphor for mere obedience. As a person, she can scream or sing (220, 260), is the recipient of verbal abuse (258), and is disabled by oral testimony which is false (283–284). This implies that the procedure of which *dikē* is a symbol is conducted by oral exchange. Justices are declared-in-agora (280); if they are perverted, this is because lords pronounce them crookedly, so that Hesiod has to adjure the speakers to straighten their utterance (262–263). The constant imputation of crookedness more probably refers to crookedness of speech rather than, as some would have it, unfair manipulation of boundary lines in property disputes.[15] When justice is "apportioned" or "distributed" (224), while this might indicate a distribution of property through arbitration, it is more likely to reflect the distribution of words as they are pronounced in the judgment which makes the apportionment. The Homeric hero can not only "divide his thought this way and that" but can "apportion his words."[16]

The oral rule is not invariable: justice running a race or hemmed in inside a city or possessed as a quantity or as a gift given to mankind is not obviously spoken speech, though when justices are "given straight" to strangers, these could refer to oral guarantees of security like those pronounced to Odysseus, for example, in Phaeacia.

Considered as procedure, oral justice is not a symbol of punishment as such, but of redress, readjustment, repayment—verbally negotiated. The verb *apotinō* (260) so signifies. The concomitant is a condition of peace and of peaceful relations between men. This "moral" preference is perceptible elsewhere in Hesiod's poetry; it is focused in the formal antithesis he draws between *dikē* and either *hubris* or *bia*. The sense of *dikē* as mere punishment or vengeance may have crystallized in the period when legalities were becoming literate (below Chapter 16). It is not Homeric. It may be thought that when Hesiod assigns Zeus as agent of the misfortunes suffered by the unjust (239 ff.), he in effect places him in the role of inflicting "justice" as a punishment. But what he says of justice in this context is that Zeus "gives the signal for it" (*tekmairetai*) and then proceeds to impose the misfortunes. The verb is often rendered as though justice were something "ordained" by Zeus and therefore equivalent to punishment. What the god does is rather to give the appropriate "marks" or portents announcing or warning that the procedure of redress is going to be carried out. This accords with the Homeric use of the verb.

I argued in Chapters 2 and 3 that from a thematic standpoint an oral culture is incapable of conceptualizing justice apart from its pragmatic application in day-to-day procedure. In oral thought it remains a method, not a principle. Most of what Hesiod has to say about it does not violate this rule. Yet when he personifies "her" as a goddess, has he not embarked on a route that will lead to the separation of justice as idea from the activity which achieves it? Undoubtedly he has, yet how shadowy may be his approach to such a mental destination is shown in the alternative image he proposes of justice as a gift donated by Zeus. This is equally an attempt to objectify the term as an "entity" (to use post-Platonic language), but one which is logically irreconcilable with his previous image of personification.[17] We would have to say that Hesiod's "Justice," so far as it takes on the shape of a concept, is perceived not in clear vision but as in a glass darkly.

12
The Spoken and the Written Word

If Greek literature be accepted as a phenomenon whose history is initiated by Homer and Hesiod, the poem on justice offers three peculiarities which call for explanation. First, why the obsessive presence in the verse of one repeated word, this being the name not of a man or woman, but what we would call an abstraction? It is of course a Homeric word, and Homer's vocabulary employs many so-called abstractions—some, like contention and feud, honor and redress, occurring casually as the narrative mentions them, others encapsulated in aphorisms scattered through the story. But there is no precedent in Homer for such a protracted concentration of attention, such earnest didacticism inspired by and addressed to a single subject. Is the poem explicable as a kind of encomium or hymn composed in conformity with the oral rules but designed for recitation at a symposium rather than for public performance? This is possible—the format might so suggest—but the parallels that could be cited from early lyric, even when didactic, are in a different and lighter vein altogether.[1] Second, if we accept a desire on the author's part to compose such an encomium, why does he feel compelled to resort to Homer in order to put it together rather than freely compose his own thoughts on the subject? And third, why if he chooses to go to Homer for inspiration, cannot he make a better job of what he draws from his source? Why the discontinuity, the confusion of images, the disconnection of syntax, the failure to maintain a conceptual consistency of thought?[2]

Discontinuity

Within the first twelve lines of the poem: (1) Perses is challenged to hearken to the voice of justice and reject her opposite; (2) he is advised as a traveler to use an evasive route to achieve what is just, which seems to undercut the effect of the challenge; (3) Perses the traveler is replaced by justice herself as runner; (4) justice as runner is replaced by oath as runner; (5) justice is reintroduced as a girl in distress; (6) the girl is replaced by judges giving corrupt "justices"; (7) they are as abruptly replaced by justice, still a girl, but now traveling to town in disguise, and then being thrown out. The next two paragraphs have interior coherence. The argument is controlled by a simple antithesis that is easily understandable. The poet then breaks off to address certain "lords" (248–255), apparently threatening them with two statements to the effect that (1) heaven takes notice of "crooked justices" and (2) the earth is populated by an invisible army of spirits appointed to protect "justices." The scene is then transferred to Olympus (256–264), where a personal justice is discovered complaining to Zeus that men are unjust, apparently to get him to intervene; the guardian spirits previously mentioned are ignored. It becomes obscure who precisely is at fault: is it "mankind," or "the *dēmos*," or "the lords"? These last bear the brunt, for they are sternly admonished to put away "crooked justices." To this admonition are then appended (265–266) two self-contained one-line aphorisms. Two more are used to enclose a paragraph (267–273) which opens by piously affirming the omniscience of Zeus, who is gazing down on a "justice" inside some city unspecified. This moral confidence is no sooner proclaimed than it is undercut: what is the use of being just when the unjust receive greater justice? To this the concluding maxim "heaven forbid" is hastily appended. Belatedly renewing his address to Perses (274–285), the poet repeats the challenge to hear justice's voice, supporting it by a statement that converts her into a valuable gift from Zeus, and concluding with a description of justice as something uttered or disabled in the assembly.

Hesiod may be using Homer, but he does not command the Homeric coherence of style. What has happened to the narrative flow, the descriptive logic, the consistency of character drawing, the smooth transitions, the majestic ease of movement? The perfection of these qualities must have been acquired through some centuries of oral trial and error. We observe in Homer an enclave of contrived language, a technique of sophisticated speech, existing within the vernacular, which the memories of bards have mastered and made into a firm tradition. The Hesiodic style, for all its use of the oral metrical formulas, betrays that something has happened to the tradition: some kind of break has occurred. What could have occasioned it?

Rules of Acoustic Composition

The beginnings of an answer can be sought by reviewing the psychological conditions which the oral style was designed to satisfy, as these have been theoretically explored above (Chapter 3). A preliterate culture uses epic not only for entertainment but as a storage mechanism which conserves the ethos and nomos of the culture. Since conservation can occur only in the individual memories of human beings, the oral style puts a heavy premium upon those verbal devices which encourage memorization. Chief among these, aside from meter and music, is the monopoly exercised by narrative over the content of what is preserved. When, therefore, epic devotes itself to "the great deeds of heroes," it does so not merely to satisfy the romantic imagination, but to assist the primary function of repeating and recommending the mores of contemporary society.

The norms of the culture are therefore taught by indirection. Didactic statements of what the nomos and ethos require are disguised —from a literate standpoint—by being illustrated in the actions performed by agents, whether these are persons, as is usually the case, or things described as behaving like persons. The verbs of which such agents are either subjects or objects describe specific actions or situations or states as these occur in given temporal moments or temporal durations, not as they might represent general or permanent properties or states.

This kind of oral syntax is a response to psychological pressure— the need to assist retention of lengthy portions of discourse in the memory. What might happen, what could happen, if such pressure were removed? Would this pressure not be removed, has it not in fact been removed, in all societies of full literacy? Some memorization of poetry and prose of course continues, dependent on personal proclivity or sometimes serving professional advantage. But it remains sporadic, nothing like that total communal commitment to which the composer working in an oral culture has to respond.

Rules of Visual Composition

Given this theoretic analysis of preliterate storage, what would be appropriate theory to apply to the conditions of literate storage? The answer can be related to the Greek situation as it became crystallized after the written word had fully supplanted the oral for storage purposes, at whatever date that may be supposed to have occurred. A spoken language has become alphabetized, thus assuming the status of an artifact which is visible as well as retaining the status of a sound system which is heard. The spoken word continues to prevail quantitatively by an enormous margin; but it increasingly ceases to prevail in storage language: the document and its usage invade the entire culture pattern, and take over that area of communication subject to preservation. The document can be memorized but it need not be; it imposes no penalty for forgetting. It is theoretically a piece of speech placed in deep freeze, to be used and reused at pleasure. The special mnemonic pressures of the preliterate millennia are no longer operative. Automatically, the necessity to narrativize important statements is removed; the report on nomos and ethos need no longer depend on description of agents acting or behaving in response to other agents. It becomes possible to indulge in statements for the record, the subjects and objects of which are wholly nonpersonal. Of equal significance, the verbs connecting them can be ones which indicate not actions or situations which take place in time but relationships connected by a timeless logic. In particular, the verb "to be," used as a copula for this purpose, is likely to come into its own. Agents as hitherto employed in song had to be specific, being the names of this or that person or personification; the acts, happenings, or situations in which they were continually involved had to be equally specific: universals stated as subjects or predicates were avoided.

Documented discourse, in contrast, no longer needs to be phrased in specifics. It may be, of course, but it can tolerate in increasing quantity something that orally preserved speech cannot, namely, expressions which (1) state as "fact" a universal rather than a particular and (2) state it as a principle rather than as an event—that is, state that something is always so and so, rather than that something was done or occurred or was in place.

The Completed Syntax of Abstraction

In Platonism, these linguistic objectives have been achieved. They are woven into the syntax of argument, appearing there casually, without exciting attention from a literate readership which is used to using them in its own discourse. Here, for example, is how the term "justice," the topic created by Hesiod, makes its first appearance in the Platonic text which deals with it thematically, namely, the *Republic* (331cl ff.):

> What you say, Cephalus, is to the point. Now take precisely this (thing), namely, justice [*dikaiosunē*]: are we to say that it is truthfulness, absolutely speaking, and giving back anything one has taken from somebody else; or are these very (things) to be done sometimes justly, at other times unjustly?

The syntax which identifies justice as truthfulness meets the tripartite requirement: the subject is completely nonpersonal; it receives a predicate equally so; the linking verb becomes the copula; an infinitive of action is, however, added as a second predicate. In the alternative that is then posed, the verb "to be" is used to connect a neuter pronoun with a second predicate infinitive. Such characteristics as these of Plato's argumentative text we normally take for granted.

In similar fashion, when Euthyphro, in the dialogue of that name, is confronted with "piety" as the proposed theme of the argument, the presentation is as follows (*Euthyph.* 5c–d):

> So now, I implore, tell me that which you insisted just now you thoroughly knew: what kind (of thing) do you say the pious is, and the impious, in the case of manslaughter and so on; surely the holy in all action is identical itself with itself; whereas the unholy is completely the opposite of the holy, something always resembling itself, having one specific shape (*idea*) completely in accordance with unholiness, whatever the unholy turns out to be.

This particular example is more professionally stated, with profuse use of the neuter singular to express abstraction. It has the advantage of including an early instance of the word *shape* used in a philosophical context, and accepted as a technical term in developed Platonism. One cannot altogether ignore the possibility that its present reference is to shape as embodied in written language (below, Chapter 19). Be that as it may (and the problem of its usage involves a variant reading in the text), the passage makes plain the kind of syntax now available and necessary for didactic argument and the particular reliance of Socratic method upon this syntax: the subjects have to be impersonals, the verbs must take copulative form, and the predicates have to be impersonals.

It is convenient to identify Plato as the discoverer of the necessity of this syntax in its completed form—and therefore as the writer who completed the process of linguistic emancipation from the syntax of oral storage—but for good measure it is possible to cite similar symptoms from the text of an older author who was perhaps completing his work about the time when Plato began to write. Thucydides is a historian whose narrative intention does not of itself require a break with the genius of oral syntax. But the speeches he intersperses in the narrative are largely analytic, and employ an argumentative style which is notoriously abstract, so far as subjects and objects are concerned. Yet it is significant that the syntax customarily falls short of completing that degree of abstraction which requires subject, copula, and predicate conjoined in a totally theoretic statement, and that statements which approximate to this standard are comparatively rare. King Archelaus, for example, counseling the Spartans to use caution, uses the following expressions (Thuc. 1.83.1–2):

> No one need think that for men in numbers to hesitate to attack a single city is unmanliness (*anandria*). There are for our opponents also allies now contributing money; and war is not (a matter) of arms so much as finance, which makes arms effective.

The first clause uses the copula and a nonpersonal predicate to define the subject, which, however, describes a specific situation; the third uses the copula to connect two similar specifics. Or again, Diodotus, enjoining a similar caution upon the Athenian assembly, says (Thuc. 3.42.1–2):

> I hold that there are two (things) most opposed to good counsel, haste and passion; of which the one usually occurs in company with want of understanding, and the other with lack of education and limitation of intelligence.

The first clause meets all three requirements (a comparatively rare phenomenon in Thucydides); the second describes two events whose subjects are nonpersonal.

I have avoided to this point the temptation merely to pinpoint abstract nouns as in themselves sufficient index of a theoretic syntax, and have also avoided identifying such nouns as in themselves symbolic of "concepts." It should be emphasized that complete "conceptuality," if this be the appropriate word for describing this nonnarrativized syntax, depends not on single words treated as phenomena per se, but on their being placed in a given relationship to one another, in statements which employ either a copula or an equivalent to connect them. The growth of abstractionism and conceptualism in the Greek tongue is not traceable by a mere resort to lexicons, indexes, and glossaries,[3] common as this practice has become. Single words classifiable as "abstract," like *justice* or *contention* or *war* or *peace,* can be as easily personified as not. What is in question is the ability of the human mind to create and manipulate theoretic statements as opposed to particular ones, to replace a performative syntax with a logical one.

The Ear and the Eye

The genesis and refinement of a philosophical vocabulary would normally be viewed as a phenomenon of mind alone: its causation would be sought in the energies of the human intellect. Could it be really true that a mere physical change in the conditions of storage was responsible, that the mere documentation of language encouraged a basic shift in mental habits? It might be difficult to prove positively that the use of writing, now universal in literate societies, has a direct connection with the employment of abstract thought,[4] since obviously such thought is now expressible orally in discussion. But it is not difficult to show negatively that such thought does not find a welcome in orally preserved speech. What was the new positive factor added to the process of cognition of speech when speech was written down? The factor was physical. Words which from time immemorial had subsisted as sounds in the air, subject only to acoustic laws, became also shapes inscribed on surfaces, and therefore also subject to laws appropriate to vision. All laws of cognition are set by the brain, but the brain employs various senses to attain cognition. Under preliterate conditions cognition of language—of what is being said—depends on the ear. Its manufacture depends on the tongue. In literacy, the laws (or habits) of vision are used to supplement those of the ear, both in cognition and creation. The significant effects of this change register themselves in the management of language as it is used for storage purposes—language that has a knowledge content, be it legal, literary, philosophical, religious, or technical, usable for the business of living in the culture concerned.

But vision, unemployable for linguistic purposes in preliterate society, still had a storage function to perform, supplying the memory with the shapes of artifacts used and reused by the culture—artifacts which by repeating themselves in the course of successive manufacture supplied continuity and structure to behavior also.[5] This had been true in particular of the architecture, sacred and secular, public and private, which prescribed itself for any given community. It might not amount to much, but the contours of streets, meeting places, courtyards, doorways, rooms, roofs, and hearths, no less than the formal shapes of temples and senate houses, auditoria (in the open air) and racecourses, harbors and docks (where they existed), had the effect in the early city-states of guiding behavior as they were used, that is, perceived. The way of life, the nomos and ethos of society, aside from being recorded and preserved in contrived speech, embodied itself in structures seen by the eye, which in this way could serve to supplement the ear as an instrument of storage.

As storage speech became an artifact, the eye if it chose could exercise upon it that kind of architectural expectation to which it had long become accustomed. Language as it presented itself to be read became a physical material amenable to an arrangement which was structural—or "geometric," if that term is preferred. This meant rearrangement, for whereas the previous need for oral memorization had favored sequences governed by the laws of sound, it was now possible to supplement these by dispositions suggested by the laws of shapes. This is a theoretically bald way of stating a process which was pychologically subtle and lay below the level of conscious purpose. The eye joined partnership with the ear, as it has ever since, but it did not replace it.

Selection of Names

The lifting of the mnemonic requirement made the choice of non-agents as subjects theoretically easier. But what sense or what instinct would actively engage itself to seize this opportunity, if not the architectural and selective eye? In orally preserved storage, the agents commonly are identifiable by their personal names. The new possibility is open of using names of nonpersons—mere "nouns," as we say. The nouns on which attention will be focused—by a composer of didactic temperament—will be those that are names particularly relevant to nomos and ethos; they will be names of behavior.[6] These are scattered incidentally through the narrative; they tend to show their presence particularly in aphorisms and moral formulas. The architectural eye can proceed to rove over the script now presented, selecting and collecting the names of nonagents relevant to didactic purpose, in order to make them the subjects of new "stories" telling about nomos and ethos.

The composer has to start somewhere, and the only place to start from is epic storage, now rendered visible. This is the only material available and suitable for such manipulation. His first "architectural" collection of such names will include with them the kind of actions or events or situations in which they occur in mythos. His eye will assemble what has been said about a given name; the series so assembled will reflect the activist contexts in which it has previously occurred.

The Poet as Proto-Literate

So much for theory, which if deemed acceptable would go far to explain those peculiarities of Hesiod's poetry already noted. They can be viewed as symptoms of a compositional process which is proto-literate, one which has begun to feel release from narrative pressure, and therefore free, or freer, to select impersonals as subjects for discourse; but also one which has not yet mastered the new kind of syntactical connection which would be necessary to give such discourse its own continuity: the laws of narrative sequence are being discarded, in part at least, but the laws of logical sequence have not yet been discovered. The poet's technique falls into place when it is seen as initiating a transition from the oral to the written word.

The entire work of which the poem on justice forms a part never undertakes to tell a single compendious narrative, but attempts a series of observations attached to such topics as contention and feud, work, wealth, family, war and peace, vice and virtue, counsel, respect. These identify themselves as specific names used and reused in the verse. More generally, activities are described such as farming, trading, navigating, house building, and the like, all these being supported by aphorisms which attach themselves to the topics where they seem pertinent. The inspiration for many of the topics and aphorisms can be discerned in Homeric contexts; others have drawn upon the oral reservoir at large, which in addition to epic included some specialist or craft poetry, such as calendars. The overall effect is miscellaneous: the smooth associative mechanisms of oral poetry do not seem to be at work. More plausibly, this represents the work of the collecting eye rather than the associative ear.

As noted in Chapter 1, the cultural and stylistic vocabulary which normally imposes itself upon us when we seek to understand oral poetry requires us to employ literate metaphor for a nonliterate process. Terms like "theme," "structure," "pattern," "program," and even "composition" itself, imply that language is being arranged visually rather than acoustically, and even touched and handled on the page, as though we were looking at contours rather than hearing echoes and assonances and dissonances. With Hesiod, the literate metaphors begin to fit: the era of true "composition" in our sense has begun, however tentative the beginning.

The Names of Justice[7]

Within the miscellany, the poem on justice stands out as the single most coherent example of such compositional effort centered on a single name. Its energy of concentration makes it an illustration, as complete as can be gained, of how the laws of proto-literate composition work, when undertaken in the service of a didactic purpose, and of the means which are used. Seeking to construct a summary statement, compendious of its kind, of what the nomos and ethos of his society "really are," what the rules may be which regulate proper behavior in the early city-state, Hesiod chooses the name *dikē* and attempts to write a poem about it-or-her. His selection is not arbitrary or personal to himself; it continues the didactic function of storage epic, but now at a more explicit level rendered possible by the existence of such epic in visible form. Nomos and ethos are not something he is free to invent. The only place he can go for suitable materials is that enclave of orally contrived language in which they are already present. So he instinctively chooses a "name" which is thematic to both epics. He "remembers" it as any member of the oral community would, by the way it comes up in the stories as they are told—two great stories, the master-stories of the culture. The *Iliad* narrated how a "justice" was broken and restored, and the proper manner and method of doing this; the *Odyssey*, how the outrageous were the opposite of the just, and how the two types behaved in given situations. Hesiod weaves together the two justices of the *Iliad* and *Odyssey* to compose his own story of justice. He does it by making *dikē* and *hubris*, instead of Agamemnon and Achilles and Odysseus, the subjects and objects of his discourse. But whereas it would be an easy matter for oral memory to recollect what Agamemnon or Achilles did or what happened to them—for they were the overt agents or "characters" of the story, and their names were reiterated—the names of *dikē* and *hubris* and related terms were buried deep in the oral matrix. To rely on oral memory not only to recollect but to collect what happened to them would be beyond existing capacity. But place the language of the story visibly before the eye, so that the flow is arrestible and the words become fixed shapes, and the process of selection and collection can begin.

Homer Alphabetized

The metrical (as distinct from the moral) formulas employed in Hesiod's verse have encouraged some critics to include it in the general category of oral poetry as defined by Parry, Lord, and their followers. It is also commonly held that Hesiod was a writer, though this need only mean that he wrote down what had previously been composed "Homerically" in his head. My thesis goes further, and argues that what he did depended not merely on his ability to write but on his ability to read, and that a vital part of his own reading, addressed though it was to his own text as he put it together, was addressed also to a text of Homer. We cannot be sure that this was the complete text of both epics as we have it now. But his procedure compels the conclusion that either at the time when he began his career as a bard—a career of which he was self-consciously proud—or at some prior period the larger portion of the *Iliad* and the *Odyssey* had become alphabetized. Such papyri (or else parchments, but the expense would be severe)[8] were in circulation, however limited, and Hesiod had access to them. A great moving river of sound had been arrested and, as it were, frozen.

We normally speak of these oral compositions as being committed to writing at some date. This way of putting it describes an operation which under modern conditions occurs ten thousand times an hour all over the literate world. The original act was rather different; its occurrence was something like a thunder clap in European history, which our bias of familiarity has converted into the rustle of papers on a desk. It constituted a cultural intrusion which had dynamic and, some would say, destructive effects. It certainly began to undermine an oral way of life and oral modes of thought. This is an extreme way of putting it, intended to dramatize a fact about ourselves. We as literates, inheritors of twenty-five hundred years of experience with the written word, are removed by a great distance from the conditions under which it first entered Greece, and some effort of the imagination is required to comprehend what these were, how they affected the manner in which the event took place, and what the consequences have been in the long term. It is possible to argue that the alphabetization of Homer set in motion a process of erosion of "orality,"[9] extending over centuries of the European experience, at the end of which our modern culture has been left unevenly divided between oral and literate modes of expression, experience, and living.

Liguistic Sound and Verbal Shape

Hesiod's image of justice, if that is the best word to use, is the fruit of an uneven partnership between ear and eye, memory and vision. The structure of the poem is at times evidently acoustic. It is hard to pinpoint the exact place where association of sounds yields to architecture of shape. *Dikē* itself is both a sound and a shape: the sound pounds its way through the poem even as the shape duplicates itself in grouped symmetries. Occasionally sound prevails to the point of turning the Greek into a pun, as in lines 270-272 (*dikaios . . . dikaion . . . dikēn . . . adikōteros*) or line 243 (*limos, loimos, laoi*). The overall structure is oral, to the extent that it follows a rhetorical schematization, in which there is a first movement (213–247) introduced by the formula "O Perses, I pray you," a second (248–273) introduced by "O lords, I pray you," and a third introduced by repeating the first formula, in the manner of ring compositions. The shift to a new theme when the poem has concluded is marked by a shift in formula: "To you I speak, most foolish Perses" (286). Within and between paragraphs echo and assonance play their parts. Rewards of the just and misfortunes of the outrageous are linked together by pairing of equivalent sounds furnished by introductory correlatives: "they who . . . for them: they who . . . for them" (225–227 and 238–239); by Zeus, who "betokens war" and "betokens justice" (229, 239); by "given works" and "given to works" (231, 238). These linkages are consistent with the fact that both these paragraphs, as noted above, move forward with an easier fluency. The verse seems to be obeying an oral control not elsewhere perceptible in the poem to the same degree. The second paragraph in its conclusion mentions the "considerations" of Zeus, a noun which seems to have assisted the transition to an appeal to lords to "consider deeply" and then to an image of immortals who "consider all" (245, 248, 250). The "false oath" of line 282 is promptly echoed in the "true oath" of line 285; the "generation" of the lost is echoed in the "generation" of the saved (284–285).

The ear thus accompanies and guides the eye in the task of composition. The ear's prevailing power is perhaps most evident in the poet's memory of the plots of the two epics taken as wholes, for it is these that have led him to recognize, however obscurely, the themes, or rather roles, of justice and of just men as these are variously played out in the course of the mythoi. He did not need a careful reading of papyri to lead him to these as his subject. They were supplied to the consciousness of his culture by the epics themselves as they were recited and recollected.

Nevertheless, in the actual assemblage of materials to form a poem, one is tempted to say that the eye has prevailed over the ear, so far as transitions between paragraphs are disjunct and abrupt, as though they were pieces picked up out of diverse contexts into which they orally fitted and placed in a new series where the arrangement depended upon the visual repetition of the same verbal shape, regardless of "fit."

A Field of Meaning

So we return to a view of that "freedom," linguistic or verbal, which Hesiod gained as a reader, a proto-literate, who did not have to rely exclusively on oral memory and manipulation of acoustic associations as methods of placing statements in linked sequences. What did he achieve, and what were the limits of his achievement? He took the initial step of separating out nomos and ethos from their narrative container by identifying a key "name," or two such, those of "justice" and the "just person," and assembling examples of their occurrence as they lay before him in the text. In Homer, justice is an impersonal, singular or plural, symbolizing legal procedure or procedures, or (in association with the just person and just thing) a pattern of behavior which (in the *Odyssey*) is generous and peaceful. Hesiod cannot, in assembling the story of the symbol, bring himself to treat it consistently as an impersonal. Sometimes that is what it is in his verse, either singular or plural. But just as often the "it" becomes a "she": an agent functioning as the subject or object of action, in the remembered idiom of narrative. Whether as impersonal or as a woman, "it" or "she" is called upon to play opposed roles: justices are preserved but also perverted; justice is powerful but also powerless.

When one word is used in so many diverse situations, it is tempting to treat the problem as an example of a limitation in the Greek vocabulary, which has to be got around by supplying variant translations to suit context—as though this were an extravagant instance of homonymy, as when the word "suit" can refer to a legal petition or a coat and trousers, or a "sentence" can signify a grammatical unit or a judicial penalty. Thus the Loeb version of Hesiod renders *dikē* in the singular variously as "right," as "justice," and as "punishment"; in the plural, as "judgments." The Penguin version allows itself a larger indulgence, using for the singular "right," "justice," "verdict," "punishment," and "law"; the plural becomes "judgments" and "law-suits," or else is omitted through paraphrase; the adjectives *dikaios* and *adikos* are taken to signify "an honest man," "a just man," and "a felon."

Command of such flexibility may be thought commendable; the style of translation has been "improved." By adjusting translation to the variety of contexts in which the word is placed, the disjunction between the hexameters is smoothed out. But the intention of the poet and the difficulty he has in achieving it are masked by this procedure. What in effect he is trying to do is to define a "field of meaning"; he is not playing with a concept which has been delimited and hardened by the resources of literate definition. To substitute a variety of terms for the single one which is obsessing him is in effect to destroy his topic, to conceal the act of integration which he is performing upon those epic situations from which he is extracting the new "subject" of discourse. In oral speech, the sound is the sign of the meaning. If a sound keeps repeating itself like a refrain, the effect is most faithfully rendered in another tongue if the refrain is imitated. The word "right," its plural, "rights," and its adjectives "rightful," "righteous," and "unrighteous" could in English achieve something of this effect. The variety of applications to which the word is subject goes back into English preliterate usage. Given the definite article, "the right" symbolizes an abstract principle, also indicated in the antithesis "right" versus "wrong." But pluralize it, and we get the "rights" and "wrongs" of a situation, which are more specific, as also is "the divine right of kings," identifying a source of authority whick kings alone control. Again in the plural, to speak of "my rights" is to identify claims against individuals or communities as if these were pieces of property; the "rights" of a legal case symbolize the claims as argued and given verbal form. As adjective, "right" can indicate either correctness—"this is the right road to take"— or propriety—"this is the right thing to say under the circumstances"; as an adverb, the word describes movement in a straight direction—"keep right on going"; and, of course, it designates the "right hand" from the left, possibly a basic signification.

The Greek *dikē* and its correlatives perform a similar diversity of symbolic functions, which Hesiod is endeavoring to assemble into his "field of meaning."[10] The field had to be prepared for the later growth of a conceptual tree, to the definition and description of which Plato was to devote his most famous treatise. The name of the tree became *dik-*

aiosunē, a concept still translatable as either "justice" or "righteousness."

Yet the poet's intention was surely subject to frustration. The composition which had put these sequences together might be an act of integration, but only in embryo, for the discontinuity is extreme. Neither on the one hand is there narrative coherence in which characters behave consistently, nor on the other logical coherence in which the terms of an argumentative discourse retain fixed meanings. The reason is that although Hesiod is on his way to constructing a first term of a Platonic propositional syntax, a second and a third are missing altogether. We are not given an impersonal predicate by which justice can be explained, and we are never told that justice "is" something or other, but always what she or it is doing or being done to, or else what the just person is doing or refrains from doing. Hesiod as he is proto-literate is alos proto-conceptual. Justice as principle precisely and exhaustively defined apart from its application in given instances has not yet made her entrance on the stage of the Greek experience; she is in the anteroom, awaiting the assistance of a fuller literacy than is at present available.

13

The Early History of the
Verb "to Be"

❁

The Platonic question Is justice truth? used to initiate the argument of the *Republic,* has a beguiling simplicity, concealing the fact that in order to use this kind of language certain logical (I prefer to say syntactical) requirements have to be met. Not only must both subject and predicate be completely stripped of personality and specificity, but the verb to be used to connect them must be invested with the function of denoting not an act, or an event, but a relationship which is both logical and static, or, as Plato would say, "immovable." We have seen indications that neither the poetry of Homer nor that of Hesiod was capable of enunciating such a statement in its "Platonic" form, and this not just because it was poetry, but because it was oral poetry composed to meet the syntactical requirements of memorized speech. Hesiod can say what justice does, what is done to it, but not what it is. The effort to topicalize has succeeded; so far so good. But the movement toward definition has only just begun. Those who would agree that this may be true of the justice poem might be inclined to argue that surely the Greek tongue—even Hesiod's Greek—can say what a thing "is" if it wants to; it is only that *dikē*—a specially difficult case—does not happen to get this kind of treatment. They would argue that the Platonic model so far quoted is a particularly stringent example of the use of the verb

233

"to be," not typical of the copula as routinely employed in attaching a specific subject to a generic predicate: "the house is big"; "that horse is lame"; "the Greeks are our enemies." Are not such statements the commonplaces of language? Platonism, to be sure, expended considerable energy in *eliciting* their logical structure. But it is one thing to give Plato credit for rationalizing the functions of the verb "to be," as a verb which identifies or denies identity or classifies or invests with absolute existence; it will seem quite another if I suggest that before Plato the Greek tongue had to "learn" how to make such statements: that oral language found it very difficult to make them—perhaps impossible, depending on one's judgment of idiom—and that they were only entering into the common parlance of speech about the time when Platonism placed them under examination and accelerated their usage. Students of this problem have perceived that archaic Greek preserves "locative" and "existential" usages of the Greek verb *einai,* but it has seemed a matter of common sense to assume that the copulative use was prior and original.[1]

How, precisely, does *einai* behave in Homer? It surely is common enough. The first book of the *Iliad* contains fifty-seven examples of its utterance, which will serve as an illustrative sample, the more so since the book, in comparison with many others, contains much argument and little action.

Acoustic Values of *Einai*

We are dealing with orally memorized language and therefore with the acoustics thereof. It is relevant to observe a basic distinction which lies between Homeric and English expressions of the verb "to be." "Am," "is," "are," "was," "were," and "be" are colorless monosyllables, often scarcely heard or noticed; they have become copulative conveniences, unless, for special purposes, rhetorical or philosophic, we arrange them so as to pronounce them with a special stress: "To be or not to be, that is the question." Such expressive usage is unusual unless practiced within the confines of the kind of discourse conducted by logicians or metaphysicians.

The overwhelming proportion of the forms of the verb that occur in Homer are disyllables, trisyllables, or quadrisyllables, and they carry corresponding rhythmic weight in the line. Their sound is an important component of what is being said. The exceptions, depending on dialect, are the second singular of the present indicative, *ei,* and the first and third singulars of the past, *ēn*. None of them occurs in the first book of the *Iliad*, where in the angry encounter between the two leaders English translators find it only too natural to insert "you are" and "he was" and "I was." In the two instances where the first book uses the past tense in the singular (ll. 381 and 593), it prefers the "epic" lengthened form, *ēen*, which supplies the terminal foot of the line, completing its cadence. Rarely Homer uses the monosyllable *ēn* (equals "was") in expressions, such as "it went hard for," where the adverb and the verb combine to form an emphatic rhythm. It is noteworthy also that his ear, if using the second person singular *ei*, may choose to add a consonant converting it into *eis* or into *essi*. The monosyllabic forms, when they occur, are always long and carry corresponding rhythmic weight, as opposed to "is" and "are," "was," "were," and "be" (and, be it added, to many equivalents in modern European tongues).

To suggest that considerations of onomatopoeia should play some part in the understanding of the role of *eimi* in oral poets is not frivolous.[2] Its pertinence can be indicated by noticing the curious tendency in Homeric verse for the forms of the verb to occur closely together in groups of two, three, or four. The first book yields the following examples; for a moment I shall follow the convention which translates these instances by the verb "to be":

1. Achilles having convoked an assembly, the seer Calchas rises to speak:

70   Who knew the things being and about to be and being before [*eonta, essomena, pro-eonta*]

2. Agamemnon addresses Achilles: you can go home for all I care:

176 You are most hateful [*echthistos essi*] . . .
178 even if you are very strong [*karteros essi*] . . . [repeated in 280, below]

3. Athene restrains Achilles from killing Agamemnon:

211 assail him with words how indeed it will be [*essetai*],
212 for this I declare, that which accomplished shall be [*esetai*]
213 truly one day for you threefold gifts will be present [*paressetai*]

4. Achilles accuses Agamemnon of shirking a risky encounter with the enemy:

228 that seems to be [*einai*] like death to you.
229 Oh yes, it is [*esti*] much preferred to stay with the Greek army . . .

5. Nestor, addressing Achilles, seeks to arbitrate his differences
with Agamemnon:

280 if you are [*essi*] strong . . .
281 yet he is [*estin*] superior . . .

6. Hera complains that Zeus is conniving with Thetis:

541 ever dear to you, it is [*estin*] being [*eonta*] removed from me to plan
in secret

7. Zeus, replying, admonishes her that she cannot expect to share
in all of his conversations:

546 difficult will they be [*esontai*] to you though being [*eousēi*] my wife

8. Zeus in exasperation threatens her:

562 all the more removed from my heart
563 will you be [*eseai*] and horrible that will be [*estai*]);
564 if it is [*estin*] thus, then it is going to be [*einai*] what I want

9. Hephaestus tries to reconcile his parents:

573 sorry work will this be [*essetai*] and past endurance . . .
575 nor of goodly banqueting
576 any pleasure there shall be [*essetai*]

10. He recalls his father's violent temper:

581 he far superior is [*estin*];
582 you must address him with words that are soft;
583 surely thereupon the Olympian gracious will be [*essetai*] to us

Are these groupings accidental? They constitute twenty-four usages
out of a total of fifty-seven. They occur within a total of only 21 lines
out of a total for the book of 611 lines. In short, once the groupings are
observed and isolated, they become obtrusive. In examples 1, 6, and 7
the verb is repeated within the compass of a single line. In example 8 it
occurs four times in 2 lines. In examples 2 and 10, a whole line separates the repetition, and in example 9 two lines intervene, yet an echo

principle seems to be at work; in numbers 2 and 9 *essi* and *essetai* are repeated (as also in number 3); and in example 10 *estin . . . essetai* are applied to the same subject.

Why employ onomatopoeia as a way of managing this particular verb? Surely such repetition, with something of the force of a pun upon the word, suggests that behind the sound of the verb lurks a meaning that is not so neutral and innocuous as the English copula. In fact, in the last nine of these groupings the expressive force of the verb is heightened by a context of hostility or exasperation (numbers 2, 4, 6, and 8) or earnest and emphatic warning (numbers 3, 5, 7, 9 and 10). One can almost hear the hiss of hatred expressed in the *essi . . . essi* of example 2. What precisely is the "meaning" of the word which the ear of a composer can so manipulate?

Einai as Presence

It is convenient, and perhaps also correct, to begin by viewing those instances in which *einai*, being qualified by an adverb or prepositional phrase, is used to indicate location. It may later appear probable, after all other usages are reviewed, that this locative sense is the primary one, signifying a "presence":

63   for indeed a dream from-Zeus-presents-itself [*ek Dios esti*]
338   let the pair of them as witnesses stand-in-presence-before-gods-before men-before the king [*estōn pros theōn,* etc.]
541b you-staying-in-separation-from-me [*emeu aponosphin eonta*]
566   all the gods that-reside-on-Olympus [*eisi en Olumpōi*]
587   you dear-remaining-in-my-eyes may I not see beaten [*eousan en ophthalmois*]

The locative sense becomes more explicit when the verb is compounded:

213   one day gifts to-you-thrice-as-many-will-be-at-hand [*pote toi tris tossa paressetai:* alliteration rivets the formula together]
258   who in counsel and for fighting above-the-Greeks-prevail [*peri . . . Danaōn, peri d'este . . .*]
287   yes, but this fellow wants above-all-others-to-prevail [*peri pantōn emmenai allōn*]

The force of *peri* corresponds to the colloquialism "be all over somebody."

593 little to me was breath-left-in [*moi enēen*]

Very commonly, the adverb or prepositional phrase is replaced by a dative of a person. In the traditional classification of grammarians this becomes a dative of "possession," of "interest," of "person judging": of "agent." But in the Homeric text it can more naturally be interpreted as a variant way of expressing location, as in "next to," "in the presence of," or "before the eyes of."

107 ever to you evil [words] present-themselves-in-mind as-desirables-to-prophesy [*aei toi-kaka-esti-phila-phresi-manteuesthai* where a word like *epē* is understood]

153 not to-me-do-they-stand-accountable; they never raided my cattle etc. [*ou ti moi aitioi eisin*]

176 chief-enemy-you-stand-to-me of god-nurtured lords [*echthistos moi essi*]

300 of the other [prizes] which to-me-are-lying-beside-swift-ship [*tōn allōn ha moi esti thoēi para nēi;* dative and prepositional phrase combined cf. 563a below]

321 the pair to him . . . stood as . . . heralds and ready assistants [*tō-hoi-esan*]

325 either he gives her to me or I will come and take her myself, that which to-him-indeed-unpleasant-will prove [*hoi rhigion estai*]

380 Apollo heard him for to-him-very-dear-he-stood [*mala hoi philos ēen*]

546a my words hard-to-you-will prove [*chalepoi-toi-esontai*]

563a apart-from-my-heart-to-me-you-will-stand [*apo thumou . . . emoi eseai;* dative and prepositional phrase combined as in 300]

563b that which-to-you-indeed-unpleasant-will prove [*toi kai rhigion estai* if 325]

583 Zeus propitious-will-prove-to-us [*essetai hēmin*]

Twice the prefix and preposition *epi*, signifying "on top of," serves in place of the fuller *epesti*, "to be placed as a burden on."

335 not you on-me-rest-accountable [*ou ti moi ummes epaitioi;* a variant on 153, above]

515 not on-you-lies-fear [*ou toi epi deos*]

Einai as Status

As one examines the various Homeric predicates of *einai*, it comes as something of a surprise to find how many signify rank or status, often in the comparative and superlative degrees. If these constitute a species to which special favor is shown, it is tempting to see the usage as an extension of the locative into the social context, indicating position among other men (and women): subject X not only "is present" in or near or above Y, but also is an "extended presence" within or above a Y which may or may not be expressed. In such contexts *einai* calls for some such translation as "stand," "remain," or "constitute oneself"; it acquires a force not unlike that of the intransitive aspects of the Greek verb *histanai.*

91   who now far the greatest-of-the-Achaeans-claims-to-stand [*nun . . . aristos . . . euchetai einai;* predication includes time as well as status]
131   not so indeed, though great-standing, O godlike Achilles, not so shall you use craft . . . [*agathos per eōn*]
178   you may stand-strong, but a god surely gave you that [*karteros essi*]
185   that you may know how much I-stand-superior-over-you [*pherteros eimi*]
267   most-strong-they-stood and with strongest fought [*kartistoi esan*]
275   nor do you though-great-standing take the girl from him [*agathos per eōn;* a reuse of 131]
280   you may stand-strong, and a goddess mother bore you
281   but he superior-stands, for he rules over more [*karteros essi,* reusing 178, and *pherteros estin*]
580   suppose he wish to fling us out of our seats
581   for he supreme-stands [*phertatos estin*]

In fact the usage is extendible to signify the negative, that is, loss of status, deposition in rank:

118–119   of the Argives I alone-be-left-prizeless [*agerastos eō*]
171   I do not intend here-dishonored-staying to accumulate riches for you [*enthade atimos eōn;* the predicate includes location as well as status]
515–516   then I may well know
          how far I among-all-most-dishonored-goddess-am-left [*meta pasin atimotatē theos eimi;* the predicate once more includes both location and status]

To be sure, a narrative context in which two powerful men are struggling for supremacy is likely to encourage this type of predication; even Nestor in his capacity as elder statesman feels it necessary to compete (267). But this does not apply to the case of Zeus (580) and Thetis (515). Moreover, these predicates of magnitudes (for that is what they are) have more extended applications:

114   I have preferred her above Clytaemnestra for she-from-her-stands-not-inferior [*hethen esti chereiōn*]
239   This [that I say] before-you-large-oath-shall-prove [*toi megas essetai horkos;* location and status both included]
259   The pair of you stand-younger-below-me [*neōterō eston emeio;* i.e., "lower than"]

The predicate need not be an adjective; status can be symbolized by title:

144 one-man-as-captain-director-must-be-appointed [*heis archos anēr boulēphoros estō*]
546b [my words] hard-to-you-will-prove [above, 546a], wife-though-standing [*alochōi per eousēi*]

It is easy to see how so many of these examples tempt the translator to be content with the copula. What seems more natural than to say: "you are my wife"; "you are both younger"; "you may be a great man"; "he is superior," and so on? If this is done, some original force of the Greek has been lost. If it functioned as the "colorless copula," it would occur in a wide variety of routine statements in which an implicit presence, often involving some force or energy, was not in question. But such is not the case.

Einai as Presence in Time

If the qualification attached to the verb is temporal rather than locative, the significance of *einai* shifts from presence to duration, in time rather than place. It is doubtful, however, whether Homeric Greek could conceptualize the difference:

272 with those [of my generation] none of those who now-as-mortals-are-present-upon-earth could fight [*nun brotoi eisin epichthonioi;* where not only time but place is implicit]
290 the gods-ever-living made him warrior [*aien eontes;* on this, see further below]
352 Mother: for you love me-though-living-for-a-little [*minunthadion per eonta*]
494 then indeed to Olympus went the gods-ever-living [a reuse of 290]

Temporal force reiterated can dispense with *einai* altogether:

416 for now to you the portion (remains) little indeed, not at all very long [*epei nu toi aisa minuntha per ou ti mala dēn,* a variant on 352]

Or it may inhere in the predicate alone:

117 I want the people safe-to-remain (still) [*sōn emmenai*]
388 He uttered a word-in-threat, which (now) indeed-accomplished-stands [*dē tetelesmenon esti;* once more the idiom is as much locative as temporal]

The future tense projects a presence forward in time, imagining it as a fact already achieved "at that time," so that some sense of action or process completed enters into the meaning of *einai:* "to turn out"; "to prove":

136 having prepared a prize according to desire, how it equivalent-shall-prove [*antaxion estai*]
211 assail him with words, how indeed it-shall-turn-out [*hōs esetai per*]
212 Thus do I declare, which indeed accomplished-shall-prove [*kai tetelesmenon estai;* cf. 388]
573 indeed sorry works these will-prove-to-be-and-no-longer-supportable [*essetai oude eti anekta*]
576 nor any pleasure of goodly feast will-be-felt [*essetai hēdos*]

Seven other instances, involving locative predicates attached to the future forms of *einai,* have been already cited (213, 239, 325, 546a, 563a, 563b, 583). Their frequency supports the suggestion already made that the temporal sense is an "extension" of the locative.

Neuter Predication

In a majority of the instances so far listed, *einai* attaches predicates to persons. In eleven, the subject, though impersonal, is specific and personified to the degree that it is treated as a presence or as something done or performed (a dream, prizes, gifts, breath, words, words, oath, word, prize, works, pleasure). Three others place *einai* in a different predication:

212 thus do I declare, that which indeed accomplished-shall-prove
325 either he gives her to me or I will come and take her myself, that which to-him-indeed-unpleasant-will-prove
563b that which to-you-indeed-unpleasant-will-prove

To these can be added:

228 you have no stomach to arm for war or join an ambush, that which looks to you to constitute death [*to de toi kēr eidetai einai*]
564a if thus-this-stands,

And:

564b to-me-it-bodes-to-stand-dear [*ei houtō touto estin, emoi mellei philon einai;* an instance of repetition within a single hexameter]

In each of these six, *einai* attaches itself to a neuter subject which has reference not to a person or thing but only to the general sense of what has been just said. With these can now be conjoined three more, in which the "subject" to which *einai* is attached virtually becomes an infinitive:

169   to go home indeed much superior-is-presented [*polu pherteron estin oikade imen*]
229   indeed much preferable it-presents-itself-to-take-gifts-away [*ē polu lōion esti . . . dōra apoairesthai*]
541a   ever-to-you-dear-it-presents-itself . . . -in-secret-to-arbitrate justice [*philon estin . . . dikazemen;* cf. 541b, above]

Are we to say that *einai*, used in these eight contexts to connect neuter subjects to neuter predicates (with the exception of *kēr* in 228), has assumed the role of a true copula, that to translate it as "prove to be," "constitute itself," "present itself" is an overtranslation? This would mean that *einai* is expressing a logical relationship and nothing but that. To the extent that this is true, we must observe that such a condition for the verb is not created by the verb itself, but by the company it keeps: the attached subject has been depersonalized; it is "what has been said" or "going home" or "taking away gifts," to which a neuter impersonal predicate is conjoined: we recognize a degree of abstraction, of conceptualization, present in such idioms (which are infrequent). But what has been conceptualized is still an activity, a happening: something qualified by contingency of place and time, even if this is only implied. It is still an event "presenting itself" through the medium of *einai*, in some specific guise and with a locative complement either explicit (325, 228, 564b, 541) or implicit.

Absence of Predication

Yet even the first book of the *Iliad* can yield five instances of *einai* which reveal a qualitative difference from any so far reviewed:

70   [the priest] knew what-are-present and what-will-be-present and what-are-before-present [*ta eonta, ta essomena, (ta) pro eonta*]
290   gods-ever-living [*aien eontes;* reused at 494]

It is these participial idioms that hold the key to the future development of *einai* as a logical copulative. We have already viewed the participle placing a person in a particular contingent position of place, circumstance, or status:

131   though great-standing [reused at 275]
171   here-dishonored-staying

352 though-living-for-a-little
541b you-staying-in-separation-from-me
587 you dear-remaining-in-my-eyes

But what are we to make of the participle when it is stripped of any contingency, standing naked and alone? Only one subject can serve in such a role—the eternal gods, who have no context in time at least (though they have in space). But even they can be eliminated, their place taken by the participle itself—in the plural, to be sure, for the Homeric mind still sees the total environment of man as a plurality. It will be left to the philosophers to reduce this to a single reality, a "being." The "existential" image of *einai* is therefore predictable out of Homer, but can we say that the copulative is also?[3]

Appositional Equivalence

Probably we cannot, simply because Homeric verse is capable of employing copulative idiom without using *einai* at all. It normally uses *einai* to express a personal subject (or something behaving as such) as present in a given role determined by a second presence "of," "to," "by," "from," "above," or the like, either expressed or implicit. An X functions as a Y in conjunction with a Z. Suppose the Homeric mind wishes for any reason to present an X connected in some way to a Y but disconnected from any function which would involve a Z? This could amount in effect to expressing a kind of equivalence between the two. Under such circumstances the presence of *einai* would have too strong an impact; one wants a colorless connection. How to achieve it? The answer is to avoid achieving it: X and Y are each stated alone and placed side by side:[4]

80 more powerful (is) a lord what time he rages against an inferior [*kreissōn basileus*]
116 if that (is) better [*ei to ge ameinon*]
156 many things (are) in between [*polla metaxu*]
167 if ever distribution (of booty) comes (in question), to you the prize (is) much greater [*soi to geras polu meizon*]
177 ever to you contention (is) dear and wars and battles [*aiei . . . toi eris te philē*, etc.]
217 for thus (it is) better (to do) [*hōs ameinon*]
274 for to obey (is) better [*peithesthai ameinon*]
404 he (is) superior to his father [*ho gar . . . . ..ameinōn*]
525 this out from me among immortals (is) greatest

526 signal; for mine (is) not recallable or evadable
527 nor unfinishable, whatsoever with head I may nod [*touto . . . megiston . . . ou gar palinagreton,* etc.]
589 formidable (is) the Olympian to confront [*argaleos Olumpios antipheresthai*]

The translator in modern tongues readily supplies the copula, classifying the lord as powerful, the contention as dear, and so on. The Greek idiom reveals that oral language did not readily express classification, but only equivalence. The standard grammatical explanation, that the verb "to be" is "understood,"[5] is misleading. The appositional construction simply invites the mind to jump from one term to the next.

These examples express equivalences which are generally the case, either as applied to given persons (where some contingency is added or implied) or universally so, where the subject is cast in the neuter singular. That precisely is why *einai* is not there, for if it were, it would intrude the notion of a presence limited to particular circumstances, valid "now" or "sometimes," "somewhere" or "somehow." The appositional idiom therefore becomes compulsive in aphorisms of all descriptions, illustratable in a citation of some familiar examples from other books of the *Iliad:*

2.204a Not good-thing (is) plural-command;
204b a single commander must preside [*estō;* a neat example of a generic apposition and a specific *einai* juxtaposed]
205 a single lord to whom Cronus' son of devious device has given
206 scepter and settings, that he may decide counsel with them.
6.146 even as of leaves (is) the generation, so also (is it) of men;
147 leaves—some of them—the wind scatters groundward and others the wood
148 burgeoning grows and the season of spring comes on [cf. 21.464].

The conference held in Book 9 between Agamemnon's embassy and Achilles and the addresses delivered by Achilles and Phoenix on this occasion offer unusual opportunity for the intrusion of such reflective syntax:

9.318 equal the portion (is) to one remaining behind, or if he should engage in war,
319 in equal honor (is) both the inferior man and the goodly;
320 alike dies the man who does nothing and he who does much
401 Not to me (is it) worth the price of my life—neither all the goods that they say Troy acquired . . .

406 seizable (are) cattle and sheep,
407 acquirable (are) tripods and horses,
408 but the life of a man to come back (is) not seizable
409 nor takable when once it shall cross over the barrier of teeth.

497 turnable (are) the gods, even they,
498 and of them indeed greater (is) honor and force,
499 and yet them with sacrifice men turn aside praying

505 Ruin (is) strong and nimble, which is why
506 she far outruns all prayers.

In these examples, reflection is initiated by an aphorism, which is then extended into a commentary which lapses into that narrative syntax normally required for memorized speech. The aphorisms come as near as oral language can manage to a "Platonic" syntax of conceptualization. It is as though the effort of general reflection, which we can call the logos of the passage, as it interrupts the narrative flow, can be sustained only briefly before seeking support in a resumption of mythos.

The Absent Copula

It may now become more apparent why it does not occur to Hesiod, let alone Homer, to tell us what justice "is." Neither poet even supplies an aphorism which places it in verbless equivalence. The moral formulas of the *Odyssey* which employ the adjective "just" as a predicate (none of them name "justice" as such) conform to the rules already elicited. The suitors "(are) not just": this is their permanent role in the mythos; so in this expression *einai* is not used. But when Greeks or Phaeacians on given contingent occasions, which are stated, "proved to be not just," the past tense is used. The formula used four times which proposes a generic antithesis between "men (that are) just" and "men (that are) savage" omits the *einai*; but when the "savage" are qualified by the locative statement "the mind in-them-is-present not-god-fearing," the verb is used. In order to pronounce the aphorism that "(it is) not (a) just thing to mistreat a stranger," the *einai* is omitted: neuter adjective and infinitive are placed in equivalence.[6]

Hesiod likewise cannot use the copula. His use of *einai* is locative, as shown in the lines which introduce the entire argument of the *Works and Days*:

So then, there-was-not-present only one
family of contention, but over-the-earth-
there-are-present two.

Similarly, in the justice poem the "immortal guardians" are described as (249b):

near-at-hand-among-mortals-being-present

to which is appended (252):

present-are-thrice-ten-thousand-upon-the-much nourishing earth.

Hesiod therefore can tell us only where justice and the just person stand or stay or remain (or else what they are doing or having done to them). He does not say "Justice is the maiden daughter of Zeus" or "Justice is renowned on Olympus," but phrases it in a sentence which begins "And she—the maiden—stands [*esti*] (as) Justice born of Zeus," and adds the locative "renowned and revered of gods who inhabit Olympus." He does not say "justice is not a trait of the animals" but "justice is not present among them" (*esti meta autois*). He does not say "it is no good for a man to be just, so it is impossible for me to be just," but only "I myself among mankind would not (wish) just-to-remain, if . . ." (*meta anthrōpoisi dikaios eiēn . . . kakon andra dikaion emmenai*: where the locative phrase qualifies both verbs, which are linked together by onomatopoeia, as so often in Homer).

On the other hand, in cases where we would attach a predicate with *einai* "understood," Hesiod leaves the two terms of the statement in appositional equivalence: "outrage (is) evil"; "the road (is) superior"; "peace (is) nourisher-of-*kouroi*"; "evil counsel (is) most evil"; for a man just-to-remain (is) evil."

But justice figures in one idiom so far unnoticed. As he begins his summing up, the poet wants to rank justice as "by far the most excellent." To use *einai* would be to rank *dikē* by locating it in a position among or above others. He wants to say something like "justice is supreme," without qualification of place, time, or circumstance (and no such qualification is attached). The verb he uses to link the subject to its predicate under these conditions is *ginetai*, literally "is born" or "becomes." Applied in this fashion, the verb comes as near to an unqualified copula as oral speech is capable of managing. Hesiod, to put the matter in platonic terms, is not interested in the "becoming" of justice but in its "being." But sheer being applied veridically cannot yet be phrased; the image of process, responding to the narrative syntax of memorized speech, still prevails.

I return to the problem of the copula as it was raised at the beginning of this chapter—the general problem of predication as practiced now in common speech. The poetry of Homer and Hesiod is formulaic not by accident, but inherently so. How then does one counter the objection that, even admitting the behavior of *einai* in oral poetry to be such as described, it need not have been so restricted in the vernacular? Is not the formulaic style after all a straitjacket from which the vernacular is freed? We can never, of course, know the vernacular in question,[7] but there are a few considerations which may shed some indirect light on whether or how far it used the copula, or avoided using it. For one thing, there was no metrical reason to bar the use of abstractly stated sentences in the hexameter, as shown, for example, in the fifth-century aphorism: "In righteousness [*dikaiosunē*] comprehensively all virtue is (found)." *Einai* is still obviously locative, but given the character of subject and predicate and the conceptual nature of the adverb, location comes close to bring a metaphor for a logical relationship. This kind of statement would be unthinkable in Homeric or Hesiodic diction, and why so, if not also unusable in the contemporary vernacular?

It is true that the copula in modern vernaculars has become a routine method of indexing not merely rules and principles, like "Honesty is the best policy," but the "facts" of everyday life: "this house is large"; "the horse you sold me is lame"; "the corn is green"; "the Japanese are our enemies"; "he is very ill." Are we so sure that it was used in this routine way in archaic Greek speech? An acquaintance not only with nonepic poetry, but with the comedy and the prose of the high classical age, raises some doubts about this presumption. Would not such speech prefer idioms like: "this house looks-like large" or "is built large"; "the horse walks lame"; "the corn grows green"; "the Japanese make war on us"; "he feels very ill" or "he ails"? This is not to deny that *einai* could be used with such simple subjects and predicates or some of them, but if used, would it not impart the notion of a presence "standing or looming in the distance" (in the case of the house), or "confronting us" (the Japanese)? The fact is that a vernacular tends to reflect the rules of syntax obeyed in preserved speech. Hence today, in order to speak "well," we speak a "literate" speech; under nonliterate conditions would one not have to obey "nonliterate" idiom in order to speak "well"? A member of a society restricted to oral communication would be more likely than his literate counterpart to invest his statements with a kind of dynamism. He would tend to perceive his environment not as a series of objects placed in relation to each other, but as a series of activities and processes in which objects play roles. His own experience of such would modulate itself in a series of actions and reactions to such activities.

The mastery of the copulative "to be" over common speech which has increased since oral Hellenism ceased to exist can be perceived in the extended use of the verb in European tongues as an auxiliary to denote voice or mood or tense. Even if we allow for certain usages of the Greek *einai* which can be classified as "auxiliary," such a complete neutralization of the verb, making it totally subservient to the sense of what it accompanies, would be highly uncharacteristic. The same observation applies to the tendency to replace psychological verbs—"he rages, he hungers, he loves"—with psychological statements: "he is angry, is hungry, is a lover of."

In sum, it is reasonable to conclude that it would not have occurred to a Greek of the archaic age to ask himself "What is justice?" or to get into an argument with his neighbor about its "nature." Would he even be able to think about justice as anything except something that occurs or is stated incidentally in a procedure in which men gather to judge and arbitrate their differences? And if he could neither state it nor come to terms with it otherwise, how can we say that justice "existed" for him, as concept or as principle?

14
The Justice of Solon

❦

Hesiod by an act of recomposition brought justice into the realm of discourse; it became a topic or subject consciously chosen for description and exposition. This event, so far as we can tell from the remains of Greek literature available for inspection, does not happen again for perhaps two hundred and fifty years. Plato's *Protagoras* is the next document which, on the record, devotes some direct attention to the role of justice in society, and his *Republic* is the first to attempt a systematic definition. Why this enormous delay in following up what from a modern standpoint seems to be a concept of central moral significance for civilized society? To be sure, *dikē* and it associated symbols begin to recur in certain authors, but always incidentally, as their use may be suggested by their connection with other matters, never as the central focus of what is being said—until Plato.

Hesiod, Parmenides, and Plato

There could be one simple answer, the clue being supplied by Hesiod's own difficulties, which were linguistic and syntactical. He had managed to isolate the topic; that is, to choose an impersonal in place of a Homeric agent as the subject of what he wanted to say. But he had not been able to discard the dynamism which characterized all Homeric predicates, that is, all predicates employed in speech orally memorized.

The veridical copulative statement that X *always* "is" Y, or that Y is *always* true of X, was not available to him: the verb "to be" remained imprisoned in its locative and existential dimensions. The energies of analytic discourse were still asleep. The spell had to be broken. The thinker chosen by the Greek historical process to begin the task of breaking it, as Plato himself would acknowledge, was the philosopher Parmenides, in the first half of the fifth century. Only when his work and that of his disciples was completed was the way left open to make affirmations about justice which would satisfy the syntactical require-ments which Parmenides proposed for statements about the universe. It was said in antiquity of the Socratic dialectic that it brought down philosophy from heaven to earth. In logical terms, this meant that the single eternal "being of the cosmos," the "is" which always is and never "is not" and never ceases to be, should be applied also in the realm of what we would call human values. Justice too must have its being.

For an investigation of the history of justice as a concept, Hesiod's poem and Plato's *Republic* are the only two primary sources, the only two available "conceptual" sources, despite the chronological gap between them; and one would think that an examination of each parallel to the other, widely separated as they are in style and scope, would perhaps expose how the break between them occurred within a continuity which they shared but which is not rendered visible by any other method. One observes, for instance, Plato's own sense of his closeness to Hesiod: even the guardians of his ideal state can be viewed as a reminiscence of the thirty thousand spirits appointed to protect "justices" in Hesiod's poem.[1] Accepting the thesis that Hesiod's isolation of the topic was prompted by the documentation of language in visible form, one may ask whether Plato's further rendition of the topic owed something to the same causes. Was it Plato the writer—the first Greek author, so far as we know, of a substantial corpus of didactic prose rivaling the Homeric poems in their encyclopedic range—who was able to complete a vision of the concep-tion of justice because the language suitable for such a vision—a veridi-cal language—was now also becoming available in visible form, on an extensive and systematic scale, projected beyond the consciousness of the writer, enjoying a stability of documented existence denied to the oral tradition?

A Metaphysical Version

Yet a method of exposition which would pass directly from Hesiod to Plato faces an obstacle placed there less by such ancient sources as intervene between the two than by the interpretation placed upon what these sources say by some modern historians of Greek thought. The substance and wide dissemination of this interpretation can be conveniently illustrated by a statement which Bertrand Russell included in his *History of Western Philosophy* (1945): "The idea of justice, both cosmic and human, played a part in Greek religion and philosophy which it is not altogether easy for a modern to understand . . . this conception of justice—of not overstepping eternal fixed bounds—was one of the most profound of Greek beliefs." Russell is here presumably following the guidance supplied in Germany in 1933 by the first volume of Werner Jaeger's *Paideia* (English translation, Oxford 1939), which, in a chapter entitled "The Greek City State and Its Ideal of Justice" observes (pp. 102–103): "The long succession of Ionian epigrams and poems which extol Justice as the basis of human society runs from the later portions of the Homeric epics through Archilochus and Anaximander down to Heraclitus . . . Throughout these centuries we hear the call of *dikē* growing constantly more widespread; more passionate and more imperative." Accordingly, in a subsequent chapter, "The Discovery of the World Order," Jaeger says of Solon and the Milesian philosophers: "Solon's idea was this: Dikē does not depend on human earthly justice . . . her power is immanent, manifested in the process by which all inequalities compensate themselves in time . . . Anaximander's idea of the eternal power of dikē ruling natural phenomena implies the idea of a cosmos . . . Anaximander's doctrine of the systematic justice of the universe reminds us that the most important idea in the new philosophy, that of Cause, was originally the same as the idea of retribution." And again, Jaeger says of Parmenides (p. 175): "He means that his own *dikē* . . . is the necessity implicit in the conception of Being." Language like this argues that the *dikē* of the *Odyssey*, and the *dikē* occasionally mentioned subsequently in a very few authors of the archaic period, identified (1) an accepted political principle informing the existence of the early city-state, and (2) a comprehensive cosmic principle of metaphysical proportions.

In forming this view of the character of the early Greek mind, the influence of German idealist philosophy can no doubt be detected. Its effect on modern scholarship is visible in two articles by Gregory Vlastos, "Solonian Justice" and "Equality and Justice in the Early Greek Cosmogonies" (1946, 1947), and more recently, though only incidentally, in H. Lloyd–Jones's *The Justice of Zeus* (1971; see pp. 80–81 and notes), where, however, the focus is on justice primarily in its religious context. Such views are not unanimously held. *The Presocratic Philosophers* (1957) of Kirk and Raven avoids this kind of language altogether, as does the first volume of W. K. Guthrie's *History of Greek Philosophy* (1962–1975), though in the second (pp. 346 ff.) some concessions are made to it. But it has proved attractive to a generation of scholars, and found its way into much popular history of Greek thought. Language like this is overblown.[2] Frail evidence in support of it can be sought only in a few isolated expressions, one (or perhaps two) used by Solon of Athens, one doubtfully attributed to the philosopher Anaximander, four quoted from Heraclitus, and two from Parmenides.

Justice as Due Process

What does Solon the lawgiver have to say about justice? Here is a kind of father figure presiding over the history of Hellenism. His stature would probably increase if time had been kinder to the record of his life and the remains of his works. Already by the middle of the fifth century he had become a character of legend. His law code, it would appear, whatever its content, addressed itself to the specifics of legal situations;[3] that was its genius. As to any general views he may have entertained about the nature of justice,[4] one has to resort for guidance to his poetry. Its remains, meager as they are, address themselves to two areas of concern which are recognizably different. One group of poems is didactic and employs the present tense: these are for the most part his elegies. They offer general reflections bearing on the Greek life-style of his day, or any day, and on the condition of Athens; they advise, admonish, and exhort. In the other group of poems he speaks in the past tense; these are the fragments of his tetrameters and iambics, along with some six to nine lines of elegy. The tone is specific and the purpose is political, as he reviews what his policies have been and defends their results. In each style he employs the vocabulary of justice, but understandably in different ways.

A fragment (24.D) of twenty-seven iambic verses offers a kind of *apologia pro vita sua*. In the first seven lines he defends himself against the charge that he left much business unfinished, and then continues:

Many to Athens their god-built country
I brought back that had been sold for export, this one extra-justly,
that one justly, and others under necessity
pressed into exile for debt, ceasing to utter the Attic tongue,
diversely scattered as they were;
while those right here enduring slavery ignoble,

trembling before the moods of their masters,
I set free. These (things), by (using) power
fitting close together force [*bia*] with justice [*dikē*],
I achieved and completed as I had promised.
And laws [*thesmoi*] according with the lowly and the noble
by fitting justice [*dikē*] straight to each man
I inscribed [*egrapsa*]. If someone other than I had taken the goad—
some ill-conditioned and covetous man—
he would not have restrained the demos; if they had wanted
what at one time pleased the opposition
and at another what the other side were proposing against them,
our city would have been widowed of many men;
that is why I contrived (to gather) my strength from all sides,
twisting and turning like a wolf in a pack of dogs.

The symbols of justice employed here are procedural. They recall the "justice" of the *Iliad*. Athenians can be sold abroad; the act as performed can occur "justly" and also "outside of justice," that is, within or without "due process"; the legality of sale as such is not in question.[5] Besides due process, one can use force; *bia* is also a procedure, a method of action. So Solon can imagine the two methods combined as partners; overall, this is what his political policy amounted to. By implication, he is correcting Hesiod, who had placed them in antithesis, equating force with aggressive arrogance.[6] Solon's poetry more than once rejects the latter (1.11 and 16; 3.8 and 34; 5.9). He is not so sure about force: he is perhaps ambivalent about it (23.20). He is not a utopian like Hesiod; he has to practice as well as preach, and he is also living in a more literate age. So he is able to penetrate more closely into the nature of procedural justice, the kind dramatized in the *Iliad*. What he has now "inscribed" are "laws"; they enjoy a fixed visible existence. Justice, however, is something he adjusts to each case, making a "straight fit." Under preliterate conditions, both *themis* and *dikē* (or their plurals) were spoken, not written, so that epic tended to confuse their application. Solon's language accepts a working distinction between rules as written and as applied. Does he intend to claim that the laws themselves as inscribed are worded with flexibility? A recent reconstruction of his law code suggests that it was drafted to cope with a great variety of legal situations.[7] Yet when he says the "fit" of his justice is "straight," the adjective he uses is traditional, recalling the idiom of oral management. *Dikē*'s reference is to a process of adjustment, of negotiation. This is necessary because the measurements made are proportionate, are relative to status and circumstances; they have to be "fitted" individually. The question here is of equity, not equality. He accepts as Hesiod does the status of the lowly and the noble as facts of life. Hesiod had observed that aggressive outrage can afflict both; by implication justice, being the opposite, can benefit both. Here Solon indicates how this is brought about.

The first seven verses of his apologia, to which we now return, read as follows:

For myself, why from the purposes for which I assembled
the demos did I desist, before achieving them?
There will be at my side a witness to testify about this in (the) justice of
time—
she, the mother supreme of the Olympian spirits,
full well (she will), even black earth, whose marker stones did I on a time
abolish, stuck in the ground everywhere.

A good deal has been made of the phrase "in (the) justice of time"[8] as though time should be capitalized as a kind of metaphysical entity imposing the rule of justice upon events. Greek linguistic usage in the archaic epoch renders this improbable; the phrase is likely to mean "during a just procedure carried out in the course of time." To translate, as some do, "in the court of time" catches the legal coloration, but it is questionable whether the narrower sense of *dikē* as a court of justice had yet been realized.[9] The dimension of the apologia is imaginative. Solon in Homeric fashion had "assembled" (either literally or metaphorically) an agora of the *dēmos;* in his vision it is still sitting, or will be sitting, when earth comes forward to testify, but this procedure will take time, will have to wait on time, as indeed it does in the *Iliad* to the point where Agamemnon is ready to testify on oath. Why is the procedure necessary, and why so prolonged? Solon faces the complaint: what have you achieved? The mortgage-markers had been removed, that is one thing; the restoration of the "black earth" to full productivity is another. It will take time, in the course of which the blossoming earth will herself set the record right; and so, esteem lost by Solon will be restored by her testimony; the "justice" of time will be reciprocal in its effect.

Justice as Equity and Equanimity

That legal procedure would be in the forefront of a lawgiver's thought is to be expected. But there is a wider dimension to Solon's policies. He can earn the title, as far as the record goes, of the first statesman on the European scene, through his program of impartial protection for rich and poor, noble and commoner, powerful and power-less. He describes in a famous passage how he

stood with my strong shield cast round both parties.

By this he probably meant that he protected them from each other, for he adds:

I did not suffer either party to prevail nonjustly,

where the adverb indicates the gaining of an unfair advantage, that is, one out of proportion to what a man of given status should properly have, though what sets that proportion Solon does not state. The rules are still those set by a propriety, which is established by the existing nomos and ethos, not otherwise defined. The ideological novelty lies in the recognition that Athens—and presumably any city—consists of at least two classes, the rich and the poor, and that what is required is an accommodation between them.[10] Solon's traditional support for such a perspective on human affairs lies in the *Odyssey*, just as his procedural notions find their prototype in the *Iliad*. The just man of the *Odyssey* showed his quality by his treatment of the traveling stranger, and also of the poor and destitute; what he should grant them is equity. For Solon this is a matter which it is not enough to celebrate in poetry; it is to be implemented in policy. When he refers to it, however, he does not use the language of justice, though perhaps he comes near to doing so in the following couplet:

From the winds (as they blow) the sea is perturbed. But if
no one quickens it, it prevails-most-just of all (things)

Only here in his surviving poetry does the adjective *dikaios* occur, linked in the superlative of status to a locative use of the verb "to be," as in similar Homeric examples. Whatever the context may have been, the lines constitute an aphorism, perhaps of his own contriving, built, like so many such, round an ambivalence of meaning in one key word. In what sense can the sea be "just"? It is not there to be contemplated as a force of nature, but as a surface to be sailed on. It is "just" to the traveler who uses it, but only if the winds let it alone. It can furnish that equity and equanimity which in the *Odyssey* the voyaging traveler should justly receive from human beings. But at a second level of meaning, the sea is itself a metaphor for the citizens of a city-state. Archilochus had (probably) invented the formula of the "ship of state," which became a cliché. His comparison was between the city and the storm-tossed vessel. Solon transfers it to the sea itself, realistically one would think, because crews do not normally subvert themselves by quarreling, but the sea continually does just that to itself. The gales that threaten its stability are those of civic discord, the dangers of which are so prominently advertised in his poems. But, left undisturbed, the city's condition is one of complete justice, meaning it is a haven of hospitality to all who live in it.[11] Can we conclude from this wording that the symbolization of *dikē* has been extended beyond civic procedure to cover the concept of the civic order within which the procedure takes place? Has it become a "justice of the state" as Plato would have understood it? There is otherwise no warrant for such an equation in Solon's verse. To be sure, he extols the effects of law and order (*eunomia*)[12] in contrast to lawlessness (*dusnomia*) and perhaps personifies these twin terms,[13] but he does not do this in direct connection with justice, who when symbolized earlier in the same poem is assigned a different role. Solon need mean no more than that civic order is hospitable to a peaceful and civilized life-style.

Solon and Hesiod

Of the didactic elegies, two that survive are of some length. One of seventy-six lines is included in an anthology of worthy commonplaces compiled by Stobaeus in the fifth century of our era. Another of thirty-nine lines (presumably incomplete) was quoted in the course of a speech delivered by Demosthenes. Each contains a reference to justice, in terms which have been interpreted to support the view already cited that for Solon "*Dikē* does not depend on human earthly justice; nor does she act by sudden temporary strokes of divine punishment . . . her power is immanent, manifested in the process by which all inequalities compensate themselves in time; and that inevitable process is the 'punishment of Zeus' or 'divine requital.' "[14]

This kind of language overstates the implications of Solon's Greek, which is best understood against a background furished by the genre—or, perhaps better, the ground rules—within which both elegies are composed. Structurally, they have been put together out of units consisting of self-contained aphorisms, a majority of which coincide with the couplet. They have, however, been chosen and contrived with some care to produce an effect of continuous argument, assisted by enjamb-

ment between couplets. The first twenty-five lines of the longer poem
(1. D), here offered as a sample, arrange themselves as follows:

1–2	Invocation of Muses of Pieria daughters of Zeus and Memory:
3–4	May the gods grant me prosperity and fame,
5–6	a comfort to my friends and a terror to my enemies.
7–8a	My desire is for property but not if acquired nonjustly;
8b	justice never fails to follow after;
9–10	god-given wealth lasts,
11–12a	but if pursued by aggressive arrogance [*hubris*], it arrives improperly;
12b–13a	it follows reluctant in obedience to nonjust works;
13b	disaster [*ate*] swiftly pollutes (the mixture);
14–15	the beginning is small as of a fire, slight at first, destructive at the last;
16	the works of aggressive arrogance are short lived.
17a	Zeus oversees the end of all,
17b–24	simile of a spring wind scattering clouds, stirring sea, and destroying fair works on land—till the sun shines;
25	such is the retribution [*tisis*] of Zeus.

The Hesiodic technique at once becomes evident.[15] The earlier poet
had initiated the practice of excerpting and recording Homeric sentiments specifically relevant to the practice of the Greek nomos and ethos.
Solon carries the method a stage further. His poem sustains a more
consistent level of reflection; it manages with a fair amount of success to
avoid relapsing into the narrative mode, except in the simile. The verbs
maintain themselves in the present tense, as usually in Hesiod, but more
importantly, the images employed are not disjunct: one tends to lead
into the next. Lines 3 to 16 present a consistent sequence of impersonal nouns as subjects or objects of the statements the author wishes
to make (prosperity–property–justice–wealth–disaster–beginning–
works). This level of abstraction is not, however, sustained in the rest of
the poem. The diction, as commentators have observed, remains impreg-
nated with the formulaic vocabulary of epic, adapted to the elegiac
rhythm. Solon cannot turn a line without resorting to it. Is his debt a
general one, to the oral reservoir upon which presumably both Homer
and Hesiod drew? Prosperity and fame won under the gods' favor is a
commonplace aspiration of Hellenism, whether heroic, archaic, or classical, as also is the acceptance of the existence of friend and enemy as
facts of life, to be dealt with accordingly. The simile has a more specific

ancestry in the Homeric description of Zeus's wrath, kindled by the expulsion of *dikē* from the agora and venting itself in a flood which destroys the "works" of men. Solon, who goes on to remark (line 26) that Zeus, however, is never overhasty in anger, may intend an "improvement" upon his model.[16] Prevailingly, the poem feels the remote control of Hesiod's *Works and Days,* which to begin with had converted the mere anger of Homer's Zeus into a conscious policy of divine retribution. Solon follows this lead (*tinō* and *tisis,* the retributive verb and noun, occur four times in the poem; cf. *W.D.* 260) and also adopts Hesiod's doctrine of postponed retribution falling on the descendants of the guilty (*W.D.* 284 and Solon 1.31-2). It is even possible that the emphasis on the "works" of mankind as the significant test of human quality (the noun recurs seven times in the poem) was suggested by Hesiod's theme. The couplet invoking the Muses which forms the proem is formed in recollection of the proem to the *Works and Days,* and includes their parentage as it had been defined in the *Theogony.*

When, therefore, we find Solon's poem uttering warnings against "nonjust works" which are also "the works of aggressive arrogance" (1.11, 12, 16), when again he warns not only that "justice never fails to follow after" (1.8) but that "disaster swiftly pollutes," and even concludes his poem with the aphorism that "disaster raises its head afterward: Zeus sends her (it) to exact retribution" (1.75-76), we recognize that his language falls into the same pattern of recollection. It was Hesiod who had constructed the explicit antithesis between *dikē* and *hubris,* and by linking *dikē* associatively with *atē* had conjoined their powers in one personality. Is it even possible that when Salon speaks of ill-gotten wealth following "reluctant in obedience to (the dictates of) nonjust works"—a curious metaphor—he is recalling that *dikē* of Hesiod who "followed weeping to the city and haunts of men"? Solon's Zeus who "oversees the end of all (things)" (1.17) and who is never caught unaware (1.27) is Hesiod's Zeus, whose "eye sees and notes all" and from whom likewise nothing "is hidden" (*W.D.* 267-268).

Justice Personified

The shorter elegy contains within a passage of three lines (3.14-16) a personification of Justice, in terms as explicit as anything said about "her" in pre-Platonic literature. They have to be understood in their context. The poem opens with a proud assertion that "the city which is ours shall never perish," the reasons given being that she is protected by Zeus, by the gods generally, and especially by the uplifted hands of Pallas Athene (3.1–4). He then continues (5–18):

It is the townspeople who a great city in their folly
persist in destroying, obedient to (the temptation of) money;
nonjust (is) the mind of the leaders of the demos; for them (it) is prepared
to endure many pains (issuing) from great arrogance;
they lack skill to contain greed or to enjoy in orderly fashion
the pleasures available in relaxed ease of feasting;
they grow rich yielding to (the temptation of) nonjust works;
sparing neither sacred possessions nor public property,
they steal; their rapacity is indiscriminate;
nor guard they the holy foundation-roots of Justice—
she who in silence is aware of what comes to pass and was before,
and who in course of time by all means comes ready-to-exact-retribution.
This is the wound that to the whole (or every) city comes irremediable
and (the city) quickly comes into dire slavery.

The lines breathe a native pride in Athens which continues to inspire the rest of the poem, adding fervor to his warnings against any conduct that threatens her. But they too have an ancestry. When Hesiod celebrates justice, the city is never far from his thoughts as he composes. The road *dikē* follows leads to the city; it is the city that profits from just dealing, and comes to grief when it is ignored, as Zeus inflicts retribution. But Solon's Athens, "our very own city,"[17] is not destined to suffer such a fate at Zeus's hand. Solon rejects Hesiod's pessimistic alternative, and in the same breath proceeds to recall Hesiod's warnings. His attention—or his recollection—would appear to be directed in particular to one passage, a rather crucial one: Hesiod had warned certain *basileis* that "the gods nigh at hand take consideration of those employing crooked justices," and that "thirty thousand spirits roam the earth invisibly guarding justice." Then followed the personification of *dikē* on Olympus, where she "sings the nonjust mind of men—that it pay retribution—even the demos for the excesses of the *basileis* who pervert justice." Four lines later, the figure of justice is replaced by Zeus, "whose eye sees all, minds all, who will take a look now if he wishes nor is caught unaware of the kind of justice the city is keeping inside." There are several points of comparison, which taken together can hardly be accidental. Hesiod's syntax first allowed *dikē* to complain against mankind, and then substituted the demos, who suffer for the sins of their princes: Solon first reproaches the townspeople, but then substitutes the "leaders of the demos," thus reproducing the ambiguity of his prototype as well as reusing the formula "nonjust mind." Adopting Hesiod's personification, he enlarges the model by attaching attributes drawn from the context of the model. The rapacious element in the civic population withhold from her (in the singular) the "guardianship" which has been accorded to her (in the plural) by Hesiod's thirty thousand. In her silent but ominous and omniscient awareness of what is going on, she assumes the role assigned by Hesiod to these same gods and spirits ominously and invisibly present among men, and in particular the role of Zeus, from whose observant eye nothing escapes. In Hesiod, she could complain of mistreatment and ask for a penalty to be imposed; here she inflicts the penalty herself. Two more of her attributes are drawn from reminiscences of the *Theogony*. Her "foundation-roots" are Solon's addition to what might be called her iconography. It is unlikely that they are intended as a metaphor for an imaginary "temple of justice." He is exploiting a rare but epic word (*themethla*) applied in Homer to the "roots" of eye or gullet; the metaphor is not architectural but physiological, and is used by Hesiod to describe the home allotted by Zeus as a reward to the three giants by those assistance he had overcome the Titans. The Titans were banished "beyond the gods, beyond Chaos," that is, excluded from the cosmos. The giants were treated differently (*Theog.* 815–816):

> the illustrious assistants of Zeus
> have their home-and-habitation upon the foundation-roots of Ocean

This location, also referred to as

> springs and bounds of earth, Tartarus, sea and heaven,

confers on them an intimate seat within the cosmos, one which can also be thought of as its source. Does the Justice of Solon now occupy this seat? Does his metaphor allow her briefly to migrate from men into the cosmos? It would be a unique departure, and one not easy to assimilate to her claim on men for protection and her power to pursue them with retribution. That he might wish to do this for her—that is, give her a theogonic status—might perhaps be inferred from the fact that he assigns to her a knowledge of events "present, future, and past" modeled upon the claim that the author of the *Theogony* makes for himself—or for his muse—in the introduction to that work.[18]

The Absence of the Copula and of Conceptual Clarity

Space forbids an exhaustive review of both elegies, which would uncover many more comparisons of this order. Those already disclosed are sufficient to make clear what is happening as Solon sets out to put together poetry of this character. He has the text of Hesiod's verse in his memory, and also visually before him. In dealing with his model, he continues a process begun by Hesiod when dealing with *his* model. The results achieved are more sophisticated. Solon belongs to a more literate age: command over the syntax required for reflection has increased; there is a greater sense of logical connection in passing from one aphorism to the next. The didacticism, correspondingly, has become more overt. Solon says (3.30):

this is what my spirit bids me instruct [*didaxai*] the Athenians [cf. 22.7],

whereupon he proceeds to dilate upon the positive effects of law and order (*eunomia*) and the negative effects of its opposite (*dus–nomia*). Many of his sentiments recur in the remains of the didactic poetry ascribed to Tyrtaeus before him and Theognis after him, even to the repetition of formulas and whole lines. The didactic genre, born with Hesiod out of Homer, begins to attain its own specific format; it becomes a literature of clichés, visible also in the choruses of Athenian tragedy (below, Chapter 16), serving as a transmission line for the consolidation of those common proprieties, embedded in epic, which had guided Greek culture in the oral period of its development.

What Solon has to say about justice in the didactic portions of his verse is incidental to this process of composition. He contributes some further poetic metaphors with which to surround the symbol. Such imagery is a function of its immediate context; no overall consistency is attempted: *Dikē* is praised, and then replaced by a second personage, *Eunomia*: their respective powers are celebrated in variant versions. For this again he had the authority of Hesiod, who had made them sisters, daughters of Zeus. To *Eunomia* he also assigns the function of "straightening crooked justices." This is the traditional language of procedural "rights" argued and judged in the agora, without benefit of personification. The symbolic assignment of *dikē* still covers a field of meaning, both singular and plural, without conceptual clarity.

This is the less surprising when it is observed that Solon's vocabulary can employ the verb "to be" only within the limits of Homeric usage. There are twenty-two instances in the preserved fragments; none are copulative. Three happen to occur together, grouped acoustically within two lines in the Homeric manner (1.38–39). No more than Hesiod does Salon command a syntax suitable for telling what justice "is" or what it really "means."

To suppose that concealed in such imagery lies some conceptual grasp of a profound moral and cosmic principle is to misconceive what is actually happening in the usage of the Greek tongue during the archaic period of its development. The last three lines of the passage quoted from the shorter elegy (3.16–18) contribute a further clue to the completely nonphilosophic, nonabstract, nonconceptual character of Solon's composition. These have been phrased so as to be connected in sense and sound by the verb "come," occurring in each line in three variant forms at identical metrical positions. Logically, they leave the reader to solve a dilemma: is it justice who "comes" to punish, or the inevitable wound that "comes" to the city, or the city that "comes" to slavery? Such a logical test is inappropriate: the rules of composition still encourage acoustic echo. Solon is a writer of verse which still invites memorization.

He never discusses justice as a topic, in the way Hesiod had done. In his pragmatic account of what his policies had been he indirectly does something to clarify the character of *dikē* as procedural method. His elegies make no conceptual contribution which carries one beyond Hesiod. To be sure, the longer elegy is preserved in Stobaeus' anthology under the heading "Concerning Justice," as though this were its formal subject. But such classification, though it has influenced modern interpretations of Solon, is the work of a later and literate age. It is in fact Platonic, for the term "justice" has become no longer *dikē* but *dikaiosunē,* a distinction with a difference (below, Chapter 17).

15

The Justice of the Pre-Socratics

❦

The Milesian Formula

Anaximander of Miletus lived perhaps forty years after Solon. The doxographical tradition of later antiquity, derived from Theophrastus' *History of the Opinions of the Physical Philosophers,* ascribes to him the doctrine that the "material principle of things" was something he called "the Infinite," which was not any one "of the four elements so called but some other infinite body from which was generated all the heavens and the worlds in them." The account then continues: "(He says) that into those (things) out of which genesis exists for existing (things) does destruction also occur according to necessity; and that they give justice and penalty [*dikē, tisis*] to each other for nonjustice [*adikia*] according to the order of time, using in this way rather poetic terms to say so" (*FVS.* 12A9). Few passages of the doxographical tradition have generated more problems of interpretation. What precisely is the logical connection between the two last sentences as cited, and what in turn is their joint relationship to the doctrine of the Infinite? The different answers that have been given do not affect the conclusion to be drawn about the role of justice. What the doxography actually reports is a metaphor, by which a physical alternation, or oscillating rhythm, in all probability that of the seasons, is illustrated from legal procedure between human beings, that procedure being based on the rule of reciprocity, as in the *Iliad*. *Dikē* in the citation cannot possibly represent a justice in the sense of a comprehensive principle embracing the universe and its processes, for it is itself an item which is exchanged or bartered in the course of the process. Equilibrium and an end to reciprocal action would occur when, as Odysseus says to Achilles and Agamemnon: "You will not be left holding any thing lacking of justice, and you too will prove to be more just" (Chapter 7). The point of Anaximander's metaphor is to deny that in nature this kind of equilibrium ever does occur; the reciprocal give and take is perpetual. The phrase "order of time" has been linked with Solon's "justice of time" to draw the inference that time should be capitalized, becoming the "judge" (*Jaeger*, p. 159) of the cosmic process, and the neutral term "order" (*taxis*) converted into an "assessment" levied by Time (as in the Athenian tribute lists: so also Kirk and Raven, p. 120).[1] All this amounts to putting rather routine Greek phraseology upon the rack in order to extract a metaphysical confession from it. "Order of time," like "justice of time," refers to regular durational intervals within which the reciprocal process occurs.[2]

The dimensions of a cosmic justice would probably never have been fastened on the Greek were it not for the phraseology of the preceding clause, the authenticity of which has been called in question. Indeed, it is quite uncertain how much, if anything, of the whole citation (reported in indirect speech) is faithful to an original text, which the Lyceum may or may not have possessed at the time when Theophrastus wrote his history, despite reference to the "poetic vocabulary" employed.[3] But faithful or not, it stays away from any language which would be appropriate to the expression of justice as a philosophical concept or principle.

Heraclitus

Dikē had considerable symbolic significance for Heraclitus; the term is employed in four of his surviving sayings:[4]

1 (frag. 80) Necessary to understand war as-prevailing-communal
     and justice as feud [*dikēn erin*] . . .
2 (frag. 94) Sun will not step beyond measures;
     otherwise the Furies, assistants of justice, will find out where
     he is.
3 (frag. 28) Illusions the most illustrious (man) knows how to guard.

> But mark for all that (how) justice shall lay hold of the
> artificers and testifiers of falsehoods.
> 4 (frag. 23) The name of justice they would not have known,
> if these (things) did not exist.

Heraclitus' diction is pregnant, allusive, and often manipulated to render more than one layer of meaning. These sayings are no exception. The first is a reminiscence of two lines from different books of the *Iliad*, one of which is reworded and the other (as was noted in antiquity) contradicted. But Heraclitus has more than mere lines of Homer in mind. He is recollecting the rhythm of the narrative in which they occur, the action of which had undergone two abrupt reversals. Achilles, on hearing of Patroclus' death, experiences a revulsion of feeling. He vows to abandon his quarrel with Agamemnon, exclaiming, "Would that feud [*eris*] from among gods and men might perish!" Then, as the Trojans continue to press their advantage, he appears on the Greek fortifications and signals his decision to reenter battle by a great shout. Polydamas on the Trojan side counsels Hector to fall back on the defensive; Hector refuses the advice:

Ares (is) communal; before now he has killed the killer.

This is an aphorism, which in Hector's mouth at this moment of crisis becomes prophetically ironic. War is something which responds to the rule of reciprocity. But in this case reciprocity will require that the slayer of Patroclus shall himself be slain. Heraclitus offers the comment that what Hector says is correct and what Achilles had said was wrong.[5] The logic of war (*polemos*) and the logic of feud (*eris*) must be united—the logic of the battlefield and the logic of the agora. Both involve reciprocal processes. As are enemies in war, so are contestants in a civil feud. Homeric *dikē* as a symbol could be interpreted in two different ways, for it referred both to the process of argument and arbitration between contending parties and to the settlement which ended the process. Heraclitus opts for the former as the only version appropriate to explain the behavior of the cosmos.[6] The epic aphorism, following the oral rule, had been appositional: "Ares (is) communal." Heraclitus, converting it, substitutes the impersonal "war" (*polemos*) and inserts the locative participle of the verb "to be"—"extending-communal" (*eonta xunon*)—to indicate the idea of a formula which reaches over into opposites. But from the wording of Achilles' exclamation he eliminates the verb "perish" and substitutes the noun *dikē*, forcing both *dikē* and *eris* into an appositional conjunction where they become equivalents. Could it be that this kind of management of the Homeric text becomes possible because the text is now available in visible form, to be perused by the eye, instead of being merely recollected by the ear?[7]

The second and third sayings revive the personification of justice applied by Hesiod and Solon, but neither is philosophically very serious. Both exhibit a quality of sardonic humor which seems to have been recognized in some of the apocryphal anecdotes told about the philosopher in later antiquity. The measures of the sun have a twofold regularity: he appears and disappears at morn and eve, and he travels up and down the heavens between summer and winter. The limits of both journeys are set, an example of the regularity of cosmic behavior which was an article of faith with all pre-Socratic thinkers, except perhaps Democritus. But imagine the sun straying; one way he might be tempted to do so would be to dally underneath the earth, reposing who knows where. This possibility need not worry us; the Furies are down there too; they will find out where he is and arrest him and bring him back. The rule of regularity in the cosmos, that is, of "justice," requires this. But "she," as personified in Hesiod, is on Olympus. To enforce her complaints against the sun, she needs the Furies as "assistants" who can get at him when he is below the earth.[8] In support of this explanation, one can note that, if Solon's phrase "the foundation-roots of justice" was correctly explained as a reminiscence of that dwelling place set upon the "foundation-roots" of Ocean, with which Zeus had rewarded the three giants who had been his "assistants" (*epikouroi*), then Heraclitus is putting the same context to a different use, identifying not the giants but the Furies as "assistants" serving the interests of a cosmic order identified as "justice" instead of "Zeus." After all, it was the giants who enabled Zeus to restore his orderly reign over gods and men after the Titan rebellion.

Of the third saying,[9] it has been well observed that it belongs to a considerable group of such which attack the credentials of other persons of whom it is claimed that they are men of wisdom or intelligence, among whom Homer and Hesiod and Archilochus and Xenophanes are named; the language used suggests that the target was not only the poets themselves but those who recited their works in public gatherings. The philosopher's teachings, now ignored, would one day supplant them; the attacks have a tone of personal bitterness, and the present one is no exception. His target is "the man of evident reputation" (*dok-imōtatos*) who "has the ability to guard the (things) seeming" (*dok-eonta*). The characteristic pun sardonically calls attention to an irony which might be rendered (as above): "the illustrious guards only illusions," or else as "the most impressive guards only impressions." Who is this illustrious person, presumably a type? Is he statesman or general? The clue is supplied in what follows: "justice will lay hold of artificers and testifiers of falsehoods." The term "artificer" could be applied professionally to a poet; the term "falsehoods" had already been applied by Hesiod to certain kinds of poetry; the "testifier," as opposed to the artificer, is the reciter of poetry. The two clues can be combined to support the inference that the "testifiers" refers not to participants in legal proceedings, but to recitation of the poet's works, which from Heraclitus' point of view (supported by the accepted didactic functions of oral poetry) amounted to a witness to their authority. But that authority was illusory. Heraclitus' judgment in this matter was shared by other pre-Socratics, notably his successor Parmenides. If such be the nature of his target, this would explain the phrase "knows how to guard" (as read in the manuscript: *ginōskei phulassein*); the infinitive indicates the oral function of "holding in the memory" (Chapter 7, note 6). The reciters can learn to memorize, but the content memorized is illusory.

Justice "will catch up with" such people. How can this occur? Does Heraclitus mean they are going to be literally arrested and tried in court, or even pursued and harassed by Furies? This does not seem possible. More probably, he means they will not enjoy their reputation forever: the philosopher, (or his teaching) will take their place in public esteem; hence the savage emphasis on *dokimōtatos*. What then is "justice" except again, the rule of reciprocity required to keep "regularity" in affairs both cosmic and human? As they lose their *doxa*, he shall gain it. But the verb "catch up with" indicates that his imagination is still tending to dramatize the rule by personifying it.[10]

Dikē as the rule of regularity would seem to embrace the reciprocal process overall. Yet, depending on context, it can also symbolize one pole of the process: the retributive act which corrects previous injustice. This ambivalence haunts the term throughout its history in pre-Platonic thought. Anaximander (if the diction attributed to him is trustworthy) had expressed the narrower sense. The fourth remaining saying of Heraclitus probably does likewise. Its text relies on a plausible emendation. Previous attempts at interpretation have been convincingly corrected by G. S. Kirk,[11] to give a sense which harmonizes with the philosopher's doctrine of opposites. The pronominal adjective "these things," whether or not part of the quotation, must refer to what passes for "nonjustice"; justice subsists in virtue of its antithesis to the nonjust: neither can be known without the other.

The saying may intend to make a further point. The justice of which men become aware is a name; it exists as a name.[12] Is the philosopher advertising the fact that Hesiod's poem had indeed converted *dikē* into a "name" serving as a subject of discourse, and so becoming overtly recognizable as a topic? The wording, in fact, recalls the Homeric formula "they knew not formularies or justices," meaning that they did not possess or use any memorized version of them. Now, *dikē* has become known not only by its application but as a name to be identified; and as such, Heraclitus wishes to assert its relative nature.

Parmenides

The central preoccupation of the philosopher Parmenides is with the behavior and meaning of the verb "to be." The nature of his doctrine—difficult to decipher precisely because of those syntactical limits placed upon the Greek tongue which he is laboring to amend—need not concern us here,[13] except insofar as the term "justice" intrudes itself three times in what remains of his philosophical poem. It occurs only once in the expository portion, where, if anywhere, the term *dikē* might be taken to bear a serious philosophical meaning. He is giving a lengthy account of the properties (if that is the right word) of the "is," also named as "the being (thing)"; it is "unbegotten, indestructible . . . one, continuous," and so forth (8.3 ff.); "nor will the force of conviction permit that anything can become from not-being alongside of it; and therefore justice never lets it loose to become or perish by slackening (it) from fetters" (8.12–14).

The use of "justice" as a metaphor for describing cosmic situations has by now become familiar. Here "she" becomes a jailer, "her" prisoner being the unbegotten and indestructible and continuous "is." Parmenides is committed to the proposition that his "being" is the sole reality. How could he imagine it as the prisoner of something else? Such a metaphor would be philosophically acceptable to him only if *dikē* represented this same reality by another name, so that it could be imagined as its own prisoner. What sense of "justice," as established in Greek usage, would encourage such an image? The only and obvious one would be the traditional one, of justice as regularity, as custom, as accepted order, as what is expected and normal behavior, otherwise undefinable. Parmenides' application of the term—whether cosmic or logical, it is hard to say which—is in the mode employed in fragment 80 of Heraclitus, but leads to a different conclusion: the overall regularity of process is replaced by the regularity of immobility. "Justice," so far from being explained by having expository predicates attached to it, is itself attached as a kind of self-explanatory predicate to the dimension of what he is really interested in exposing—the character of the "is."

Hesiod, who first personified *dikē*, was directly interested in what the symbol might mean; Parmenides is not. His disinterest comes out in the fact that he can (given his repetitive style of exposition) reuse the metaphor of the jailer while substituting alternative terms to fill it, as when he says "forceful necessity [*anankē*] holds (the is) in bonds of limit which embrace-and-confine it"; and again, "Nothing other either is or shall be outside of the being, since fate [*moira*] has fettered it to stand [*emenai*] whole and immovable." It is not enough to describe *dikē*, *anankē*, and *moira* as "deities keeping company with each other." That is just what they do not do in Parmenides' poetry. For Parmenides to offer such alternatives is to indicate indifference on his part to the choice of terms, provided they recall traditional powers employed to dramatize a very nontraditional and sophisticated doctrine. The phraseology in "forceful necessity" and "fate has fettered" is Homeric, as is "embrace-and-confine," all three being drawn from disparate contexts in the *Iliad* which describe constraints imposed on people (Andromache, Hector) and on oxen, and have nothing to do with cosmology.[14] Their use exemplifies a principal habit of Parmenides' poetic method, one which assembles a multitude of tags and echoes from Homer and Hesiod, reworking them as necessary to serve non-Homeric purposes.

This allegorical patchwork of doctrine has earlier been placed in the mouth of a goddess, unnamed in her immediate context (is she the traditional Muse?), who introduces it to the philosopher in the following words (1.26–28):

Welcome! for it is no evil fate [*moira*] that escorted you forth
to travel along this way; for indeed it lies [*estin*] far outside of the treading
of men.
No, it was the law [*themis*] and justice [*dikē*].

Justice, so far from being a jailer, is here an escort provided for a journey. The model is Homeric. The story of the *Odyssey* placed emphasis upon the "justice," that is, propriety, of providing an escort for travelers; such was a special virtue of Odysseus, as recalled by Penelope.[15] *Dikē* here is conjoined with *Themis* to assert that the route of Parmenides, for all its apparent novelty, is that approved by traditional norms. For good measure, it is possible to detect memories of two more Homeric tags in the idiom of the lines.[16]

It is improbable that statements of this kind are inspired by "religious feeling." What we observe, rather, is that in Parmenides the "justice" which his verse symbolically employs carries the sense which underlies the ways in which it is applied in Homer and in archaic Greek thought generally. Personified, it can shift from role to role in a variety of performances, precisely as Parmenides asserts that reality should not. This applies with full force to "her" first appearance in the poem. As the philosopher travels on an allegorical journey toward the doctrine which is to be recited to him (as Hesiod recites his doctrine to Perses), his escort consists of "maiden Heliades" (did he invent them?) who, "leaving the halls of night behind proceed into light," and reach a certain place (1.11–14):

There stand [*eisi*] gateways of paths of night and day,
and lintel above encompasses them and stone threshold;
these high in sky are filled with great doors;
of them justice much penalizing holds the alternate keys . . .

The escorts cajole this personage into unlocking the doors and they pass through, to be received in due course by the unnamed deity. The quoted lines combine two memorable images, from the *Odyssey* and the *Theogony*, the latter the prevailing one. The role of justice is added by Parmenides; the unrelenting jailer of the later part of the peom is here preceded by the compliant janitor. But significantly "she" is equipped with keys. Hesiod had spoken of night and day approaching from opposite directions and briefly greeting each other as they pass each other by, alternately crossing and recrossing the threshold of the house they share, but never together.[17] The passage is one of the great poetic contexts of the Greek tongue. Within that mysterious house is somehow located the voice that speaks Parmenides' doctrine. But the place is now protected (as it is not in Hesiod) by two doors, alternately opening and closing to admit egress and ingress of day and night. For the philosopher to gain ultimate knowledge requires that both doors be opened at once, as they are (1.19). Justice is supplied as the doorkeeper to perform this function: normally she lets in one at the same time as letting the other out, executing in this way that reciprocal regularity of the cosmos which was also assigned to her by Heraclitus in connection with a different but related phenomenon, that of the sun's passage. That is why she "keeps punishing"—first day, then night—as she alternately confines them. A reminiscence of Hesiod's goddess demanding human penalty is applied to the diurnal rhythm of nature.

We conclude that justice in the thought of the pre-Socratics does not exceed the logical limits of that propriety and regularity which was the fundamental norm of Homeric society. The novelty lies in its application, now extended operationally to cover the behavior of the external world. The meaning remains circular; what is conserved is what is always (or should always be) done; or rather, in Parmenides' language, what always is. Once convert such a notion into a person—something that the pre-Socratics, in the manner of Hesiod and Solon, are always tempted to do—and "she" tends to disappear into a medley of roles assigned according to the convenience of the context. We are still not told what justice formally and definitively *is*.

16

The Justice of Aeschylus

The *Agamemnon* as printed in modern texts runs to 1673 lines. Within this compass the Greek verb "to be" in one form or another occurs seventy-eight times, to which can be added eight instances of compounding with the prefixes "in," "with," "from," and "on" (*en-, para-, apo-, epi-*).[1] Monosyllabic forms total nineteen, of which ten represent the past tense of the third person singular, *ēn* (plus one instance each of *ep-ēn* and *par-ēn*). The third singular present (*esti*) occurs twenty-three times (and add *par-esti* thrice). In comparison with Homer, it is to be remembered that a "line" of tragedy (as printed) is rarely as long as a hexameter, and frequently, as in choruses, contains only a third as many words. Overall these statistics, for what they are worth, may indicate an increase by the beginning of the fifth century of the ready employment of the verb—and possibly therefore of movement toward its copulative usage, particularly as may be indicated in a preference for *esti* above other forms—but proof would depend on a word count applied to more than one play and more than one author.

The Syntax of the Verb "to Be" in Drama

Such figures do, however, invite attention to what may be called the acoustic behavior of the verb, which, as in Homer's case (and also

Hesiod's), may have some bearing upon its semantic significance, prompting the question: does its role in the rhythms of the verse exhibit any peculiarities? One is discernible which is shared with Homer. The verb, though widely dispersed through a tragic diction of great virtuosity, variously employed for dialogue, choric song, and chant, in twenty instances intrudes itself in pairs separated by only a few words (ranging from two to eight)[2] and also once recurs three times in four lines.[3] This echo habit—if that is the right word—ceases at line 549 and is resumed at line 1203. In fourteen instances (a few of which overlap with the twenty), the syntax is epigrammatic, meaning that *einai* serves as verb in a sentence of between two and four words.[4] In five others, it is placed metrically first in the line but syntactically last in its clause, which gives it a kind of postponed emphasis.[5] In four others it terminates both line and clause simultaneously.[6] The significance of such eccentricities of arrangement taken singly may seem slight, but statistically (if we allow for occasional overlapping between instances), they add up to a total of forty-four usages of the verb (twenty-three in pairs and threes, twenty-one in single positions) out of a total of eighty-six (including compounds). What these statistics may suggest is a continuation of the propensity observable in epic for the verb to carry that kind of emphasis in pronunciation which provokes the habit of either echoing it or isolating it. Such emphasis would be compatible with a semantic content more significant, more colorful, than a merely copulative use of the verb would imply.

And indeed, once the verb is perceived and examined not as a single word but in its syntactical connections (or lack of such) with subjects and predicates of given types, it is possible to discern that its semantic usage, while advancing beyond Homeric norms, has nevertheless not departed very far from them, as the following tabulation may reveal:

67–68   "(it) stands where (or how) now (it) stands [*esti . . . esti*]"; an absolute use, lacking subject and predicate, and untranslatable, in the manner of Parmenides; the Greek supplies no "it." This paired example is locative, as indicated by the adverbial conjunction.

104   "I prevail-with-authority [*kurios eimi*] to tell of the voyaging might of men . . ."; an instance of linkage to a status word as predicate.

160   "Zeus, who-ever-precisely he stands-to-be- [*hos tis pote estin*], if this (thing is) acceptable to him being-named . . ."; the verb

connotes an identity which constitutes the existence or real nature of a person, in this case in the form of a name: the sense is close to the existential.

168–170 "nor even who-precisely formerly waxed-great [*hos tis . . . ēn megas*] luxuriating in all-conquering élan—not even (he) will be celebrated as [or "though"] previously existing [*prin ōn*]"; a second pair, the predicates indicating both status and position in time.

217 "(I pray that it) may-turn-out-well [*eu eiē*]"; what the optative-future projects in time is an event, indicated by the predicate adverb, but the event has no subject; the employment of the "impersonal absolute" construction in such commonplaces is deceptively casual.

259 "just-propriety stands-firm [*dikē esti*] to honor a commander's wife." The use of an infinitive of general action as predicate foreshadows a syntax of abstract definition. But the idiom of English, as of other modern tongues, by paraphrasing as "(it) is justice to honor . . ." goes too far, supplying a nonexistent subject so as to convert the verb from locative-existential to copulative usage.

269 "(I pronounce) Troy (as) being-in-possession-of-Achaeans [*Troian Achaiōn ousan*]"; epigrammatic and locative.

272–273 "what (is) the guarantee? Is-there-present-to-you-of-these evidence [*esti tōnde soi tekmar*]? (It) is-present [*esti*]"; a third pair, with locative sense.

325 "of vanquished and victors diversely to-hear-the-voices-is-present-fact [*dicha phthongas akouein esti*]"; the grammars define this usage by the paraphrase "(it) is (possible) to hear," thus supplying a subject and predicate, both nonexistent, which convert what is essentially a locative usage into a copulative. The real subject is an event—a diverse hearing of voices, generalized in the infinitive, which "presents itself" to the ears.

367–383 This strophe contains the following:

367 "The stroke of Zeus they have-and-can declare;

368 Yes, there-is-present [*par-esti*] this thing to track-to-discovery

374 To descendants is-manifested injury (?) . . .

376 of (those) puffed up more than in-just-propriety . . .

378 let-it-prove (or persist) nonpenalized (for me) [*estō a-pēmanton*]

380 . . . for there-is-present [*esti*] no defense of (in) wealth

381   to [against?] surfeit for (him) who
382   kicks over the altar of justice."

The first and third examples (368 ,380) are locative; the second projects into the future (cf. 217) an act of separation indicated by the privative; *par-esti*, like the use of *esti* in 325, is commonly disguised by the paraphrase "(it) is possible (that) . . ." The strophe, a characteristic choric meditation, aphoristic in style and thought (but with dubious text) calls attention to the impersonal use of *einai*, with or without an infinitive as subject or predicate, which now, developing in such gnomic passages as this, seems to anticipate its philosophic conversion into an instrument of definition

412   "There-is-present [*par-esti*] dishonored silence (?) . . . to see"; the text is uncertain, but the locative sense is clear, though disguisable, as in 368 (above).

427–428   "the woes (set) in houses beside the hearth are-these-lying-there [*tade esti*]"; a locative usage, as the complementary predicates indicate, despite the temptation to translate copulatively "the woes are these."

463–465   "The Erinyes in time (a man) proving-successful [*tuchēron onta*] without justification . . . render dim-and-dark"; the participle carries both temporal and locative predication: "in time," by its position, accompanies both verbs.

The first eighteen instances of *einai* in the *Agamemnon* have now been reviewed. The nineteenth introduces a new type, to be observed separately. It will be appreciated that none of the eighteen is copulative. They fairly represent usage in the rest of the drama (if we ignore for the moment the group represented by the nineteenth). The primary and most persistent sense is locative, with location in time, personal status, or personal identity as secondary aspects. Such usage is typically Homeric. But the syntax of the verb also shows a tendency to employ idioms in which the subject or predicate may be expressed as an infinitive of "general action"; or else either subject or predicate may be absent altogether; and not rarely the verb can occur absolutely without any qualification. Such syntactical habits, perceptible but infrequent in Homer, may point toward a linguistic future in which *einai* will come to represent on the one hand the notion of existence and on the other the act of definition or verification, expressed in the strictly copulative use. It need not therefore surprise us if the philosopher Parmenides, living in the same epoch in which this play was composed, found himself pursuing with intellectual vigor the problems presented by these syntactical usages.

A "Generative" Usage

The nineteenth instance in the text furnishes a type which, while expressive of these same tendencies, deserves separate classification. It is deceptive in the way it tempts the translator to treat *einai* as the copula, but in fact the verb is found attaching itself to predicates describing activities, and so is used to indicate an involvement of the subject in action, as follows:

472 "(I pray) may I neither become-a-city-destroyer [*eiēn ptoli-porthēs*], nor on the other hand taken-prisoner beneath another eat away life"; the predicate is essentially a verb [*porthō*] disguised as an adjective; the idiom is the equivalent of "may I never destroy cities"; the predicate attached by *einai* to its subject is not a property, quality, or class, but an action. It is tempting to call this a "generative" use of *einai*. Whether or not this be a suitable desigation, the usage plays a prominent role in Aeschylus' diction.

542 "you-took-possession of this disease [*ēste ep-ēboloi tēsde nosou*]"; location is also implied.

593 "By such statements I was demonstrated (as) being-cast-adrift [*plank-tos ousa*]"; again a locative implication.

796 "eyes-are-not-for-hiding-from . . . [*ouk esti lathein ommata*]"; a periphrasis for "would not be able to hide," where the paraphrase "it is not possible for eyes . . ." converts into copulative usage.

869 "if he was-found-dead as (often as) the stories accumulated" [*ēn tethnēkōs*]"; the predicate, as in 796, is actually a verb. Similar idioms are classified as "periphrastic," the verb acting as an "auxiliary," to complete tense and voice, but its force is stronger than that.

989 "acting-as-witness-in-person [*auto-martus ōn*]"; the context is also locative, the equivalent of "witnessing in person."

1037 "Zeus has set you to-be-present-as-participant of lustral water [*koinōnon einai*]"; the predicate is equivalent to "to participate in"; the context again locative.

These seven illustrate the type sufficiently. The text furnishes no less than twenty-one more: at 1050 (she stands-there . . . equipped . . .); 1060 (uncomprehending-standing); 1094 ([as] keen sniffer like a dog

. . . she appears-to-be-acting); 1099 (informed-we-stand); 1105 (un-knowing-I-stand); 1140 (you-go-god-carried); 1179 (shall-emerge-look-ing); 1195 ([as] false-prophet I-function-door-knocking-babbling); 1206 (he-acted-[as]-wrestler-upon-me); 1211 (how un-scathed-did-you-remain?); 1232 female of male [as]-murderer-does-function); 1302 (abiding-enduring-out-of-well-enduring mind); 1360 (I too hold-my-self-similar); 1375 ([as]-friends-seeming-to-behave); 1395–1396 (if [it] could stand-done-fittingly . . . [it] would stand-as-done-justly, where adverbs replace verbal nouns or adjectives); 1421 ([as] listener . . . a judge-severe-you-behave); 1488 (which of these stands-not-god-ordained?); 1505 (unaccusable-you-stand); 1561 (hard-battled-they-stand to judge); 1571 (hard-to-be-borne-though-standing); 1637 (sus-pected [as] enemy-I-stood-from-far-back).

In these usages, adjectives, participles, and adverbs are rendered into predicate verbs linked to their subjects by *einai*. Such linguistic preference reflects a mental one, which would prefer to see the image of a simple action performed by or upon a subject replaced by an image of the subject presented in separation from the act, which becomes "his" predicate. This behavior of *einai*, I suggest, like others already noted, marks an increasing tendency[7] to use a language of predication either supplementing or replacing a language of dynamic imagery; it antici-pates a direction which both language and thought are going to take, as they proceed to convert the concrete into the abstract, the narrative into the analysis, the image into the concept, the particular into the uni-versal. But the direction is only incipient. The true oral ancestor of the veridical statement as expressed by a copula, namely, the appositional conjunction of two equivalents without a verb, still prevails in the diction of this play as in all others.[8] So far, however, as the direction exists, it could be taken as a symptom of the fact that the syntactical habits of tragedy reflect an increasing invasion of the spoken word by the written.

The Mythos of the *Oresteia*

The theme of the trilogy—the only surviving one—of which the *Agamemnon* forms the first part, is on the face of it a family curse, or better, a fatal family destiny, transmitted in the male line through three generations, from two brothers, Atreus and Thyestes, to their respective sons, Agamemnon and Aegisthus, and from Agamemnon to his son, Orestes. Atreus had had his brother's children (all but one) killed and eaten unwittingly by their own father. This event had occurred in the building before which the action of the first play of the trilogy takes place. Thyestes, discovering the identity of what he had eaten, had invoked a curse on Atreus and his house and fled with the surviving child, Aegisthus. As the curse proceeds to take effect, the female line becomes involved. Agamemnon performs a ritual murder upon his daughter Iphigenia; her mother Clytemnestra then murders Agamemnon, with the conspiratorial assistance of Aegisthus, who becomes her consort; Agamemnon's daughter, Electra, then assists her brother, Orestes, to accomplish the killing of both Aegisthus and Clytemnestra. Burdened by the commission of this act against his own mother, Orestes in turn is hounded by demons of vengeance, relentless and physically repulsive, who are represented as being commissioned by her ghost to undertake the duty of destroying him. The march of events is thus tightly controlled by a series of murders. Rather than being a blood feud waged between rival families, the narrative is one of internecine conduct within a single family, or between two branches of it, which threatens the family's destruction.

This formula does not cover all the facts in the case, though it adequately accounts for what goes on in the second and third movements of the trilogy. The first movement, the *Agamemnon*, which is much the longest, involves its audience in the contemplation of still more crimes and consequences peripheral to the family tragedy yet involved with it. Agamemnon's brother was Menelaus, whose wife was Helen (she also happened to be Clytemnestra's sister). She, succumbing to the seductions of Paris, had deserted her husband despite his love for her and had absconded to Troy, the city of Paris' father, Priam. The crime brings retributive destruction upon Troy, inflicted by Agamemnon on behalf of his brother. It was to further this purpose that he had his daughter killed, to appease a divinity who was temporarily preventing the punitive expedition from setting sail. The motivation for this particular crime had therefore nothing directly to do with the family curse; the instructions came from another quarter.[9] Agamemnon's success against Troy in turn encourages aggrandizement on his part, a feature which he displays on returning from the wars to greet his wife, and which contributes to his downfall at her hands. The same events have created one more victim. Cassandra, Priam's daughter, survives the total destruction of her home and city to become a prize of war. The conqueror brings her home as his concubine. After he withdraws into the palace, inspired by prophetic frenzy she announces his impending and foreordained doom, and also her own, at the hands of the outraged wife. This duly occurs.

So far considered, the trilogy resembles an exercise in Grand Guignol, horror for horror's sake, an effect which, to say the least, is not mitigated when two corpses in each of the first two plays are produced and displayed on stage by their respective murderers to mark the triumph of their vengeance. Of course, a large portion of the events which we feel to be included in the action is not action in the stage sense. It takes place only in memories and reflections, reports and prophecies, as these are variously offered by characters and chorus by way of commentary on what is going on. Their emotional impact is therefore mitigated: they are not seen, only heard. It is a method of dramatic enlargement common to all Greek tragedy, never more so than in the *Agamemnon*, which is constructed so as to indicate the historical background which has predetermined the present and the future.

It remains true that one of the most powerful impressions conveyed by the *Oresteia* is that of human beings caught in a web of continuous crime from which they cannot escape. Yet escape occurs. The opening of the third play is so arranged as to introduce the question: can the most recent agent of murder (Orestes) be absolved of his act and restored to civic society? The audience, having heard the whole trilogy, would sense that this question was not addressed to his act alone. The perpetrator himself, appealing for a judicial solution, recalls the fatal series, from the point where Troy was sacked, and states, "I killed my mother by penalty of reciprocal killing for my father" (*Eum.* 457–464). Can the series now be halted? The *Eumenides* devotes itself to dramatizing the way in which this might take place. The solution is to create an institution[10]—it is actually created on stage—namely, a court of legality, in which murder and counter-murder are replaced by verbal argument from contending parties and by judicial decision, implemented by the vote of a jury.[11] Shall the most recent perpetrator of murder be destroyed in his turn? By the narrowest of decisions, the vote is no; the series can end.

The dramatic climax is thus a legal transaction, we might almost say a negotiation, between contending parties under the presidency of an arbitrator (the goddess Athene) who shares responsibility for final decision with a panel of jurors (the court of the Areopagus). The procedure over which they preside is still an *agon*, a confrontation between opponents (*Eum.* 677, 744, etc.), though now conducted by persuasion, instead of violence as in the first two plays (a fact noted in the drama itself). As such, it furnishes both a counterpart and a likeness to what has gone before. Viewing the trilogy as a whole, we become aware of a continuing series of transactions, carried out violently to be sure, but exhibiting a kind of law of reciprocity. These successive slayings have had their own rationale, which is replaced by the procedures of litigation and judgment. The *Oresteia* is not a simple story, still less a mere horror story. The characters can be viewed as trapped: but from another point of view they successively take up burdens, even duties as they conceive them, imposed on them. Each act of murder is an attempt to correct an imbalance in human affairs, to restore an equilibrium, we can say even an equity, symbolized in the biblical phrase "an eye for an eye"; the trouble is that each attempt fails because the results achieved —the injury inflicted and the guilt involved—prove excessive. Confrontation, being a fact of life, poses the problem of containment. The rhythm of human affairs needs to be kept within measure, rather than overturned on one side or the other. What is needed is reciprocal accommodation, not reciprocal murder.

The Symbols of "Justice"

A story of this kind can be perceived as consisting of a series of attempts to aim at something called "justice," mostly regarded as penalty or punishment imposed at any one point in the process, but also extendible to a view of the process as a whole. Much of Greek tragedy turns on this theme, but it is a particular preoccupation of the *Oresteia*, whose diction is saturated with the symbol *dikē* and its correlatives as these are applied in a great variety of contexts to explain what has happened, is happening, or will happen. These form a kind of symbolic system.[12] In the *Agamemnon* the noun (*dikē*) occurs seventeen times, accompanied by the adjective "just" (*dikaios*) thrice; "justly" (*dikaiōs*) thrice; "nonjust" and "nonjustly" (*adikos adikōs*), one each; two verbs of "adjudication" (*dikazō, dikaiō*), one each; a noun "adjudicator" (*dikastēs*), once;[13] and a variety of compound derivatives (*anti-dikos, pro-dikos, sun-dikos, en-dikos, euthu-dikēs*, one each; and *dikē-phoros* twice); for an overall total for the play of thirty-six. This leaves out of account fourteen instances of *dikēn* used as an adverbial preposition governing the genitive, meaning "just like." As will appear, this "system" covers a field of meaning, resembling but not imitating the same phenomenon in Hesiod's poem. It has no single frame of reference as that would be defined to meet conceptual standards.[14] It covers legal process as a whole[15] and its various aspects—the court, the plea, the hearing, the judgment, the sentence—no doubt in this area reflecting the growing prominence of legal process in the Athens of the day. But its reference can shift backward to indicate Homeric and traditional aspects of "justice," viewed as the propriety of expected behavior or the exchange and adjustment of "rights" through compensatory behavior. But yet again, it can focus intensely upon retribution, as simply retaliation inflicted through physical injury and death.

The *Eumenides:* Justice as Legality

In the third play of the trilogy,[16] the legal dimension of *dikē* understandably prevails (though not without competition), as is made clear near the beginning when Apollo promises the exhausted fugitive that at Athens he will find "adjudicators" (*dikastai*, 81).[17] Accordingly, Orestes, reaching the sanctuary of Athene's temple, announces as he clasps her image, "I await here the outcome of judicial process" (*telos dikēs*, 243; using the term *dikē* in the context of Apollo's promise). The demonic chorus, having pursued him into the temple, protest that he is requesting "to become subject to judicial process [*hupo-dikos*] in a suit for debt" (260). Athene, entering in person, inquires the identity of those present. The chorus, speaking as litigants, state the case against Orestes which has justified their pursuit. Athene replies, "Two parties are present but only one half of the argument" (428), and turns to Orestes: "Declare your country, family and circumstances, and offer defense against the complaints made, if indeed you are embracing this image because of your trust in judicial process" (*dikē;* 437–440). Orestes responds to the opportunity thus afforded by putting forward his half of the case, concluding with the appeal: "Be your part to judge the justice of it [*krinon dikēn*], whether I have acted justly (i.e., legally) or not [*dikaiōs;* 468], for it is before you that I have acted-the-transaction" (*praxas,* referring to legal action, 469). So far, the machinery invoked is assumed to repose in the authority of a single magistrate, resembling the *basileus* who figures so prominently in Hesiod (though even Hesiod prefers the plural). This is not going to be enough; what we have so far witnessed is a preliminary hearing. She replies: "The transaction [*pragma*] is too important for a mortal to judge-the-justice [*dikazein*] nor on the other hand is it lawful for me to assess the "justices" [*diairein . . . dikas*] of a homicide subject to fierce wrath" (472); and she adds an interesting legal point by way of explanation: sanctuary, reached by Orestes in her temple as approved by the antique nomos, is her province; the alternative of a judicial trial will require a different authority (473–475), even though, as it turns out, she also participates, thus melding old and new. She proceeds to meet the problem by announcing the formation of a permanent body of "adjudicators" (*dikastai*, 483), thus fulfilling the terms of the promise previously made by Apollo, and invites the two sides to submit "testimonies and sworn evidencies to assist the judicial process" (*dikē*, 486; possibly the distinction is between oral guarantees and objects produced for visible display, as in the *Iliad*, though the only "object" to be produced will be Apollo himself). At the sound of a trumpet, the people and the "senate" are convoked (566–568) and the senate is seated (629). Apollo appears to "join in the judicial proceedings" (*sun-dikein*: he is something like a "friend of the court"). "Bring on the case," he says to Athene, "and complete-and-conclude the justice of it [*dikē*] as you know how." The chorus as prosecutor and Orestes as defendant then argue; Apollo offers his testimony on behalf of the defendant, the chorus offer rebuttal. Athene addresses the people who are "conducting judgment upon the first justices [*prōtas dikas*][18] concerning shedding of blood" (681–682), and after reaffirming the permanence of the present "council of adjudicators" (*dikastōn . . . bouleutērion*, 684) indicates where they will sit and in general terms what their judicial functions and influence are to be (690–697): the latter will depend on the city's retaining deterrence as a factor in legal proceedings: "Does any man stay within justice [*endikos*, i.e., within legality] when he has nothing to fear? So keep within justice [*en-dikōs*] by trembling before the majesty of this court" (699–700). A vote is then requested "to decide justice" (*diagnōnai dikēn*). The chorus and Apollo continue to match arguments against each other while ballots are cast into two urns; Athene claims the role of "judging justice" last (*krinai dikēn*). She "will add her vote to Orestes personally for all to see" (*tēnde egō*, 734–735), and then she states that Orestes wins even on an evenly split vote. The urns are emptied, the ballots counted. She pronounces that Orestes "has got off a judicial trial [*ekpepheugen dikēn*] for bloodshed" (752).[19] To the protests of the chorus she rejoins: "the judicial process [*dikē*] came out even-voted" (795–796).

This review of legal usage, even though not exhaustive (in some instances the text is too corrupt to be usable), reveals its frequency, and also its fluidity within the sphere of the legal. The "justice" in question may be that of the procedure taken as a whole or that expressed in any aspect thereof, identifying the pleas offered, the judgment given, or the overall rule of legality within which these occur, something you do not "step outside of." Such growing identification of "justice" with legal process may well reflect institutional changes in its management, as these may have been set in motion since the time when oral "formularies" were entrusted to writing. Documentation of law would, one would think, encourage greater formalization of procedure and increasing professionalism in its administration. In place of the *histōr*, the *dikaspolos*, the elders, or a particular *basileus* (whatever their overlapping roles may have been in oral society), we have a jury of *dikastai* with fixed attendance (570) and a presiding officer who convenes a sitting and calls for a vote. Mere oaths orally asseverated before an audience are no longer enough to carry conviction before a body equipped to weigh evidence (429–432): the oath that is important is the one sworn to by this body (483, 680, 710, 749). Instead of decisions orally formulated, reflecting a consensus reached as a result of responding to competing varieties of rhetoric, we have a ballot cast in silence (on the part of the balloters) and arithmetically counted. In the play, the court established by Athene is that which sits on the Areopagus. Since the duties and powers of this body were "reformed" about the time of the play's production, it has been debated whether Aeschylus in constructing his plot was responding to contemporary interest in this event, and perhaps taking sides either for or against the reform. It is probably more to his purpose to dramatize the whole movement toward increasing legality, which he might regard as characteristic of the genius of his city ever since the day of Draco and Solon. The remains of Draco's code, as these have been recently reexamined,[20] could be used to support this hypothesis.

Justice in Homeric Dress

But leaving aside the fine points of legal history, it is equally to be noted, as we pursue the problem of the presence or absence of justice as a philosophical conception, how much of Homeric practice still lingers on in the action of the *Eumenides*. The chorus represent the past confronted by the present; their cause is that of the "older gods." This role is basic, and would seem designed to meet the expectations of the audience, whatever additions were contributed by Aeschylus' own imagination.[21] The emphasis on their seniority (cf. 731, 848, 1027), now brushed aside by upstarts, suggests for them, despite their sex, the role of "elders," who in an earlier and simpler age were treated automatically as the source of authority and counsel (above, Chapter 7). At the opening of their first stasimon, devoted to a description of their nature and functions, they introduce themselves with the claim phrased in traditional idiom: "We are straight-justiced" (312). When despite their protests legal proceedings are opened, they would like to require the defendant to affirm his innocence on oath or otherwise deny him speech. They are relying on the kind of time-honored oral procedures conducted in the agora which Homer and Hesiod take for granted. Athene objects: "You prefer to 'hear' (what is said) justly rather than transact business justly," meaning that they are rejecting legal process, with its apparatus of testimony and evidence, in favor of a more primitive method. The Furies are puzzled: "You are the expert; please explain." She replies: "I pronounce that nonjust (statements) cannot prevail by means of (mere) oaths." The chorus impatiently rejoin: "Anyway, prove him wrong and judge a justice straight," thus reverting again to the phraseology of antique practice, in which the "straight words" spoken in the agora by the judge are presumed to be those which conform to the winning side (429–433). Later, having ostensibly stated their case before the court, they assert that "having discharged our every arrow we wait where we are to hear how the contest is judged" . . . "we wait around to become an oral witness [*epēkoos*] of this justice" (676–677, 732–733). There is also much talk of oaths given by or received from litigants. Some of the procedures followed are also antique. Though dikasts do the voting, an assembly of the people (566, 681) has to be convoked, apparently to witness this event. What they also witness is a rhetorical contest between adversaries. To be sure, litigants continued to handle their own cases even in the fourth century, but in the drama there is as yet no mention of a body of law to guide the proceedings (such law as is mentioned is still *thesmos*) nor any thought of appealing to its text or the tradition reflected in the text, as became regular in the fourth century. Though care is taken to identify the balloting as the necessary method of reaching a decision, even while it is taking place the rhetorical contest still goes on (711–733), as though judgments were still being swayed by who turned out the winner or, alternatively, by who spoke "justice most straight." Even the vote of Athene, which receives what seems to be arbitrary weight, may recall the right of a single *basileus* either to preside or to intervene in a hearing before an agora.

More generally, it is indicated several times that the justice rendered to Orestes may be akin to that celebrated in the story of the *Odyssey*, namely, the proper reception and treatment of the "stranger-guest." Orestes had of course enjoyed the status of *xenos* in Phocis as an exile before the murder (202). After the murder, he becomes both "suppliant" and "stranger-guest" at Athens. That is how Athene identifies him when she first sees him and interrogates him (409, 436); Apollo in his turn, as a native of Delphi, identifies the jury as "stranger-hosts" to himself and to Orestes (680, 748). Despatching Orestes to Athens, he had taken care to promise the escort which in the *Odyssey* was perceived as the hallmark of the proper treatment of a traveler (91, 93). The promise is elicited by an appeal from Orestes: "You know what it is to-avoid-committing-injustice; so now please learn to-avoid-indulging-in-indifference." The couplet is a jingle, almost a pun, and its purpose is rather puzzling unless it is meant to identify justice specifically as the rule governing protection of traveling strangers. Apollo knows the rule forbids the kind of injuries commonly visited on wayfarers unprotected by their city's "justice." Will he then please apply it in this case? He answers in effect: I will. It is also to be observed that the Argive alliance offered to Athens by Orestes, himself an Argive, before the trial, and affirmed after it, represents in fact a transaction between one *xenos* and another.

Justice as Retribution

The "justice" of the *Eumenides* so far described has a rival locked in fierce competition with it. Orestes is no sooner despatched to Athens to seek the justice of adjudication than the Furies, reacting to the reproaches of the ghost of Clytemnestra, stir in their sleep, awake, and discover that Apollo has allowed him to depart. Their protest is vehement: "Who can call this a just condition of affairs?" (*dikaiōs echein*, 154); "The younger gods are responsible; their power completely exceeds justice" (*dikas pleon*, 163). Apollo replies in kind: "You belong . . . where justices are a matter of head-lopping and eye-gouging" (187); "I deny your persecution of Orestes to be conducted within justice" (*en-dikōs*, 221; cf. 699–670); "the justices (i.e., adjudications) of these matters Pallas will oversee" (224). They rejoin: "It is I who with justice shall pursue this man" (*dikēi*, if this emendation is correct). Catching up with Orestes at Athens, they continue to sustain this claim: he may want to become subject to judicial process (260); it is in Hades that he will contemplate sinners like himself "enduring what is appropriate to the justice of the case" (*tēs dikēs epaxia*). When Orestes on his side invokes the presence and assistance of Athene (288), this becomes the signal for the Furies to proclaim their own powers and prerogatives, starting with the announcement: "We stand-straight-justiced; that is what we think." Otherwise, this lengthy "binding song" (307–396) avoids mentioning their connection with justice. When Athene announces the formation.of a jury system to try the case, they are provoked into open denunciation, for if, in the course of this "justice," Orestes is acquitted—as he might be—what becomes of their own "justice" and its authority? In a passionate stasimon (490–565) they proclaim (490–493): "Now comes total overthrow, if the "justice" and injury inflicted by this mother-slayer shall prevail!"[22] It will be no use now for parents "newly smitten to cry out, O Justice! O thrones of the Furies! while the house of justice falls in on them" (508–516). The court nevertheless is summoned; legal process takes over, in which the chorus briefly participate (583–586); cross-examining the defendant, they even prompt him to offer his explanation to "those adjudicating these matters" (*dikazontas*, 601). When, however, Apollo joins in advocacy, they admonish him: "Take care; or you will overdo justice on his behalf" (*huper-dikeis*, 652). On announcement of the vote, Orestes hails the result; now he can be restored to kin and country (754–761). But for the chorus it is the hour of defeat. Their passionate anger is turned against Athens. Though they have participated in the "justice" of the court, it is to another justice they now appeal: "A canker leafless childless—ah Justice!—will cast corruption on the land!" The cry is repeated verbatim as the stanza is repeated (784–787 = 814–817).

The drama thus opposes justice to justice; the language employed leaves this in no doubt. One part of the action—the major part—celebrates justice as applied in legal procedure, and dramatizes its effects. A second part—communicated in the language of the chorus and also their acts—celebrates a justice which is injured, perhaps destroyed, in the course of these same effects. This is not to say that the drama exploits the difference as a difference. It is not a problem play; more accurately the difference is exploited, one might almost say savored, as though such an antithesis were part of the scheme of things. This comes out in several instances where the text is so constructed as to employ "justice" in punning sequences, recalling the grouped sequences in Hesiod. The mind capable of constructing such drama is aware that *dikē* covers a field of meaning, but its design is to exploit the field, not tidy it up.

Justice as Ordered Propriety

It is in conformity with this view of things that the Furies are in the conclusion reconciled, accepting house and home within the city they have threatened in the name of justice to destroy, and accepting also the ambience of those procedures of justice which have threatened their own justice.[23] In order to draw the Furies into the orbit of legality, to convert them into "Eumenides," or "Kindly-Ones," it is necessary to create some ambiguous middle ground between these two "justices"; or alternatively to confer upon the Furies' brand of justice some share in the role of its competitor. They greet Athene's decision to set up a court of justice by singing four stanzas of dire prediction: this may mean the overthrow of that justice which enforces retributive punishment for homicide (490–525).[24] They then devote four more stanzas (526–565) to associating the term *dikē* and the adjective *dikaios* with a far wider sphere of human affairs, offering a series of aphorisms and observations which can be summarized as follows: what we need is neither anarchy nor despotism; the mean is always preferable; god supervises in various ways; my utterance is commensurate; impiety breeds outrage; prosperity is the fruit of a healthy mind; I advise absolute reverence for *justice's altar;* so don't let material gain tempt you to kick it contemptuously; penalty always impends; the latter end decides. Heeding these words, we should honor parents and protect stranger-guests domestically. So shall *the just* (except in emergency) enjoy some prosperity; or at least avoid disaster. But I advise that the rash transgressor who accumulates goods forcefully *without justice* will come to grief in time; his calls for help will be vain; the *daimōn* mocks his lack of foresight; his previous prosperity is smashed on the *reef of justice,* and he goes under for ever.

The dramatist has evidently composed these four stanzas (with the assistance of several commonplaces) to descant upon those qualities of state and citizen celebrated in the poetry of Solon. The "justice" contained in this context is Solon's justice (as is also the case in a strophe of the *Agamemnon,* 750–762).[25] It has nothing to do with homicide,[26] but very much to do with sobriety in the pursuit of wealth and power. Solon's sentiments have been given lyric reformulation and assigned to the Furies in order to prepare the audience for their conversion from demons into benign spirits, whose justice of reciprocal murder can be adapted to the justice of civic order in a peaceful and prosperous Athens. It is to be noted that as the conversion begins to take place, under the persuasion of Athene, she begins to employ the justice symbols in their comprehensive (and possibly original) sense of a "propriety" in the performance of what is "expected," synonomous with a "regular" order of things. She points out that it is now possible for them to dwell in the city under the most attractive conditions, which they may refuse, but if so, "You cannot with just propriety [*dikaiōs*] direct any wrath or complaint against it" (888). If they accept, she says, "you have opportunity to be honored with just propriety [*dikaiōs*] in perpetuity as a free holder of this land" (891), and she continues, "Just-like a gardener, I am very fond of this just-and-proper people" (911–912, punning on *dikē* as preposition and adjective). In the task of protecting Athenian manhood, the Fates too have their part to play: "their apportionment is correct; they have a part in every home; their weight is felt in every season; by visitations legitimate [*en-dikois*] supremely and universally honored" (963–967). The citizens themselves, showing favor and honor to the Furies, "will adorn a land and city of just rectitude" (*ortho-dikaion*, 994). In the finale, as the moment arrives for these now benign spirits to leave, Athene appropriately summons escorts to conduct them to their underground abode "with attendants who keep guard over my image, with just propriety [*dikaiōs*], for it is to the very eye of Theseus' land that you pass." The *dikē* language of these closing pronouncements (in the last hundred and fifty lines of the play) is neither retributive (and punitive) on the one hand nor legal on the other. Associated as it is with a vision of Athens as a peaceful, well-ordered, and prosperous community, it recalls the directive "justice" of the Homeric poems, within which men should live by conserving the social norms, which can be done only by exercising a kind of reciprocal courtesy.

The situation is different when, as earlier in the play, justice is personified. As her image becomes more definite, so also it becomes narrowly punitive, as is evident in the songs of the chorus (before their conversion) and the conception they convey of their role among men. The rule of reciprocal measure becomes the rule of retribution; that is, *dikē* identifies herself not with the overall rhythm of the process but with one specific moment of it. It is much easier to achieve poetic exploitation of retributive violence, mirrored as murder or malign persecution. The fact that Aeschylus also manages to make drama out of *dikē* as merely "due process" is a paradox and a triumph of art.

The *Choephoroi*: Justice as Reciprocal Punishment

As we go backward in the trilogy, the varying modalities of *dikē* repeat themselves, but in different proportions. Space forbids more than a summary. Behind the *Eumenides* lies the *Choephoroi*.[27] Its plot, preoccupied as it is with the ritual murder of Clytemnestra, has a bare simplicity, supplying the reasons for Orestes' later predicament. The actions performed and the sentiments inspired are treated on their merits; they are unmysterious. Central to the stage setting is the tomb of Agamemnon, addressed variously and jointly by a chorus of household servants, by Electra, and by Orestes. It is called an "altar" and treated as a shrine: the murder is performed as a kind of blood offering to it, to the ghost of its inhabitant, who is passionately invoked, and in whose service the deed is performed.

These simplicities of plot are matched by the simplicity with which the vocabulary of justice is employed, as it recurs throughout the text. Its initial appearance is as the symbol of punitive retribution, and this narrowing of reference is made explicit when the chorus adjure Electra to expect an avenger to arrive (neither party is yet aware that he has arrived). She replies: do you mean an adjudicator of justice, or its executor (*dik-astēs* versus *dikē-phoros*; literally a *dikē* manager versus a *dikē* carrier, an untranslatable pun)? They reply: "Speaking explicitly, (it will be) a reciprocal killer" (120–121). Her question formulates the contrast between *dikē* applied as a mode of due process, as in the *Eumenidēs,* and *dikē* as merely the penalty imposed. Their answer makes it clear that only the latter is in question; there will be no attempt to pursue the legalities that will be dramatized in the *Eumenides.* Yet the form of her question, implying as it does the possibility of choice, may be intended to point forward to the legal alternative that will be tried after this one has run its course. The play's conclusion offers support for this suggestion. The killing is over: Orestes displays the bodies of the culprits, the blood-stained garment used to entangle his father; he expatiates upon their crime and punishment, and then turns to exculpation for himself. He apostrophizes the sun, witness of all that has been done, "to stand by me and testify in procedure (or court) of justice [*en dikēi*] one day, that when I visited this fate upon my mother it was done within justice [*en-dikōs*]. As for Aegisthus—fate is not in question; he merely received the justice [*dikē*] of an adulterer as per custom [*nomos*]" (985–990). His words, in fact, predict the legal "justice" of which, fortunately for himself, he will become a beneficiary, and which will be required to resolve the situation created by matricide. The "justice" of the murder of Aegisthus is of a different kind, symbolizing the mere act of penalizing adultery which has been sanctioned by tradition.

The "justice" of Orestes' commission in this play becomes so because the act is one of reciprocity; the vocabulary takes care to underline this rule: the "executor" is a "reciprocal killer" (121). Electra, apostrophizing her father, pronounces, "An avenger of you is to appear and the slayers are to be reciprocally slain" (143), and the chorus in a later apostrophe promise "enemy word in reciprocity for enemy word," "murderous blow in reciprocity for murderous blow" (309, 312). Orestes, in a third apostrophe, adjures his father: "At least grant us reciprocally to match one handhold with another, if indeed, being defeated, you want reciprocally to win" (498–499).

Does justice in this play then become the symbol of the reciprocal process itself—the notion of a rhythmic order of things, embracing the overall exchange that occurs when eye is compensated for by eye rather than identifying the single retaliatory act? To judge by contexts the symbol wavers between the two. When Electra says that the slayers are to be "reciprocally slain," she adds that the slaying is a "justice" (144), as though *dikē* might represent the overall process within which the two slayings are to occur. The chorus appeal to the fates "to complete matters in the way in which [or "according as"] the just (thing) [*to dikaion*] changes sides" (306–308), which seems to acknowledge rather strikingly that Clytemnestra previously had "justice" in slaying Agamemnon, which she has now "lost" in a transfer to Orestes. In the next breath (309–312), amplifying what they have just said by adding "enemy word reciprocal for enemy word . . . blow for blow," they speak of this as "Justice transacting a debt" (311), which in the context implies previous borrowing and repayment. Electra herself phrases it as "Justice from those nonjust I request-in-return" (398); Orestes more forcefully but paradoxically exclaims, "Justice collides with Justice" (461), to which Electra adds (462) the alternative formula: "Ye gods accomplish our prayers within (rules of) justice [i.e., reciprocity; *endikōs*]"; cf. above on l. 988.

Justice in Her Personification

Yet the justice "carried" by an "executor" (above, on 120) resembles in one important respect both "Justice the victory carrier," who with gods and earth is evoked by Electra from her father's ghost (148), and the "justice" by whose agency "the sword is driven into the ribs," and whose "anvil is planted for destiny the sword maker to forge and make ready" (641–646). These three contexts exploit the symbol so as to suggest an implicit word play upon "sword carrier" (which is Homeric), "justice carrier," and "victory carrier" (the three are metrically approximate), so that "Justice" becomes a warrior who in single combat inflicts the fatal blow, a metaphor applied to her at line 948, where she "grapples in hard battle" (the text, however, is dubious). In short, as sometimes in the *Eumenides,* "she" now functions as the symbol not of process but of penalty: "Justice who came visitant to the sons of Priam, (yea) heavy-justiced punishment" (935–936). In the *Choephoroi* it is this role that prevails.

As a divinity, closely associated with Zeus, she evidently reflects the efforts of Hesiod to invest *dikē* with personality. This influence could be anticipated from a passage in an earlier play of Aeschylus, the *Seven against Thebes.* Two brothers (instead of father, wife, and children) are pitted against each other in mortal combat. The shield of one of them carries the device of a warrior "escorted quietly by a woman, who as the letters read, says 'I am justice'" (*Septem* 645–646). This personage is "Zeus's maiden child" (662), a verbal echo of Hesiod's hexameter. This is also the goddess who in the *Choephoroi* "cries aloud" as she exacts debt, who is "unlawfully trodden under foot," who is "the daughter of Zeus truthfully so" (311, 642, 949). As such, like Hesiod's *dikē,* she presumably sits on Olympus. Yet first Electra (148) and then Orestes (497) appeal to their father's ghost to provide her presence, as though she were that justice who in Antigone's words "shares the house of the gods below" (Soph. *Antigone* 451). This would be appropriate to a companion of the Furies, but does she then enjoy a split personality?

Aeschylus also chooses fresh company for her.[28] She is joined in two trilogies, of "gods, earth, and justice" (148) and of "might, justice, and Zeus" (244), where she takes a place occupied by "violent force" (*bia*) in another play of Aeschylus, the *Prometheus Bound.* The equivalence is symptomatic of her retributive role.

These metaphors for status and behavior betray the kind of inconsistency characteristic of Hesiod's poem. It also becomes clear that personification as such encourages the growth of a major contradiction, perceptible also in the *Eumenides,* at a level which could be called philosophical, if philosophy were in question, which it is not. In the *Eumenides,* the drama of justice became one of due process replacing the justice of the single retributive act. The *Choephoroi* is a drama of the retributive act pure and simple. Personification might be thought to accentuate and clarify the meaning conveyed by a slippery symbol like *dikē,* and so assist in the process of conceptualizing justice with greater precision. The image is indeed sharpened, but without giving any assistance to this end; on the contrary it involves its reference in almost hopeless ambiguity. Instead of symbolizing the rhythm and order of reciprocal adjustment, or alternatively the procedures of legal negotiation which seek to preserve and restore such order, justice as person parts company with both altogether.

The "Justices" of the *Agamemnon*

Behind the *Eumenides* and the *Choephoroi* stands the *Agamemnon*. As its great retributory sequences gather momentum, the symbols of justice interpenetrate the verse with equal insistence and ambiguity. The opening words of the chorus (40–43) identify Menelaus as Priam's "great opponent-in-justice" (*anti-dikos;* the prefix may carry the sense of reciprocity), and the legal metaphor remains persistent (451, 534, 813, 1412, 1421, 1535, 1601).[29] Yet Clytemnestra describes Agamemnon's proposed ceremonial entry into his own house as being "conducted by justice," with the remaining arrangements to be completed "justly." On the face of it (for the double entendre, see below), she is talking about the propriety and appropriateness of such a reception under such circumstances, and this sense also recurs. Yet again, when Aegisthus vigorously defends the "justice" of his case as his own father's avenger (1577–1611), he is speaking of retribution pure and simple. Throughout the play, these three senses of *dikē* compete with one another. Correspondingly, as the various parties become involved in the action, the things they do or have done to them invite competing claims to a "justice" which has no constant or consistent reference. In everything said by the chorus in the parodos (40–256), justice and its symbols are ranged on the side of the Atreidae and against Troy (the description of Agamemnon's decision to slay his daughter offers no exception). Only twice near the end of the first stasimon is the diction of the verse so constructed as perhaps to convey an ironic hint that this "justice" may be in question (451, 464). The announcements of the messenger from the battlefield reporting victory confidently reaffirm the assignment of "justice" against Troy. The chorus in the second stasimon then offer some meditations upon its (or "her") effects without making clear whether they mean Troy or Agamemnon to be the victim of such effects (761, 772, 789). Agamemnon on entry reaffirms the justice of what has been done to Troy. The welcome extended by Clytemnestra marks a symbolic turning point. She continues to assign a "justice" to Agamemnon, by signifying the propriety (as she argues) of the reception he has earned by his deeds, while employing a double entendre to convey to the audience the sense of a retribution being prepared for him, as is noted in the commentary later offered by Cassandra (1229). The murder, once accomplished, can be openly defended because justice has been reversed (or, in the words of the chorus of the *Choephoroi*, "changed sides"). It now presides over Clytemnestra and her action; that is her account of the matter (1396, 1406, 1432). The chorus indignantly deny that she has any justice at all (1535, 1546). Aegisthus on entry claims justice for himself[30] while denying it to Agamemnon (1577, 1601, 1604, 1607, 1611). The chorus seek finally to strip it away from him (1615, 1669).

The modern reader is always tempted to make moralistic selection[31] among these competing claims. This tends to obscure if not distort the dramatic intentions of Greek tragedy, which so often depend, as in this case, upon exploiting a language which covers a field of meaning rather than having reference to conceptual definitions. Given these fluctuations in operational reference, where in the great trilogy are we to say that justice lies? The answer seems to be everywhere and nowhere. If we admit the Aristotelian doctrine of tragic flaw, who among this gallery of characters are the (comparatively) just persons in contrast to the unjust? We would have no doubt of the answer in a Shakespearian play. But is the question as applied to Greek drama answerable at all?[32]

A Field of Meaning

As the problem is conceptual, so also it is linguistic, created by the use of the same set of words in varying and often contradictory situations. But is it fair to treat a poet as if he were obligated to be a philosopher? Can Aeschylus not be allowed to manipulate metaphor and image with logical inconsistency but poetic effectiveness? Of course he can, but we have still to ask: Was not the poet of this epoch still fulfilling the Homeric role of teacher of Greece? The poet's business is to manufacture good theater, and for this purpose the conflicting claims of stage opponents to possess virtue are no obstacle. But there is some evidence in the *Oresteia* itself that the same poet (and Aeschylus is not untypical in this regard) can be aware not that these claims should be put right, but rather that the symbols employed in making them have a special quality of their own, that they are puzzle words, with slippery meanings that invite and yet repel definition. The evidence lies in that habit, already observed in the behavior of the verb "to be," of manipulating the symbols in groups, as though the poet were playing with them. Not infrequently the play amounts almost to a pun, at other times to a double or triple entendre. The most flagrant of all puns is the one used to indicate that retributive justice has divine status. *Dikē* is, as it were, defended as the daughter of Zeus on the basis of her verbal derivation from him (*di-kē: di-os;* the pun was "invented" by Hesiod, improved on by Aeschylus in the *Seven* (662),[33] and used etymologically by him in the *Cheophoroi* (949)). This piece of ingenuity, however bizarre, probably indicates an awareness that she has been placed on Olympus by an act of poetic imagination which needs support.

It is true that new words, sometimes key words, as they happen to be introduced in the course of what is being said, tend to repeat themselves in the same context; such is a habit of Greek poetry, perhaps a continuing response to the echo principle of oral composition. It is also true, perhaps for the same reason, that Greek verse will repeat a commonplace word where it is convenient, perhaps several times, without bothering to vary it.[34] This may explain some of the behavior of the *dikē* symbols in the *Oresteia,* but not all of it. Agamemnon, announcing his return from the wars, opens his statement as follows: "First Argos and its native gods (it is) *justice* to address, (who are) responsible with me for my return and for the *just (things)* I transacted against the city of Priam. For the *justices* the gods heard (argued before them) were deadly . . . " Two usages of *dikē* and one of the adjective *dikaios* are compressed into four lines of text. The reference of the first is to the propriety of his address; of the second and third, to a legal process he has employed (used as a metaphor for war). Within the bounds of the process, the second refers to the conduct of proceedings—a trial—and the third covers first the argument offered—the plea—and then the penalty exacted—death. Is this exploitation of meanings an accident in the choice of words? Such an explanation was not sufficient for similar phenomena in Hesiod's verse. Or again, Clytemnestra concludes her elaborate invitation to Agamemnon to step on purple cloth with the words: "that *justice* may lead you into a house unanticipated. For the rest, care immune to sleep shall dispose matters *justly*." The irony of these two statements is reinforced by a double entendre in the use of the symbol: for Agamemnon, the reference is to the propriety of his reception, for Clytemnestra, to the retribution that awaits. In similar vein, the bloody deed accomplished, Clytemnestra confidently asserts, "I exult; if it were possible to pour libation in appropriate fashion [*prepontōs*] over this corpse, then *justly* would these (curses be poured); nay, justly-in-excess." *Dikaiōs*, applied in the sense of "propriety" (as determined by *prepontōs* in the previous line), is at once converted into something much stronger than propriety, namely retribution.[35]

These are tightly controlled examples. Five more looser groupings can be perceived in the play, two in choric meditations (376–398, 761–772), one in a messenger's speech (525–534), one in an exchange between Clytemnestra and the chorus (1396–1432), and one in Aegisthus' self-defense (1577–1611); constituting a total of twenty-six occurrences out of a total for the play of thirty-six. There are seven concentrated examples[36] in the *Choephoroi* along with six looser ones,[37] and five[38] in the *Eumenides*, with nine[39] looser ones. If we allow for the extended length of the *Agamemnon*, the relative frequency of the phenomenon increases as the trilogy progresses, which might be expected, since the problems surrounding the symbol gradually tend to become more explicit. Among the "tight" examples in the *Choephoroi* can be noted the one that occurs within line 120, distinguishing between *dik-astēs* and *dikē-phoros*, playing on the ambivalence between "due process" and "penalty imposed"; another two-line example occurs at 987–988 where "in justice," meaning "in my legal trial," is repeated as "keeping within justice," meaning "retributively." Or again, in a four-line example in the *Eumenides* (430–433), "just" and "justly" are defined in one sense by Athene, to apply to legal procedure, while the Furies, replying, use "justice" in its prelegal sense. This example is typical of the ploy, in that it uses repetition not to play upon the resources of ambivalence, but rather to clarify by suggesting distinctions, even though these are not pressed conceptually (cf. *Eum.* 468–472, 699–700, 804–805, 911–912). This again accords with the progress of the trilogy toward a resolution of what in the two earlier plots seemed irresolvable. But the solution dramatized is practical, not theoretical. These passages of compulsive repetition have the effect of locating different senses of the symbolic system side by side, as if to fix them within a field of overlapping meaning. It is still the "justices" of Hesiod that we contemplate, not the "justice" of Plato.[40] The range of contradiction remains unaffected. When Orestes exclaims, "Justice collides with Justice" (*Choeph.* 461), his exultant words come near to open ackowledgment of the fact, as do those of Eteocles in the *Seven against Thebes* when, attacking the claim that is made for justice emblazoned on his brother's shield, he proposes the paradox: "Surely then in all justice would justice be falsely named."[41] Nowhere in the drama of Aeschylus can we yet find out *"what justice is."* And given the fact that the rules of language at his disposal, syntactically speaking, were not very different from those available to his successors in the genre, it may be inevitable that we should have to wait for a philosopher to tell us what we want to know.

17

The Justice of Herodotus

The language in which Plato proposes justice as the subject of a lengthy philosophical treatise shows two departures from previous usage. Besides employing a syntax which makes philosophical definition possible, he changes the name of the thing he is talking about. Although occasionally employing the traditional term *dikē,* he normally refers to "justice" by the lengthened appellation *dikaiosunē.* Is there any significance in the change in nomenclature which may have parallel bearing on the change in syntax? The question, it is fair to say, has not hitherto been raised.[1] It has on the whole been assumed by historians and scholars of Greece that when pre-Platonic authors speak of *dikē* they might just as well have been speaking of *dikaiosunē.*[2] Another way of putting it would be to say that "justice" in Greek authors is commonly assumed to represent a conceptual constant of Greek thought.

Plato, in fact, did not invent this lengthened form. It appears in the historian Herodotus perhaps two generations earlier,[3] and the manner of its appearance invites comment. It is not normal with him; the occurrences are exceptional. He regularly and frequently employs the traditional *dikē* and its correlatives. He may also be the first (so far as we know) to employ names for "nonjustice" in the abstract (*a-dikia, a-*

dikēma).⁴ His whole "justice" vocabulary surely reflects the cumulative effect of increasing legal procedure and practice in the city-states—something that might be expected as laws and legal formulas multiplied in their written versions. Some legal idioms involving *dikē*, which by the fourth century had become routine, first make their regular appearance in his text: as "paying back *dikē*" and "giving *dikē* or "taking *dikē* (as a penalty) for something."⁵ *Dikē*'s field of meaning had traditionally covered a procedural process in all its aspects: the specific reference shifted according to the context. Now the focus tends to narrow down to identifying the penalty or punishment inflicted as the result of process. It is a possibility foreshadowed as soon as the habit of personifying the symbol begins in the poets.

The intrusion of *dikaiosunē* into the historian's text marks a different mental departure. There are only eight occurrences of the word distributed over five widely scattered contexts, one each in Books 1 and 2 and 6, and two in Book 7. Each of these tells a story with moralizing overtones which could be characterized as a fable. The following are summaries.⁶

Herodotus 1.95 ff.: The Story of King Deioces the Mede

The conquest of Lydia becomes the historian's occasion to narrate the history of Cyrus the Persian, which in turn calls for a summary of the previous history of Media-Persia. The Medes, having broken away from the Assyrian Empire, "gained their freedom." Their example was followed by the entire Asiatic mainland. Their political organization was confined to the village. A certain Deioces, a man of intelligence and wide reputation, had monarchical ambitions, which he sought to realize by concentrating on the "practice" of *dikaiosunē*, for he understood clearly that in the present lawless condition of the country, there was a deep antagonism between "the just" and "the nonjust" (*dikaion* . . . *adikon*). He was accordingly chosen to be "judge" of his village. He was "straight" and "just" and "did the justicing correctly." The contrast with the decisions rendered in other villages induced neighboring villages to bring their suits to him until he had a monopoly of the judicial process. Deioces, as part of his plan, finally declined to continue this, pleading that it was "unprofitable" for him to neglect his own affairs. Faced with an increasing degree of "lack of order" (*anomiēs*, 1.97.2 and 3), the Medes held an assembly to decide policy and voted to establish a monarchy, which would bring law and order and the opportunity to get work done. Chapter 98 describes how they picked Deioces as a well-known man to be monarch, whereupon he required them to furnish a royal capital (which became Ecbatana) and a bodyguard. An architectural description of Ecbatana is followed by a description of the Persian palace ceremonial, which Deioces, says the historian, invented, its motive being to stress his own uniqueness in separation from his subjects. His legal administration became severe and more bureaucratic, requiring the submission of written briefs, but enforcing appropriate and adequate penalties for all acts of aggressive arrogance (*hubris*). His spies and agents pervaded the kingdom.

Traits in this story are recognizably consistent with the previous tradition surrounding the practice of *dikē*. This (perhaps mythical) character begins his career by dispensing oral justice in the Homeric fashion and according to Hesiodic rules. But when he is enthroned as monarch, his administration requires that legal procedures become literate. The written word (presumably the Aramaic syllabary) in this case becomes an instrument of despotism.[7] Deioces' "justice" is something that has to be applied to a political problem, namely, the isolation of small separate communities living in a state of anarchy. The *Odyssey* had portrayed this paradigm in the story of the Cyclops who "knew not justices or laws," and Hesiod's poem had envisaged the solution—*dikē* as Zeus's gift to prevent cannibalism. The policies applied by Deioces are those celebrated in Solon's poetry. *A-nomia*, lawlessness, must be replaced by *eunomia*, law and order (the latter having been already celebrated by Hesiod). It is the task of "justice" to achieve and maintain this condition, as it appears in the idealized Athens of the conclusion to Aeschylus' play. Its enemy is the traditional *hubris*.

As so far explained, it is difficult to see in the application of *dikaiosunē* anything that could not just as well be described as *dikē*. If there is a hint of a difference, it lies in the verb to which *dikaiosunē* is attached as object. It is something upon which Deioces "concentrated himself" and which he "practiced." The first expression would be appropriate to an activity personally undertaken, and the second to something which, in the language of the late fifth and fourth centuries, would be a "virtue" (*aretē*) which a man cultivated in himself. That is to say, the hint points toward a tendency to think of the justice implemented in due process as requiring also a "justice" which is an ethos in the individual who is to implement it. It marks a step toward the "internalization" of the concept.

Herodotus 2.141–152 (with Extensive Omissions): The Story
of the Twelve Kings of Egypt

Herodotus has narrated in garbled form a highly condensed version
of Egyptian dynastic history, concluding with the reign of one "Sethos,
a priest of Hephaestus" whose policies neglected the interests of the
Egyptian warriors to the extent of expropriating their land holdings. At
the conclusion of his reign the Egyptians were "liberated" (2.147.2).
But being unable to conduct their lives for any length of time without a
king, they divided the entire country into twelve districts, each with its
own king.

These twelve, besides intermarrying, governed their administration
by three rules or regulations which forbade mutual subversion and
mutual aggrandizement and which guaranteed complete mutual amity
(2.147.3). Herodotus then gives his account of the motive behind this
arrangement. As soon as they had assumed their respective kingdoms, an
oracle had foretold that one of them would be monarch of all Egypt.
Their careful observance of these three rules was designed to prevent
this. According to the oracle, the future monarch would be identified by
the fact that he would pour libation in the temple of Hephaestus from a
cup of bronze.

And so the twelve kings "employed *dikaiosunē*" and continued to
do so until, on a certain occasion, one of them seemed to fulfill the oracle
by accident. The eleven took no chances. They established by examination that he had done so without intention, so could not "decide it just"
to kill him, but they stripped him of his powers and exiled him. He had
in fact, adds the historian, been exiled once before. Being now a victim
of *hubris* (2.152.3), he planned vengeance on his persecutors, and in
due course, with the aid of "bronze men from the sea" (that is, Greeks),
he deposed the eleven and became monarch of all Egypt. This was
Psammetichus, who founded a dynasty (chap. 158 ff.).

The context in which "justice" is applied in this fable is once more
political, and its objective again is the maintenance of social order and
stability. But the conditions for achieving it are more complex. Centralized authority as a solution is not available. Peace and good order must
depend on an equilibrium between twelve independent authorities who
by compact agree to avoid aggression and enhance natural amity. As
Plato might say, each swears "to do his own thing" and not interfere. To
maintain the agreement is to practice *dikaiosunē*, which amounts to

regulating one's actions according to social rules, a traditional sense of *dike*. To abrogate the rules by victimizing one of the parties to the agreement (for whatever reason) is to commit *hubris* against him. This is corrected reciprocally when the victim retaliates, an act which has the effect of unifying the previous pluralism of twelve independent authorities under a single monarchical government. But as in Deioces' case, *dikaiosune* is the label used to identify those practices or policies which precede the establishment of monarchy.

Deioces had "practiced" justice; the twelve kings "put it to use." The second idiom again suggests that this *dikaiosune* is not after all simply an equivalent for *dike*, a procedure externally applied, but a possession of the individual who can use it, in short, a property of the person, part of his character. This tendency to internalize the notion of justice is also perceptible in the fact that the eleven in taking action against the twelfth feel they cannot "with justice" kill him because the act which gave offense, or more precisely the effect which it produced, was not premeditated. Inner motive or intention is here stated as one of the criteria of just or unjust action, as it already had been much earlier in Athens in the law code inscribed by Draco.

Herodotus 6.73 and 85–87: The Story of Glaucus of Sparta

The two Spartan kings Cleomenes and Leotychides descend upon Aegina and, in the absence of resistance, select and seize ten prominent Aeginetans, take them to Athens, a bitter foe of Aegina, and "place them on deposit" at that city. There they remained as hostages until the death of Cleomenes, whereupon, on complaint of the Aeginetans at Sparta, a Spartan tribunal found the plaintiffs to have been the victims of *hubris* (6.85.1). Leotychides, it was finally agreed, was to accompany them to Athens to take back the hostages. So Leotychides came and demanded his "deposit." The Athenians said they "did not judge it just" to comply: the deposit had been made by two kings, not one. To this Leotychides made a lengthy reply:

To restore them is an act of piety; to refuse to do so is the opposite; the choice is yours (6.86a). But I want to tell you of a "happening" in Sparta which concerned a deposit. There is a Spartan tradition about one Glaucus three generations ago who, besides being generally preeminent, enjoyed a unique reputation among Spartans for *dikaiosune*. Tradition reports that in the course of time the following thing "happened" to him. A Milesian arrived and told him: "I want to enjoy the benefit of your *dikaiosune*, which has gained wide reputation in Ionia and indeed in all Hellas. Ionia, so I have reflected, is continually insecure, and money continually changes hand, whereas the Peloponnese enjoys secure and settled conditions. I have decided to convert half my property into silver and deposit it with you, well understanding that deposit with you means security for me. Here it is, and here are the tokens you must keep. You will restore it to the bearer of corresponding tokens." Glaucus accepted the deposit on these terms. After a long interval of time the children of the depositor arrived, produced the tokens, and asked for payment. Glaucus put them off, "I don't remember," he said, "I can't carry back to any knowledge of what you are talking about. I want to recall the matter and do the 'just' thing. If I was the recipient, I would be correct to pay up. If I was not, I will apply the usual Greek regulations against you. Give me four months."

The Milesians made out that they had been disastrously robbed, and left. Glaucus resorted to Delphi, asking the oracle: shall I take oath and plunder the money? The oracle replied in seven hexameter verses to the effect that it would be more profitable to take oath, and to prevail, and to plunder the money. After all even the man of faithful oath must die. However, oath has a demonic offspring which can exterminate a man's lineage and household, whereas the lineage of the man of faithful oath can prevail.

Glaucus promptly asked pardon of the oracle, but the oracle refused: to tempt the god was equivalent to doing the deed. Glaucus restored the money. "And why, then, O Athenians, do I tell this tale? There is now no root or branch of Glaucus' line left in Sparta. The moral of this story: in the case of a deposit do not even harbor an intention of refusing payment to a claimant."

However, Athens gave no hearing to this argument, and Leotychides left. The Athenians were waiting for the Aeginetans "to give justices for previous nonjustices they had arrogantly inflicted on the Athenians" to please the Thebans. The Aeginetans in their turn, "claiming they were the victims of injustice, . . . now set about preparing to retaliate" against the Athenians.

The historical context into which the tale is inserted narrates a dispute over the rights and wrongs of political practices followed by states toward each other: Athens offers one judgment of what is just, Aegina another; each judgment is governed by the rule of reciprocity: each party, it is claimed, is the victim of *hubris*. So far, this is the traditional justice symbolized by *dikē*. The tale told by the Spartan mediator strikes a different note. The connection between tale and context is supplied by the notion of "deposit," applied politically to hostages but in a private context to money. Justice becomes the rule governing fiduciary trusteeship in business transactions. Perceptible in the fable is an emerging ethic of banking, natural concomitant of the expansion of Greek commercial enterprise. Business transactions are still guaranteed by oral oaths and promises, not documentary exchange. Sanctions to support their fidelity are still sought in the threat that violation which may temporarily profit the violator will nevertheless have negative effects on his descent, following the tradition established in Hesiod and accepted by Solon. But the tale adds a surprising codicil: even to harbor the intention to violate, apart from committing the act, is reprehensible and visited by a similar penalty. This goes much further than Draco's law code, or indeed any law code, by separating thought from action, and then arguing in effect that thought is a form of action to be regulated accordingly.

The justice which Glaucus now violates is therefore a "justice of the heart," a kind of personal integrity. It is something supposedly in his personal possession, for the Ionian tells him, "I want to take advantage of your *dikaiosunē*"; one would not say "your *dikē*," or if one did, it would mean "your rights" or "claims." It is pertinent to note that the occasion for the employment (or failure to employ, for Glaucus as it turns out enjoys the reputation but not the reality) of this inner virtue is this time a private business transaction, not a political or judicial decision.

Herodotus 7.44–52: The Story of King Xerxes and Artabanus

Xerxes on his way to Greece pauses at Abydos in order to ascend an eminence from which he can review his army and fleet. At the spectacle of such incomparable numbers of men he first congratulates himself but then weeps, whereupon his uncle Artabanus, an original opponent of the expedition, engages him in a dialogue, the purpose of which is to encourage some second thoughts about the enterprise. The conclusion in summary runs as follows:

Art.: Since nothing may deter you, take one piece of advice. Great enterprises call for correspondingly extensive calculation. Cyrus reduced Ionia to tributary status—all of it except Athens. Do not—so I advise— do not by any means lead forth the Ionians against their parents. We don't need them to win. If they join our expedition either (1) they will do what is completely nonjust by enslaving their metropolis or (2) they will do what is completely just by conspiring with her to defend her freedom. In the first case they will add no advantage to us; in the second case they will gain the capability of doing severe damage to your expedition. Remember the old saying: you don't see all the end at the beginning.

X.: Of the idea you have so far expounded this last one, which expresses fear of revolt by the Ionians, is particularly erroneous. The evidence they gave us was patent, witnessed by yourself and others, when during Darius' incursion into Scythia they could have destroyed the entire expedition and come out on top themselves. What they in fact responded with was *dikaiosunē* and loyalty with every sign of courtesy. Besides, they have left children, wives, and property behind them to remind them not to revolt. Abandon these fears. I want you to protect my household and throne. You are my sole regent.

Artabanus was then sent back to Susa.

Once more, the argument as it is arranged exposes an implicit dichotomy between the claims of "justice" as *dikaion* and the quality represented by *dikaiosunē*. For Artabanus, complete justice represents the rule that requires brother to assist brother. This is a traditional view of *dikē*—of what is "proper"; and it is supported by an appeal to the wisdom of Solon—"consider the latter end." For Xerxes justice as *dikaiosunē* is like loyalty and gratitude—a quality of the heart, something one can "put in the hands" of someone else, as a kind of gift, in this case the gift of a grateful subject to his monarch.

Herodotus 7.163–164: The Story of King Cadmus of Cos

Greece, confronting Xerxes' invasion, had invited Gelo, ruler of Syracuse, to lend her military and naval assistance, but had refused his conditions for doing this. After the departure homeward of the Greek embassy, Gelo concluded that the Greeks would probably be beaten; it was safest to play a waiting game. He accordingly despatched an agent, one Cadmus, a native of Cos, to Delphi, entrusting to him a large supply of funds. His instructions were to maintain good relations with everybody but to await the issue. If Persia won, he was to give the fund to Xerxes with the usual tokens of submission. If the Greeks won, he was to return with the money. Gelo chose Cadmus because of his past history. Having inherited the kingdom of Cos in good condition from his father, Cadmus had "deposited" his authority over Cos with the commons and gone off to Sicily. His action was entirely voluntary and prompted by *dikaiosunē*. (In Sicily he acquired Zankle from Samos and made a settlement there. The town changed its name to Messene.)

Gelo was well aware that his arrival in Sicily under these circumstances was only one instance of a general *dikaiosunē* in him. That is why he used him as emissary. Cadmus crowned the record of rightful acts emanating from himself by the following supreme example: he completely controlled the large funds entrusted to him and could have appropriated them, but refused to do so. After Salamis and the departure of Xerxes he departed, too, but this time to Sicily, and brought all the money back with him.

The story revives the theme of trusteeship, and is told to illustrate a justice exercised in both political and private contexts.[8] But in this instance the two "justices" are the same; both exemplify the practice of *dikaiosunē*. This comes about because the political justice represents not a procedure expressive of the traditional rules of *dikē* and *dikaion*, but a voluntary surrender of personal power to others, in the democratic interest: he "deposited it into the middle." Described in these terms, Cadmus is a kind of reincarnated Solon, insofar as Solon had claimed to have renounced absolutism and to have strengthened the "middle." The notion that political power is a deposit held temporarily by him who exercises it (and must therefore be surrendered at the end of a term of office) is a doctrine of Democritus. Here the deposit is carried out in the reverse direction. Such a voluntary act is equated with the equally voluntary one of returning a sum of money intact to its owner when under the circumstances several excuses could have been made for failing to do so. The moving cause of such an act must again be more in a man's inner quality than in social rules or procedures, which are powerless to enforce it. The Greek phrases it as an example of "the just works issuing from himself," a rather striking use of the reflexive, for which there are parallels in Socratic language.[9]

Herodotus' style is discursive, admitting frequent narrative digression and descriptive materials drawn from a variety of sources. The fact that these five contexts themselves wear the air of intrusion in his narrative is therefore no anomaly, nor of itself does it allow one to infer a common source. But the kind of correspondences between them which my examination has revealed does permit such an inference and the further conclusion that these eight occurrences of the term *dikaiosunē* were also supplied (in view of its rarity otherwise) from this source. What this was must remain speculative. It is barely possible that Plato later supplies a clue. When he himself proposes the subject of *dikaiosunē*, he initially connects it with the paying back of debts. The reader who later becomes aware of the majestic proportions of Plato's developing theory may be a little surprised by this rather mundane way of introducing it, but it does reflect the connection in Herodotus between justice and money deposited in trust. Somewhat later in the same context, Plato's "Socrates," citing the maxim "It is just to benefit friends and injure enemies," refers this to the authority of five worthies; four of them are Greeks, but the fifth, oddly enough, is Xerxes. Do we hear an echo of Xerxes' sentiments concerning the "just" attitude of the Ionians toward himself? From such hints a shadowy hypothesis begins to emerge. It has been proposed that the first book of the *Republic* was originally an early dialogue, addressed to a given "virtue" like other early dialogues, whether or not it was separately published.[10] The *dikaiosunē* which it problematically explores is represented as a topic familiar in Sophistic circles, one which Plato is anxious to redefine. If the word was a Sophistic invention, its original author was likely to be not Thrasymachus but Protagoras, with whom Herodotus could have been on familiar terms. A discourse of Protagoras touching on the subject would have prompted the later tradition that Plato's *Republic* owed a debt to a work of his composed on the same lines. The stories as told by Herodotus reveal some interest in constitutional theory: four of them concern kings. Their format favors the kind of dialogue in which arguments are arranged antithetically. At the same time they are stories, with a flavor of historical romance, which illustrate the effects of *dikaiosunē* by narrating what happened when it was applied. These traits accord with the tradition surrounding the content and narrative format of Protagoras' writings and his methods of exposition, and with Plato's criticism of them. They also underline the fact that the justice of Herodotus is separated from that of Plato by the same barrier which divides Plato from all his predecessors, the Sophists included—one that intervenes between two different syntactical systems. The prose of Herodotus, and we can guess also that of Protagoras, can introduce a new piece of terminology; it cannot use the kind of language, concerning this "thing" that is so named, which will explain what it really *is*, apart from what it does or what is done with it. The clean break with narrative syntax required for this kind of discourse, concerning not only justice but any other entity, is not yet achieved.

The Verb "to Be" in Herodotus

The verb "to be" proliferates in the historian's text.[11] Are we to say it is never truly copulative, or that the sense of the statements in which it is employed is never truly veridical?[12] Its existential usage, in the absolute, is clear; it has recently been the subject of attention, but it does not carry us beyond previous usage. To show the way in which the verb is advancing, as it were, toward its Platonic application, and yet stopping short of it, the first thirty-two chapters of the work provide a convenient illustration. In thirty-one of these, the present tense *esti* ("is") occurs only thrice. In the thirty-second alone it occurs nine times. When this happens, it is because narrative is interrupted by a conversation between Solon and Croesus, which is reflective. Much of what Solon is made to say consists of a series of apothegms, recalling the style and some of the substance of his elegies. The subjects of eight of the *esti* statements are "men" or "a man" or "a man's body"—generic but still personal. The remaining one is an infinitive of action. The predicates indicate location or privation or status, or else are verbal nouns or adjectives used with *esti* to indicate an action in the mode rendered familiar in Aeschylus. The advancing usage of the verb between Homer and Aeschylus has provided ample parallels. Herodotus' text, however, in comparison with Solon's elegies, for example, shows a tendency to supply the verb where it might previously have been omitted: "Man *is* wholly (a thing of) coincidence"; "the rich man *is* not more prosperous than the man who sustains himself at the subsistence level'; "many very rich *are* nonprosperous"; "no one human body *is* self-sufficient." The mere appositional equivalence favored in oral aphorisms is yielding to a notion of relationship between subject and predicate indicated by interrupting the equivalence by inserting a verb. Yet equivalence is not yet truly replaced by predication of category, property, and the like, in a way to make analytic definitions possible. This is strikingly demonstrable in a debate held in Book 3, upon the merits of three types of political constitution. It is the most theoretic passage in the entire history, yet nowhere is *esti* used in any statement in the course of three chapters which would define the natures or characteristics of the three "things" which have been made topics of discussion.

Justice Internalized

We cannot, therefore, say that justice as a concept has yet been achieved. But a step has been taken toward realizing how complex such a notion may be, by coining *dikaiosunē* to indicate that there is a justice within man as well as one which he operates in society. There was, after all some, slight Homeric precedent for such a notion. *Dikaiosunē* is something possessed by a *dikaios*, a "man of justice," and his lineaments, as portrayed in the mythos of the *Odyssey*, were primarily not those of a

litigant or an arbitrator (as in the *Iliad*) but of a host and fr
civility extended even to the stranger and the impoverished.
always represented as a response to rule and regularity, the act
havior required, involving as it did some surrender of the power o
strong as it confronted the weak, smacked of the voluntary and perso
(though of course not so recognized by Homer). The kind of transac
tion recommended in three of Herodotus' stories as representing "justice" is, at least by implication, rather similar.[13]

Plato (as we shall see) was not primarily interested in the Odyssean model of the *dikaios*. But he completed the internalization of
justice[14] as a quality of a man by placing it as a "virtue" in the psyche,
employing this word to symbolize the human personality. Psyche is a
second concept whose definition was not available to pre-Platonic authors
until the Socratic dialectic made it so.

end, whose
Although
ial be-
f the
al

18

e of Plato

Plato, as editors of later antiquity recognized, composed several dialogues each of which committed itself to the topic of a single virtue.[1]
Justice is the only one of these which receives the honor of a treatise of
ten books. To be sure, the *Republic* is read for other reasons too. It
ranges over such diverse fields as politics, economics, education,
epistemology, the theory of forms, the condition of poetry, the immortality of the soul. But these discussions are contained within the structure of a formal design which is made explicit. The first book constitutes
a dialogue which introduces the topic: what is justice? Can it be
defined? No clear answer is given; the argument ends aporetically, in
the manner of the other ethical dialogues. But the dilemma this time
must be solved. It has been propounded in order to provoke the challenge put forward in the second book: justice, the supreme virtue, must
be defined in and for itself. The rest of the treatise is then devoted to
unfolding and completing the definition, with some meticulousness. By
the middle of Book 4, preparations have been made to place justice
within the city (432b ff.) and the soul (442d ff.), respectively, this
virtue in each case being balanced against a definition of the corresponding vice. Further demonstration of its profitability at the conclusion of
Book 4 (444e7 ff.) has the effect of producing a second and extended

definition, to Book 9 (588b1 ff), one which is again formally completed after proving the misery of the corresponding vice (576b11 ff.); a mathematical ratio is even established between the two (587b4 ff.). The doctrine of the soul's immortality and its destiny which concludes the work is introduced in order to complete the account of justice by describing its rewards in this world and the next (X.608c1; 612b1 ff.). The intent to devote a literary monument to the celebration of justice and justice alone is unmistakable.[2] As previously noted, this is the first time this has happened in a formal sense since Hesiod. Justice may in a sense be viewed as furnishing the theme of Aeschylus' trilogy, but between exploitation of a symbol for dramatic purposes and an attempt to organize its meaning systematically there is a profound difference.

Dikē versus Dikaiosunē

The subject is introduced as one requiring investigation when the aged Cephalus is asked whether "one is to say that justice is simply and solely truth and giving back anything one takes from another, or . . ." Excuse for introducing the word has been furnished in the exchange immediately preceding: Cephalus, a man of substance, has been asked what he would say is the main advantage of being wealthy. His reply is genial but a little evasive: it is a great source of comfort to anyone nearing life's end to be able to reflect that he has avoided wronging anybody; he can contemplate future existence if there is one without fear of retribution. This scarcely answers the question until he adds that if you have money you can always ensure that you depart this life without having to fear that you have cheated anybody or owe anybody anything. Apparently he means that with money we can balance the books and settle up debts before we go.

The reply is worldly, but is worded so as to place what he says within a context furnished by the term "justice," as traditionally understood: one remembers, he says (330d7 ff.), the *muthoi* concerning the inhabitants of Hades, how the *doer-of-nonjustice* here gives *justice* there . . . and one reflects: have I *done-nonjustice* to anyone? Discovering in one's own life many *nonjustices,* one is frightened; but if not conscious within oneself of anything *nonjust,* one has pleasurable expectation for company; the poet will say: whoever conducts one's life *justly* and piously "communes with sweet expectation."

In this passage, the noun *dikē* and the adverb *dikaiōs,* the three privatives, *a-dikos,* the adjective, *a-dikēma,* the noun, *a-dikein,* the verb, have all been translated in obedience to the field of meaning principle previously applied to Homer and Hesiod. The mention of the *muthoi* concerning Hades is a reminiscence of the description in the *Odyssey* of the ghosts appearing before Minos.[3] There are a total of six occurrences of these terms in Plato's thirteen lines of Oxford text. *Dikē* is used, as in Herodotus, in the restricted sense of penalty; and the noun *a-dikēma* is also Herodotean. It is clear that Cephalus is thinking of "justice" (1) within its traditional sense as representing the rule of reciprocity, (2) as this is applied in particular to the duty of repayment of money, a duty which was exemplified in two of Herodotus' stories, (3) in the more restricted sense of any fine or penalty that may be incurred.

Socrates, commending the statement, asks in the same breath: "Now this very thing, *dik-aiosunē*, shall we say it is truth, and paying back what one receives . . . ?" The question is phrased so as to suggest that a topic already mentioned is being resumed. So far as the term *dikaiosunē* itself is concerned, this is not strictly true; it is not even as though Cephalus had used *dikē* in its more extended meaning. May one perceive a distinction, a new dimension, here inserted into the argument? Why could Plato not have used *to dikaion*, "the just (thing)," as the subject of his question? The terminology would have fitted Cephalus' language. Aside from Herodotus, *dikaiosunē* in our surviving sources scarcely appears in pre-Platonic authors: once in Thucydides, once very doubtfully in Damon the musical theorist, once in a possible quotation from Thrasymachus himself.[4] Its absence in the *Clouds* of Aristophanes is notable (no bar to its use in anapests), since that "Socratic" comedy stages a debate between "The Just Argument" and "The Nonjust Argument"; equally so, one might think, is its absence in the debates in Thucydides over the fates of Mitylene and Melos, in both of which the notion of "justice" is freely employed.

Justice as a Social Formula

As the dialogue advances, allowing Polemarchus to take over the role of interlocutor, the following "definitions" of the term are attempted: (1) "it means telling true (things) and giving back what one has taken" (331d2: the same formula is described at 331e4 as "*dikaion*") (2) "it is that technique which gives back benefits and injuries to friends and enemies" (332d5; cf. 334b8); (3) "it is useful for contracts" (333a12); (4) it is useful in the particular case where "money is to be placed on deposit and kept safe" (333c7); (5) and finally (this one contributed by Socrates, 335d11–336a8) it means forbidding injury to anyone, including enemies, which means repudiating the maxim previously cited. Socrates calls this maxim a "saying" (*rhēma*) and attributes it to the authority of five traditional worthies, among them Xerxes. As we have already seen, the maxim is in fact incorporated in Solon's elegy on the good life. These five formulations of "justice" place it within its traditional procedural context; it is a directive whch prescribes rules regulating actions performed by persons or groups in their relations with each other, with the strong suggestion that these rules are reciprocal. The fifth is nonreciprocal in its effects, and in traditional terms is a paradox; but it too expresses itself as a rule of behavior which is social.

Nor does this change when Thrasymachus takes over the dialogue and proposes the equally paradoxical view that *dikaiosunē* is the interest of the stronger. Although traditional *dikē* and *dikaion* as previously understood would have shrunk from any such cynicism, the reference of the term is still procedural and external, applying this time to the rules of political power and its exercise, as is made abundantly clear in the course of the argument (338e1, 341b5 and 8, 342e7, 343b5, 344a7, 345d6, 346e4; at 351b1 the term's range is extended to cover power exercised by whole communities, that is, cities, upon each other). Hesiod and Solon would have rejected the paradox, but they would have recognized the political context in which the term is applied as being natural for it, and so would Aeschylus; even the actors in his trilogy are political figures motivated by and responding to familial relationships which are dynastic. Indeed, is the "justice" proposed by Thrasymachus so very different from the *dikē* imposed by Agamemnon on Troy, by Clytemnestra on Agamemnon?

Justice as a Virtue of the Soul

Yet as the argument begins to ascend toward its summit, a new color is supplied to the term. A theoretically complete nonjustice and a theoretically complete justice have been placed in antithesis to each other, the former being designated as the more profitable; whereupon Socrates remarks: "There is something else about them I would like you to tell me. Do you name one of them a virtue [*aretē*] and the other a vice [*kakia*]?" (348c2; cf. also 353b2). This alters the reference; a "virtue," however interpreted, identifies something personal rather than interpersonal; it can be possessed independently of one's relationship to another. Is "justice" to become this also? There have been hints of the possibility in Herodotus. The focus becomes sharpened when the effects of the negative, nonjustice, are examined, as they occur "within one individual" (351e6). These (on the analogy of the communiy previously considered) take the form of "faction" (*stasis*) and a man's "lack of concord himself with himself"; he becomes "enemy both to himself and to just people" (352a7); this latter clause combines the notions of internal state and external relationship. Then, to clinch this "internalization" of *dikaiosunē*, it is proposed that it is really a "function of the *psychē*" (353d3, 6; and e7). Though the argument ends aporetically, Plato has in fact stated that justice must occupy a dimension, not previously sanctioned by tradition, which will ever afterward confer on it a bifocal meaning: the justice of the community, a social morality, and the justice of the soul, a personal morality.

One may therefore measure the distance between the justice of Hesiod and that of Plato by recognizing that in the substitution of *dikaiosunē* for *dikē* lay an enlargement of the field of meaning of "justice": it became richer and more complex by including the double reference to the polis and to the individual. Justice remains the symbol of a relationship within society—as it always had been—but now it also describes one within the human personality;[5] there presumably is an identity of some sort shared between them because of the use of the single common term. Hesiod had created the topic by grouping together in succession a variety of statements in which the symbol *dikē* and its correlatives occurred. Plato in this first book of the *Republic* resumes the task by organizing a second grouping of such statements, which, however, as descriptions of their subject, are successively offered and rejected or altered.

Justice as an Entity Which Is

A second way of measuring the distance is to recognize an advance in linguistic behavior. First, the symbol is now presented as a linguistic constant, a single "thing" and only one "thing," never pluralized. Second, it is repeatedly placed in formal antithesis to its negative—*adikia*—rather than to the symbol of another "thing" like *hubris* or *bia*. Third, certain verbal devices are employed which have the effect of suggesting its isolation, one might say its "solidity," as a self-sufficient identity, perhaps even an "entity." The first hint of this occurs when justice is first introduced: "(Take) this actual (thing, namely) justice; would you say it is . . . ?" The neuter pronoun in fact is called on to play a large role in the growing philosophic vocabulary,[6] whether in the appositional position or as predicate: "Very well; since justice is evidently not this (thing) . . . what other (thing) should it be called?" (336a9); "My question is this: what kind of (thing) justice really is in relation to nonjustice" (351a1). As the search for definition is resumed and intensified in the second book, the idiom is reinforced: what I want to hear, says the first interlocutor, is "what each (thing) of the pair (viz, justice and nonjustice) is and what force it has when present (as a thing) itself by itself in the soul" (358b5). The second interlocutor repeats the intellectual challenge: "Demonstrate to us . . . what each of the pair itself by itself does to the possessor (so that) one is a good (thing) and the other a bad (thing)" (367b4); . . . "place your stamp of approval upon this thing about justice and only this, (namely) what (justice) itself by itself does to benefit its possessor"(367d3).

One can interpret this kind of language as a response to and correction of that syntax of narrativized description previously available which had placed symbols like *dikē* in such various and contradictory contexts, had compelled it to wear such a variety of clothes, to play so many roles, in Aeschylus no less than in Hesiod; Plato is requiring that the field of meaning be reduced. It is not enough for justice to become a topic; the topic must change into a firm concept consistently stated. The Platonic (and probably Socratic) idiom par excellence applied to this purpose is the combined use of the Greek intensive (*autos*) and reflexive (*heauton*) pronouns; it is a trademark of the dialectic.[7]

To emerge in formal conceptual dress, justice must meet one more requirement; the reference of its predicates must be as abstract as its own, so that the way becomes open to identify it by properties or attributes, categories or relationships, which are as permanent, as little subject to conditional changes, as justice itself. To this end it becomes necessary to employ the services of the verb "to be" in a purely copulative capacity. In the words of the opening question: "Are we to say that justice *is* truth . . .?"; "Since justice *is* evidently not this (thing) . . . "; "My question is: What kind of (thing) justice really *is*." Such copulative usage becomes routine as the dialogue proceeds; it is shared by Thrasymachus as well as his interlocutor: "I assert the just (thing) *to be* none other than the interest of the stronger" (338c1). Homeric location in place, time, or status is now beginning to disappear.

Equipped with these tools of language, the treatise is prepared in the second book to offer the conceptual challenge "I want to hear what each (thing) of the pair *is* . . . what does each of the pair do . . . so that one *is* a good (thing) and the other a bad (thing)?" (358b5, 367b4). The challenge is met in a way which is faithful to the double dimension of *dikaiosunē* now established. It is proposed to examine it as it exists in the city (which would be its traditional habitat), and then in the soul. A suitable city having been furnished for it, the fourth book of the dialogue at last reaches that point where Plato's formal description of what justice *is* can begin.

Introduction to a Definition: The *Republic* 427c6–428a10

So (we can say), O son of Ariston, your city now *stands*[esti]-founded-and-colonized. Then the next thing: you must take a look inside it, after getting adequate light from somewhere, and not (just) you; you must call on your brother and Polemarchus and the others to come and help, in case we can see where precisely justice *might-be-present* [*eiē*] and where nonjustice, and in what the two differ from each other, and which of them must be acquired by him who intends *to be* happy, whether or not he evades the notice of all gods and men. No, no, said Glaucon: you, yes you, promised to go-searching, (it) *being* a pious act on your part to come-to-the-help of justice to the best of your power, by any and every means. True, said I, you correctly remind me and one must so perform, but you too will all have to collaborate. We will. Well, I anticipate that what we want will be discovered as follows: I presume our city, if correctly colonized, *to be* completely good. Of course. It (is) obvious that it *is* intelligent, courageous, temperate, and just. Yes. Now (is it true that) after discovering in it whatever of them we can, the leftover *will-prove-to-be* [*estai*] the (thing) not discovered? Please explain. As (in the case) of any (other) four such, if you were searching for any single one of them in anything, directly you recognized it, you would feel satisfied, and if you got to know three, by this very (fact) the one we were searching for would be recognized. For obviously it would not *turn-out-to-be* [*ēn*] other than the leftover. Then in (the case of) these also, since they actually *are* [*onta*] four, the search should be made in similar fashion. Evidently so.

Ancient Greek cannot be translated into the syntax of modern tongues without some paraphrase, which means the interposition of a metalanguage between ourselves and the original. So far as may be, this should be kept to a minimum: identical terms should receive identical renderings, without yielding to the temptation to accommodate to context or indulge in stylistic variation, in order that the coherence of any thought pattern may not be obscured; a rule applicable to Hesiod is also appropriate to Plato. When, moreover, the Greek is worded so as to have reference to concrete actions, places, colors, sounds, and the like, and to sensations of these, one should avoid translating, that is, interpreting, them as though they were metaphors for something else, such as abstract relationships or mental processes. If the direct sense of a verb is "to look at," it is better not to render it as "consider"; if it means "to seek out," this is not necessarily equivalent to "inquire." If X is said to be "inside" Y, this does not necessarily mean it is "inherent" in Y; if Y is a "part" or "portion" of X, this need not mean it is a property or quality of X.

The language makes it clear that the focus of the argument offered in Book 1 is being intensified, and the terms of the challenge offered in Book 2 are to be met. Justice is to be treated as the symbol of an identity, complete of its kind, perhaps a conceptual one, placed and fixed in an absolute antithesis to its formal negative. To expound and explain this "entity" is to be the task systematically undertaken—a conceptual task.

Prephilosophical Syntax

Why then in its inception does the language of narrative take precedence over the language of logic? A city has been colonized; bring a light to look inside it; summon allies (as in epic battle) for this purpose; they will have to collaborate with what we are doing: Socrates has forgotten what he had promised, and has to be reminded. It is as though Plato felt an instinctive need to utilize a transitional syntax in order to supply a transition to his reader, helping him to apply thought to a syntax of abstract argument which was nontraditional—and why should he not, if he lived and wrote in an epoch when this transition was taking place? Having thus temporarily wooed him, to the point where Socrates is able to say "I presume our city to be completely good," Plato allows analytic argument to take over from narrative.

Consistently with this reversion to prephilosophical language, the operations of cognition are represented as acts of vision employed upon material objects. The city (the actual existence of which is on paper or in the mind) must be inspected with the aid of a light, in order to see where justice as a resident is staying in it. There are four virtues to be discovered inside it. Then the language of cognition takes over: three of them can be "recognized," that is, known, and so also the fourth.

The verb "to be" is becoming prevalent; there are nine occurrences in this introductory passage. But its traditional usage is not shaken off: "Colonized . . . the city now stands . . . where precisely is-justice-present? . . . the leftover will-prove-to-be the nondiscovered . . . it would turn-out-to-be other than the leftover." There is a sense of location, in place or time, explicit or implicit, in these expressions. Even the propositional statement "The city is (stands) completely good" recalls the status usage familiar from Homer (and one can add the existential usage of Parmenides); and the affirmation that "to help is pious," using an infinitive of action in place of a personal subject, is equally traditional. Yet at the same time and in these very expressions the verb is moving in a copulative direction, most evident in the statement that "the city is intelligent, brave, temperate, and just"; the predicates specify no particularization of place, time, or condition. Even the instances which carry local or existential meaning are moving closer to the copulative, insofar as subject or predicate or both are rendered in a grammatical form which is neuter or else a numeral: "the leftover will be the not-discovered . . . it would not be other than the leftover . . . since they actually are four."

Having proposed the method of exhaustion as proper for reaching a determination of justice, the treatise proceeds to apply it. Intelligence, courage, and temperance and their respective locations in the city are successively identified (428a11–432b3). Justice will be what is "left over"—a rather curious way of introducing the supreme of virtues. Aside from establishing its intimate relationship with the other three, we will have to identify it in its own right. This will require some systematic exposition of what it actually *is*.

Definition of Political Justice: The *Republic* 432b2–434a2

A

Three (of the four) in the city we have now presumably looked at. As to the form [*eidos*] still left—the one still (necessary) to enable the city to partake in virtue—what pray *would it be*? (It is) of course obvious that it *is* justice.——Yes.

B

The time has come, Glaucon, for us to behave like huntsmen encircling a thicket concentrating on (the task of) preventing justice from slipping through and disappearing. Evidently it *is present* somewhere around here. So keep looking, be ready to catch sight of it, and if you happen to sight it before I do, point it out to me.——I wish I could; but you will make quite adequate use of me if, instead, you use me as a follower who can look at what is shown to him.——Then follow, and let us both pray for luck.——I will; you just go ahead.——Well here were are; this place by the look of it (is going to be) hard to get through; it is cut off from the light, it *presents-itself*-dark [*esti skoteinos*], in fact, and scarcely-to-be-tracked-through. However, let's go in.——Yes, let's go.——Whereupon I caught sight of something, and shouted, "Glaucon, we (are) probably onto a track; I don't think (the object) will quite succeed in getting away.—That's good news.

C

Really, a stupid thing has happened to us.——What do you mean? ——My dear fellow, the thing appears to have been kicking around in front of our feet all the time, and yet we didn't see it; what ridiculous fools-we-*have-been*. Sometimes one looks around everywhere for something which one is holding in one's hands all the time. So we too, instead of looking directly where we should, have let our gaze wander off into the distance; (that must be) how we have failed to notice it.

D

Please explain.——(It is) like this: I think we have been speaking of it for some time and hearing it spoken of, without realizing that in a way we were actually speaking of it.——Can't you cut the prelude short, for your would-be listener here?——All right; listen and see if this makes sense.

E

When we were colonizing the city, there was something which from the beginning we posited had to be done in everything. (It is) this something, I think, or perhaps a form of it, (which) *is* justice. Now (what) we posited and repeatedly mentioned, if you recall, (was that) each individual ought to "adopt" that one pursuit, of those pertaining to the city, for which his nature *was* naturally most-"adapted."—— Yes, we did.——Now observe this: we ourselves have often said, and we have heard from many (sources) besides, that doing one's own things rather than being-busy about many matters *is* justice.——I agree.——This then, namely, doing one's own things, when it occurs in a certain mode, (is what) justice is-likely *to be*.

F

Do you know why I infer this?——No I don't, but please tell me. ——(There is) in the city the (thing) left over from the three we have inspected, temperance, courage, intelligence. This, I believe, *is* that which has provided the potential-principle to enable all those (others) to be engendered in it and to guarantee their security, for just as long as it *is there* too. And we did say, you know, that the leftover from them, once we discovered the three, *would be* justice.——Yes, that's inevitable.

G

Now mark this: suppose we had to select which one of these, once engendered within the city, would most likely render it good: Would (it be) that concord of opinion between rulers and ruled? Or that conservation, engendered in the soldiery, of an opinion inbred by custom-law, concerning what precisely *are* (things) to-be-dreaded and not (dreaded)? Or that intelligence and guardianship which *is present* in the rulers? Or finally, (the fact) that each (person), *being* one (individual), does his own thing rather than busying himself about many matters; is it this, *being present* in child, woman, slave, freeman, craftsman, ruler, and ruled that will most likely make the city good? It *would-be-hard-to-choose* between these alternatives.——It certainly would.——Apparently then (there is) a potential-principle residing in (the fact) that each individual does his own things; this (is something which) competes with the city's wisdom, temperance, and courage in the service of the city's virtue.——Yes, indeed.——This means, does it not, that what you would have to posit as this competitor in the service of the city's virtue (would be) justice?——Correct.——

H

Look at it also from this angle and see if you agree: are you going to assign the city's rulers the "adjudicating of justices" [*dikas dikazein*]? ——Of course.——In adjudicating surely their sole conceivable aim (will be) to ensure that groups and individuals do not keep holding what belongs to others and are not deprived of what belongs to themselves.——Yes, none other.——This *being* the just (thing to do)? ——Yes.——Then from this angle too justice would mean the holding and the doing of (what is) one's own and familiar and belongs to oneself. This (would be) an agreed conclusion?——Yes, it would.

Form and Principle

That portion of this exposition which is argued demonstratively, along the lines of philosophical (or dialectical) reasoning, is represented by paragraphs A, E, F, and G: the vocabulary and syntax are expository, regardless of whether the demonstration seems convincing. The syntax of the verb "to be" generally corresponds to this demonstrative purpose: (A) what pray would the form *be?* . . . obviously it *is* justice; (E) This something or perhaps a form of it *is* justice . . . doing one's own thing *is* justice . . . justice likely *is* this; (F) the leftover *is* that which has provided a principle . . . we said the leftover *would be* justice; (G) what precisely *are* dreaded objects . . . each (person) *being* one (individual). Subjects and predicates all meet the requirement of abstraction, through the use of either impersonal nouns or neuter adjectives. In fact, the subject or predicate of five of the statements is justice itself. We feel the growing pressure to substantiate it as an entity, especially as it is predicated of the word *form* (*eidos*), used once previously as a technical term (402c), and also as it is linked with the term "power" or "potential" (*dunamis*), suggesting its elevation to the abstract level of a "principle," as my translation suggests—something Aristotle might style an *archē*. It is as a nonspecific principle that it has power to "compete" with the three specific virtues, whether it be viewed as permeating them or presiding over them.

Yet is the argument really analytic? It offers a series of hypotheses or propositions, arguing that they are linked together, but there is very little reasoning that would satisfy syllogistic requirements. The limitation is mirrored in the kind of predication here practiced. The copula is used to join identities or equivalences; it does not yet classify or categorize or qualify; the linkages are not causal. One has the feeling that for Plato at this stage of his philosophical progress it is enough to assert justice as an integral identity, logical or existential (the dispute over this alternative is unlikely ever to be settled), which must always have a constant unchanging reference, and so requires behavior which is uniformly regulated. This is probably why analytic philosophers have not found the *Republic* very interesting, in contrast to the later critical dialogues. But at least it is fair to say that in the *Republic* the idea of morality as a principle or set of principles which have an existence independent of their application has been brought to birth.

One observes also, however, the continued effort to conciliate the reader, obliged to read a demonstrative argument, by letting the discourse relapse into a syntax which narrates the activities of living subjects and objects. In B he is invited to join a hunt in a forest; justice becomes the quarry. Will it slip through the thicket? No, the hunters have spotted it! In C it becomes something lying on the ground that we have been stubbing our toes against, or some object we have been handling unconsciously without quite knowing what it is. In D it is a subject of common talk or a popular tale to which we are invited to listen (but not to read). In similar vein, the verb "to be" can "lapse" into usages which are either locative (four instances) or "generative" (four instances).

A Traditional Ethic

Yet despite the demand to conceptualize, one which a narrativized syntax seeks to mitigate, what after all is the definition that is achieved? "To do one's own thing (or things)"! The formula seems morally meager, surprisingly so.[8] To be sure, it derives, as Plato points out, from the rules governing division of labor among artisans as these were prescribed when the city was being "founded-and-colonized." "To do one's own thing" is made to appear only the ingenious extension of a principle governing technology to the field of politics. But was that its source? To say that the principle justifies Plato's tripartite division of classes and the prohibition against their intermingling is to explain its application but not its inspiration. What is it that is "one's own thing"? No operative answer seems possible: the formula does not seem explicable except in its own terms. It merely insists that the citizen do properly what in fact he is doing, accepting, we might say, his assigned role. Who or what can have assigned it, unless it be the existing life-style of the social nexus, within which he is living? And what is this, if not a description of behavior which responds to that traditional rule of propriety which has conserved and protected the existing nomos and ethos of Greek society? Is the content of his *dikaiosunē*, now that it has been conceptualized, very different from that sense of *dikē* as the rule of regularity, of not stepping outside your allotted portion (*exaisima, anaisima*), of avoiding extravagant or excessive action (*atasthala, schetlia*), which had haunted *dikē* in all its applications from Homer to Aeschylus?[9]

Plato may reveal as much in his own reference to where the formula comes from: it has been under our noses; we have been holding it in our hands; we have not only been speaking of it ourselves; we have, from away back, been hearing it spoken of. These remarks do not refer to previous statements in Plato's works,[10] but to attitudes fostered by Greek tradition, as these were expressed in the *dikē* of Homer and Hesiod and had become ingrained in the social and personal mores of the polis.[11] They had arisen in that conservatism characteristic of the society of oral communication now being rapidly superseded. By contrast, the effects of the growing apparatus of a literate democracy were disturbing and dislocating: accepted civic roles were being altered; and yet one might question whether the effects went really deep.

A traditional context for justice emerges again in the conclusion (H): the city will have rulers, one of whose tasks will be to "justice the justices"; the symbols are *dikai* in the plural and the verb *dikazein;* the combination has an antique flavor, recalling the language of Menelaus (Chapter 7). What will be the objectives of such judicial exercise? Elsewhere in the *Republic* Plato repudiates the notion that in his utopia there will be any need for litigation. Here, however, his mind is not on litigation but on the conservation of existing distributions of property and power, definable only in terms of the status quo. When in the next stage of the argument the justice of the just individual has been formulated in its turn, its effects are illustrated in the same traditional terms: the just man will not after receiving a deposit wish to deprive its owner of possession; he will stay away from sacrilege and stealing and treachery; his oaths and contracts will be completely reliable; adultery and neglect of parents and of cult service to the gods do not "fit" this kind of person; such is the kind of city and man created by *dikaiosunē* (442e4–443b6). In fact, such rules of behavior had historically owed nothing to the new morals of Plato's definition. They were the directives of the tradition, as embodied in the *muthoi* and maxims of a Homer, a Hesiod, a Solon, an Aeschylus, and as most recently applied in Herodotus to the moralities of commerce.

There is a difference, however. What Plato does not want to retain is the purely procedural aspect of *dikē*. He welcomes it as propriety, but would prefer a society where the need for adjustments required to preserve or restore propriety does not exist. He is unwilling to accept the fact of individuation, which, as I argued earlier, impelled even oral societies instinctively to formulate and adopt directives of a correctional nature—the Greek *dikē* being a leading example—which when applied would restore the pattern of nomos and ethos temporarily disrupted. Plato's justice, as writ large in the city, becomes the symbol of unchanging stability. Even the transfer of progeny from one class to another is only allowed to prevent stability from being impaired. The Greek consciousness had, of course, always revolved round the polarization between process and peace, motion and rest. Plato's justice opts for one of these, and the concessions made in his later dialogues to the necessity of admitting metaphysical motion did not essentially change his political and moral stance. It has been explained as an effect of his conservative social background. A second reason could be found in the sheer effort required, both linguistic and intellectual, to wrest from the tradition his identification of justice as a solid conceptual entity. This requirement of the mind, extended to bind subjects to predicates in permanent propositions, he wished to enforce also upon the sphere of human action.

Definition of Personal Justice

There are paradoxes in Plato's justice; perhaps no philosophical attempt to formulate such a conception can ever escape them. They illuminate the intermediary nature of his role in Greek cultural history and the mediating quality of his genius, poised between an oral past fast disappearing and a literate consciousness now coming into its own. This is especially true of his political justice. Yet when he proceeds to implant justice in the human soul, he leaves tradition firmly behind him. As already noted, an intellectual movement toward conceptualizing the human personality as the source of motive and intelligence had been proceeding, during the last half of the fifth century, in parallel with the

conceptualization of justice. Concluding the definition of political justice (and also of its negative, nonjustice, 434a3–d1), Plato turns to
study the proposition, which he takes as an agreed one, that "this form
applies also to each individual human being; that also (is) where justice
is-present" (434d3–4). To formulate this kind of justice will require
first a description of its seat, where it resides, namely, the soul. The rule
of symmetry will require that the entity, like the polis, should be
tripartite (434d2–441c8). This structure, having been expounded, is
ready to receive the four personal virtues as analogues to the four political ones. Personal justice, again reserved to the last, receives a definition
which is clinched in the following paragraph (443c9 ff.):

> In reality justice pertains not to the outward action (performed) upon
> one's (concerns), but to the inner, that which really pertains to oneself
> and to the self's concerns; the individual avoids allowing the elements
> [genē] in the soul to mind each other's business and get involved with
> each other: he actually makes a proper disposition of (what is) per-
> sonal to him [oikeia]: he personally assumes command of and organizes
> himself [auton hautou] and becomes friend to himself . . . becoming
> in all respects one out of many . . .

The energies of the psyche must be so arranged as to provide for
the same unshakeable, unchanging stability that the polis enjoys by the
equally stable disposition of its three classes of citizens. There is no
dialectical logic in this summary. Yet it establishes with clarity a firm
conception of justice as the symbol of a purely personal morality which
has endured to the days of Marx and Freud.

I say "purely personal"; the initial clause, on the face of it, seems to
imply a repudiation of a great deal of what Plato has previously said. If
justice does not apply to outward action, it becomes an inner and private
condition, a morality of the self but not of society. One notes many
passages in the later pages of the *Republic* which lend color to this
position, and others which do not; Plato's moral philosophy cannot shake
off paradox nor need we require that it should. The present statement
seems extreme, but it can perhaps be explained. Whereas Plato's description of political justice was conservative, and in many respects
avoided a sharp break with traditional notions, his psychology is as
radical as the conceptual language he wishes to employ; he wants to
press them both home. In pre-Platonic authors it is difficult to identify
idioms which will describe a purely personal morality of the inner
consciousness; in Plato it becomes much easier to do so. But while we

can today take the acceptance of such a position in moral philosophy for granted, he felt he could not. He had to impress it upon the Hellenic consciousness, to the point where it assumed priority. For, as the later pages of the *Republic* make clear, the private soul was also the seat of that intelligence which alone could understand the forms of his philosophical system.

19
A Philosophy of the Written Word

When Hesiod undertook the topicalization of justice and, as it would appear, achieved this by exploiting Homeric contexts and reassembling Homeric sentiments, this activity on his part prompted the question: Why should this kind of breakthrough have occurred at the particular historical moment when he was living and working? The answer supplied was that whereas Homeric verse had for didactic purposes supported a form of discourse, whose composition was controlled acoustically, Hesiod was able to supplement acoustics by the use of the eye. This had a twofold advantage: first, since language spoken and heard could now survive as an artifact, some of the pressure to ensure survival by memorization was relieved, and this in turn meant that the composer felt freer to exploit statements which had the names of nonpersons as their subjects and objects; second, another physical sense, that of vision, supplementing the ear in the task of composition, could in some degree rearrange phrases and lines according to visual rather than acoustic principles—a sort of architecture of the eye imposing itself upon echo patterns of the ear.

Plato the Writer

The question arises: does the Platonic commitment to a more elaborate and stringent topicalization of justice have any connection with these same causes?[1] The sheer span of time that had elapsed does not make this seem very likely. Greece, after all, had now been using documented speech for perhaps two hundred and fifty years. Surely the effects of any adjustment between auditory and visual methods of composition had run their course. However, let the proposition that in Plato's case there is some connection stand for the moment as a hypothesis to be tested by application. If it is true, certain attributes of his discourse are traceable to the effect of a growing habit of seeing language as well as hearing it, of reading it as well as memorizing it; a literate way of using and arranging words is to be perceived, which encroaches upon the nonliterate without entirely displacing it. What would such attributes be? What would the symptoms of literate usage look like? They would surely be identifiable as extending the steps away from Homer already taken by Hesiod: (1) meter as a memorizer is discarded altogether, thus freeing words to be disposed, as we say, "prosaically," in ways which will most directly convey their semantic connections; (2) subjects of didactic statements have become abstract to a degree beyond Hesiod's powers of expression; (3) predicates attached to them are equally so, this effect being achieved by the recurrent preference for verbs intended to indicate connections which are logical or causal, in place of verbs symbolizing action or situation; (4) the favorite method for achieving this is the use of the verb "to be," as a copula divested, so far as possible, of the senses of presence in location or time, of activity or existence, which have continued to haunt it in the intervening centuries of its usage. To give a simple example: Hesiod would be able to say, "Ten thousand spirits guard the justices and reckless works of men"; Plato could say, "Justice *is* that principle which preserves the city as one and *is* the opposite of nonjustice." The latter mode of language, according to the hypothesis, has been encouraged by increasing documentation.

But surely the source of the syntax of Plato's dialectic, if source is to be sought, would lie in the conversations of Socrates, who never, so far as we know, used the written word for didactic purposes. This objection will fail if two things are true: first, that the conversations of the Platonic dialogues as we have them are not reports of oral originals, but are compositions carefully written to conform to the linguistic rules of abstract argument; second, that even so, Socrates' own method, in so far as it employed dialectical definition, was exploiting a type of vocabulary and syntax for which the increasing documentation of that day was responsible, he himself, however, being an oral traditionalist. The intellectuals who were his contemporaries were writers, but for the most part not Athenians. This is not the place to entertain a consideration of the Socratic question. But to raise it at all is to realize afresh how Plato as writer occupies a mediating position between two forms of communication. This is fairly evident from his preference for dialogue as a method of exposition, a preference which declines as he grows older. The purpose of the format, viewed as a literary convention, resembles that of the narrativized portions of his argument noticed in the previous chapter; it is a technique for wooing and conciliating a public which is half audience and half reader. It has even been suggested that the written dialogue was a teaching device designed to be read aloud in the Academy.[2] This would make it a compromise beween traditionally oral methods of communicating instruction and the kind of communication that is experienced in a library.

Does Plato himself have anything to say which would lend color to the hypothesis? Are there indications in his text, even slight ones, that it is being composed with attention to visual values, that language as he is using it is in some respects changing, not so much because it is written, as because it can be seen? One might point to the fact of the text's very existence and its bulk. Here is the first extant body of Greek prose composed with didactic purpose, comparable in range to the Homeric epics (and, indeed, exceeding them in length) or to the poetic output (including the lost plays) of any given dramatist. The preceding histories of Herodotus and Thucydides were not written till the last half of the fifth century, and only the second of these was composed in the dialect of Athens. Their format still conformed to the epic requirement that the syntax of what is said be that of narrative, even though there is much in Thucydides which anticipates Plato's management of abstractions. Whatever impression the philosopher wished to convey of preferring the spoken to the written word, he exists as Plato only because he was a writer and author of phenomenal industry, which he applied to a genre of language, namely, expository prose, never before attempted in Greek or indeed in any prior language known to us, the Old Testament not excepted. This is his professional definition which has given him such an overpowering impact upon intellectual history, and the conversational format chosen for much of his writing must not be allowed to obscure it. In one of his works—the *Phaedrus*—which contains considerable ironic disparagement of some of the written work of his contemporaries, there is a passage which dilates upon the superior advantages of his own dialectic as orally employed in the instruction of pupils.

It reads like a professional defense of the kind of classroom exercises conducted in the Academy. But what he says has to be placed in proportion in the context which surrounds it, one which shows keen awareness that a growing body of written work by his contemporaries now exists, that it is recent, that it is not limited to the texts of speeches orally delivered, and that he has to come to terms with it himself;[3] reluctantly he is doing so by his own conmitment to writing, though he would still like to be thought of as an oral teacher.

Plato the Reader

So far so good. But to point to his ability as a writer, or even an awareness that he was a writer, falls short of any demonstration that the actual visibility of the language before him, his own and that of others, was still registering some novel effect on the way it was being composed. The question to be put sounds a little esoteric; it turns on the psychology not of the writer but of his counterpart, the reader. If there is an answer, it must be in the text itself. Are there forms of expression, idioms, mannerisms which give it away?

To test such a suggestion, the passage already reviewed and partially translated in which the definition of justice is prepared by first defining the three other virtues will do as well as any. The argument was arranged so as to focus upon the existence of four terms, intelligence, courage, temperance, and justice, each of which is to be made the subject of a discourse describing what the term means, or what the thing it stands for is. In achieving this purpose, Plato is aware that he is engaged in a process of "naming names," fixing them, we might say, as new names, new insofar as they are now to become symbols of conceptual identities. It is as though he had realized and was rationalizing the task first undertaken by Hesiod, who had in effect named Homeric *dikē* as the new subject of poetry. Accordingly, Plato's text uses and reuses four verbs which index the act of naming: "to attach the appelation" (*pros-erein*); "to call" (*kalein*); "to name" (*onomazein*); "to attach the term" (*pros-agoreuein*). There is nothing unexpected here; the text expresses itself in the traditional idiom of orality; what one is asked to think about is what is said to one. But there is a countervailing thrust in the language, and a more powerful one, which invites the reader to accept the metaphor of vision as supplying the method of his comprehension. He is repeatedly asked to see, seek out, to look or look at or look for, to gaze, to inspect, to discover. Within the passage devoted to the definitions of the four political virtues (427c6–434a2), there are some forty instances of such terms, the most frequent being "see" (*horan* with derivatives), ten times; "seek out" (*zetein*), six times; "discover" (*heuriskein*), eight times; "look" (*skopein* with derivatives), seven times; "scrutinize" (*apoblepein*), four times. The common reader is likely to make nothing more of this than a convenient idiom of current use—current to this day—employing our vision of the environment as a metaphor for cognition. But there are reinforcements of this effect. Treating of courage, a virtue which requires training through habituation, Plato uses a simile which elaborately compares it to a dyed color. Justice is presented as a quarry which we are looking for rather anxiously in a thicket. The colony which is to house the virtues has been founded in order to be ready for visual inspection. There may also be some significance in the use three times of "put in place" to mean something formally stated. Such language is typical of Platonism, as indeed of abstract discourse since Plato. But could it ever have been typical of a Homer or an Aeschylus? I pointed out in an earlier chapter that much of the critical vocabulary employed in literature, philosophy, or science (subject, theme, thesis, program, code, composition, construct, and the like) relies on metaphors drawn from sight or touch but not from hearing; this is true even of the word *literature* itself. Do we perceive in Plato the beginning of the establishment of such a vocabulary, and does its appearance reflect his own unconscious response to seeing the substance of what he thinks as it is alphabetized on the paper before him?

Two metaphors have pecularities which put them in a class by themselves. "The colony has been founded," says Socrates to his interlocutors. "So get a light from somewhere to take a look at it." The layout of this city has previously been described in some detail, schematically no doubt, but it is still an actual city, in a given location, of a given size with a given population, exposed in panoramic view. What would be the use of a lamp to inspect such a scene? For that matter, why is a light needed at all? Why cannot the city be viewed by day? But if the author at the moment is thinking of his creation in its documented form, so many words or lines drawn on papyrus, the request makes sense, especially if one thinks of it as being looked at indoors, in a room poorly lit, or in the evening. Again, at the point where justice becomes an animal pursued by hunters in a thicket, we are warned that the quarry may "slip out"; so far, so good. But the Greek then adds: "and become invisible after being obliterated," which disrupts the metaphor. To obliterate would in pre-Platonic Greek most naturally mean to kill or destroy, and that is exactly what the hunters would want to do, rather than avoid doing, and if they were successful, the quarry instead of disappearing would remain highly visible. The language would retain sense, though not coherence, if "obliterate" (the Greek means to remove from sight) referred to deletion of writing, a meaning it was acquiring by the end of the fifth century. This would explain the resultant invisibility of the object once deleted. Plato has slipped into imagining the definition of justice as embodied in script. To grasp and understand it means to read the script; to miss it is to lose the script, to leave it unread.

A similitude occurs several times in the dialogues which points in the same direction; it is the one which employs the letters of the alphabet. A conspicuous instance arises at the original point in Book 2 where the challenge to define justice once and for all is accepted. The method to be followed, says "Socrates," will be to enlarge the object of search artificially to make it more visible, "as if people who could not see very well were assigned letters to read from a distance (which were too) small, till the idea occurred that the same letters exist on a large scale elsewhere and in a larger medium. I imagine it would be a windfall for such people to (be able to) read the large ones first, and then take a look at the smaller." The interlocutor, admitting this to be true, goes on to ask: "why propose this kind of viewing (as an analogy) in pursuing a search, the object of which is justice?" Socrates gives one kind of answer, explaining how the analogy fits what he is going to do. We need another, explaining how it came to be used in the first place. The topic of a discourse is surely being thought of as existing in written form. Plato is relating himself, albeit unconsciously, to his script; it is a relationship which his audience must share.

If, then, metaphors of vision play an intensive role in Plato's text, compared with previous Greek discourse, I suggest that this reflects a growing if unconscious domination of the written over the spoken word, of the word as seen over the word as heard. The condition is not idiosyncratic with Plato: he shares a situation which is becoming general in his lifetime.

The same explanation might be applied to the master metaphor of his entire system. For what is the Theory of Forms if not a visual metaphor applied to mental objects, one which we still apply when we call them "ideas." They are "shapes" (*eidos idea*) which yet cannot be seen. How explain this extraordinary paradox? Persuasively, a source has been argued for it in the previous use of "shape" for a geometric figure expressing theoretic relationships, or alternatively in its use to describe a type or sort or class of objects, as in some pre-Socratic thinkers. But suppose it also owes some of its inspiration to the fact that the programed statements and definitions of Platonism had come into existence as visualized statements, or, more accurately, had been created in the course of a historical process which rendered language increasingly and fluently visible? The Form after all is that which is, an abstraction, a principle, a concept, or essence, depending somewhat on context. If such objects had been alien to speech as recited and memorized, and had proved acceptable and manageable in speech as visualized in the document, was it not tempting to call them shapes?

Platonism versus Poetry

Documentation, then, made Plato's philosophy possible, not in the superficial sense of providing a medium for its transcription, but in the deeper sense of providing the means for its formation.[4] One may fruitfully compare the role that inscription must have played in the formation and rationalization of a growing body of law. But surely Greek discourse in the form of poetry had been documenting itself for two and a half centuries without producing a Plato. Why then does the role of the written word suddenly become so crucial, even allowing for the fact that some of the symptoms had appeared before Plato, in the work of the pre-Socratics and the historians and Sophists of the fifth century? If it really was the instrument par excellence required for the creation of a fluent philosophical language, why only now? One can only reply by pointing to the fact that previous documentation, so far at least as the Greek mainland was concerned (for Herodotus was not an Athenian), had indeed remained poetic. Accepting that the rhythms of poetry had the original function of rendering important statements memorizable, that the evidence of this function is to be seen in the earliest Greek texts we have, that these in all likelihood were inscribed not earlier than the first half of the seventh century, and perhaps later—one is tempted to conclude that if subsequent authors continued to use documentation in the service of poetry exclusively, they were still composing primarily for listeners and memorizers, and only secondarily for readers. Their works, though written, continued to be performances responding to audience control. Plato's authorship (as that of Thucydides) occurred at a time when the control was drastically reduced, though throughout later antiquity it never wholly ceased. Why this may have happened so long after Homer is a problem beyond the scope of the present work to answer.[5]

This would mean that, despite the efforts of a Hesiod, the syntax of Greek literature retained commitment in the main to the oral rules of narrated action, not analysis, to the description of active performance, not causal definition, to personification, not abstraction. Even when discourse became reflective, this would still apply. The *Oresteia*, for example, could not manage the theme of justice in any other way. Symbolic systems under these conditions could not be programed consistently. Does justice mean retribution or arbitration, punishment or propriety? Is it a goddess or a rule of procedure? It is asserted to represent what is right for Agamemnon to do to Troy, for Clytemnestra and Aegisthus to do to Agamemnon, for Orestes to do to Clytemnestra and Aegisthus, for the Furies to do to Orestes. It represents the conflicting claims of contending parties, claims which cannot be reconciled, which are in fact hostile to each other. Logically, this is a condition of moral confusion, one which haunts many Greek tragedies. Zeus and Prometheus, Antigone and Creon (to name two well-known examples), each respectively asserts his own claim to justice, while condemning the non-justice of his opponent.

Such contradictions can be dramatically effective, and the contemporary audience could accept them with equanimity. Was there not the chorus always present, speaking to it, confirming its accepted notions of social stability? But suppose linguistic need and opportunity should arise to stabilize "justice per se" as a symbol of uniform reference, or at least as one which should "ideally" have such reference. The modern critic is prone to estimate the moral conflicts of Greek drama as though this had already happened, as though Plato had done his work, as though *dikaiosunē* reigned in the minds of the Greek audience as queen of virtues, a moral standard of the inner man and his outward society, existing beyond the action of the play, so that it could be imposed as an instrument of moral judgment upon the protagonists, who are to be sorted out according to whether their words and acts come close to or depart from this criterion, or, alternatively, whether they can somehow be reconciled, accommodated within it. So the claims to justice on behalf of a Zeus or an Antigone are approved, those of a Prometheus or Creon dismissed as misleading or false. A head-on collision between an Oedipus and an Apollo is to be understood as an expression of a deeper tragic morality which somehow unites them in a common "meaning." Such moralizations can be carried out only at the cost of doing violence to the text of the plays, to the sum total of what is actually said in them.

If, however, it is realized that the plots of Greek drama are contrived within the proprieties of an accepted culture pattern not otherwise defined, that it is a function of the drama to continue the Homeric task of recommending these proprieties by illustrating what happens to people when they are defied, that the primary function of the chorus is to underline the lesson by repeating what the proprieties are, that the symbols of justice and other virtues are pronounced as part of the action, accentuating the tragic tension between competing moral claims; if, finally, it is perceived that by Plato's day the time was ripe and the Greek language ready to state what justice *really is always*—then we begin also to understand the probable source of Plato's astonishing hostility to poetry, to Homer, and in particular to Greek drama.[6] Aside from his objections to poetry's disturbing emotional effects, his deepest repudiation is epistemological. He had said, in establishing justice as a condition of the psyche, that it was not concerned with "outward action." When he comes to write the last book of his treatise, he adds (603c4 ff.) that "mimetic (poetry) imitates human beings acting out actions enforced or voluntary, who think that it is (only) action that conduces to their welfare or otherwise; they grieve, they rejoice, wholly within such limits." Using this kind of language, he is describing the genius of speech as orally preserved; it has to be narrativized, a panorama of actors and acts, never of conceptual relations. We with our post-Platonic consciousness can impose those relations by way of critique and interpretation; that is why we find Plato's rejection so puzzling; but they are not there in the Greek verse. To him all poetry *qua* poetry is of this general character; what he says allows no exception. For it is always a mimesis. The report given by mimesis, so he has just argued (596d8 ff.), can be compared to physical appearances reflected at random in a revolving mirror, offering an optical deception which communicates contradictory reports concerning what should be identical objects; by way of contrast, the calculative element in the soul corrects such distortion by measurement and number and so avoids contradiction within the same; it should be impossible to entertain contrary opinions which defy the science of measurement.

The Poetic Is-and-Is-Not

Could there be a better way of describing how the symbols of justice have behaved in the previous poetic tradition? Earlier, in his dialogue the *Euthyphro,* Plato had ironically complained (or his "Socrates" on his behalf), in response to the interlocutor's attempts to define piety, that "your statements [*logoi*] evidently will not stay still but keep walking about. You want to accuse me of being the Daedalus who makes them do this; but you are far more skilled at this than Daedalus."

Euthyphro is no poet, but the *logoi* he offers as definitions of the virtue under discussion have a family resemblance to the way the symbols of any virtue would behave in Greek poetry as Plato knew it. For that matter, had the behavior of *dikē* in Hesiod's poem been any different? The persistence of an activist syntax made mobility inevitable, and it is an activist syntax which even Euthyphro continues to employ. Socrates pleads with him to state what piety *is;* all he can do (11a) is "to state something that happens to it [*pathos*], what is done to it, for instance, that it is loved by all gods, but without getting to the point of stating what it *is* when loved." Using the term *pathos,* a rough equivalent of both affects and effects, as opposed to essence (*ousia*), to describe what Euthyphro is talking about, Plato is also describing what, from his standpoint, epic and drama have always talked about. The connection emerges in the *Republic.* The definition of justice given in the fourth book is to be expanded and refined in the ninth. To prepare for this will require an epistemological foundation, which can be exposed only by expounding a fundamental principle of Platonism. It is a philosophy employing a "method" of discourse and of thought which always has for its subject or topic "that which is." There is a contrasting type of discourse and of mentality, one whose content is "that which both is and is not." The one deserves the name of "knowledge," the other earns the title of "opinion."

"So we have discovered, it seems, that the many customs-and-conventions [*nomima*] of the many concerning the beautiful and so on roll to and fro between what is not and what is . . . Those who are viewers of the many beautifuls, but do not see beauty per se, nor can follow another who would conduct them to such, who view the many justices [*dikaia*], but not justice per se and so on—let us call them all "opinionators," who do not know anything of what they "opinionate" (479d3 ff.).

It is a mistake to interpret Plato's target by limiting it to any group of professionals like the Sophists. The "viewers" have already been identified as the audiences at dramatic entertainments (475d2 ff., 476 b4). He is looking back on the Greek poetic tradition which had hitherto nourished and preserved the nomos and ethos of his society. He is applying philosophical standards to it, and in the light of those standards he judges it wanting. For the justice of Agamemnon was not that of Clytemnestra, nor was the justice of Orestes that of the Furies who pursued him; traditional *dikē* in Plato's terms both is-and-is-not.

Poetics after Plato

Aristotle thought that his master's rejection of poetry was unfair, and set about remedying the matter by restoring to drama the moral intentions Plato had denied it, using the doctrine of the heroic ethos and the heroic flaw for this purpose. In his generation, the sense of tension between literate and nonliterate types of communication was passing away. The struggle to achieve a conceptual syntax was completed, as his own works testify, and in a more relaxed mood the results could be used as a tool to analyze the previous poetic discourse on its own merits. But it is a question whether he was a better critic of Greek poetry than Plato, who had sensed its historical function, inherited from the oral condition of Greek society, to be the educator of Greece, a function which he judged was becoming an anachronism, and correctly so. It is no accident that as the influence of Plato's philosophy prevailed, tragedy died—at least, tragedy in the high classical mode. Reborn in a later age, and recast in a different spirit, it was to furnish characters who would allow right and wrong, virtue and vice, to play out their parts on the stage with a greater degree of explicitness than had ever been possible before him, in ways which he might conceivably have approved.

Epilogue

Though the investigation now concluded has been confined to certain works of Greek "literature," the style and substance of the argument have not been "literary." The authors in question have been treated less as autonomous writers than as voices of a culture, or more precisely of two interacting cultures, the oral and the written. As noted in the Prologue, this kind of approach touches on the professional concerns of many—oralists, anthropologists, philosophers of language and ethics—who do not normally interest themselves in classical philology. This may be the place briefly to indicate some points of contact and difference.

In the developing story of human culture, speech, on the one hand, and the invention of tools, on the other, have played central roles. In estimating their relative importance it is now commonly agreed that speech has priority.[1] My own reconstruction of the Greek experience has been guided by a further assumption: the significance of speech which is placed in storage for reuse has priority over its employment in day-to-day communication.[2] The control of culture lies in information that is accumulated and recalled, and language used for this purpose exhibits certain important differences from what is casually spoken in interpersonal relations.[3] From this I have deduced that the oral epic in all language is devised to be a storehouse of memory, not a vernacular

335

pastime, and that its literate successor is the prose contained in the vast accumulation of knowledge, both humanist and scientific, which now lies in the libraries of the world—an accumulation which threatens to become unmanageable.

To accept language as the clue to culture, yet to insist that its function as a storage mechanism has priority, is to accept much that has been said by others, but also to reject much. For example, even in the restricted area of Homeric criticism, the oral poetry of the Balkans, although it yields empirical evidence of the use of a formulaic style common to all speech as orally preserved, no longer carries the responsibility of recording cultural information for reuse. The conduct of the "business" of the Balkans, meaning the politics of power, the laws of property, the historical and moral consciousness, has relied on literate record for over two thousand years. But in archaic Greece it was oral Homer who carried this responsibility. So in the last resort the "singer of tales" fails as an adequate analogue for Homer.[4]

In the larger literary perspective of the American "oralist" school, responding to the growing influence of McLuhan's *Gutenberg Galaxy* and subsequent writings, critics have recently been compelled to take "oral cultures and oral performances"[5] with greater seriousness. My own readers will quickly perceive my sympathy with one principle of McLuhan's argument—summed up in his aphorism "The medium is the message"—that the character of a given technology of communication exercises considerable control over its content. But I would prefer to perceive in the shift to a "linear" literacy an improvement in storage method which has produced many liberating consequences for the mind, where oralists might prefer to place the accent on psychological restriction. Modern media which do not require literacy in their use constitute an addition to the apparatus of a literate society, but scarcely a replacement of it, in the fundamental sense in which a Plato did replace a Homer.

Social anthropology, accepting the term "myth" as a central category of the oral experience, and organizing the empirical data of field studies accordingly, has variously interpreted the content of myth to be an account of natural phenomena (Max Mueller), a ritual reenactment (Frazer, Durkheim, Jane Harrison), tribal history (Rivers), sociological system (Malinowski), or finally a way of thinking which arranges experience according to polarities (Lévi-Strauss).[6] My reader will infer that the theory offered here of epic function is closest to Malinowski's view of mythic function[7] and that the account of Homer's content in

Chapters 6–10 is designed to show the theory at work in the composition of the two poems. But I would plead for the supersession of the term and concept "myth" by the alternative term "epic" as a more comprehensive and useful category, on the ground that it indicates a single genus of the preserved oral word, the "tribal encyclopedia," of which the variants of myth so far discerned are species.[8] Myth has enjoyed a prestigious and privileged position,[9] as though it indicated some fundamental quality either of the oral mind or of all minds. But the noun does not appear to have entered the English language till the nineteenth century. May it not be true that its present connection with religion, its supposed sacral nature, its enshrinement of "beliefs," its message of "duty," all represent conceptions which are sophisticated rather than savage? Certainly they are not easy to render with satisfaction into ancient Greek, and I suspect the same would be true of the languages employed by the American Indians or the Trobriand Islanders. Are these not rather the terms used by a European sensibility which has grown up in the course of a historical experience both post-Platonic and also Judaeo-Christian?[10] Does not the act of conserving cultural information in language respond to social needs which are primarily secular, as these are mirrored in the Homeric poems?[11]

The structuralist method offers a special case because of the special character of the materials used to support it. These have been drawn in the first instance from compilations of field reports of the American Indians north and south, starting with Franz Boas' at the turn of the century. To what extent have the observer's own literate habits encouraged a remodeling of what is said into forms which may help to suggest structure? The question is probably unanswerable, but it should at least be asked, as indeed it has been. It has also recently been argued with vehemence that only experience of an actual performance with its variant intonation and gesture can be faithful to the genius of what is said.[12] While agreeing so far, in that the technique of performance is incorporated in the oral message, I would see in this a method of group imprinting and group memorization, historically speaking, rather than a means of personal self-expression.

The American Indian materials reflect a more drastic limitation. Their content is confined to the linguistic ambitions of peoples who over varying periods of time, in some instances several centuries, have been robbed of their autonomy. Effective regulation of their politics and law, of powers to make war and peace, rules of mating and inheritance, rights of land tenure and technologies of food supply, is no longer vested in the word pronounced and recalled, but has long passed into the hands of literate conquerors. The art of the preserved word, robbed of such responsibilities, degenerates into the mere telling of stories, with a notable concentration upon purely domestic preoccupations, nonpolitical in character, centering rather pathetically on copulation and digestion and excretion; no Homeric stuff here. Concomitant with this loss of responsibility has been the decay of the musical skills originally cultivated to support it, so that the so-called myth, a mere shadow of its epic forebears, declines into a kind of rambling semirhythmic prose.[13]

Structuralism brings one out of an anthropology appropriate to primitive societies into philosophical procedures of some sophisticaton. The capacity to detect patterns of opposition and synthesis in orally preserved speech (whether in the anthropology of a Lévi-Strauss or the linguistics of a Jacobson)[14] is categorical, and would consequently be viewed, from the standpoint of this book, as itself a product of alphabetic literacy. Insofar as polarity and symmetry recur in orally preserved speech—as they certainly do—I would prefer to ascribe their presence to an obedience to the acoustic law of responsion, conveniently summed up in the word *echo*, a law essentially mnemonic rather than expressive of any deep structures of the mind.

If it is true, as indicated in the previous chapter, that Plato is the first author of record with fluent command of propositional language, then in the field of philosophy proper a reconsideration may become due of two related matters: the status of those kinds of statements which in a general sense can be described as conceptual in some form (veridical, or existential, or propositional, whether synthetic or analytic); and the status of ethics, conceived as a set of rules or principles governing what we call "morality."[15] As to the former, the view of J. L. Austin, that the syntax of a natural language is oriented towards the performance of speech-acts, has evident connection with the character of pre-Platonic syntax as I have sought to expound it. As far as ethics are concerned, it is unmistakably the Kantian metaphysic of morals, with its reliance on the doctrine of the categorical imperative, itself the philosophical fruit of nearly two millennia of Christian conditioning, which has pervaded the consciousness of what is loosely called "the west," to the point where it appears to be a natural and inevitable mode of thinking. Is it possible that this "morality of the soul," so far from being implanted in our human nature, was born when Plato proposed what was to be the first of many doctrines of justice still being offered to the present day, doctrines which have encouraged the growth of a more compulsive consciousness rather different from the ease of character and pragmatism of conduct diffused in preliterate societies?[16]

Classical scholarship itself has, in fact, shown recent awareness that the Greek archaic mentality was not quite like ours, and in particular that notions of moral responsibility familiar in our culture either were absent in Greece or, at least, expressed differently.[17] This kind of argument inevitably provokes its counter-argument, reasserting the primacy of the notion of a universal law of justice in Greek thought.[18] Both parties to the dispute may in their different ways be postulating questions inappropriate to the period. The habit of looking for the absence of what we are used to, or conversely of reaffirming that it must be there, is hard to shake off.

It has recently been stated that "we shall never develop an effective oral poetics if we *begin* by reading Homer. The *Iliad* and *Odyssey* come to us already written down, edited and recopied an unknown number of times."[19] This way of putting it, while recognizing that the poems have become a phenomenon of European literature, reverses the original truth and turns Homer upside down. The "primary oral cultures" whose stories are offered by anthropologists as the preferred material are not really primary at all. The Homeric epics considered as records of the orally preserved word, whether or not we choose to call that word "mythic," meet the following criteria of authenticity: (1) they have been framed in a society free from any literate contact or contamination; (2) the society was politically and socially autonomous, both in its oral and its literate periods, and consequently possessed a firm consciousness of its own identity; (3) so far as responsibility for the preservation of this consciousness rested upon language, that language had originally to be a matter of oral record with no exceptions; (4) at the point where this language came to be transcribed, the invention necessary for this purpose was supplied by the speakers of the language within the society itself; (5) the application of the invention to transcribe anything and everything that might be both spoken and deemed preservable continued to be controlled by Greek speakers.

I am not aware of any material now in use by anthropologists which meets all these requirements simultaneously. If I have ventured to cite the naive reports of early voyagers in the Pacific (Cook), recorded memories of the Scottish highlands (Smout), and a West African tribal "myth" (Goody), it is because the first meets criteria 1, 2, and 3, the second 2 and 4, and the third 2 and 3. I have, however, cited them in the interest of commending to the notice of all students of human culture two epics in ancient Greek, the recitation of which, at least as early as the sixth century before Christ, was judged to be the responsibility of a guild or society called "The Sons of Homer" or, perhaps more accurately, "Homer's Men."

Notes
Works Cited
Index

Notes

❧

References have been restricted where possible to author's names; titles have been shortened. Complete bibliographical information appears in the Works Cited.

1. From Homer to Plato: The Contours of the Problem

1. For some recent controversies, and bibliographies, see Combellack, "Milman Parry" (1959) and "Some Formulary Illogicalities" (1965); Russo, "Homer" (1968); Lord, "Homer" (1967); Anne Parry (1971); Russo, "How and What" (1976).

2. Theagenes *FVS* 8.2. Xenophanes 21B10, 11. Heraclitus 22B57, 42. Herodotus 2.53. In general, citations from Homer, critical or otherwise, by Herodotus and Thucydides presuppose a didactic view of his function.

3. *Frogs* 1053–1055, 1009 ff; Guthrie, *History,* III, 29–30. Richardson elucidates the didactic presumptions which guided Homeric criticism in the same period, as applied by Sophists and intellectuals.

4. *Rep.* 2.376e2–377d6. This and all other translations, unless otherwise indicated, are mine.

5. *Rep.* 10.598d7–600d6 with omissions; see Havelock, *Preface,* p. 28.

6. Milman Parry, pp. 408–413; cf. also p. 376: "It is wrong . . . to . . . suppose that heroic poetry . . . is due to any law in the growth of literature . . . Its proper study is even more anthropological and historical."

7. Below, Chap. 6, "The Sentiments of Sarpedon."

8. Parry's *L'épithète traditionelle dans Homère* appeared in 1928. A late eighth-century B.C. date for the alphabet was first defended by Carpenter in 1933 and 1938.

9. Page, "Archilochus," p. 121.

10. Kirk, *Songs*, p. 130; Snodgrass (pp. 436, 416 ff.) would place the Greek "renaissance" around the mid eighth century.

11. Hanfmann.

12. R. M. Cook observes (p. 16) that geometric represented not a peasant style but an urban one, abstract in conception and analytic in expression.

13. Below, Chap. 2, n. 10.

14. Mayr, pp. 635–636, 650–652; below, Epilogue, n. 1.

15. For a working definition of the term as used in this book see the discussion by Leach in "Culture," pp. 24–32.

16. Examples are codes, models, structures (Lévi-Strauss), charters (Malinowski), and most recently "perspectives" (Ong); on this last, Frank Kermode remarks, "He uses this distressingly visual word more than once and even apologises for doing so, but somehow it turned out to be indispensable." Lacan (p. 14) gives the revealing definition: "By 'letter' we designate that material support which concrete speech borrows from language."

17. Use of visual terms to describe spoken sounds goes back to Aristotle; Havelock, *Origins,* p. 10.

18. With the qualifications noted in the conclusion of the Epilogue.

2. The Function of Epic in Preliterate Societies

1. Goody and Watt, especially the Introduction and first paper (pp. 1–67). Goody, *Domestication,* has now related writing to cognition.

2. The reader will bear in mind the qualifications surrounding the use of this word.

3. Leach, "Ourselves," p. 772: "The ordering of cultural systems . . . is a structure like that of language . . . Our problem is to reach down into the grammar of the other culture."

4. In this case, Lattimore.

5. Cf. *Od.* 8.582–583. Structuralist theory would encourage a wider interpretation of Helen's dilemma: she has not been properly "exchanged" within a given kinship "model," but has invaded it, the model being indicated by primary and secondary terms for kin. Hence the "directives" (as I call them) of the terminology do not work for her; cf. Scheffler's account (pp. 77–88) of the kinship problems and issues presented by Lévi-Strauss.

6. Teeter, pp. 95–96.

7. Not to be confused with what Malinowski calls "new drives and new desires" created by "new needs" (*A Scientific Theory,* p. 143); these may result in "imperfection in technical performance, the disobedience of the rule of cooperation and the mishandling of objects or people," but such errors "provide ultimate punishment to the organism by the miscarriage of the instrumental sequence" (p. 142); this kind of process is envisaged in biological terms as self-regulating.

8. Beaglehole, pp. 174–176, 186; cf. the Epilogue.

9. I urge this point, in contradistinction to those who, relying exclusively on a communication concept of language (Epilogue, n. 2), would emphasize that in oral societies "all beliefs and values, all forms of knowledge, are communicated between individuals in face-to-face contact" (Goody and Watt, pp. 28–29).

10. The terms appear conjointly at Hesiod *Theog.* 66, the earliest instance (Havelock, *Preface,* p. 62): Ostwald reviews later usage under literate conditions; but see also his comments on pp. 9–10 and 21, with footnotes.

11. Smout, p. 115.

12. Such as would provide some stability to oral history, modifying the pessimistic view of Jacoby (*Atthis*), that only the fixity of written record is reliable.

13. Beye, "Homeric Battle," treats extensively of acoustic association.

14. See also the Epilogue, n. 7.

15. The oral poet must "reinforce his society's ethos": David Buchan, p. 171.

16. Beaglehole, p. 175; cf. also pp. 541–544.

17. Nor is it noticed by Moses Finley, pp. 38–39.

18. Smout, p. 22, who elsewhere (pp. 137–138) notes by contrast how toward the end of the sixteenth century "law rested on a Roman basis that took no account of unwritten tradition." However, as late as 1693 a Scottish chief could be "accused by the bard of abandoning his Highland home, and dismissing his poets and musicians" (p. 315).

19. In part by Aristarchus, more extensively by modern editors (Leaf's edition). It is an example of "rhetorical storage" (below, Chap. 6) inserted in the narrative.

20. As described at *Od.* 9.5–11.

21. Richards, "Future of Reading," p. 5.

22. Radin expresses the contrary view.

3. The Psychology of Rhythmic Memorization

1. In the Greek view, these two could form a combination indicated by the term *cheironomia* (Lawler, p. 12). Fitton's lecture "Greek Dance," published posthumously, is an inspired reconstruction of the physical dynamics of Greek dancing and the role it played in a poetic culture, though its mnemonic functions as I have described them are not noticed.

2. Recent excavations at Chternigov in the Ukraine point to the use of mammoth bones as percussion instruments in paleolithic times (Bibikov).

3. Both percussion and wind instruments used in preliterate contexts can of themselves convey powerful directive messages. American plantation owners forbade the playing of the drum, on penalty of death (Negro spirituals provided a pacific substitute). In the Basque country under Franco, not only were priests arrested for preaching in Basque, but "people playing the chiustu, a flute-like instrument, have been accused of giving 'subversive signals'" (*New York Times,* May 25, 1975), which may shed incidental

light on Plato's censorship of music. Music as the servant of oral statement tends to remain monodic. Johnson's *Music and Society* offers a view of the complex historical relationship between the two in Scotland; less satisfactory is Tedlock's "Towards an Oral Poetics" (Epilogue, n. 13). It is possible to speculate that the quantitative measures upon which the Greeks concentrated (Newton "Meter and Stress") gave superior technical assistance to verbal memorization, hence enlarging its content—i.e., the content of early Greek "literature." These measures in turn would have been consonant with the use of wind and (to a lesser extent?) strings, rather than straight percussion. Thirty years before Parry, Béla Bartok had in the Balkans and Central Europe begun to collect and record "oral music," identified by him as grounded in national cultures, expressing the "inherent simplicity" of peasant societies (Bártok, *Essays*). On drum music see Ong, "African Talking Drums."

4. A matter of frequent note in the earliest Greek authors, e.g., *Od.* 17.518–520, *Theog.* 98–103; cf. Havelock, *Preface*, pp. 152–155.

5. Thomas A. Johnson reporting from Bathurst, *New York Times*, March 9, 1973. This may be considered primitive stuff to compare with Homer, till one observes similar rules of memorization at work, even if vestigially, in a materially more "advanced" culture: "The resonant lines" which provide "the introductory chord and announce the major theme of *The Tale of the Heike* . . . are still learned by every Japanese school child"—from Ivan Morris' review of the translated version.

6. See Chap. 13.

7. *Introduction*, pp. 211–218, and Stroud, p. 40 and n. 36 (the comparable Hittite formula).

8. C. P. Roth, p. 335.

9. From the review of A. R. Luria's *Mind* by Harding.

10. The pictorialization of data recommended by mnemonists achieves the same kind of syntax, converting an item into an event.

11. See the Epilogue on the usage of "epic" and "myth."

12. Goody, p. 7, notes some Homeric analogy. The myth has two parts, the White Bagre for initiates and the Black Bagre for sophisticates.

13. Quoted from the review in *Times Literary Supplement*, July 21, 1972, p. 848. For myth as performance see Goody, pp. 41–43, 56; popular participation, p. 39; instrumental accompaniment, pp. 47, 58; instruction in memorization, pp. 49, 56–57, 59–60, 79; guidance for seasons and crops, pp. 53, 79–80; for health, p. 39; political decisions and cultural identity, p. 42.

14. Goody (p. 61) notes the mediation of a literate interpreter, "the extent of whose contribution is rarely clear"; the culture concerned, in fact, is not strictly oral: a song sung at funerals greets "all diviners that use the stick . . . the owners of books with their pens . . . those who read the sand" (p. 51).

15. See above, n. 3, on the possible advantages of a quantitative measure.

16. Goody, pp. 62–63; all four appear in the Black Bagre.

17. Havelock "Preliteracy and the Presocratics," pp. 49–50, and nn. 13, 14. J. Harrison's acute sense that the Homeric gods were artificial, "mere

things of thought" (pp. xi, xxi) brought her near to perceiving their function as an apparatus.

18. Judges 5; cf. Pfeiffer, *Introduction,* pp. 151, 326–327; the tribes numbered only ten at the time of composition.

4. The Society Reported by Homer

1. Chadwick, p. 180, Finley, *World,* p. 35. Lawrence, p. 88, is explicit and dogmatic: "Homer . . . ignores the present; he is concerned purely with legends of Mycenaean glories and transmits as faithfully as possible all the details of that ancient life."

2. Stubbings, noting discrepancies between Homer's Ithaca and the actual island he is presumed to be describing (*Companion,* pp. 398–421) concedes that "Homer was writing an epic not a guide-book"; but the concession is confined to this instance.

3. Kirk, *Songs,* pp. 110 ff., 179 ff., reviews the evidence.

4. In Milman Parry's telling phrase (p. 411), Homer was "the heroically magnified reflection of their own life."

5. Webster in *Companion,* p. 454, *From Mycenae,* pp. 157, 221–222.

6. Webster, *From Mycenae,* chap. 8, "Late Elements in the *Iliad* and the *Odyssey.*"

7. Page, *History,* pp. 120 ff., Webster, *From Mycenae,* p. 122.

8. Page, *History,* 151–152.

9. Nilsson, "Kataploi."

10. By Nilsson, ibid.; the case for a Mycenaean origin of the Achaean catalogue is argued by Page, *History,* pp. 120–134.

11. J. M. Cook detects invention at work in some of the names, and signs of topographical acquaintance with Lydia and Caria available to an Ionian poet. He also observes the awkward presence (from a Mycenaean standpoint) of the Phrygians, and that archaeology fails to supply a Mycenaean presence in Lycia "beyond Xanthus."

12. *Od.* 7.237–238 (Arētē to Odysseus), 24.298 (Laertes to Odysseus); cf. 8.550–553 (Alcinous to Odysseus); Xenoph. B22.4.

13. Webster in *Companion,* p. 454, and *From Mycenae,* p. 157.

14. Even if Ionian commercial expansion did not predate 700 (Roebuck, Hanfmann), small agricultural surpluses and miscellaneous artifacts must have been traded seasonally by sea prior to that date by the same men who grew and made them, and in their own boats (Hesiod *W.D.* 618–632, 641–648, 672–688). Moses Finley, *World,* p. 75, defending the "heroic" context of the *Odyssey,* points to the absence of a word for "trader" (*emporos* at 2.319; 24.300–301 means a passenger, as distinct from a shipowner). But Odysseus in one of his tall tales becomes the temporary trading partner of the owner (14.295–296). Laertes, greeting him, accepts maritime itinerancy as a fact of life (24.298–299; cf. 7.238). The model for the boat (*schediē*) he builds is a *phortis* (5.250). In Phaeacia he is taunted by being called a ship's captain (*archos,* a title used in the Catalogue) with a crew of entrepreneurs and an eye for profit rather than an *athlētēr* capable of competing in the games. The snobbery is dramatically effective; professionalism among

athletes became obnoxious (Xenoph. B.2). But it does not validate the notion that "the ethics of the world of Odysseus prohibited the practice of trade as a vocation" (Finley, *World*, p. 73); trading as described by Hesiod is not yet a separate vocation.

15. See Chap. 5.

16. Above, n. 1.

17. *Il.* 12.5–34; the wall had been built without being properly "blessed" (1. 6), perhaps a reference to a civic ritual required for such an undertaking; *Il.* 24.446: the gates opened for Priam.

18. Webster, *From Mycenae*, pp. 214–220; Kirk, Songs, 186–187.

19. *Companion*, pp. 504–522 (Stubbings, "Arms and Armour") concludes by stating: "But what has already been demonstrated in relation to other items of equipment applies here too: in general the poet mentions no features that would not be appropriate to Greek chariots of any age." Kirk, *Songs*, pp. 190–192, would distinguish intermingled references in the *Iliad* to a Mycenaean long shield and long thrusting spear, as against the round shield and short thrown spear.

20. "Any kind of room" (Wace, *Companion*, p. 493).

21. Blegen in the *Companion*, p. 425, describes a (probable) "clerestory" in the palace of Nestor.

22. Gray argues for a Mycenaean context, including the *orsothura*, a unique feature: cf. also Webster, *From Mycenae*, p. 113. I have quoted from Butcher and Lang's translation to illustrate the grandiloquence which is felt to be appropriate to "heroic," i.e., Mycenaean descriptions. I prefer to interpret *orsothura* and *laurē* in the light of probable etymology and classical usage (L.S.J. s.v.). The *klisia* of Achilles built for him by the Myrmidons (*Il.* 24.449–456) and the farm buildings of Eumaeus built by himself (*Od.* 14.5–14, where surely *rhutos* means dragged, not "grooved," as also at 6.267) represent that level of archaic domestic architecture, using a combination of wood, stone, and thatch, which has not survived for archaeological inspection.

23. The stockman is twice identified as *orchamos andrōn* (*Od.* 20.185, 254). The swineherd regularly carries the epithet *dios* (17.508; 21.80; 22.157, 162).

24. Shipp, 1st and 2nd eds.

5. Some Elements of the Homeric Fantasy

1. Idomeneus is only inferable from the presumed feminine form. The scale of Webster's identifications (pp. 115–121), using the tablets, is generous; Kirk, *Songs*, p. 36, is conservative: "fewer Homeric counterparts than might be expected." It may be more relevant to Homer's "real world" that a Hector, an Ionian king, may have ruled in Chios in the ninth or eighth century. (Wade-Gery, pp. 6 ff.; Webster, *From Mycenae*, p. 152).

2. Lesky, p. 41. For attempts to supply one, see N. Austin, n. 4.

3. Havelock, "War as Way," pp. 51–52.

4. "For such are the disposition of men in general in these voyages that

they are seldom content with the hardships and dangers which will naturally occur, but they must add others which hardly ever had existence but in their imaginations . . . thus posterity are taught to look upon these voyages as hazardous to the highest degree." James Cook's *Journals*, pp. 460–461, quoted in Beaglehole, p. 266.

5. Pfeiffer's *Hebrew Iliad* interprets by this title the biblical records bearing upon the occupation of Canaan and the careers of Saul and David.

6. It has lately become fashionable to interpret them in the light of supposed lists of people and materials in the Linear B tablets: (as in Webster, *From Mycenae*, passim).

7. In the aphorism at *Il.* 2.204–205 *koiranos* in the first line is supplanted by *basileus* in the second. At *Od.* 1.181–184 Athene pretends to be a "lord-king" of the Taphians (*anassein*) who is at present a maritime metal trader. In each case the verbal pattern combines the antique and the contemporary.

8. *Anax* at 4.18, 290; 6.451; 7.296; 17.160. *Anassein* at 24.202; cf. also 20.180.

9. The same formula for Priam appears at *Il.* 5.464 and nowhere else so far as I know. *Il.* 18.288 mentions Troy's wealth dissipated through forced sales to Phrygia and Maeonia; 24.234, 278 describe gifts given by Thracians and Mysians.

10. The formulas "Priam and Priam's people," "Priam's city," "Priam's sons," "X son (or daughter) of Priam" recur with regularity.

11. With the entry of Priam "onstage" at 24.162 (*en messoisi*), forms of *gerōn* and *gerousios* applied to him recur 44 times before the epic ends; otherwise, *gerōn* affixed as a title to his name appears only at 13.368; 21.526; 22.25; but cf. the *teichoskopia*, where he is one of a company of aged (3.149–150, 181, 191, 225).

12. See Chap. 9. Penelope in her role of object of the suitors' addresses is twice styled *basileia*, it would appear sarcastically (4.770, 17.370); Eumaeus once applies the same title respectfully (17.513). Hecuba is wife and mother, never queen.

13. M. Finley, "Homer and Mycenae," p. 142, argues that *basileus* is applied differently in Homer.

14. At *Il.* 24.404 the *"basileis* of the Achaeans" have difficulty in restraining their troops from resuming hostilities.

15. Gagarin, "Dike in Works," nn. 50, 51, observes the variety of nomenclature in that poem and the descriptive difficulty.

16. G. H. Calhoun, "The Homeric Picture," *Companion*, 431–452.

17. See Chap. 7.

18. See Chap. 7.

19. Above, Chap. 4, n. 22.

20. *Od.* 21.120 ff. requires an area extensive enough for the archery contest. The floor is dug up and then stamped down. Would any real megaron floor (even if it were a dirt floor) be so treated? The denouement of the drama requires that the combatants operate in a kind of amphitheater. Dinsmoor, p. 32, cautiously observes, "The classical Greek house by no means fits

the action of the story . . . Homer's ancestors . . . carried with them the tradition, or memory at least of the northern or mainland type of palace."

21. Finley's view (*World*, p. 29) that *hērōs* is a class term for the whole aristocracy is difficult to defend.

22. Hesiod *W.D.* 157–160. So also Pindar *Pyth.* 1.53; at *Pyth.* 4.58 the Argonauts are included; at *Nem.* 3.22 Heracles. Homer at *Od.* 6.303 (a dubious text) had perhaps included Alcinous, who like Heracles had a share in the Argonaut legend. Standard authorities on hero cults (for example, Farnell, Rose) have foreborne to distinguish as firmly as I have done between Hesiod's *genos* of Trojan "heroes" and the civic cults of local "heroes."

23. The ritual interpretation placed on this word by Jane Harrison (pp. 11 ff.) appears to have no connection with Homer.

6. The Method and Manner of Homeric Storage

1. In Malinowski's terms (*A Scientific Theory*, pp. 165–166) this "encyclopaedia" would contain not only "the charter of the tribe-nation" but also "the charter of the tribe-state . . . that unwritten but never absent constitution of authority, power, rank and chieftainship."

2. The view taken in this chapter of the structure and intentions of Homeric verse would seem to be in agreement with a recent dictum: "one must in dealing with Homeric resources renounce a large area of normal literary criticism" (Combellack, "Milman Parry," p. 196).

3. Bowra, pp. 112, 154.

4. Described as "juxtaposition of formulae" in Adam Parry, pp. 195–200. Claus, "Aidōs," p. 22, perceptively observes the effect of ll. 326–328 in "transforming the original homily."

5. In 1660 James Duport, Regius Professor of Greek at Cambridge, published his *Homeri Gnomologia Duplici Parallelismo Illustrata*, the parallels being drawn from (1) the Bible and (2) popular writers. Quaint as this long-forgotten work may now appear, it had a virtue denied to Homeric scholarship of the nineteenth and twentieth centuries: it took the didactic intentions of the poems for granted, and detected that there existed buried in the verse an extensive substratum of maxims and sayings designed to this end.

7. The Justice of the *Iliad*

1. For an overall view of the semantics of legal terminology, see Gernet. Oral *themis*, and later *dikē*, were given divine status, which I interpret as a mnemonic device, part of the "god apparatus," rather than as a response to religious feeling (see Chap. 3 and Havelock, *Preface*, p. 170), but it has encouraged a treatment which (as, for example, in Jane Harrison's *Themis*) would explain them as religious imperatives rather than understand them as oral procedures. Gagarin's two recent articles on *dikē* (1973, 1974) have given welcome proof, adequately documented, that archaic usage of the term referred in general to legal process, not moral values (cf. also Rodgers),

though the reader of Chaps. 9 and 10 (below) will realize that such process was not limited to relations of property.

2. I cannot follow Dodds in insisting (p. 5 and nn. 16, 17, 18) that Homeric *atē* excludes the notion either of "personal agent" or of "objective disaster." It furnishes a conspicuous example of a vocabulary which under preliterate conditions can have double reference (in this case subjective and objective); cf. Frankfort, and for further treatment of this passage, see Chap. 11.

3. As Heraclitus perceived; see Chap. 15.

4. Nilsson, *Homer and Mycenae,* p. 265.

5. Ostwald, p. 156; see also Jeffery on the later role of the assembly in the constitution of Chios.

6. Lattimore translates "the sons of the Achaians carry it in their hands in state when they administer the justice of Zeus." Such simplified wording has proved influential (cf. the title of Lloyd-Jones's *The Justice of Zeus*), but it ignores the following: (1) the text incorporates two different nouns, *dikai* and *themistes*; (2) the text uses two different verbs meaning "manage" (the root in *dikaspolos*) and "protect" (*eiruatai*); (3) both *dikai* and *themistes* are pluralized; they symbolize some specifics of action or speech, not an abstraction; (4) *pros dios* does not mean "of Zeus" but "under (the authority of) Zeus"; the *themistes* are not Zeus's personal property, or even his creation, though he keeps an eye on them, or, more correctly, on their proper protection by the *dikaspoloi.* It is *themistes* in the plural that matter in Homer and give substance to the symbol in the singular, whether used impersonally or as a proper name (*Il.* 15.87 and 93; 20.4; *Od.* 2.68; see n. 1, above). In the context of Greek preliteracy, I would interpret "protect" to mean "conserve in memory" (this is not, however, the sense of *eiruto* at *Il.* 16.542). The *themistes* are the oral maxims, in all likelihood expressible as case law (see Chap. 3, n. 7) to be cited and applied where appropriate, whereas *dikē* and *dikai* covered the procedures conducted on given occasions, with some flexibility, calling for "management" but also requiring an ability to cite from memory the appropriate maxims; these would be the "collections of legal rules," whereas the *dikai* are "rulings" (C. Roth, however, p. 333, would draw no distinction, and Wilamowitz, commenting on *W.D.* 218–224, argued for *themis* and *dikē* being synomymous). Were the "managers" professionals? In some cases they function as such (see Chap. 9), but the litigant himself could act, for knowledge of oral formularies was to some extent general. So Achilles speaks and acts here, as Menelaus later does, in his own cause. The *skēptron,* a wooden club, serves less as a permanent badge of rank (except in Mycenaean memory) than as a signal that whoever is holding it commands the audience.

7. See Chap. 10.

8. See Chap. 13.

9. See Chap. 5.

10. Dodds, Chap. 1.

11. "The concept of *dikē* which denotes both the overall system for settling opposing claims and also each claim itself," says Gagarin in *Aeschylean*

Drama, p. 23, where he also observes that such "illogical" ways of thinking are characteristic of oral communication.

12. Cf. the discussion of the early legal sense of this verb in Stroud (pp. 42–45), who aptly quotes H. J. Wolff, *"dikazein* means to state the right"; see also Kells, pp. 129–134 (cited by Stroud). The sense recurs in drama (see Chap. 16).

13. So far as etymology has any relevance to actual usage, that proposed by Benveniste (the root *dik*, meaning "say," "speak," as in Latin *dico, judico*) provides a simpler explanation than the one advanced by Palmer (followed by Kirk, *Heraclitus*, pp. 127–128, and Gagarin, "Dike in Hesiod") which proposes a root *deik*, splitting into the two senses of "boundary mark" and "characteristic."

14. The rendering of *aissō* (506) is crucial. It means "start," "swoop," "dash," "rush," an action appropriate only to the activities of the litigants, never "stand up" (so Gagarin, "Dike in Hesiod," p. 84, applying it to the elders). The subject therefore changes to litigants either at 505 (where they are holding the club which commands the audience) or at 506 (where they "rush up to them," i.e., the elders, or else, if the change occurs at 505, "gesture with these," i.e., the clubs). I have preferred "rushed up to (the elders)" as more consistent with the plural; cf. the dative with *ep-aisso* (L.S.J., s.v.), with which there is a possible phonetic association in *ep-eita* in the same line. *Dikazon*, active instead of middle, has been held to exclude the litigant (Kells) but this is not true of Menelaus, nor of Orestes in Euripides *Orestes* 580, and the *dikē* which in a different situation is driven out of the agora (*Il.* 16.388) is that of the litigant. The audience could hear *dikazon*—to conduct a *dikē*—as referring both to litigants and to judges. Line 508 refers to the litigant who wins because his statement of *dikē* is spoken straightest, as in Menelaus' case; this would also mean it was judged straightest by an audience.

15. See Chap. 11, n. 15.

8. The Legalities of the *Odyssey*

1. Or "top men." The archaic usage of *aristos*, as Adkins has perceived, responds to a "success ethic," and renderings which suggest power or influence rather than moral qualities are preferable.

2. As noted by Gagarin, *Aeschylean Drama*, p. 11.

3. See Chap. 13.

4. Gagarin (*Aeschylean Drama*, p. 169, n. 31), correctly observes that Odysseus' killing of the wooers is in Greek terms a "wrong" and yet uniquely goes unpunished, though I think one should add that due process rather than punishment is the mode expressed by *dikē* in the epics and applied in the present case, as also not infrequently in drama (see Chap. 16). But in alleging that "the relatives of the suitors finally accept their (shameful) weakness and drop their demand for compensation" he seems to me to misinterpret the action of the finale and its intentions. They had in fact taken up arms.

5. Kirk, *Songs*, pp. 249–250.

6. I am unable to follow Kirk's reasoning (*Songs*, p. 248) that the problem of purging blood guilt and reconciling the dead men's relatives would have seemed urgent to an audience of the classical age but "obtrusive" in the eighth and early seventh centuries. Are we then also to assign the story of *neikos* and reconciliation in the *Iliad*, or the portrait of legal process on Achilles' shield, to this same "classical age"?

9. The Moralities of the *Odyssey*

1. *Il.* 4.66–67 and 71–72, 166–168.
2. On *aisima, aisula*, and *exaision* (4.690), see Chap. 10.
3. Cf. the maxim expressed at *Il.* 1.80.
4. N. Austin, p. 12, n. 18, compares *Od.* 1.60–62; 2.233–234; 16.424–430; 20.209–213.
5. See Chap. 10.
6. In the text of the *Odyssey*, *xeinos* and its associated terms, once noticed, leap to the eye (and ear); the entire epic is pervaded by them. They supply explanations for twists and turns in the story which are otherwise puzzling. Yet despite recent attention bestowed on thematic structures in both epics, if any exhaustive study of this one has been undertaken, it has escaped my attention. Its recognition is not aided by a "heroic" conception of the poems. For the role of *proxenos*, see Phillipson, I, 147–156.
7. Cf. the early inscription cited in Havelock, "Preliteracy of the Greeks," p. 380 and n. 25.
8. Zeus *xenios* and Zeus *hiketēsios* were two aspects of a single "international" function, of prime importance in the early Greek maritime complex.
9. For a ritualistic interpretation of the symbolism of this adventure, very different from the one given here, see Burkert.
10. On the importance of this, see N. Austin, p. 4, n. 10 (citing Calvin Brown).
11. His words (19.583–587) are urgent and solemn; he does not just "approve." There is no need to argue, as Kirk does (*Songs*, p. 245), for inconsistency between this passage and Automedon's statement at 24.167.
12. See Chap. 8.
13. Once the thematic function of the *xeinos* motif is appreciated, objections to Penelope's insistence here as "poorly motivated" (Kirk, *Songs*, p. 247) disappear.
14. See Chap. 10.

10. The Justice of the *Odyssey*

1. Cf. also Nestor at *Od.* 3.244.
2. Hirzel, Ehrenberg, Palmer, Gagarin ("*Dike* in the *Works*," pp. 82–83, with nn. 6, 7) share this view, though differing in the etymologies proposed. The sense of "characteristic" as expounded by Gagarin and assigned to the *Odyssey* involves a habit of logical classification which is unlikely to have preceded the post-Homeric history of the verb "to be" as described below in Chaps. 13–18).

3. See Chap. 18.

4. See Chap. 7. The future *esseai* is commonly rendered (e.g., by Lattimore) as an imperative, and *epi allōi* as referring to conduct toward others, as though Odysseus were a schoolmaster enjoining upon Agamemnon a moral lesson in good behavior for the future—surely an incongruous touch; cf. also Gagarin, "*Dike* in the *Works*," p. 87 and n. 31.

5. It is difficult to avoid visual metaphors for acoustic phenomena; cf. the responsions detected by Lohmann between Homeric speeches and identified as "mirror effects."

6. Like other preliterate vocabulary (see Chap. 7, n. 2) it combines the subjective (or psychic) attitude and its objective application in a single aspect; cf. Dodds, p. 31, "arrogance in word or deed or even thought."

7. Ostwald, p. 63 and n. 2, who, however, insists on a distinction between the meanings "personal conduct" and "social condition" which for Homeric vocabulary (see previous note) seems to me artificial.

8. The formula "most just of mankind" is applied in the *Iliad* (13.6) to a people called Abioi, a name which, whatever its origin, may have been interpreted by the users of the formula to mean "nonviolent" (Ehrenberg, *Aspects*, p. 57).

11. The Justice of Hesiod: An Essay in Detection

1. Notopoulos (1960), Edwards (1971).

2. Havelock, "Thoughtful Hesiod."

3. West's review of Edwards in the *Classical Review* proposes that Hesiod "rewrote," a suggestion congenial to the analysis of Hesiod's method presented in the next chapter.

4. Recent scholarship has leaned toward the autobiographical interpretation: a lawsuit between brothers as described in the poem actually occurred; Gagarin, "Hesiod's Dispute," with notices in nn. 1 and 2. The author of Prolegomenon B to the scholia (Pertusi, p. 3) seems to have thought otherwise.

5. This explanation removes difficulties in a passage otherwise obscure; Wilamowitz, at ll. 218–224, explains that *rhothos*, initially signifying the roar of the sea, here describes "das Murren des Volkes das auf dem Markte dem Prozesse beiwohnt." Such a scene could then correspond to that in which *dikē* is expelled from the agora, though here she is "dragged out." Denying that *rhothos* can apply to an individual Wilamowitz observes that *dikē* "wird nichtmurmeln, sondern schreien." It is true that *rhothos, rhotheō, rhothion,* when applied personally, are used only of plural voices (Pindar, however, calls his poetry *rhothia, Pae.* VI 129), but I would propose here a reminiscence of the screaming (*boē*) of Andromache, with the proviso, that a listener to Hesiod's elliptical line could hear in the word both the screams of *dikē* and the uproar in the audience (from proponents and opponents?). The line caused difficulty in antiquity; the scholiast reports Plutarch's explanation that *rhothos* was Boeotian for a mountain path!

6. See, however, Wilamowitz, ibid.

7. Reading *epaurei*.

8. Solmsen, p. 78.

9. *Il.* 5.601; 13.633; 15.287; 17.587; 21.57; *Od.* 1.32.

10. Herodotus 4.106: the man-eaters are "savages who are not accustomed to *dikē* and do not employ nomos at all."

11. The breaking of the armistice by Pandarus, suggested above as the "model" behind l. 240, may also be operative here. Oaths cut or sworn, and foresworn, trampled, destroyed, with disastrous consequences for the guilty and their children, are thematically obsessive between *Il.* 3.68 and 4.162.

12. Most recently, West, pp. 40–46, and also his note on *Theog.* 84 with bibliography. Sellschop's systematic attempt to give Hesiod priority over the *Odyssey* is convincingly refuted by Edwards, pp. 187–189, who stresses that Sellschop "adopts too rigid a view of the process of composition" common to Homer and Hesiod as poets working in an oral tradition. Krafft's demonstration of Homer's priority is guided by the assumption that both poets were writers.

13. I see no need to follow editors in bracketing ll. 124–125.

14. West, comparing *Theog.* 84 ff. with *Od.* 8.170–173, would reverse this judgment on the grounds that respect would be due to a king (Hesiod) but not to an orator (Homer). This misconceives the ethos of a preliterate society, which accords status to eloquence whether or not the speaker is a king.

15. Straight speech, *Il.* 18.508; 23.580; *W.D.* 263 (reading *muthous*); twisted tongue, *Il.* 20.248. *Skolios,* in the physical sense of "curved," "bent," is not Homeric; it is applied by Pindar (frag. 201) to *apatai,* and at Sparta to a *rhetra* (Tyrt. 3.6; Plutarch Lycurgus 6); at Pind *Pyth.* 2.85 the "crooked ways" are those of speech.

16. *Il.* 20.249; cf. *W.D.* 402–403 and probably *Pyth.* 2.86 (previous note), despite the commentators.

17. Unless the reference is to a father bestowing a daughter on men to live among them? (Cf. *meta autois* at 278.)

12. The Spoken and the Written Word

1. Under preliterate conditions the need of private poetry to be "published," i.e., find an audience, was met by the symposium, an occasion which encouraged the convention of personal address. By contrast, epic, composed for public recital, invited the cooperation of the Muse. The proem to the *Works and Days* combines the two.

2. Teggart (1947); Van Gronigen (1958); Havelock, "Thoughtful Hesiod" (1966); Beye, "The Rhythm" (1972). Cf. West's note on *Theog.* 94–97: "this kind of inconsequence, a series of thoughts ABC, where A and B or B and C make a coherent sequence, but ABC taken as a whole seem to lack all cohesion, is characteristic of archaic Greek literature."

3. Cf. the perceptive observation of Ostwald (p. 10) concerning the advantages of what he calls a "semantic" method: "Its characteristic is that it proceeds inductively from the particular contexts in which each of the two terms [sc. *thesmos* and *nomos*] is found, in order to define the variety of usage of each in different areas of Greek thought and action."

4. "The kind of mind that is capable of reflecting on its own thoughts and on the opinions of others could develop only through the stimulus of reading and writing"; Ivor Richards, "Future of Reading," p. 2. Those who recall the same author's *Principles of Literary Criticism* will recognize in the present chapter a debt long postponed and at last paid to that pioneering work. See also Goody, *Domestication*, pp. 112–162.

5. "Most of the information which is the heritage of a culture is stored in physical objects . . . the environment is not a natural thing; it is a set of interrelated percepts, a product of culture"; Leach, "Culture," p. 25.

6. "The name is what first makes a thing visible"; Nietzsche. Claus, "Defining Moral Terms," observes how Hesiod desires "to stimulate an imaginative response to the use of thematically significant words," a particular example being "the dense use of *dikē.*"

7. Cf. Chap. 15, n. 12.

8. Jeffery in *Companion*, pp. 556–557.

9. In the Greek case this was gradual (Havelock, "Preliteracy of the Greeks"), rather than a quick and complete shift resulting in that rapid declension in quality of oral composition envisaged by Kirk. Andrewes, p. 51, expresses the prevailing view: "The new invention spread very rapidly and from an early date a high proportion of the Greek people were fully literate."

10. Wilamowitz comments on *W.D.* 217 as follows: "*Dikē*, die ueber die *hubris* siegt, ist Recht und Gerechtigkeit, in *exelthousa* ist es der Rechtshandel. Es gehoert sich, dass die noch nicht zu aristotelischer Fixierung der Wortbedeutung erzogene Logik den Unterschied uebersicht." The same phenomenon, from a different perspective, is brought under observation by Stanford.

13. The Early History of the Verb "to Be"

1. The view here taken of the behavior of *einai* in archaic Greek differs from that presented in Kahn's *The Verb "Be"* (a pioneering study which has placed scholarship in its debt), but is consistent with the morphological parallelism between *einai* and Greek verbs signifying "go," "make to go," and "stand" (among others), and with the fact that "*eimi* and its cognates are after all unquestionably verbal in form" (Kahn, p. 9). It is sympathetic to the belief expressed by Gilson in "L'être et l'essence" (quoted by Kahn) that "que l'on dise *il est, il existe,* ou *il y a,* le sens reste le même," though my view of the causation of this linguistic phenomenon is technological rather than ontological. My radical argument is that such "copulative" statements as that "X is the state of the case" (styled by Kahn "veridical," p. 23 and chap. 7) or that "X is a so and so thing" did not become a matter of linguistic routine until after the (Socratic?) dialectic had made them so. To suppose otherwise is to read back into pre-Platonic texts a state of affairs which I believe is not there. Kahn's classifications therefore exhibit major differences from my own: (1) my estimate of the sense of *einai* in given cases is guided by its position in an extended context; (2) once this is taken into account, a large volume of instances which at first sight (which means "literate" sight) appear copulative emerge as statements of "being present"

in space, time, or status; (3) usage in Homer and archaic authors cannot safely be illustrated from postarchaic authors, least of all from the fourth century. Within the context of this kind of semantic treatment, the problem of accentuation (covered in Kahn, appendix A) loses relevance.

2. That is, unless one rejects the view, taken throughout the present work (and I suppose most professionals in linguistics would reject it) that language as employed and remembered acoustically, in a cultural context exclusively oral, performs certain referential functions differently from language as habitually seen and scanned.

3. In Kahn's view (p. 350, cf. p. 455), *Il.* 1.70 is "veridical"; in mine it is "existential," in the sense expressed by Kahn on p. 457: "facts or events that *actually occur* or *will occur*" (my italics).

4. The so-called nominal sentence (Kahn, appendix B) embraces a much wider category; see the next note.

5. Kahn's arranging of "parallel sentences with and without the verb" (p. 444 ff.) concludes that "there cannot be any general difference of structure or *meaning* [my italics] between the nominal sentence and the sentence with the verb." This, however, applies to instances where the omitted *einai* would indicate a presence, rather than mere equivalence, and it is "presence" that pervades the examples cited, as Kahn himself partially concedes (pp. 449–451); what I have identified as "appositional equivalence" is not recognized as a semantically separate category, one where absence of *einai* is not a mere "stylistic convenience."

6. Hence L.S.J. s.v. correctly avoids listing any copulative use for Homer.

7. Kahn, p. 443, observes the same of Attic conversation.

14. The Justice of Solon

1. At 469a Plato quotes a variant of *W.D.* 122–123, itself a variant of *W.D.* 252–253; the formula "guardians of mortal men" is shared by the three versions: these are Hesiod's "race of gold" (Adam's note on *Rep.* 468e).

2. Cf. Ostwald's criticism (p. 69) of the similar view that Solon's *eunomiē* "is meant to be a transcendent and absolute ideal of universal validity."

3. Ruschenbusch proposes an organization of the code under no less than 42 headings.

4. Ehrenberg, *Die Rechtsidee* (along with Wilamowitz, p. 68, n. 1, criticizing Ehrenberg's thesis of historical development for being pressed too hard upon word usage); Solmsen, pp. 112–123; Ostwald, pp. 67–68; Gagarin, "Dike in Archaic," pp. 190–192.

5. Woodhouse, p. 132.

6. Gagarin, "Dike in Archaic," n. 41.

7. See above, n. 3.

8. By Jaeger and by Vlastos, "Solonian Justice," followed by Kirk and Raven, p. 120, and Lloyd-Jones, *Justice*, p. 80.

9. See Chap. 17 on legal terminology in Herodotus.

10. Havelock, *Liberal Temper*, pp. 145–147.

11. Vlastos, "Solonian Justice," p. 66, cites the fragment as an illustration of the law of cause and effect in nature. The "no one" who is the subject of the second clause indicates that in Solon's thought the winds have become persons. Cf. also Gentili, "La giustizia del mare."

12. Ehrenberg, *Aspects*, pp. 70–93, Solmsen, pp. 114–115, Ostwald, pp. 64–95.

13. Ostwald, p. 66 and n. 4, denies they are "divine persons" but styles them "poetic persons," which would seem to assign them to the "god apparatus" as described above in Chap. 3.

14. Jaeger, pp. 159–160.

15. Solmsen, pp. 107–123, Ostwald, pp. 63–67; cf. the numerous parallels from both Homer and Hesiod cited in Diehl's text (1958).

16. Ostwald, p. 67, comparing Solon's *dusnomiē* with Hesiod's, argues that Solon "deliberately contrived these changes."

17. *Hēmetera polis:* the possessive instead of the definite article; the polis in question is not Hesiod's (*W.D.* 240, 269) but "ours."

18. *Themethla* may intend a pun on Themis, whose powers of prophecy are here conferred on Dikē: cf. the "altar" (or platform?) that is "kicked over" in the *Oresteia* (Chap. 16, n. 25).

15. The Justice of the Pre-Socratics

1. Cf. Chap. 14, n. 8.

2. McDiarmid, pp. 141–142, who goes as far as to argue that "order of time" represents Theophrastus' paraphrase of the original.

3. Suspicion of Peripatetic reformulation has long surrounded such phraseology as "genesis exists for existing things . . . destruction occurs." I would extend it further: *didonai dikēn* and *adikia* otherwise do not occur earlier than Herodotus (see Chap. 17) and *adikia* is not a "poetic onoma," being metrically difficult, and impossible in epic and elegy. The personification appearing uniquely on a red figure vase (Beazley, I, p. 11) is epigraphically dubious.

4. I do not feel confident enough of the authenticity of frag. 102 to include it; objections are noted by Kirk, *Heraclitus*, pp. 180–181, who, however, accepts it.

5. Aristotle (*FVS* 22A22) identifies the latter as Heraclitus' target. I cannot follow Guthrie's reasoning (*History,* I, 447) that the saying is also a "covert attack" on what Hector says and therefore also on the imitation by Archilochus (frag. 38D). The reasons for hostility to Archilochus were more general (see below, n. 9).

6. Hence the saying is not an "amendment" (Kirk and Raven, p. 195) of Anaximander's formula, but an amplification. Most of the corrections of "erring predecessors" (Guthrie, *History,* I, 448) commonly detected in the pre-Socratics seem to be imaginary; they were not engaged in competitive scholarship.

7. See Chap. 12.

8. In Homer the Erinus (singular) keeps company with Moira (singular) and Zeus (*Il.* 19.87); in Hesiod the Moirai (plural) keep company

with Dikē among the daughters of Zeus and Themis (*Theog.* 901–904). So in Heraclitus Dikē keeps company with the Erinues (plural) in a formula which explains how Dikē, complaining to Zeus, can in this instance obtain instruments to achieve her demand that penalty be imposed (*W.D.* 260). In Aeschylus the Erinues and Moirai are equated (*Eum.* 172), while Dikē accompanies Moira (E. Fraenkel on *Agam.* 1535).

9. Explication in Havelock, "Preliteracy and the Pre-Socratics," pp. 56–57.

10. Guthrie, *History*, I, 472, interprets *dikē* here as "divine judgment," citing an association with frag. 80, and also with 94, where, however, Kirk and Raven (p. 203) describe her role as "the personification of normality and therefore regularity."

11. Kirk, *Heraclitus*, pp. 125–129.

12. Cf. *onoma* in frag. 32 and *onomazetai* in frag. 67, and the cogent observations of Kirk, *Heraclitus*, pp. 117–119.

13. Its direct influence upon the history of the verb "to be" as expounded in this book is taken for granted; space forbids more than a reference to Mourelatos' *The Route*, in particular the first two chapters, and the perceptive review of this work by G. B. Kerferd.

14. See 6.458; 13.706; 22.5; also *Theog.* 751.

15. Cf. also *Od.* 17.117 (Nestor's escort for Telemachus).

16. *Il.* 1.418 (but the philosopher will not suffer Achilles' destiny); *Od.* 9.119 (like Odysseus he has reached a place unpenetrated by man: cf. also Havelock, "Parmenides").

17. *Theog.* 748, itself a reminiscence of *Il.* 8.15 and *Od.* 10.86.

16. The Justice of Aeschylus

1. The *Agamemnon* is chosen here to typify Aeschylean usage of *einai* because of its unique length and its role as the lead member of a trilogy in which the symbolism surrounding *dikē* is uniquely exploited.

2. At 67–68, 272–273, 378–381, 511–512, 547–549, 1203–1206, 1359–1360, 1395–1396, 1497–1499, 1636–1637.

3. At 1605–1608.

4. At 67–68, 170, 217, 269, 273, 904, 958, 1110, 1231–1232, 1249, 1306, 1354, 1410, 1426.

5. At 68, 1094, 1099, 1131, 1232.

6. At 989, 1488, 1608, 1633.

7. But this "generative" usage, as I have called it, was not a post-Homeric invention; see, for example, the passage quoted above in Chap. 4, describing Odysseus' first view of his house, which includes the idioms "are recognizable" and "are fitted"; the speaker, however, is looking at objects "present" to his vision.

8. The epigrammatic sentiment uttered at Aesch. *Septem* 592, "He wishes not to seem but be (stand) best" (a famous line) still retains *einai* within the Homeric context of status. At *Agam.* 788, in the variant expression "many of mortals give prior esteem to seeming to be," *einai* notably

stands alone, signaling its future philosophic role. Do such idioms reflect the growing linguistic influence of Parmenides and his followers?

9. Which makes it difficult to ascribe Agamemnon's "fearful dilemma" to the mere fact that he "is the son of the guilty Atreus" (Lloyd-Jones, *Justice,* p. 91).

10. On *thesmos* at *Eum.* 391, 484, 571, 615, 681, see Ostwald, pp. 12–13.

11. The *thesmos* (which may be intended to recall Draco rather than Solon; see below, n. 21) replaces the Homeric and Hesiodic agora as the venue, though in the finale the citizen body is reintroduced.

12. In contrast, the role of "justice" in the Promethean trilogy (Lloyd-Jones, *Justice,* pp. 95 ff.), though no doubt significant, lacks comparable philological support.

13. Not found in earlier authors; at 483 they are actually appointed.

14. For a summary of the contrasting view, that the message of Aeschylean justice is coherent and uniform, cf. Page's note on *Agamemnon,* 184 ff. (a pasage which does not mention justice): "Aeschylus tells us that justice is not manmade; it is a rule of life imposed on earth by Zeus."

15. Cf. Fraenkel's notes on *dikas* (813) and *dikēphorou* (1577).

16. Recently translated with introduction and notes by Lloyd-Jones; no adequate English edition of the original exists.

17. See above, n. 13, and also Chap. 17. Possibly in an earlier age he would have confronted *ephetai,* or *basileis?* (Stroud, pp. 45–48).

18. See below, n. 20.

19. A solution of the tie-vote problem, with a review of previous opinions, is offered by Gagarin, "Vote of Athena."

20. Stroud, passim.

21. Stroud argues very plausibly that Draco's code was a response to the blood feud situation created by Cylon's conspiracy. If a memory of this still lingered, it would contribute a touch of realism to Orestes' dilemma and its solution.

22. This rendering avoids the dilemma of choosing between subjective and objective use of the genitive. Lloyd-Jones, *Justice,* p. 92, agrees with Dover, *"Political Aspect,"* in preferring the latter.

23. Lloyd-Jones, *Justice,* pp. 93–94, stresses their partnership in the settlement.

24. See above, n. 22.

25. The "altar of dikē" (*Eum.* 539; *Agam.* 384) could be a reminiscence of Solon's *themethla dikēs* (see Chap. 14). The puzzling phrase at *Agam.* 383–384, "kicking the altar into disappearance" (see the note in Page, *Agamemnon,* p. 103) could refer to the extinction of the "Solonic," i.e., oral tradition surrounding *dikē*: the "kicking," which mixes the metaphor, recalls the "kicking over" of the polluted table (*Agam.* 1601).

26. Lloyd-Jones, *Eumenides,* p. 43, explains the passage as referring to the Erinyes acting as agents who administer Zeus's law.

27. *Libation Bearers,* translated with introduction and notes by Lloyd-Jones, but like *Eumenides* lacking a comprehensive English edition.

28. See Chap. 15, n. 8 (with *Agam.* 1535).

29. Page, *Agamemnon,* on 1. 41.

30. E. Fraenkel, note on *Agam.* 1577.

31. At 772 the phrase *"dikē* glitters in smoke-begrimed dwellings" is translated and interpreted (Lloyd-Jones, *Agamemnon*) as referring to a (pure) justice illuminating the abodes of humble people. But *duskapnos,* like similar compounds, is surely pejorative (cf. 818–820, the *kapnos* of Troy), and *lampei* describes a flashing light (cf. the usages cited in L.S.J. s.v.), that is, the lightning of vengeance; cf. *ainolampes* in 389. The dwelling is the palace of Agamemnon (cf. 469–470, as emended by Page, and 1180–1182).

32. "In Aeschylean drama there are no Iagos"; Gagarin, *Aeschylean Drama,* p. 137.

33. Dawson, note on 1. 661.

34. Page, *Agamemnon,* notes as an example ll. 966 ff.

35. Simple hyperbole, as in "just, no, more than just" (Lloyd-Jones, *Agamemnon*), "deserved, more than deserved" (Lattimore, *Oresteia*) would be stylistically feeble, and meaningless to a Greek, since there is nothing beyond *dikē.*

36. At 78(?), 120, 398, 461–462, 935–936, 949, 987–988.

37. At 144–148, 241–244, 308–311, 639–646, 805–812, 987–990.

38. At 430–433, 468–472, 699–700, 804–805, 911–912.

39. At 217–231, 511–516, 483–486, 579–582, 610–619, 682–684, 719–734, 749–752, 888–891.

40. Hence Aeschylean justice cannot be described as "cosmic" or "universal" in any meaningful sense of the terms, popular as they are with interpreters of the plays.

41. *Septem* 670–671, where Dawson notes "three powerfully juxtaposed words." This play, in fact, exploits two large groupings of *dikē* symbols, between 598–610 and 646–673.

17. The Justice of Herodotus

1. Kirk, however, commenting on the semantic history of *dikē* (*Heraclitus,* pp. 127–128), observes that *"dike* is not identical with the later *dikaiosune,* implying an abstract principle." Cerri, p. 14, n. 13, notes the nonarchaic provenance of *dikaiosune.* When Jaeger, p. 105, observes that "the next age coined the word 'righteousness' or 'justice,' *dikaiosune,"* he is still referring to the archaic period. Adkins in his fourth chapter, entitled " 'Justice': Homer to the Fifth Century," employs the term *dikaiosune* as though it were both Homeric and archaic.

2. That is, using the concept as such, without of course implying the elaborate content put into it by Plato.

3. And otherwise very rarely before Plato; see Chap. 18.

4. See above, Chap. 15, n. 3; the order of appearance of the nouns, for what it is worth, appears to be *dikē* and *eudikia* (Homer), *dikaiosunē, adikia, adikēma* (Herodotus), *dikaiotēs* (Plato). D. S. Robertson (in a note in *Classical Review*) argued for the presence of *adikia* in a fragment of Pindar but observed that the scholiast used *dikaiosunē* to paraphrase *dikē.* It

seems to me only too likely that it was the scholiast who supplied the Platonic antithesis.

5. The entries in L.S.J. s.v. IV suggest common usage in Herodotus and Sophocles, which on other grounds might not be surprising; *dounai dikēn* occurs at *P.V.* 9 (cf. 614) but not in the *Oresteia*, where, if fourth-century legal usage were the model, one would expect to find it.

6. Havelock, *"Dikaiosune"* (1969) provides the basis for the present chapter.

7. Cf. Havelock, *Origins*, pp. 37–38.

8. At 3.142 a parallel story tells how Maeandrius, the ruler of Samos, proposed a transfer of his authority "into the middle," his motive being "to become the most just of men." The proposal this time is aborted; cf. also 4.161, narrating the reforms of Demonax at Cyrene, which "placed all the power of the kings into the middle."

9. Havelock, "The Socratic Self."

10. Guthrie, *History*, IV, 437, reviews opinions held on this question.

11. Kahn, p. 442, n. 18 (using Giraud), notes the "extreme scarcity of nominal sentences"; but cf. my next note.

12. Kahn, pp. 352 ff.

13. If one accepts the attractive suggestion of Lloyd-Jones (*Justice*, p. 102) that the Zeus of the *Prometheus Bound* surrendered his monopoly over *dikē* in the sequel by giving her to men (cf. *P.V.* 186–192), this would involve the god in a similar transaction. Is it possible that, if we had the text of the lost plays, we would find *dikaiosunē* performing as the preferred symbol, supplanting the *dikē* of the *Oresteia?*

14. Leading perhaps to that "internalizing of conscience" of which Dodds (pp. 36–37) says, "It is a phenomenon which appears late and uncertainly in the Hellenic world."

18. The Justice of Plato

1. An English version of the table of titles preserved in Diogenes Laertius is reproduced in Grote, I, 162. The alternates are usually omitted in modern printed editions. Tigerstedt (pp. 110–111) believes that the second titles were supplied by Plato himself: cf. also Guthrie, *History*, IV, 434, n. 1 (citing Hoerber, *Theme of Plato's Republic*, as also does Tigerstedt).

2. Havelock, *"Dikaiosune,"* p. 49 and n. 2. Guthrie, *History*, IV, 434, n. 2.

3. See Chap. 10. A reminiscence of Homer, in a context which involves *dikē*, seems to me more likely than a reference to "Orphic" beliefs about the afterlife.

4. Havelock, *"Dikaiosune,"* pp. 64–65.

5. Exposition of the doctrine of "psychic" justice is completed at 443c9 ff.; cf. Guthrie, *History*, IV, 475: "The quest is ended."

6. Cf. Snell, Chap. 10, on the philosophical potential of the Greek article, pronoun, and adjective.

7. Havelock, *Preface*, p. 256.

8. A "mouse-like result" is Guthrie's phrase (*Greeks and Gods*, p. 126).

9. Guthrie, *History*, IV, 166–167 (with notes), discusses usage and possible sources of the formula "to do one's own." Vlastos, "Justice and Happiness," concludes (I think wrongly) that there is "no discernible link with ordinary usage."

10. *Charmides* 161b.

11. The distinction drawn by Gagarin (*Aeschylean Drama*, pp. 14–16 and 26–28) between legalistic *dikē* and moralistic *dikaiosunē* is therefore too sharp.

19. A Philosophy of the Written Word

1. The argument of the present chapter should be compared with what is said in Goody and Watt, pp. 49–55, under the heads of "Plato and the Effects of Literacy" and "Logic and the Categories of Understanding." They note Wilamowitz's observation (*Platon* I. 389) that Plato was "the first true author."

2. The view that the dialogues were published orally, some at the games and others at private sessions (Ryle, chap. 2)—a view consistent with my own conclusion that literacy even in the fourth century B.C. was a recent achievment (*Preface*, pp. 39–40)—does not affect the question of Plato's personal use of a visual strategy in composition.

3. *Phaedrus* 257b–258e, 274b–275a, 276d, 277b–e, 278b–279a.

4. I detect some connection here with Dover's conclusion (*Greek Word Order*) that word order in later Greek (which would mean fully literate Greek) shows a tendency to move from a reliance on rhetorical rules toward patterns determined by syntax. Kahn's attempt (p. 433, n. 19) to refute this in the case of *einai* usage is compromised by his view that copulative usage is common in early Greek.

5. Havelock, "Preliteracy of the Greeks," reviews some of the evidences and the answers they may lead to.

6. Havelock, *Preface*, chaps. 1–3.

Epilogue

1. Mayr, pp. 634–635. Malinowski seems to place almost equal emphasis on artifacts (*A Scientific Theory*) and on language (*Myth*). In popular accounts of anthropology (e.g., those associated with the names of Leakey and Bronowski) language is virtually ignored.

2. Communication and its rules are viewed as the fundamental support of Lévi-Strauss's anthropology by Scheffler, p. 70.

3. See Chap. 2, n. 9.

4. Adam Parry, pp. 214–215.

5. A recent issue of *New Literary History* (vol. 8, no. 3, 1977) carries this title.

6. Malinowski, *Myth*, pp. 11–19, reviews some of his predecessors; see also the summary by Kirk, *Myth*, pp. 3–7, and Détienne. Kirk's own eclectic approach (but leaning toward structuralism) relies heavily on Near Eastern documentation. For a critique of the evidential value of this material for reconstructing oral originals, see Havelock, *Origins*.

7. The relevance of E. R. Leach's views is also to be observed (cf. above, Chap. 1, n. 15; Chap. 2, n. 3). I have presented Homer in the guise of what Malinowski (*Myth*, p. 19) calls "a pragmatic charter of primitive faith and moral wisdom," though I would prefer to discount the term "primitive."

8. Kirk, *Myth*, p. 22, argues against assigning to myth any "unique function." The word *epic*, however, does not occur as an entry in his index, an omission which might have surprised Milman Parry (see above, Chap. 1, n. 6).

9. The message of Frazer's *Golden Bough* was mediated to classical scholarship through the influence of Jane Harrison's writings. Fontenrose's *A Ritual Theory* furnishes a counterblast from a professional classicist.

10. Dover, "Some Neglected Aspects," perceives the same sensibility at work in much current interpretation of Greek drama.

11. Malinowski's functionalist view of what cultural behavior is all about (*A Scientific Theory*) accords well with the character of Homer's content. The "speculative aspects" of myth stressed by Kirk (*Myth*, pp. 83, 253) would in my view attach itself only to a "literate" mythology, so far as the Greeks are concerned.

12. Tedlock, pp. 515–517.

13. Hence Tedlock, p. 507, denies the presence of verse epic in what Ong calls "primary oral cultures" and assumes that "narrators in primary oral cultures do not sing stories but *speak* them." The formalisms of oral epic may become more sophisticated in sedentary societies than in nomadic ones.

14. Scheffler, pp. 72–74, reviews the interrelation between Lévi-Strauss's structuralism and Jacobson's "binary opposition."

15. Cf. R. M. Hare, in particular Part I, section 4, "Decisions of Principle"; but also *Ethics and Language* by Charles Stevenson, to whom this book owes some debt incurred in conversations held at Yale University thirty-five years ago. John Rawls' *A Theory of Justice*, as indicated by the title, pursues the conceptual possibilities of the term to their limit.

16. Dover's *Greek Popular Morality in the time of Plato and Aristotle* would appear to add pertinence to this question.

17. Dodds, *The Greeks and the Irrational*; Adkins, *Merit and Responsibility* (with a critique by Long in *Journal of Hellenic Studies*, 1970, and a reply by Adkins, *Journal of Hellenic Studies*, 1971); and most recently the first chapter of Gagarin's *Aeschylean Drama* ("The Early Greek World View"). Impetus for such "revisionism" in the scholarship of early Hellenism was imparted by the developmental or genetic approach adopted in Bruno Snell's pioneering work *The Discovery of Mind* (*Die Entdeckung des Geistes*) and by Hermann Fraenkel's scrutiny of archaic language as used to describe notions of time (*Wege und Formen*, pp. 1–22) and selfhood (*Dichtung und Philosophie*, pp. 83 f.). (David Claus, *Toward the Soul* [Yale] will appear in 1978.) One can observe the somewhat parallel approach taken to the intellectual history of Egypt and the Near East in Frankfort's *Before Philosophy*.

18. As in Lloyd-Jones, *The Justice of Zeus,* a book influenced, as the Preface (p. x) acknowledges, by Walter F. Otto's *Die Goetter Griechenlands.* The point of view from which the German work was written becomes visible in the title of the American translation (by Moses Hadas): *The Homeric Gods: The Spiritual Significance of Greek Religion.* Appropriately enough, the motto chosen for *The Justice of Zeus* (p. vii) is a quotation from Otto which asserts that the morality of the Greek gods has its own laws, and becomes comprehensible only when one takes into consideration the great gulf that separates gods from men. Milton would understand this, as he sought to "justify the ways of God to men." and so would the Hebrow prophets. But it is difficult to see how anyone contemplating the Parthenon frieze with dispassionate regard could apply such a judgment to the Athens of Pericles.

19. Tedlock, p. 507.

Works Cited

Adam, James. *The Republic of Plato*. 2 vols. Cambridge, 1920.

Adkins, A. W. H. *Merit and Responsibility: A Study in Greek Values.* Oxford, 1962.

—— "Homeric Values and Homeric Society." *Journal of Hellenic Studies,* 91 (1971) 1–14.

Andrewes, A. *The Greeks.* New York, 1971.

Austin, J. L. *Philosophical Papers. Oxford,* 1961.

Austin, N. "Name Magic in the Odyssey." *California Studies in Classical Antiquity,* 5 (1972), 1–19.

Bartók, Béla. *Essays.* Selected and edited by Benjamin Suchoff. New York, 1976.

Beaglehole, J. C. *Life of Captain James Cook.* Stanford, Calif., 1974.

Benveniste, E. *Le vocabulaire des institutions indo-européennes.* Paris, 1969.

Beye, C. R. "Homeric Battle Narrative and Catalogues." *Harvard Studies in Classical Philology,* 68 (1964), 345–373.

—— "The Rhythm of Hesiod's Works and Days." *Harvard Studies in Classical Philology,* 76 (1972), 23–43.

Bibikov, Sergei. *The Courier.* UNESCO Publications. New York, 1975.

Bowra, Maurice. *Homer.* New York, 1972.

Buchan, David. *The Ballad and the Folk.* London and Boston, 1972.

Burkert, Walter. *Homo Necans: Interpretationen altgriechischer Opferriten und Mythen.* Berlin, 1972.

Butcher, S. H., and A. Lang. *The Odyssey of Homer.* London, 1921.

Carpenter, Rhys. "The Antiquity of the Greek Alphabet." *American Journal of Archaeology,* 37 (1933), 8–29.

—— "The Greek Alphabet Again." *American Journal of Archaeology,* 42 (1938), 58–69.

Cerri, G. "La terminologia sociopolitica di Teognide." *Quaderni Urbinati di Cultura Classica,* 6 (1968), 7–32.

Chadwick, John. *The Mycenaean World.* Cambridge, 1976.

Claus, D. B. "Aidōs in the Language of Achilles." *Transactions of the American Philological Association,* 105 (1975), 13–28.

—— "Defining Moral Terms in *Works and Days.*" *Transactions of the American Philological Association,* 107 (1977).

Combellack, F. M. "Milman Parry and Homeric Artistry." *Comparative Literature,* 11 (1959), 193–208.

—— "Some Formulary Illogicalities in Homer." *Transactions of the American Philological Association,* 96 (1965), 4–56.

A Companion to Homer. Ed. A. J. B. Wace and F. H. Stubbings. New York, 1936.

Cook, J. M. "Two Notes on the Homeric Catalogue." *Studi Miceni ed Egeo-Anatolici* (Rome), 2nd ser. 1967, pp. 103–109.

Cook, R. M. *Greek Painted Pottery.* 2nd ed. London, 1960.

Dawson, C. M. *The Seven against Thebes.* Translation with commentary. Englewood Cliffs, N.J., 1970.

Détienne, M. "Introduzione." *Il Mito: Guida Storica e Critica.* Rome, 1975.

Dinsmoor, W. B. *The Architecture of Ancient Greece.* 3rd ed. London, 1950.

Dodds, E. R. *The Greeks and the Irrational.* Berkeley, Calif., 1956.

Dover, K. J. "The Political Aspect of Aeschylus' *Eumenides.*" *Journal of Hellenic Studies,* 77 (1957), 230–237.

—— *Greek Word Order.* Cambridge, 1960.

—— "Some Neglected Aspects of Agamemnon's Dilemna." *Journal of Hellenic Studies,* 93 (1973), 3–19.

—— *Greek Popular Morality in the Time of Plato and Aristotle.* Oxford, 1974.

Edwards, G. P. *The Language of Hesiod in its Traditional Context.* Oxford, 1971.

Ehrenberg, V. *Die Rechtsidee im fruehen Griechentum.* Leipzig, 1921.

—— *Aspects of the Ancient World.* Oxford, 1946.

Finley, M. I. *The World of Odysseus.* London, 1956.

—— "Homer and Mycenae: Property and Tenure." *Historia,* 6 (1957), 133–159.

Fitton, J. W. "Greek Dance." *Classical Quarterly,* 23 (1973), 254–274.

Fontenrose, J. *The Ritual Theory of Myth.* Berkeley, Calif., 1971.

Frankfort, H., and H. A. Frankfort. *Before Philosophy.* London, 1949.

Fraenkel, E. *Aeschylus: "Agamemnon."* Edition and commentary. 3 vols. Oxford, 1950.

Fraenkel, H. *Dichtung und Philosophie des fruehen Griechentums.* American Philological Association Monograph 13. New York, 1951.

———— *Wege und Formen fruehgriechischen Denkens.* Munich, 1955.

Die Fragmente der Vorsokratiker (FVS). Ed. H. Diels, rev. W. Kranz. 5th ed. 3 vols. Berlin, 1934–1937.

Gagarin, M. "Dike in the *Works and Days.*" *Classical Philology,* 68 (1973), 81–94.

———— "Dike in Archaic Greek Thought." *Classical Philology,* 69 (1974), 186–197.

———— "Hesiod's Dispute with Perses." *Transactions of the American Philological Association,* 104 (1974), 103–111.

———— "The Vote of Athena." *American Journal of Philology,* 96 (1975), 121–127.

———— *Aeschylean Drama.* Berkeley, Calif., 1976.

Gentili, B. "La giustizia del mare: Solone fr. 11 D." *Quaderni Urbinati,* no. 20 (1975), 159–162.

Gernet, L. *Récherches sur le développement de la pensée juridique et morale en Grèce (étude sémantique).* Paris, 1917.

Goody, J. *The Myth of the Bagre.* Oxford, 1972.

———— *The Domestication of the Savage Mind.* Cambridge, 1977.

———— and I. Watt. "The Consequences of Literacy." In *Literacy in Traditional Societies,* ed. J. Goody, pp. 27–68. Cambridge, 1968.

Gray, D. H. F. "Houses in the Odyssey." *Classical Quarterly,* n.s. 5 (1955), 1–12.

Grote, George. *Plato.* 3 vols. London, 1875.

Guthrie, W. K. C. *The Greeks and Their Gods.* Boston, 1950.

———— *A History of Greek Philosophy.* Vols. 1–4. Cambridge, 1962–1975.

Hanfmann, G. M. A. "Ionia, Leader or Follower." *Harvard Studies in Classical Philology,* 61 (1953), 1–37.

Harding, D. W. Review of A. R. Luria, *The Mind of a Mnemonist. New York Review of Books,* April 9, 1968, pp. 10–12.

Hare, R. M. *The Language of Morals.* Oxford, 1952.

Harrison, J. *Themis.* Cambridge, 1911.

Havelock, E. A. *Liberal Temper in Greek Politics.* New Haven, 1957.

———— "Parmenides and Odysseus." *Harvard Studies in Classical Philology,* 63 (1958), 133–143.

———— *Preface to Plato.* Cambridge, Mass., 1963.

———— "Preliteracy and the Presocratics." *University of London Institute of Classical Studies Bulletin,* no. 13 (1966), 44–67.

———— "Thoughtful Hesiod." *Yale Classical Studies,* 20 (1966), 61–72.

———— "Dikaiosune: An Essay in Greek Intellectual History." *Phoenix,* 23 (1969), 49–70.

———— "The Socratic Self as It Is Parodied in Aristophanes' *Clouds.*" *Yale Classical Studies,* 22 (1972), 1–18.

———— "War as a Way of Life in Classical Culture." In *Classical Values and the Modern World,* ed. E. Gareau, pp. 19–78. Ottawa, 1972.

—— *Origins of Western Literacy.* Ontario Institute for Studies in Education Monograph Series, 14. Toronto, 1976.

—— "The Preliteracy of the Greeks." *New Literary History*, 8 (1977), 369–391.

Heike, *The Tale of.* Trans H. Kitagawa and B. Tsuchida. Tokyo, 1975.

Hirzel, R. *Themis Dike und Verwandtes.* Leipzig, 1907.

Jacoby, F. *Atthis.* Oxford, 1949.

Jaeger, W. *Paideia: The Ideals of Greek Culture.* Vol. I: *Archaic Greece: The Mind of Athens,* trans. Gilbert Highet. Oxford, 1939.

Jeffery, L. A. "The Courts of Justice of Archaic Chios." *British School at Athens, Annual,* 51 (1956), 157–167.

Johnson, David. *Music and Society in Lowland Scotland in the Eighteenth Century.* Oxford, 1972.

Kahn, C. H. *The Verb "Be" in Ancient Greek.* Foundations of Language Supplementary Series, 16. Dordrecht, Holland, 1973.

Kells, J. H. "Euripides, *Electra* 1093–5 and some uses of *dikazein*." *Classical Quarterly,* 10 (1960), 129–134.

Kerferd, G. B. Review of A. P. D. Mourelatos, *The Route of Parmenides. Archiv für Geschichte der Philosophie,* 54 (1972), 89–92.

Kermode, F. Review of W. Ong, *The Presence of the Word. New York Review of Books,* March 14, 1968, pp. 22–24.

Kirk, G. S. *Heraclitus: The Cosmic Fragments.* Cambridge, 1954.

—— *The Songs of Homer.* Cambridge, 1962.

—— *Myth: Its Meaning and Functions in Ancient and Other Cultures.* Berkeley, Calif., 1970.

Kirk, G. S., and J. E. Raven. *The Presocratic Philosophers.* Cambridge, 1957.

Krafft, Fritz. *Vergleichende Untersuchungen zu Homer und Hesiod.* Hypomnemata 6. Göttingen, 1963.

Lacan, J. "The Insistence of the Letter in the Unconscious." *Yale French Studies,* 36 and 37 (1966), 112–147.

Lattimore, R. *The Iliad of Homer.* Translated with an Introduction. Chicago, 1951.

—— *Aeschylus: "The Oresteia."* Translated with an Introduction. Chicago, 1953.

Lawler, L. B. *The Dance in Ancient Greece.* Middletown, Conn., 1964.

Lawrence, A. W. *Greek Architecture.* Baltimore, 1957.

Leach, E. R. "Culture and Social Cohesion." *Daedalus,* Winter 1965, pp. 24–38.

—— *Claude Lévi-Strauss.* New York, 1970.

—— "Ourselves and Others." *Times Literary Supplement,* July 6, 1973, pp. 771–772.

Lesky, A. *A History of Greek Literature.* Trans. J. A. Willis and C. de Heer. London, 1966.

Liddell, H. G., R. Scott, and H. S. Jones. *A Greek Lexicon* (LSJ). 9th ed. Oxford, 1940.

Lloyd-Jones, H. *Agamemnon, Libation Bearers, Eumenides.* Translations with commentary. 3 vols. Englewood Cliffs, N.J., 1970.

—— *The Justice of Zeus.* Berkeley, Calif., 1971.

Lohmann, D. *Die Komposition der Reden in der Ilias.* Berlin, 1970.

Long, A. A. "Morals and Values in Homer." *Journal of Hellenic Studies,* 90 (1970), 121–39.

Lord, A. *A Singer of Tales.* Harvard Studies in Comparative Literature, 24. Cambridge, Mass., 1960.

—— "Homer as Oral Poet." *Harvard Studies in Classical Philology,* 72 (1967), 1–46.

Luria, A. R. *The Mind of a Mnemonist.* New York, 1965.

Malinowski, B. *Myth in Primitive Psychology.* New York, 1926.

—— *A Scientific Theory of Culture.* Chapel Hill, 1944.

Mayr, Ernst. *Animal Species and Evolution.* Cambridge, Mass., 1963.

McDiarmid, J. B. "Theophrastus on the Presocratic Causes." *Harvard Studies in Classical Philology,* 61 (1953), 85–156.

McLuhan, Marshall. *The Gutenberg Galaxy: The Making of Typographic Man.* Toronto, 1962.

—— *Understanding Media.* New York, 1964.

Morris, Ivan. Review of H. Kitagawa and B. Tsuchida, trans., *The Tale of Heike. New York Times Book Review,* Feb. 8, 1976, pp. 23–24.

Mourelatos, A. P. D. *The Route of Parmenides.* New Haven, 1970.

Newton, B. E. "Meter and Stress in Greek." *Phoenix,* 23 (1969), pp. 359–371.

Nilsson, M. P. "Kataploi.' *Rheinisches Museum für Philologie,* 60 (1905), 161–189.

—— *Homer and Mycenae.* London, 1933.

Notopoulos, J. A. "Homer, Hesiod, and the Achaean Heritage of Oral Poetry." *Hesperia,* 29 (1960), 177–197.

Ong, W. J. *The Presence of the Word.* New Haven, 1967.

—— "African Talking Drums and Oral Noetics." *New Literary History,* 8 (1977), 411–429.

Ostwald, M. *Nomos and the Beginnings of the Athenian Democracy.* Oxford, 1969.

Page, Denys. *Aeschylus: "Agamemnon."* Edited with J. D. Denniston. Oxford, 1957.

—— *History and the Homeric Iliad.* Berkeley, Calif., 1959.

—— "Archilochus and the Oral Tradition." *Fondation Hart Entretiens X Vandoeuvres-Genève,* 1963, pp. 119–163.

Palmer, L. R. "The Indo-European Origins of Greek Justice." *Transactions of the Philological Society* (Oxford), 1950, pp. 149–168.

Parry, Adam. "Have We Homer's *Iliad?" Yale Classical Studies,* 20 (1966), 177–216.

Parry, Anne. "Homer as Artist." *Classical Quarterly,* 21 (1971), 1–15.

Parry, Milman. *The Making of Homeric Verse: Collected Papers.* Ed. Adam Parry. Oxford, 1971.

Pertusi, A. *Scholia Vetera in Hesiodi Opera et Dies.* Milan, 1955.

Pfeiffer, R. H. *Introduction to the Old Testament.* New York, 1941.

—— *The Hebrew Iliad: The History of the Rise of Israel under Saul and David.* Trans. from Greek and Hebrew. New York, 1957.

Phillipson, C. *The International Law and Custom of Ancient Greece and Rome.* 2 vols. London, 1911.

Radin, Paul. *Primitive Man as Philosopher.* New York, 1957.

Rawls, John. *A Theory of Justice.* Cambridge, Mass., 1971.

Richards, I. A. *Principles of Literary Criticism.* London, 1924.

—— "The Future of Reading." *American Academy of Arts and Sciences Bulletin,* 24 (1970), 2–12.

Richardson, N. J. "Homeric Professors in the Age of the Sophists." *Cambridge Philological Society Proceedings,* 201 (n.s. 21) (1975), 65–81.

Robertson, D. S. "An Unnoticed Pindaric Fragment." *Classical Review,* 2nd ser. 9 (1959), 11–12.

Rodgers, V. A. "Some Thoughts on Dike." *Classical Quarterly,* 21 (1971), 289–301.

Roebuck, C. "The Economic Development of Ionia." *Classical Philology,* 48 (1953), 9–16.

—— *Ionian Trade and Colonisation.* Archaeological Institute of America Monograph 9. New York, 1959.

Roth, C. P. "Kings and Muses in Hesiod's Theogony." *Transactions of the American Philological Association,* 106 (1976), 331–338.

Ruschenbusch, E. *Solonos Nomoi: die Fragmente.* Wiesbaden, 1966.

Russell, Bertrand. *A History of Western Philosophy.* New York, 1945.

Russo, J. A. "Homer against His Tradition." *Arion,* Summer 1968, pp. 275–295.

—— "How and What Does Homer Communicate?" *Classical Journal,* 71 (1976), 289–299.

Ryle, G. *Plato's Progress.* Cambridge, 1966.

Scheffler, H. W. "Structuralism in Anthropology." *Yale French Studies,* 36 and 37 (1966), 66–88.

Sellschopp, I. *Stilistische Untersuchungen zu Hesiod.* Hamburg, 1934.

Shipp, G. P. *Studies in the Language of Homer.* 1st and 2nd eds. Cambridge, 1972.

Smout, T. C. *A History of the Scottish People, 1560–1830.* London, 1972.

Snell, B. *The Discovery of Mind.* Oxford, 1953.

Snodgrass, A. M. *The Dark Ages of Greece.* Edinburgh, 1971.

Solmsen, F. *Hesiod and Aeschylus.* Ithaca, 1949.

Stanford, W. B. *Ambiguity in Greek Literature.* Oxford, 1939.

Stevenson, C. *Ethics and Language.* New Haven, 1944.

Stroud, R. S. *Drakon's Law on Homicide.* Berkeley, Calif., 1968.

Tedlock, D. "Toward an Oral Poetics." *New Literary History,* 8 (1977), 507–519.

Teeter, K. V. "Linguistics and Anthropology." *Daedalus,* Summer 1973, 87–98.

Teggart, F. "The Argument of Hesiod's *Works and Days.*" *Journal of Hellenic Studies,* 8 (1947), 45–77.

Tigerstedt, E. N. *Interpreting Plato.* Stockholm, 1977.

Van Gronigen, B. A. *La composition littéraire archaique Grecque.* Amsterdam, 1958.

Vlastos, G. "Solonian Justice." *Classical Philology,* 41 (1946), 65–83.

———— "Equality and Justice in the Early Greek Cosmologies." *Classical Philology,* 42 (1947), 156–178.

———— "Justice and Happiness in the Republic." *Platonic Studies* (Princeton), 1973, pp. 114–123.

Wade-Gery, H. T. *The Poet of the Iliad.* Cambridge, 1952.

Webster, T. B. L. *From Mycenae to Homer.* London, 1960.

West, M. L. *Hesiod: "Theogony."* Oxford, 1966.

———— Review of G. P. Edwards, *The Language of Hesiod in its Traditional Context. Classical Review,* 23 (1972), 19–20.

Wilamowitz-Moellendorff, U. von. *Hesiodos Erga.* 2nd ed. Berlin, 1962.

Wolff, H. J. "Judicial Legislation among the Greeks." *Traditio,* 4 (1946), 71–78.

Woodhouse, W. J. *Solon the Liberator.* Oxford, 1938.

Index

✹

Abstraction, syntax of, 221, 223, 224, 257
Academy, 326, 327
Acoustic composition, 220ff, 229ff, 230, 324, 338. *See also* Memory
Adikēma, 296, 309
Adikia, 264, 296, 312
Adikō, 211, 309
Adikos, 194, 231, 267, 297, 309
Adversary relations, 88ff
Aegina, 300
Aegisthus, 184, 278, 293
Aesop, 28
Africa, 41, 53
Agamemnon, 272–277, 292, 293
Agōn, 133, 279
Agora: in Ithaca, 76–78, 79, 101, 119–121, 139–149, 152, 153, 166, 167, 174, 180, 210; in Troy, 64, 65; in Phaeacia, 92, 93, 113, 200; in *Theogony,* 114; of the Greek army, 127–133, 152, 198; on Achilles' shield, 135, 136; watched by Zeus, 136, 258; *Works & Days,* 213, 219
Aisimos, 151, 153, 180, 183; *enaisimos,* 155, 183, 320; *exaisimos,* 181, 320
Aisulos, 151, 153, 183
Aithousai, 100

Alphabet, 9, 10, 64, 221, 228f, 329
Altar of justice, 275, 287, 289
American Indian, 336
Amphinomus, 170
Anandria, 223
Anankē, 269
Anassein, 65, 96
Anax, 95, 96, 98
Anaximander, 251, 252, 263
Andromache, 86, 205
Antidikos, 292
Antigone, 291, 331
Antilochus, 133, 134, 197
Antinous, 78, 97, 145, 148, 168, 175
Anomiē, 297, 298
Aphorism, *see* Saying
Apology of Agamemnon, 131
Aramaic, 298
Archein, 65
Archelaus, 223
Archilochus, 9, 251, 266
Architecture: domestic, 82ff; of speech, 225–226, 229
Archos, 97
Areopagus, 279, 283
Ares, 265
Arētē, 113, 158
Aretē, 151, 298, 311

Aristocracies, 98
Aristoi, 75, 97, 108, 120, 129, 140
Aristophanes, 6, 34, 71, 81, 310
Aristotle, 14, 104, 128, 189, 293, 318, 334
Armor, 81–82
Arnold, M., 7
Artabanus, 302
Assonance, 229
Atasthalia, 176, 184
Atasthalos, 152, 154, 181, 183, 185, 204, 320
Atē, 125, 126, 131, 132, 195, 207, 208, 212, 257, 258, 287, 301
Athemistos, 155. *See also* Formulary
Athene, 59, 67, 77
Athens and Aegina, 300, 301
Athletes, 109
Athloi, 172
Atreus, 174, 277, 278

Bagre, myth of, 474
Balfe, 101
Balkans, *see* Jugoslavia
Banking, 302
Bards, 82, 99
Basileus: on Achilles' shield, 58; two meanings of, 94–97; in Lycia, 107, 109, 112, 114; in Ithaca, 126, 152, 153, 179; in Greek army, 129; in Hesiod, 208, 219, 229, 259; in *Eumenides,* 284
Beggar, 161–165, 166, 167–175
Being, 251, 268
Bellerophon, 113
Bia, 136, 213, 253, 291. *See also* Hubris
Binding song, 286
Blaprō, 207
Black Sea, 63, 66
Boas, F., 337
Boundary line, 216
Bouleuterion, 282. *See also* Council
Bow of Odysseus, 172, 175, 189, 211
Briseis, 132, 198
Bronze, 70
Bypassing, 134, 196, 197

Cadmus, 303
Calypso, 85, 139, 156, 160, 209
Cannabalism, 212, 213
Carians, 66
Cassandra, 174, 278
Catalogue, 59ff, 64ff
Categorical imperative, 338
Cephalus, 222, 309, 310

Chalcas, 143
Chalepos, 186
Chariots, 82, 133, 134, 197
China, 35, 36
Chios, 64, 70
Choephoroi, 288–292
Chryseis, 198
Chryses, 142
City-state, *see* Polis
Cleomenes, 300
Cloudburst, 130, 199, 214
Clouds, 310
Clytemnestra, 141, 278, 288, 292, 293
Compensation, 131–132, 135
Confrontation, 89–90, 126, 176. See also *Eris; Neikos*
Conrad, J., 50–51
Conspicuous consumption, 93–94
Contradiction in poets, 331
Cook, Capt. Jas., 20, 21, 31, 32, 40, 63, 339
Copper, 71
Copula, 14, 42, 45, 122, 221–223, 232, 250; absent in Homer and Hesiod, 245, 246; and Solon, 261; appears in Herodotus, 305, 306; realized in Plato, 313. See also *Einai*
Cos, 303
Council: in Ithaca, 78, 207; Phaeacia, 92; of gods, 100, 139; Greek army, 128, 131, 152; in *Eumenides,* 282
Crete, 16, 97
Croesus, 306
Crooked (versus straight), 136, 137, 196, 199–201, 208, 215, 216, 219, 261
Cyclops, 79, 80, 159ff, 161, 172, 180, 213, 298
Cyrus, 297, 302

Dance, 39, 40, 85
Daedalus, 333
Dante, 30
Darius, 303
Dark Age, 10
Debts, 309
Deilos, 196
Deioces, 297
Delphi, 301, 303
Demiourgoi, 85
Democritus, 266, 304
Demodocus, 89
Demon, *see* Atē
Demos, 67, 68, 98, 135, 136, 142, 145, 171, 201, 202, 219, 254, 259; demos-eater, 208

Demosthenes, 256
Deposit in trust, 300, 302, 303, 304, 310, 320
Dialogue format, 326
Didactic genre, 261
Didaxai, 261
Dikaios, 132, 179, 184–186, 189, 191, 200, 231, 255, 281, 287, 288, 290, 297, 303, 306, 309, 333
Dikaiosunē, 13, 222, 247; in Theognis, 247; in Stobaeus, 262; replaces *dikē* in Plato, 296, 309; in Herodotus, 296–302; in Thucydides, Damon, Thrasymachus, 310
Dikaspolos, 113, 179, 283
Dikastēs, 281–283, 289
Dikazō, 134, 135, 281, 286, 320
Dikē: as master symbol, 124; personified in Hesiod, 206 ,207, 217; as spoken, 216; in Solon, 258–259; in pre-Socratics, 266, 268, 269; as penalty, 289, 291; in *Choephoroi,* 290, 291
Dikēn as adverb, 279
Dikēphoros, 289
Diodotus, 223
Directives, oral, 22, 45
Disable, 134, 207, 208, 219. See also *Blaptō*
Disaster, see *Atē*
Disconnection, in Hesiod, 196, 219
Documentation, 12, 15, 16, 26, 221ff, 328; of law, 283, 297, 330; in Plato, 325, 330
Doing one's own, 182, 183, 299, 319, 320
Dokeonta and *dokimōtatos,* 266
Doxa, 267, 333
Drama, 48, 96
Draco, 283, 300, 302
Dryden, 40
Due process, 252, 288, 289
Dunamenos, 97, 183, 318
Durkheim, 336
Dusnomia, 256, 261

Ecclesia, 128. See also Agora
Ecbatana, 297
Echo systems: in *Odyssey,* 155, 160, 189, 190; in Solon, 262; in drama, 273, 294; producing structures, 338
Education, oral, 32
Egrapsa, 253
Egypt, 299
Eidos, 318, 329, 330. See also Shape

Einai, acoustics of, in Homer, 234; in Solon, 262; in Aeschylus, 272, 273; usage of in Homer, 237 (presence), 238 (status), 240 (time), 241 neuter predicate), 242 (no predicate), 243, 244 ("understood"); in vernacular, 247; as auxiliary, 248; in Parmenides, 268; in *Agamemnon,* 272–277; in Herodotus, 305; in Plato, 313–318, 333
Elders, 76, 128, 131, 158, 283. See *also* Council
Electra, 278, 289, 290
Emporio, 70
Enclave of speech, 30, 31, 34, 48, 123, 220, 227
Enclosure of suitors, 210–212
Endikos, 282, 285, 290
Eneiman, see *Nemō*
Epic, storage function of, 29, 46, 48, 337
Ēpeiroi, 64
Epēkoos, 284
Equity, 252
Equivalence, appositional, 243, 266
Erga, 85
Erinus, 125, 141, 169, 264, 266, 267, 275, 278, 281, 284, 285, 287, 288
Eris, 89, 125, 126, 150, 265. See *also* Feud; *Neikos*
Esan, 146. See also *Einai*
Escort of *xeinos,* see *Pempō*
Estin, 131, 181, 182, 272; See also *Einai*
Ētheios, 153
Ethics, as system, 338
Ethos, *see* Nomos
Euclid, 42
Eudikiai, 153, 179, 203
Euēgesiē, 153, 176
Euergea, 152
Eumenides, 279, 281–288
Eunomia, 137, 147, 215, 256, 261
Eurymachus, 170, 174
Euthyphro, 330
Exaggeration of dimension, 93
Exhaustion, method of, 316

Fantasy, Homeric, 56, 57, 88–105
Fee-eaters, 199, 208. See also Demos
Festival, 59, 78, 173, 210
Feud, 124, 126, 131. See also *Neikos*
Field of meaning, 230, 280, 286, 293, 310, 313
Fixity of statement, 15

Foreigners, foreign speech, 66, 70, 71, 157
Formularies, 99, 131, 180, 197, 199, 213, 214
Formulas: moral 110ff, 113, 190; within narrative, 114ff; units of meaning, 118; table of, 184ff; shared by archaic poets, 261
Frazer, J., 336
Fury, *see* Erinus

Gambia, 41
Gelo, 303
Geometric period, 10
Germany, 16
Gifts, 93, 113, 146, 160, 173
Gignetai, 246
Glaucus, 8, 107, 115, 300, 301
Goatherd, 167
God-apparatus, 50
Grammar, anthropological, 17, 25
Granville, Lord, 7
Grouping of terms, in *Oresteia*, see Punning
Guardians, 205, 206, 219, 250

Hammurabi, 43
Hardy, T., 35
Hēgētores, 97
Helen, 18, 152, 162, 172, 278
Hephaestus, 56–58, 117
Heraclitus, 5, 251, 252, 265, 266, 267, 268
Heralds, 79, 128, 134, 136. See also *Kērux*
Hero, 49, 50, 53, 192, 220; as term, 101, 102; hero cults, 103
Herodotus: view of Homer and Hesiod, 5; introduces term *dikaiosunē*, 296; describes monarchies, 299, 302, 303, 305; use of *einai*, 305; use of prose, 326
Heroic age, 101–104; ideal, 8, 81, 90, 107, 108, 115; later concept of, 104
Hesiod: instructor of Greece, 5; isolates *dikē*, 13; world like Homer's, 58, 71; creator of Heroic Age, 104; critic of fees, 113; *dikē*-poem, 193–213; post-dates Homer, 214, 215; proto-literate, 226; a reader of Homer, 230; recalled in, *Choephoroi*, 291; in Herodotus, 302; in Plato, 311
Hiketēs, hiketēsios, 157
Hikōmetha, 160
Histōr, 135, 136, 283. See also *Istō*

Hittites, 88
Hodos, 196, 197
Homer, 9, 214, 228, 339
Homeridae, 64, 340
Hoplites, 81
Hubris: in *Odyssey*, 75, 185, 187; in *Iliad*, 192; in Hesiod, 195, 196, 203, 204, 227; in Solon, 257; in Herodotus, 298–301
Hubristēs, 186
Hubrizō, 154, 185
Huperdikō, 286
Hupodikos, 281

Icarius, 120
Idealism, German, 251
Identity, syntax of, 319
Impersonals, 225, 226, 230
Indirection, 51, 176, 220
Individual in Plato, 312
Individuation, 19, 321
Intention, 207, 208, 300, 301
Internalization of justice, 302, 305, 312
Ionia, 10, 63, 64, 66, 69, 301–303, 305
Iphigenia, 278
Iron, 10, 70
Ithudikēs, 194, 203
Istō, 163
Ithaca, life style in, 67

Jacobson, R., 338
Jaeger, W., 251, 264
Japan, 16
Journey, as theme, 91, 176
Judeo-Christian, 337, 338
Judicial process in *Oresteia*, 279
Justice: mismanaged, 129; managed, 131; of Menelaus, 133; orality of, 135; name of 227; as entity, 321; interpreted as a universal, 339
Jugoslavia, 58, 104, 336

Kakia, 311
Kakoergiē, 176
Kakos, 176
Kakotēs, 148
Kalessō, 146
Kant, 338
Kērux, 120
Kings and queens, 58, 86, 92
Knower, see *Histōr*
Koiranos, 97
Kouroi, kourētai, korai, 105

Kosmētōr, 97
Ktesippus, 173

Laertes, 70–72
Laos, 67, 98, 113, 120
Laurē, 84
Leaf, W., 65
Legality, 147, 279, 289, 297
Leotychides, 300
Libraries, 336
Lincoln, Abraham, 34
Linear B, 9, 64, 88, 97, 100
Linear thought, 336
Literacy, 13ff, 221, 228, 298, 325, 334
"Literature," *see* Documentation
Lo Dagaa, 47
Logoi, 333
Loeb version of Hesiod, 230
Lords, *see* Basileus
Lycians, 66, 107, 109, 112, 115
Lydia, 66, 297
Lyric, recitation of, 218

Maidservants, 166, 170, 172, 174
Malinowski, 336
Maritime complex, 177; commerce, 69, 70
Maxim, *see* Saying
McLuhan, M., 336
Medon, 148
Medontes, 97
Megaron, 93, 100, 101
Melantho, 170, 173
Melos, 310
Memory (mnemonic), 26, 27, 37, 44, 45, 135, 220, 225, 229, 257, 267, 324, 325, 330
Menelaus, 133, 135, 154, 156, 197, 320
Mentor, 96, 146, 152
Mesopotamia, 15
Metaphysics, 250, 256, 264
Miletus, 65, 66, 300, 301
Milton, 30, 104
Mimesis, 332
Minos, 101, 179, 180, 310
Missile, 168, 170, 174
Moira, 269
Monarchy, 297, 299, 305
Moral formulas, *see* Formula
Moral responsibility, 339
Mueller, Max, 336
Muses, 60, 62, 89, 257
Muslim, 47

Muthoi, 64, 216, 309, 310. *See also* Mythos
Mycenae, 9, 10, 13, 56, 58, 59, 62, 68, 71, 77, 82, 87, 88, 98, 100, 101, 121, 180
Myth, 46, 47, 336
Mythos: equivalent to epic, 46, 123, 124, 132, 226; two themes of, 176; of *Iliad,* 64, 133, 150; of *Odyssey,* 143, 177, 183
Mytilene, 310

Naming: in Hesiod, 225, 227, 230; in Heraclitus, 265; in Plato, 327
Nausicaa, 157, 158, 163
Neeion, 70
Neikos, 89, 125, 132, 136, 144, 147, 148, 150
Nemō, 197, 200, 201
Nestor, palace of, 83
Neuter pronoun, 312, 313
New England, 17, 84
Noēmones, 185
Nomima, 333
Nominal sentences, 243ff
Nomos, 212, 216
Nomos-ethos, 11, 13, 24, 30, 34, 90, 109, 117, 118, 124, 133, 147, 177, 182, 225, 227, 230, 257, 333, 334
Nostos, see Journey
Nouns, 225

Oaths, 23, 76, 132–135, 143, 148, 196–198, 205, 212, 213, 219, 283, 284, 301, 302
Occupations, Homeric, 84
Odysseus: house, 82–84, 161, 168–170; name of, 88; character, 151–153; identity, 160, 168; dog, 167; receptions of, 158, 162, 171, 172, 173; rejections of, 167, 170, 173; vindication of, 175; mother, 181
Oedipus, 205
Old Testament, 23, 28, 31, 36, 43, 47, 49, 52, 91, 170, 205, 326
Opinion, *see* Doxa
Oresteia: use of Homer, 149, 283; mythos, 277–280; justice vocabulary, 280, 292; legality, 281; retribution, 285; propriety, 286; punishment, 288; personification, 290
Orestes, 277, 278, 281, 282, 284, 286, 289, 290
Orientalizing period, 10
Orsothura, 84
Orthodikaios, 288

Ousia, 333
Outrage, *see* Hubris

Palaces, 82
Pandarus, 205
Pan-Hellenes, 57, 73, 74, 85, 177
Papyrus, 228
Parmenides, 250–252, 269, 270, 271
Parry, M., 54, 78, 107, 228
Peirar, 135
Peirazō, peirētizō, peirō, 164–166.
    See also Test
Peisenor, 120
Pempō, pompē, 171, 174, 269, 270
People-eater, *see* Demos; Fee
Performance statement, 45, 338
Pericles, 87
Persephone, 181
Perses, 194, 195, 212, 219, 229
Personality, *see* Psyche
Personification, see *Dikē*
Phaeacians, 88, 89, 92, 158, 159,
    187, 200–202
Phaedrus, 326
Phemius, 82
Philotes, 148
Phocaea, 64, 65, 71
Phoenicians, 10
Phoenix, 119, 126
Phulassein, 267
Pisistratus, 156
Plato: on education, 6, 55, 81; intro-
    duces *dikaiosunē,* 14, 231–233,
    296, 310; use of copula, 234, 312–
    314; and Hesiod, 250; and He-
    rodotus, 304, 305; and Protagaras,
    305; on political justice, 310, 311,
    316–318; on personal justice, 311,
    321–333; doctrine of forms, 318,
    319; on Homeric justice, 321; as
    writer, 324–326; naming of names,
    327; as reader, 327–330; as opponent
    of poets, 330–334; on mimesis, 332
Polemos, in Heraclitus, 265
Poliētai, 65, 78
Polis: early classical presence in Homer
    denied, 56; portrayed on shield, 57,
    58; festivals in, 58, 79, 173; in
    Phaeacia, 58, 203; in Troy, 58, 59,
    65, 66; in Ithaca, 77–79, 148, 212;
    nonexistent for Cyclops, 79, 80;
    gates of, 80, 81; in Greek army,
    80–82, 127, 128; kouroi of, 105,
    202; orality of, 118; interpolis rela-
    tions, 177; in Hesiod, 200–202,
    204, 205, 208–210, 212; Solon, 255,

256, 259; *Eumenides,* 287, 288;
    Plato, 314–318, 328
Polarization, moral, in Odyssey, 150,
    190
Polemarchus, 310
Pollution of house, 212
Pope, Alexander, 40
Poseidon, 134, 139, 160, 209
Pragma, prattō, 281
Pragmatism, oral, 36, 217
Prattein ta heautou, see Doing
Preliteracy, Greek, 9ff
Priam: presides over agora, 64, 65;
    performs humble tasks, 86; extended
    family, 93; diverse titles and roles, 95
Principle, 13; versus procedure, 137,
    181, 212, 213, 264
Procedure and process, *see* Principle
Prometheus, 209
Prometheus Bound, 291
Propriety: preliterate, 13, 24, 53;
    linguistic, 17, 27; social, 34; in
    Lincoln's oratory, 34, 35; domestic,
    in Homer, 73–75; "international,"
    177; recommended by Achilles,
    129; by Odysseus, 132; implicit in
    Solon, 255; Parmenides, 269; pre-
    Socratics, 271; *Eumenides,* 287, 288;
    Agamemnon, 292, 293; Plato, 320;
    Greek drama, 332
Prose, composition of, 325
Protagoras, 249, 305
Proto-literate, 189, 191, 226ff
Psammetichus, 299
Psyche, 307, 312, 322
Psychology of *Iliad,* 126, 127
Ptōchos, 157; theme of 161ff. *See also*
    Beggar
Punning: in Hesiod, 229; in *Eumen-*
    ides, 286, 288, 295; in *Choephoroi,*
    289, 290, 293, 295; in *Agamemnon,*
    292–294
Pylos, 155

Queens, *see* Kings

Reception: by Eumaeus, 162ff; by
    Penelope, 171; by stockman, 173;
    of a prophet, 166. *See also* Odysseus
Reciprocity: in Anaximander, 264; in
    Heraclitus, 267; in *Oresteia,* 279,
    280; in Herodotus, 300, 301
Redress, 123, 130, 216
Reflexive pronoun, 304, 313, 322
Republic, structure of, 308, 309

Rheithron, 70
Rhema, 311
Rhetoric: in oral epic, 49; storage function of, 118–122; in agora, 133, 135, 136; as instrument of *dikē,* 137; in Hesiod, 213, 229; in *Eumenides,* 283, 284
Rhodes, 64
Rhoges, 83
Rhythm, 25, 26, 37
Right, rights, terminology of, 231
Rivers, 336
Russell, B., 251

Salamis, 304
Samos, 64, 71
Sanctuary, 281
Sarpedon, 8, 98, 107ff
Saying, 24, 28, 45, 114–116, 190, 204, 219, 311
Scepter, 95, 127–131, 136, 140, 141; as symbol, 99–100
Schetlios, 160, 170, 180, 183, 204, 320
Scotland, 24, 25, 32
Scythia, 303
Section, see *Temenos*
Senate, 282. *See also* Elders
Sethos, 299
Seven Against Thebes, 291, 295
Seven wise men, 45
Shakespeare, 57
Shape, 225, 228ff, 329, 330
Shield of Achilles, 58, 100, 135
Sicily, 175
Siege-warfare, 81
Similes, Homeric, 86, 87
Skeptron, see Scepter
Smyrna, 64, 65
Socrates, 250, 304, 313, 325
Solon, 87, 109, 178; on due process, 252; on time, 254; on equity, 254; on ship of state, 256; on justice personified, 258; on *atē,* 258; his law code, 252; apologia, 253; Hesiod, 253, 254, 256, 259–261; Homer, 255; pride in Athens, 259; use of *einai,* 261; in *Agamemnon* and *Eumenides,* 287; Herodotus, 298, 302, 304, 306, 311
Son, only one: in Homer, 144; in Hesiod, 208, 210
Sophists, 305, 333
Sophocles, 205, 291, 331
Soul, *see* Psyche
South America, 15

Spring of town, 78
Stobaeus, 256
Storage: cultural, 10ff, 29, 336; preliterate, 12ff, 54, 220; in Homer, 105–122; rhetorical, 118; literate, 221, 224; in artifacts, 225
Story versus epic, 338
Straight, *see* Crooked
Stranger guest, see *Xeinos*
Strategos, 97
Structuralism, 338
Suitors, 67, 69, 73, 75, 79, 93, 97, 140, 142, 143ff, 147, 150, 151, 153, 154, 161, 162, 168ff., 173, 181, 185, 187, 204, 210
Sun, 266, 289
Symposium, 218
Syracuse, 303
Syntax: of narrative, 41; of abstraction, 221ff; of copula, 222; in Plato, 315, 319

Tahiti, 20–22, 31, 32, 40, 47
Taphians, 70, 71
Tekmairetai, 217
Temenos, 58, 109, 112, 115
Temese, 70, 71
Tennyson, 57
Terminology, literate, 226
Test, 159, 164ff, 168, 170. See also *Peirazo*
Testifiers, 267. *See also* Witness
Thalamos, 83
Thales, 66
Theagenes, 5
Themethla, 260
Themis, 101, 121, 122, 134–136, 160, 180, 253
Theoclymenus, 174
Theognis, 261
Theogony, 207, 258, 260
Theophrastus, 263, 264
Thesmos, 253, 279, 284
Thetis, 131, 142
Thrasymachus, 305
Thucydides, 310, 326
Time, 254, 264
Tisis (tino), 126, 148, 207, 257, 258
Titans, 260, 266
To be, see *Einai*
Tools versus language, 335
Topicalization, 226, 312
Township, *see* Demos
Tragedy, death of, 334
Tribal encyclopedia, 337
Trobriand Islanders, 337

Trojan war as theme, 90, 91, 148.
　See also Warfare
Troy, 59, 65, 67, 72
Twelve Kings, 299
Tyrants, 99
Tyrteaus, 81, 261

Utopia in Hesiod, 20, 202, 214, 215

Virtue, *see Aretē*
Virtues, four cardinal, 316, 322
Vision, 229, 230, 324, 325
Visual composition, rules of, 221ff

War and Peace, 92
Warfare as theme, 53, 81, 89–91,
　148, 265. *See also* Polemos
Warrior, 85, 86

Warnings given by Odysseus, 167,
　170, 173
Witness, oral, 133, 135, 143, 213,
　267, 289
Woman, abused, 197
Wood, R., 7
Works, 199, 257
World War II, 16
Writers as intellectuals, 325, 326
Written word in drama, 277

Xanthus, 66, 107, 112
Xenophanes, 5, 69, 108, 266
Xenos (xeinos), 85, 146, 186, 187,
　201, 202, 307; as theme, 155ff; as
　title, 168; in *Eumenides* 285; *xeinēia,*
　156, 160; *philoxeinos,* 157
Xerxes, 302, 303, 305, 311
Xunon, in Heraclitus, 265